GEGE AKUTAMI

You got a problem?

GEGE AKUTAMI published a few short
works before starting *Jujutsu Kaisen*, which began
serialization in *Weekly Shonen Jump* in 2018.

JUJUTSU KAISEN

VOLUME 15
SHONEN JUMP EDITION

BY GEGE AKUTAMI

TRANSLATION Stefan Koza & John Werry
TOUCH-UP ART & LETTERING Snir Aharon
DESIGN Joy Zhang
EDITOR John Bae
CONSULTING EDITOR Erika Onabe

Printed in Italy

Published by VIZ Media, LLC
P.O. Box 77010
San Francisco, CA 94107

10 9 8 7 6 5 4 3 2
First printing, April 2022
Second printing, April 2022

VIZ MEDIA
viz.com

SHONEN JUMP

ratings.viz.com
RATED T+ OLDER TEEN

PARENTAL ADVISORY
JUJUTSU KAISEN is rated T+ for Older Teen and is recommended for ages 16 and up. This volume contains fantasy violence.

JUJUTSU KAISEN

15

THE SHIBUYA INCIDENT
—TRANSFORMATION—

STORY AND ART BY GEGE AKUTAMI

JUJUTSU KAISEN

CAST OF CHARACTERS

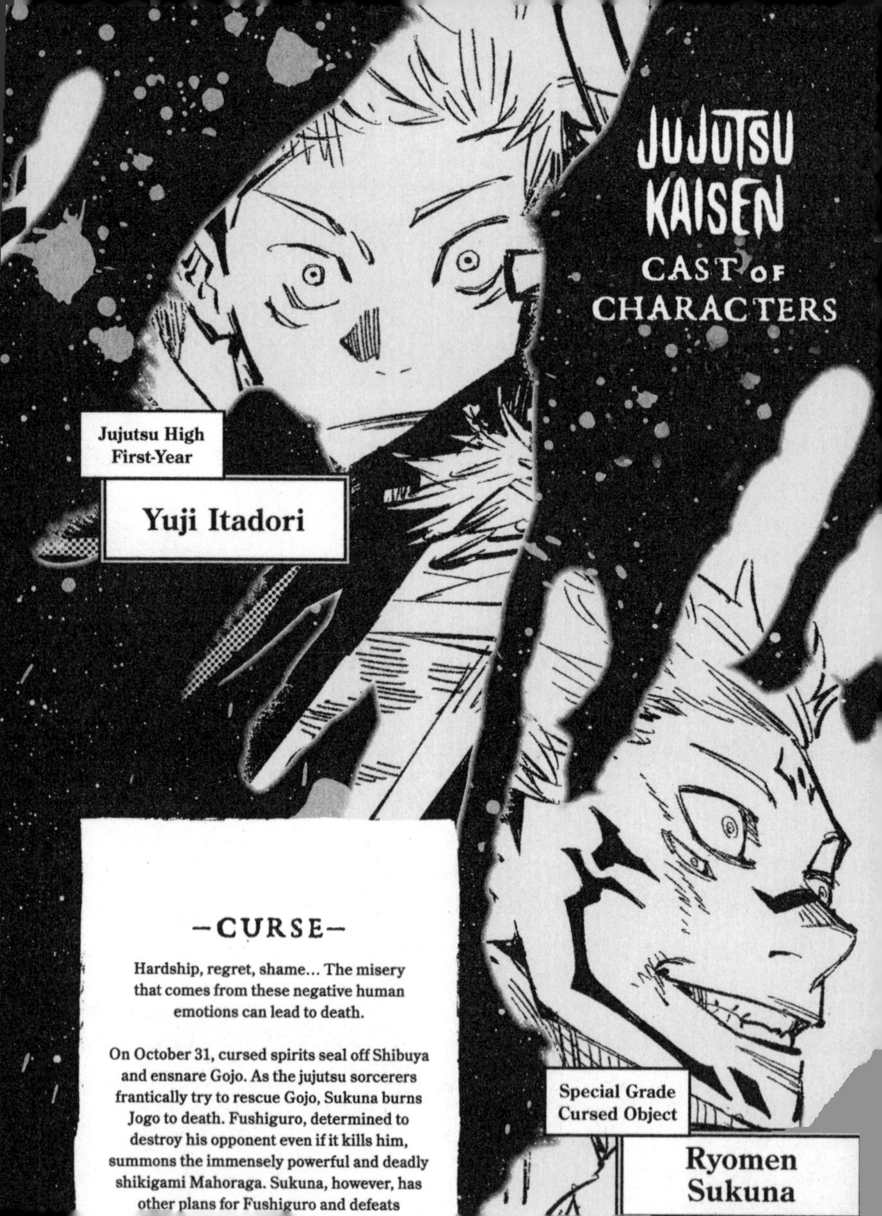

Jujutsu High First-Year

Yuji Itadori

Special Grade Cursed Object

Ryomen Sukuna

—CURSE—

Hardship, regret, shame... The misery that comes from these negative human emotions can lead to death.

On October 31, cursed spirits seal off Shibuya and ensnare Gojo. As the jujutsu sorcerers frantically try to rescue Gojo, Sukuna burns Jogo to death. Fushiguro, determined to destroy his opponent even if it kills him, summons the immensely powerful and deadly shikigami Mahoraga. Sukuna, however, has other plans for Fushiguro and defeats

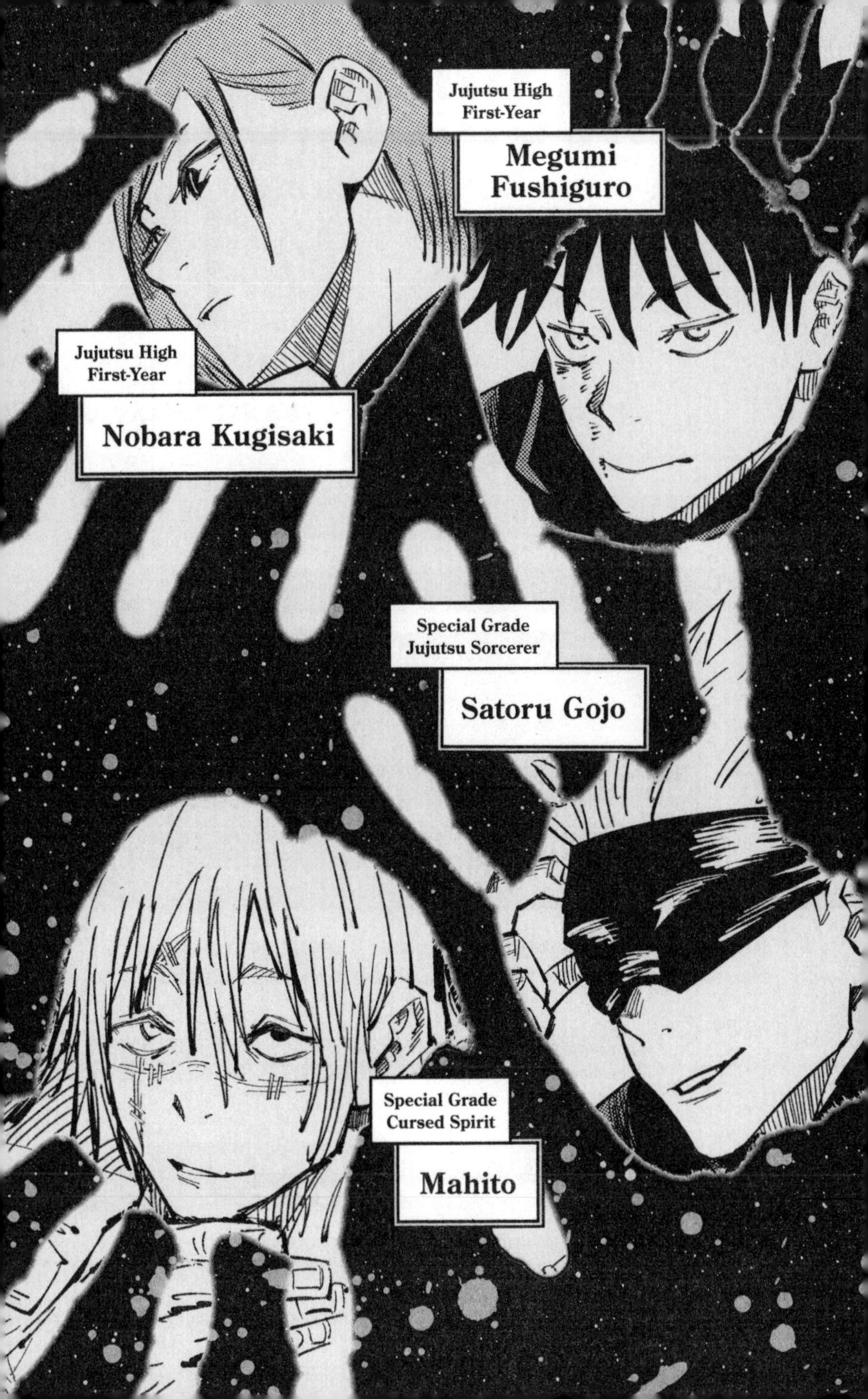
Jujutsu High First-Year
Megumi Fushiguro
Jujutsu High First-Year
Nobara Kugisaki
Special Grade Jujutsu Sorcerer
Satoru Gojo
Special Grade Cursed Spirit
Mahito

JUJUTSU KAISEN

15

THE SHIBUYA INCIDENT —TRANSFORMATION—

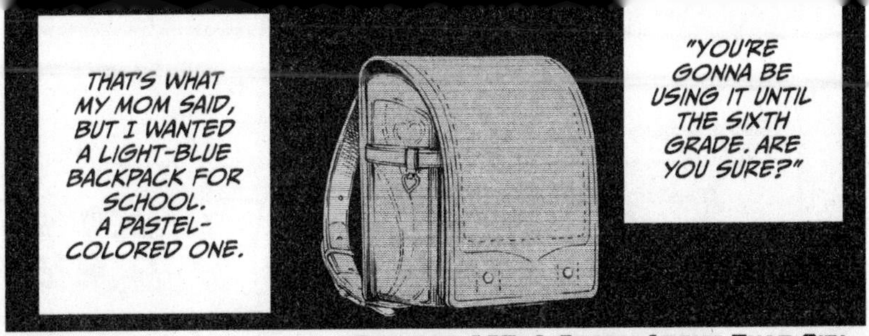
"YOU'RE GONNA BE USING IT UNTIL THE SIXTH GRADE. ARE YOU SURE?"
THAT'S WHAT MY MOM SAID, BUT I WANTED A LIGHT-BLUE BACKPACK FOR SCHOOL. A PASTEL-COLORED ONE.

CHAPTER 125: A STORY ABOUT THAT GIRL

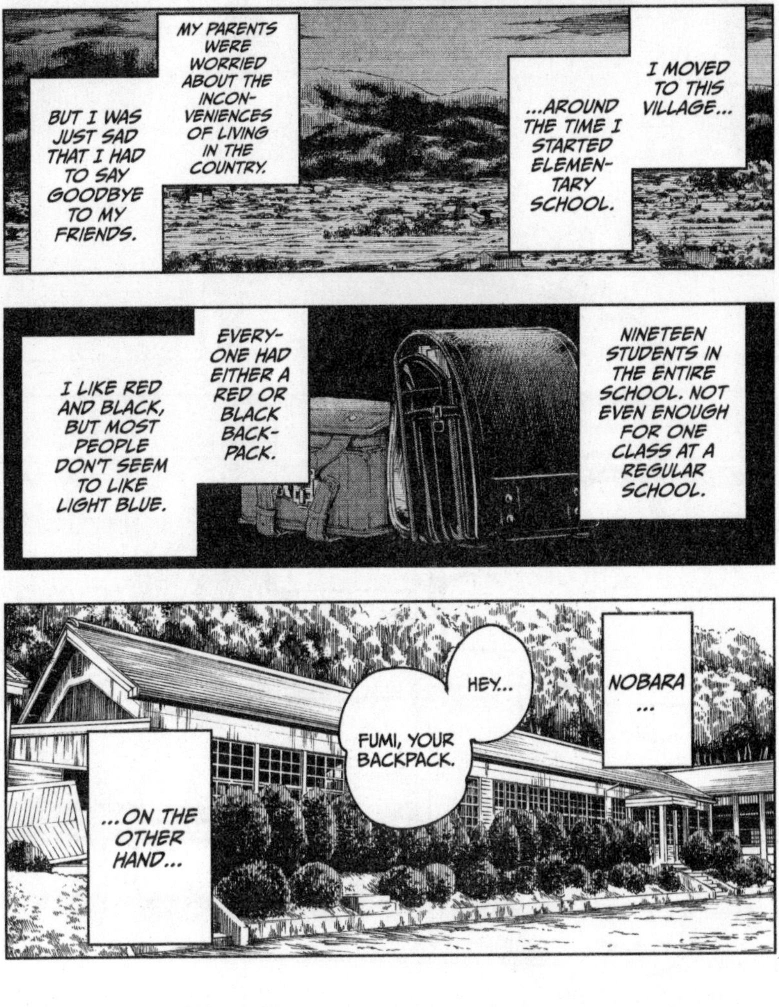
I MOVED TO THIS VILLAGE...
...AROUND THE TIME I STARTED ELEMENTARY SCHOOL.
MY PARENTS WERE WORRIED ABOUT THE INCONVENIENCES OF LIVING IN THE COUNTRY.
BUT I WAS JUST SAD THAT I HAD TO SAY GOODBYE TO MY FRIENDS.
NINETEEN STUDENTS IN THE ENTIRE SCHOOL. NOT EVEN ENOUGH FOR ONE CLASS AT A REGULAR SCHOOL.
EVERYONE HAD EITHER A RED OR BLACK BACKPACK.
I LIKE RED AND BLACK, BUT MOST PEOPLE DON'T SEEM TO LIKE LIGHT BLUE.
NOBARA ...
HEY...
FUMI, YOUR BACKPACK.
...ON THE OTHER HAND...

LET'S TRADE!

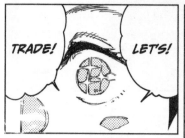

TRADE! LET'S!

HUH? ...

...BACK-PACK.

...WANTED MY...

HUH...?

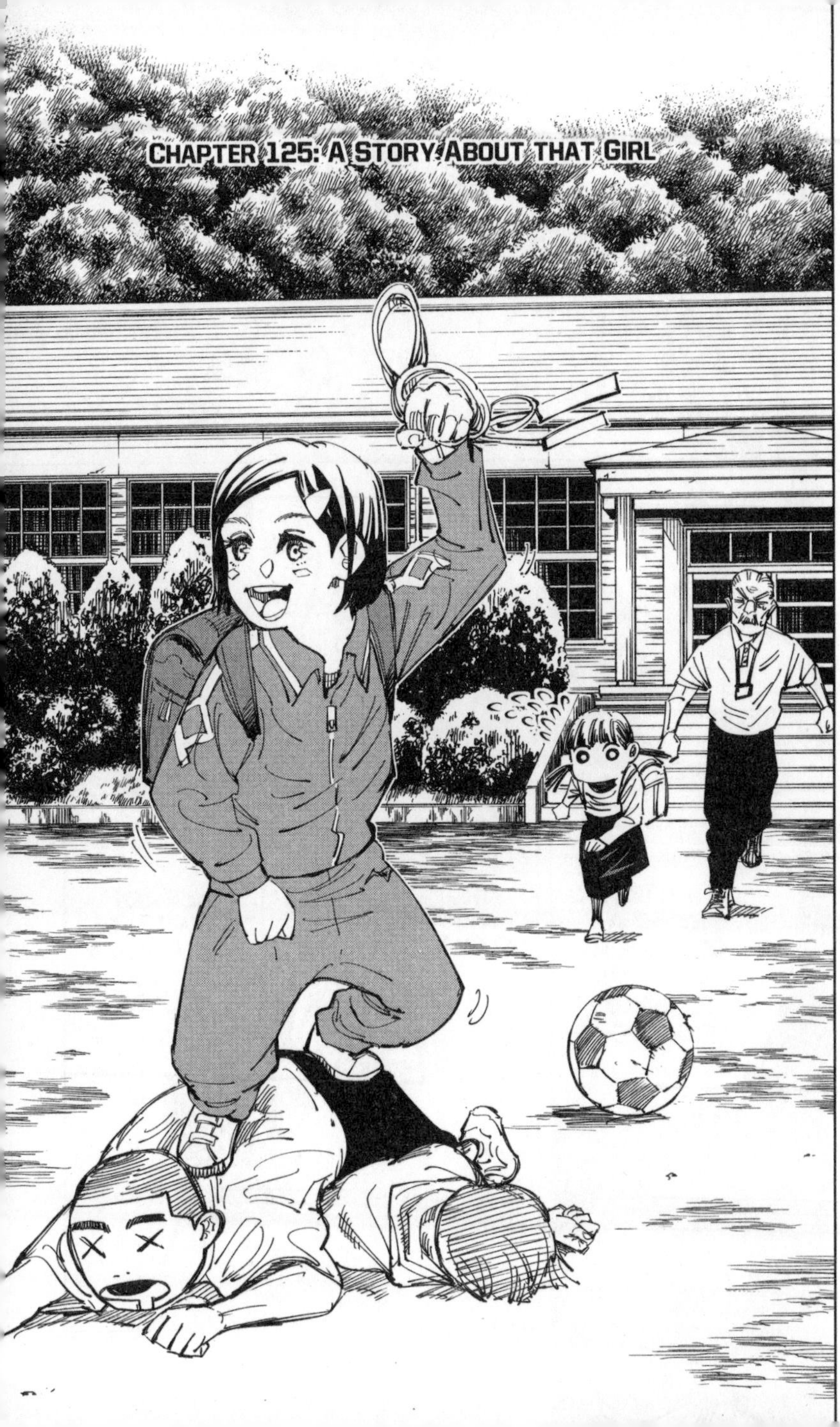
CHAPTER 125: A STORY ABOUT THAT GIRL

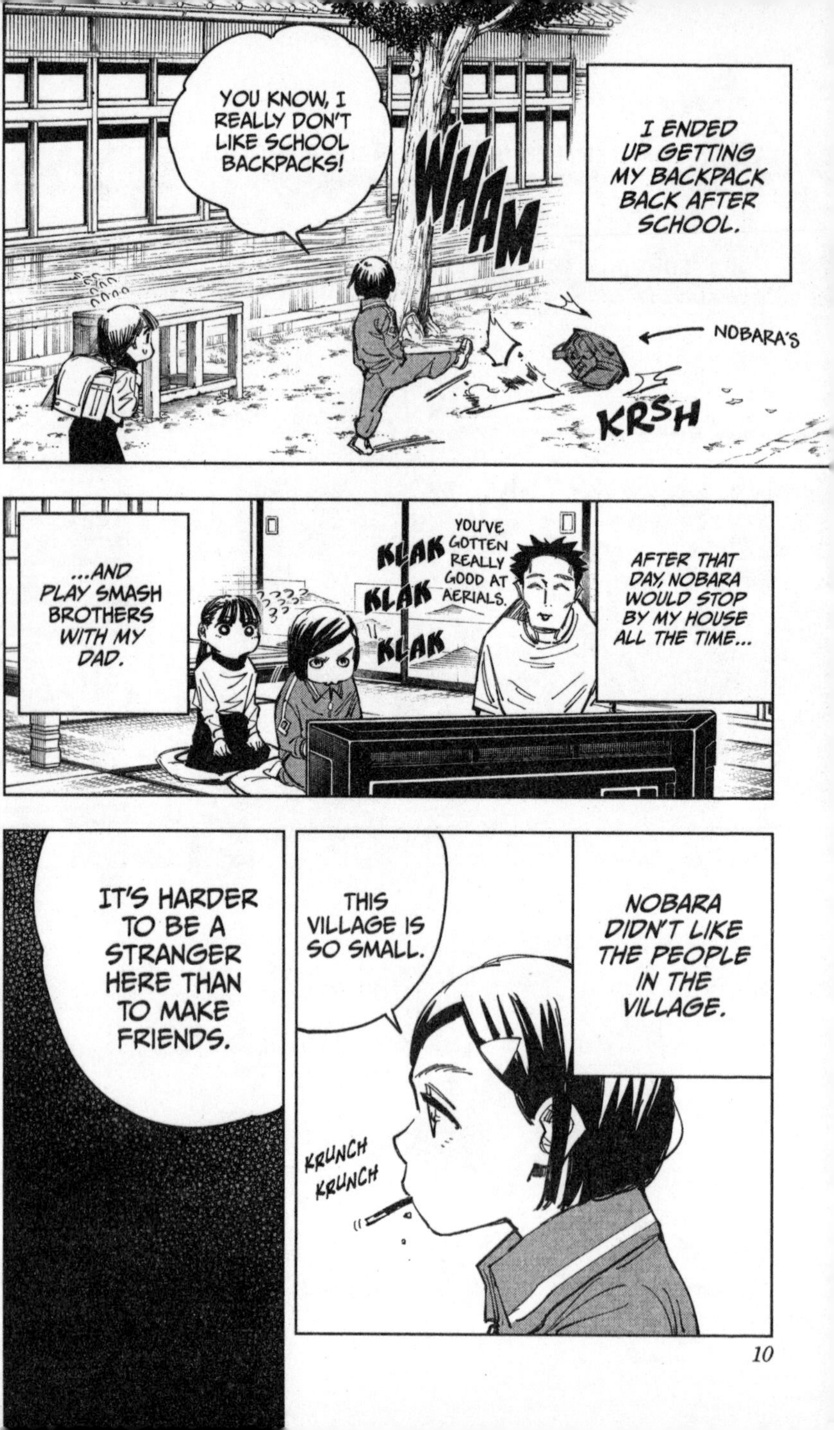
I ENDED UP GETTING MY BACKPACK BACK AFTER SCHOOL.
NOBARA'S
WHAM
YOU KNOW, I REALLY DON'T LIKE SCHOOL BACKPACKS!
KRSH
AFTER THAT DAY, NOBARA WOULD STOP BY MY HOUSE ALL THE TIME...
YOU'VE GOTTEN REALLY GOOD AT AERIALS.
KLAK KLAK KLAK
...AND PLAY SMASH BROTHERS WITH MY DAD.
NOBARA DIDN'T LIKE THE PEOPLE IN THE VILLAGE.
THIS VILLAGE IS SO SMALL.
KRUNCH KRUNCH
IT'S HARDER TO BE A STRANGER HERE THAN TO MAKE FRIENDS.

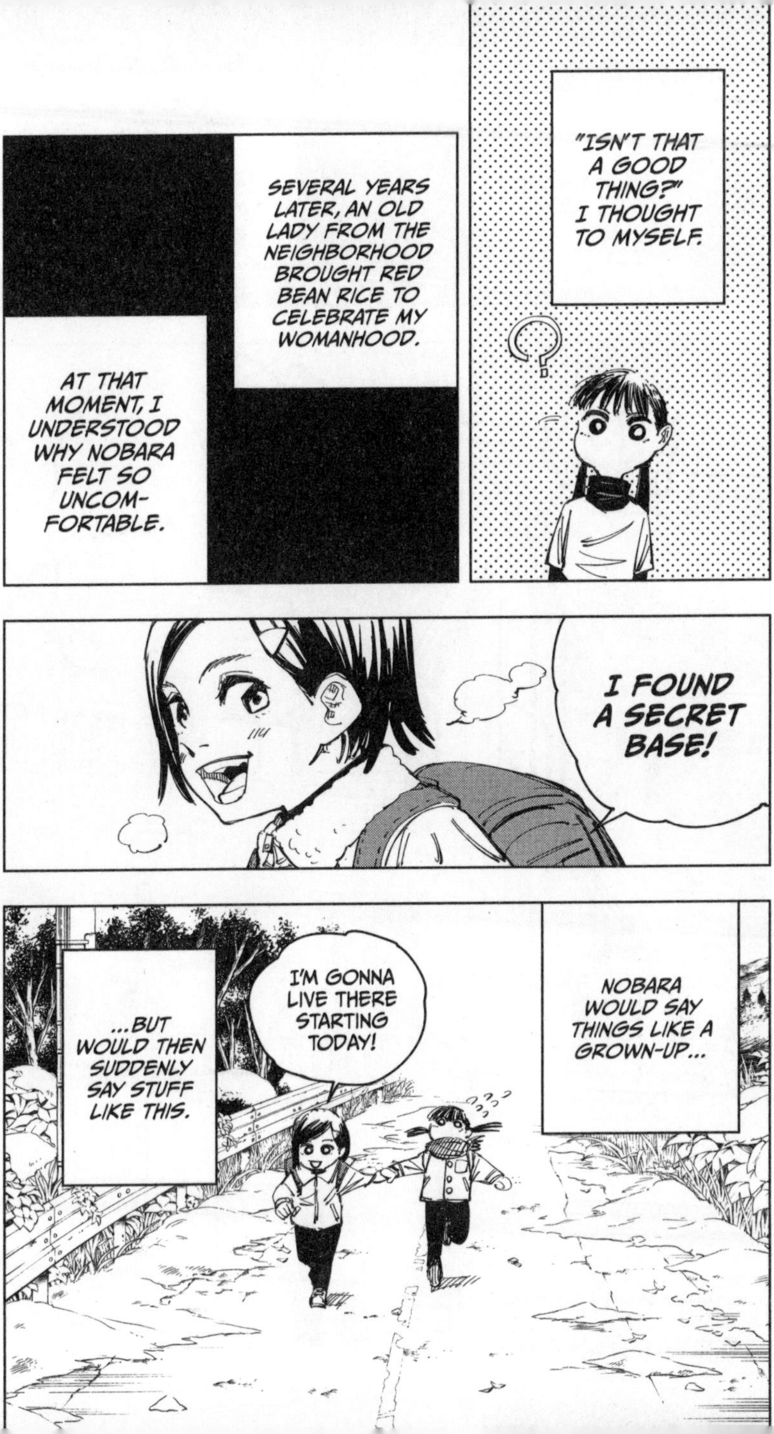
"ISN'T THAT A GOOD THING?" I THOUGHT TO MYSELF.
SEVERAL YEARS LATER, AN OLD LADY FROM THE NEIGHBORHOOD BROUGHT RED BEAN RICE TO CELEBRATE MY WOMANHOOD.
AT THAT MOMENT, I UNDERSTOOD WHY NOBARA FELT SO UNCOM-FORTABLE.
I FOUND A SECRET BASE!
NOBARA WOULD SAY THINGS LIKE A GROWN-UP...
I'M GONNA LIVE THERE STARTING TODAY!
...BUT WOULD THEN SUDDENLY SAY STUFF LIKE THIS.

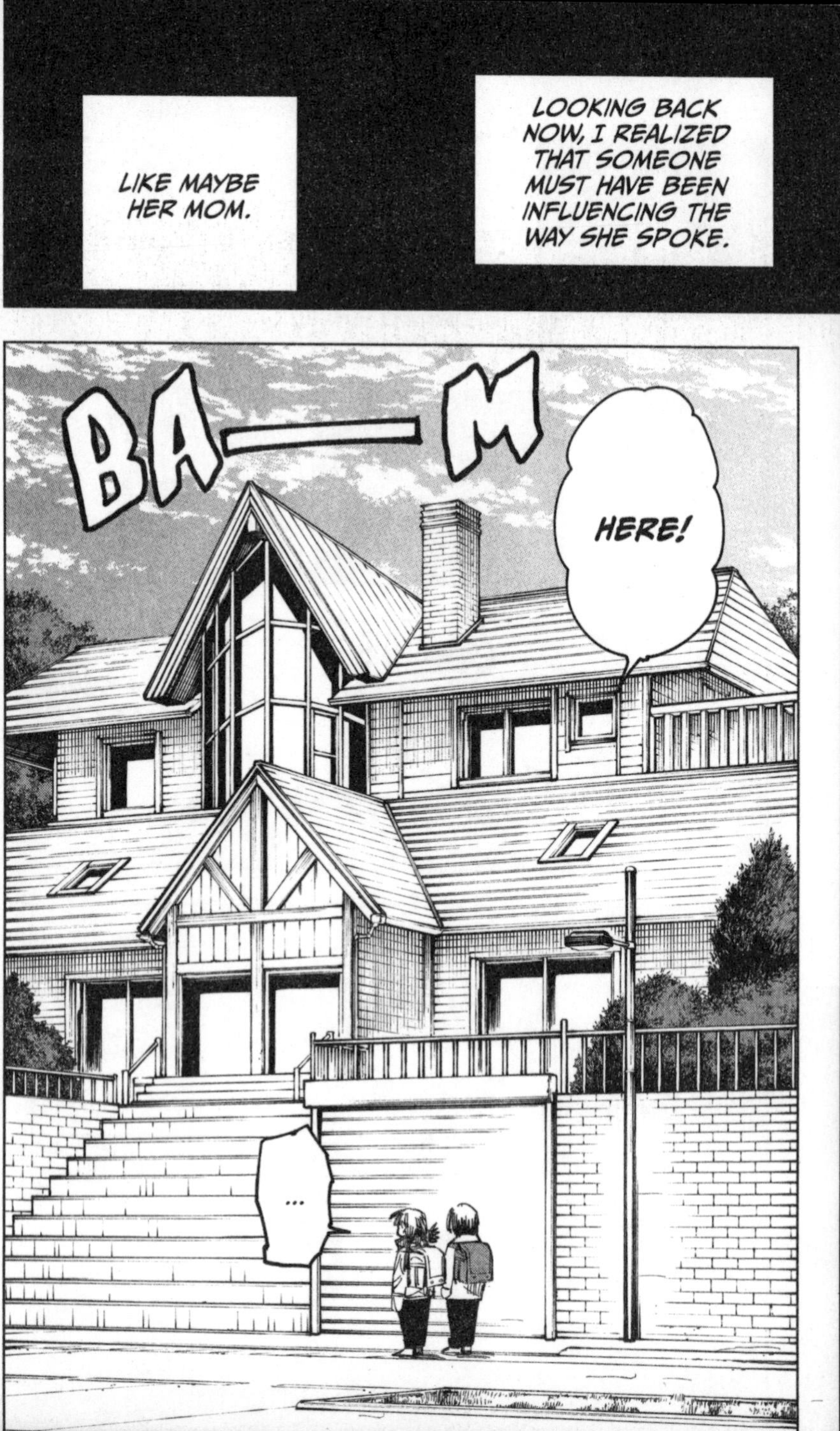
LOOKING BACK NOW, I REALIZED THAT SOMEONE MUST HAVE BEEN INFLUENCING THE WAY SHE SPOKE.
LIKE MAYBE HER MOM.
BA—M
HERE!
...

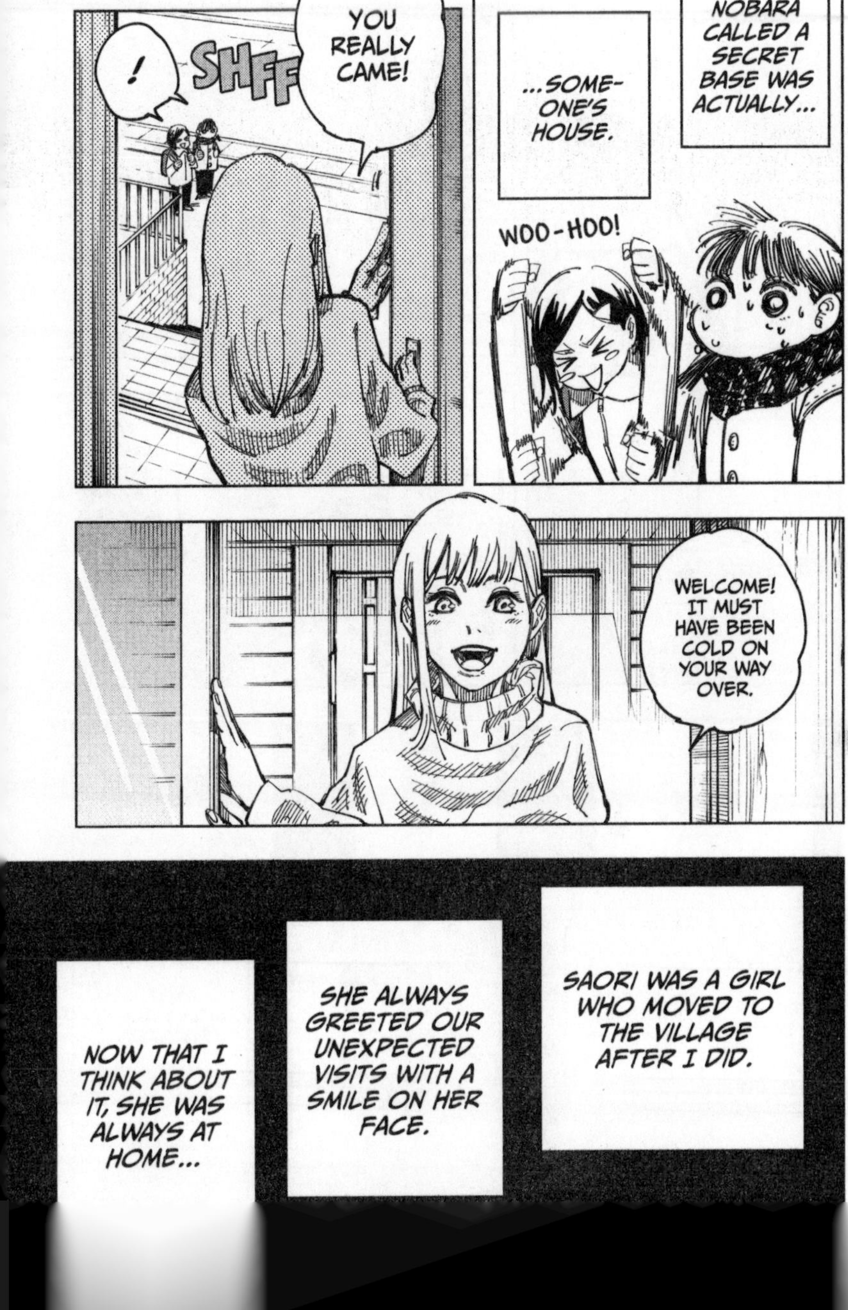
WHAT NOBARA CALLED A SECRET BASE WAS ACTUALLY...
...SOME-ONE'S HOUSE.
WOO-HOO!
YOU REALLY CAME!
SHFF
!
WELCOME! IT MUST HAVE BEEN COLD ON YOUR WAY OVER.
SAORI WAS A GIRL WHO MOVED TO THE VILLAGE AFTER I DID.
SHE ALWAYS GREETED OUR UNEXPECTED VISITS WITH A SMILE ON HER FACE.
NOW THAT I THINK ABOUT IT, SHE WAS ALWAYS AT HOME...

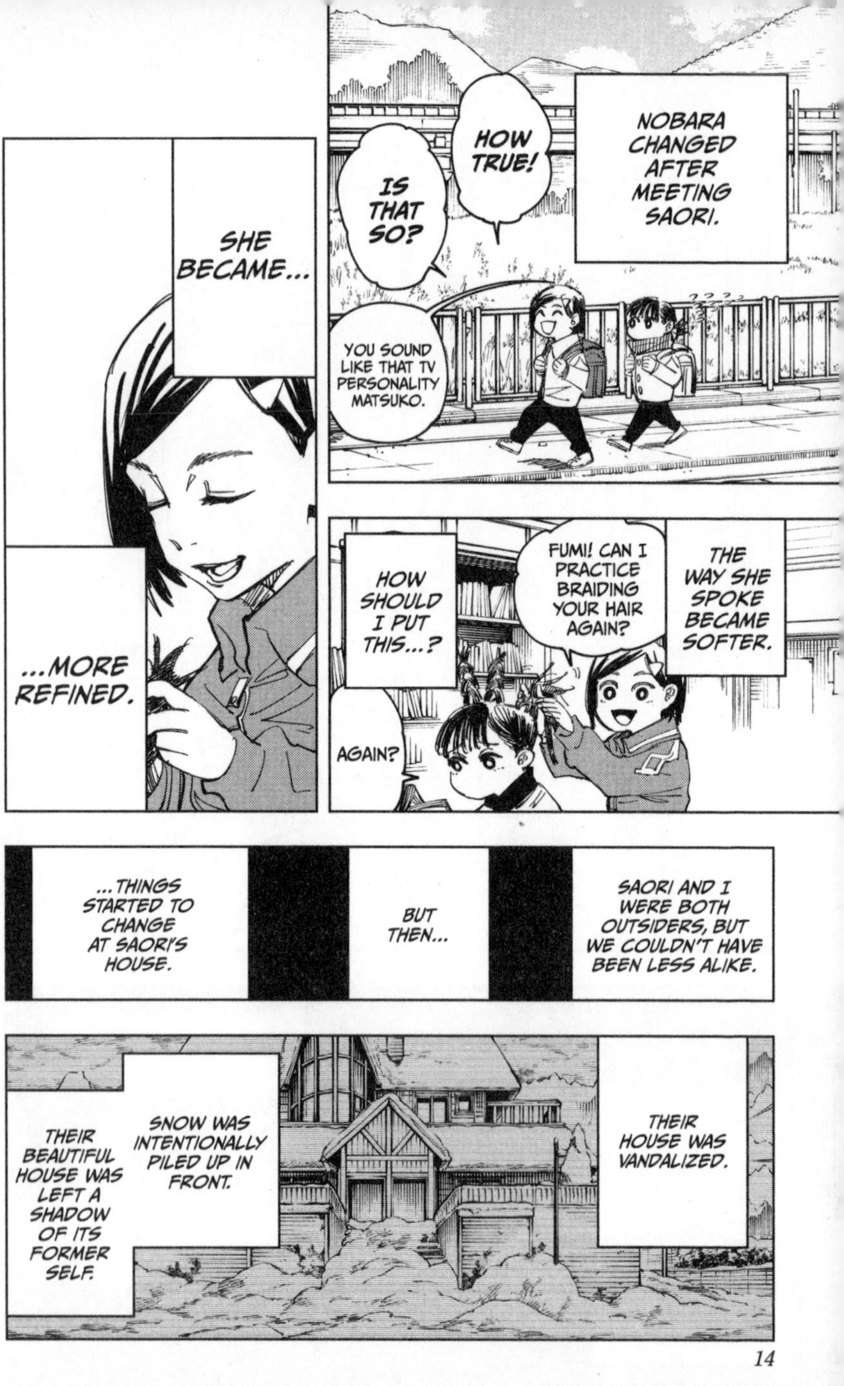
NOBARA CHANGED AFTER MEETING SAORI.
HOW TRUE!
IS THAT SO?
YOU SOUND LIKE THAT TV PERSONALITY MATSUKO.
THE WAY SHE SPOKE BECAME SOFTER.
FUMI! CAN I PRACTICE BRAIDING YOUR HAIR AGAIN?
HOW SHOULD I PUT THIS...?
AGAIN?
SHE BECAME...
...MORE REFINED.
SAORI AND I WERE BOTH OUTSIDERS, BUT WE COULDN'T HAVE BEEN LESS ALIKE.
BUT THEN...
...THINGS STARTED TO CHANGE AT SAORI'S HOUSE.
THEIR HOUSE WAS VANDALIZED.
SNOW WAS INTENTIONALLY PILED UP IN FRONT.
THEIR BEAUTIFUL HOUSE WAS LEFT A SHADOW OF ITS FORMER SELF.

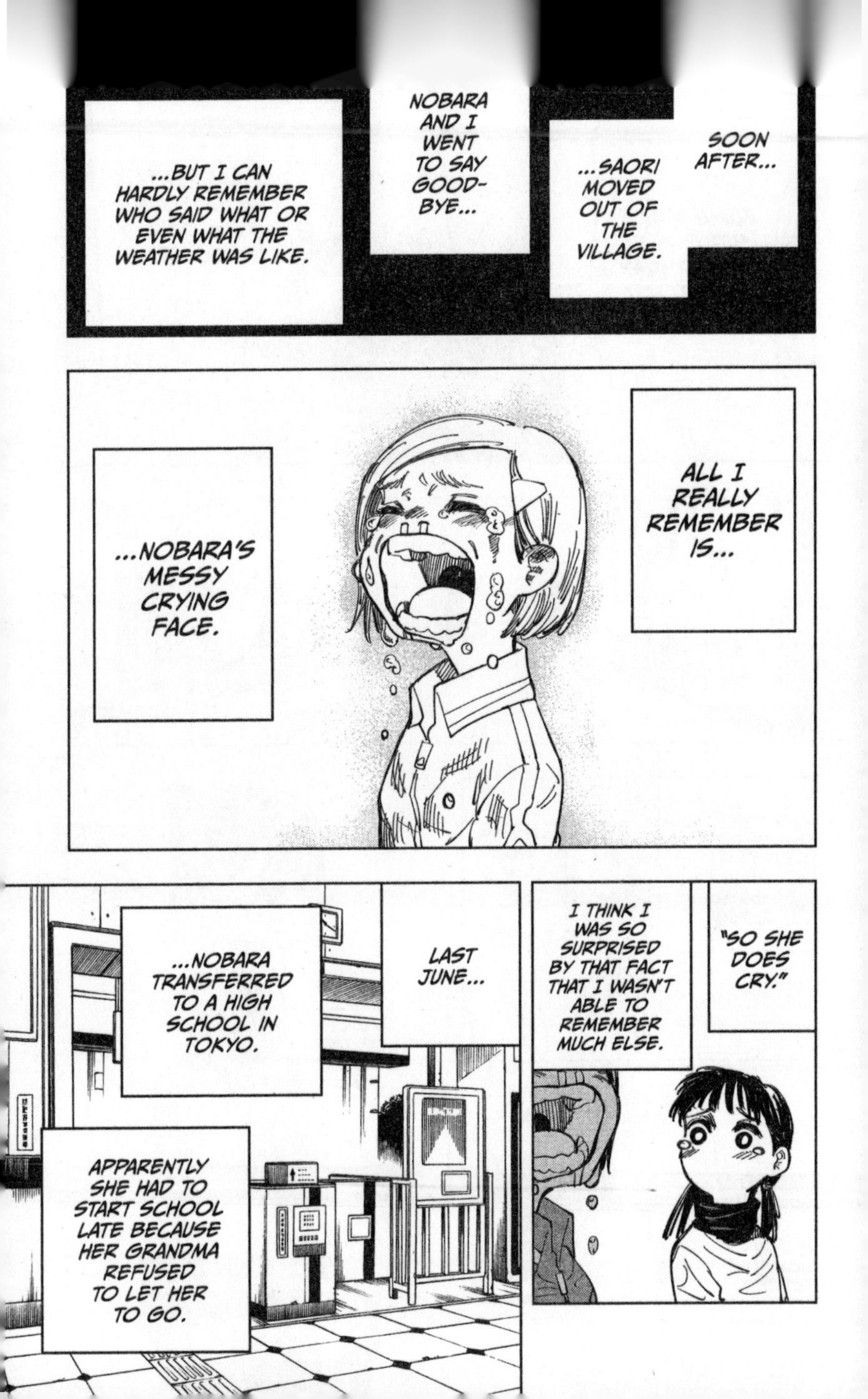
SOON AFTER...
...SAORI MOVED OUT OF THE VILLAGE.
NOBARA AND I WENT TO SAY GOOD-BYE...
...BUT I CAN HARDLY REMEMBER WHO SAID WHAT OR EVEN WHAT THE WEATHER WAS LIKE.
ALL I REALLY REMEMBER IS...
...NOBARA'S MESSY CRYING FACE.
"SO SHE DOES CRY."
I THINK I WAS SO SURPRISED BY THAT FACT THAT I WASN'T ABLE TO REMEMBER MUCH ELSE.
LAST JUNE...
...NOBARA TRANSFERRED TO A HIGH SCHOOL IN TOKYO.
APPARENTLY SHE HAD TO START SCHOOL LATE BECAUSE HER GRANDMA REFUSED TO LET HER TO GO.

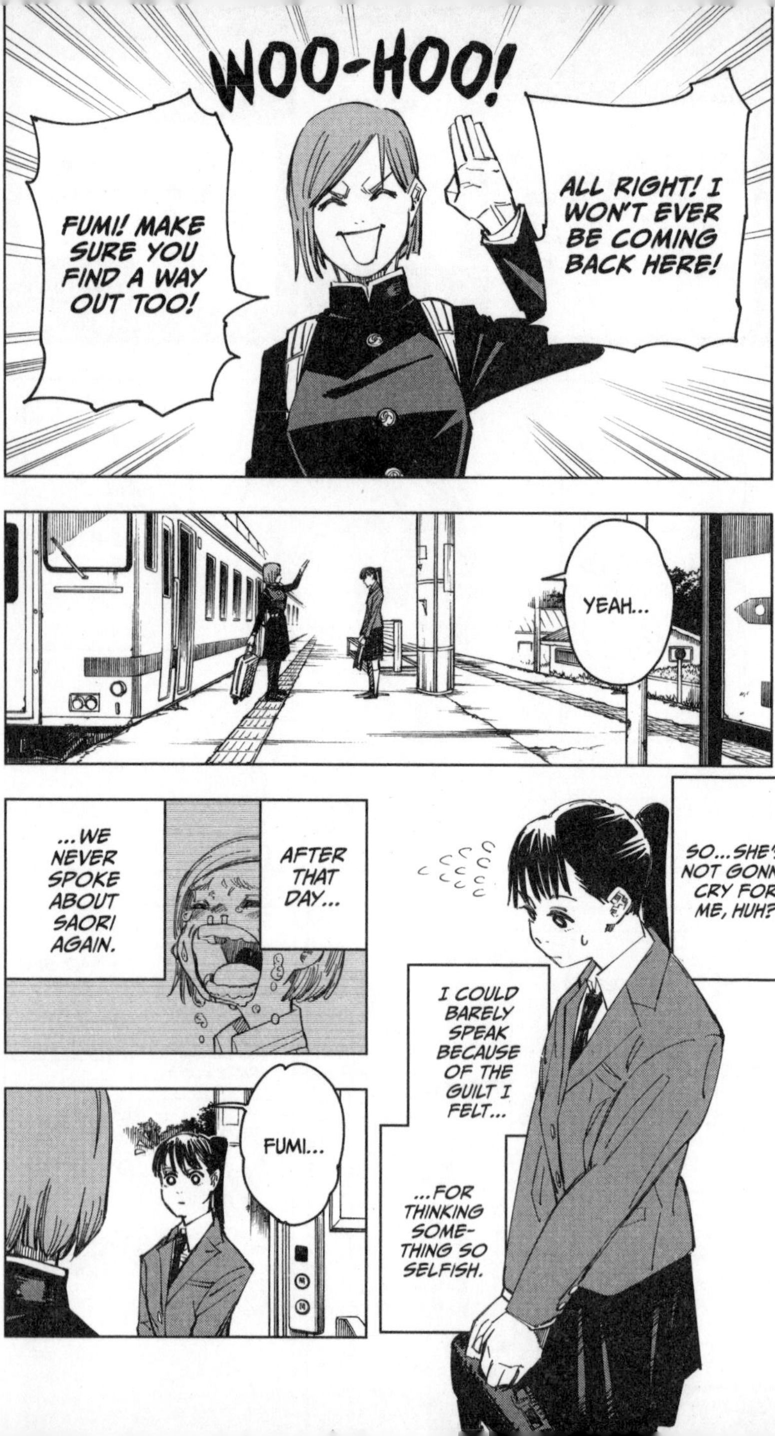
WOO-HOO!
ALL RIGHT! I WON'T EVER BE COMING BACK HERE!
FUMI! MAKE SURE YOU FIND A WAY OUT TOO!
YEAH...
SO...SHE'S NOT GONNA CRY FOR ME, HUH?
I COULD BARELY SPEAK BECAUSE OF THE GUILT I FELT...
...FOR THINKING SOMETHING SO SELFISH.
AFTER THAT DAY...
...WE NEVER SPOKE ABOUT SAORI AGAIN.
FUMI...

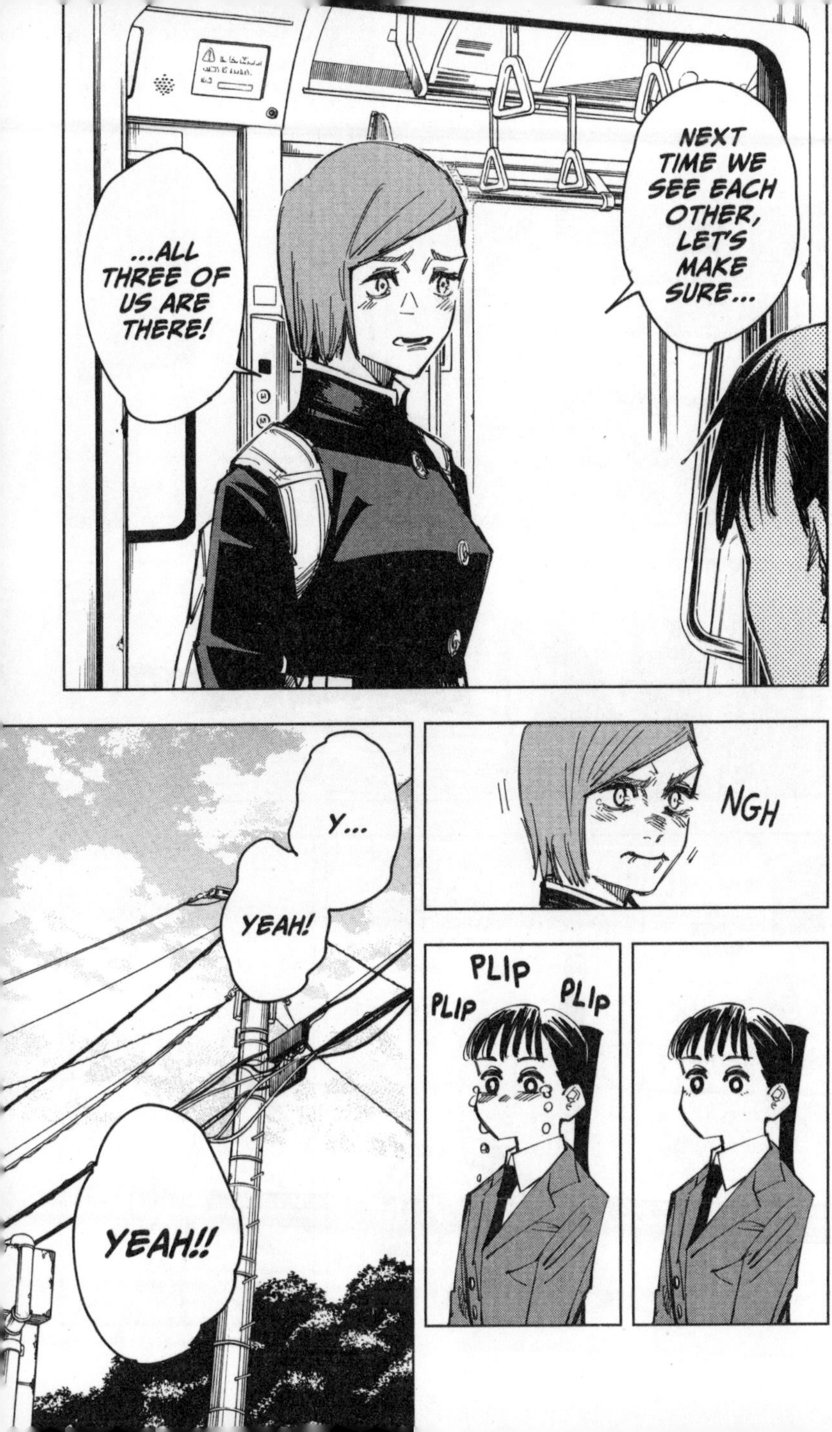
NEXT TIME WE SEE EACH OTHER, LET'S MAKE SURE...
...ALL THREE OF US ARE THERE!
NGH
PLIP
PLIP
PLIP
Y...
YEAH!
YEAH!!

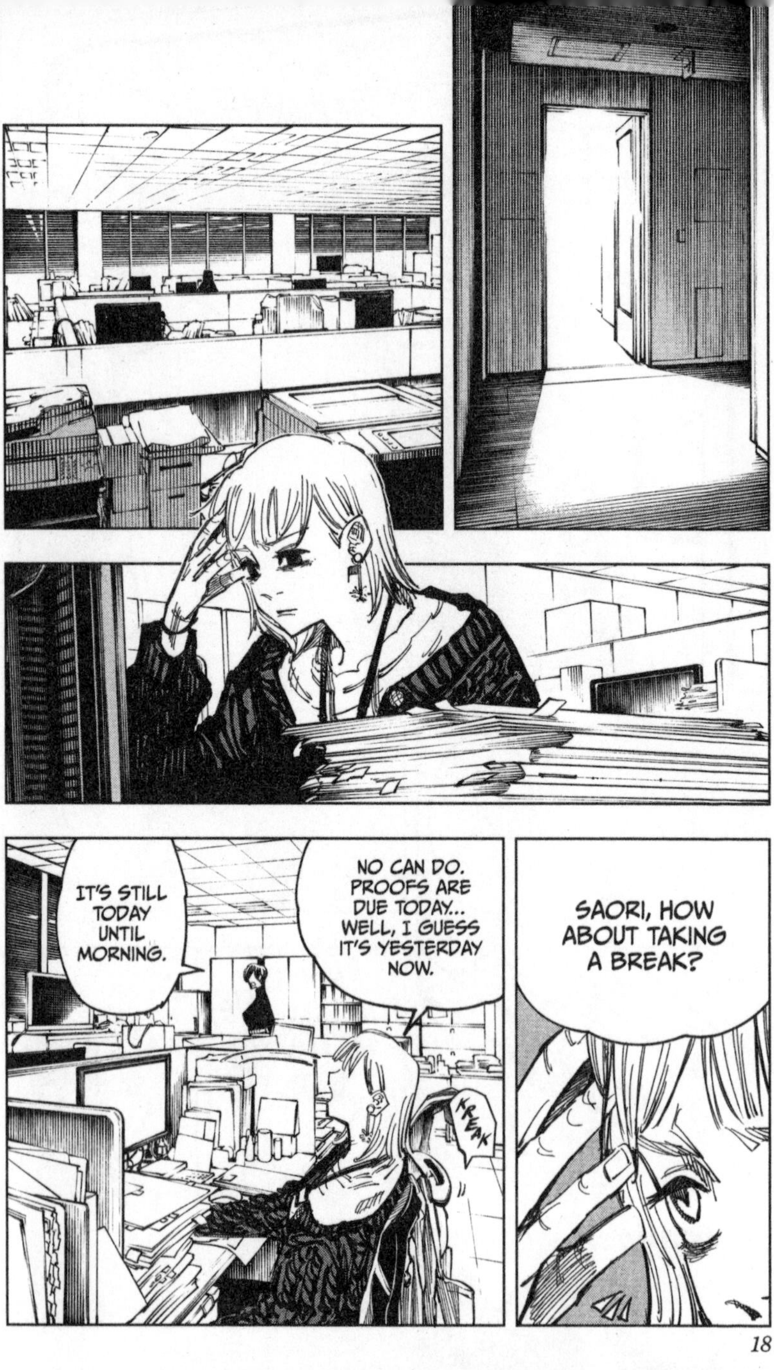
SAORI, HOW ABOUT TAKING A BREAK?
NO CAN DO. PROOFS ARE DUE TODAY... WELL, I GUESS IT'S YESTERDAY NOW.
KREAK
IT'S STILL TODAY UNTIL MORNING.

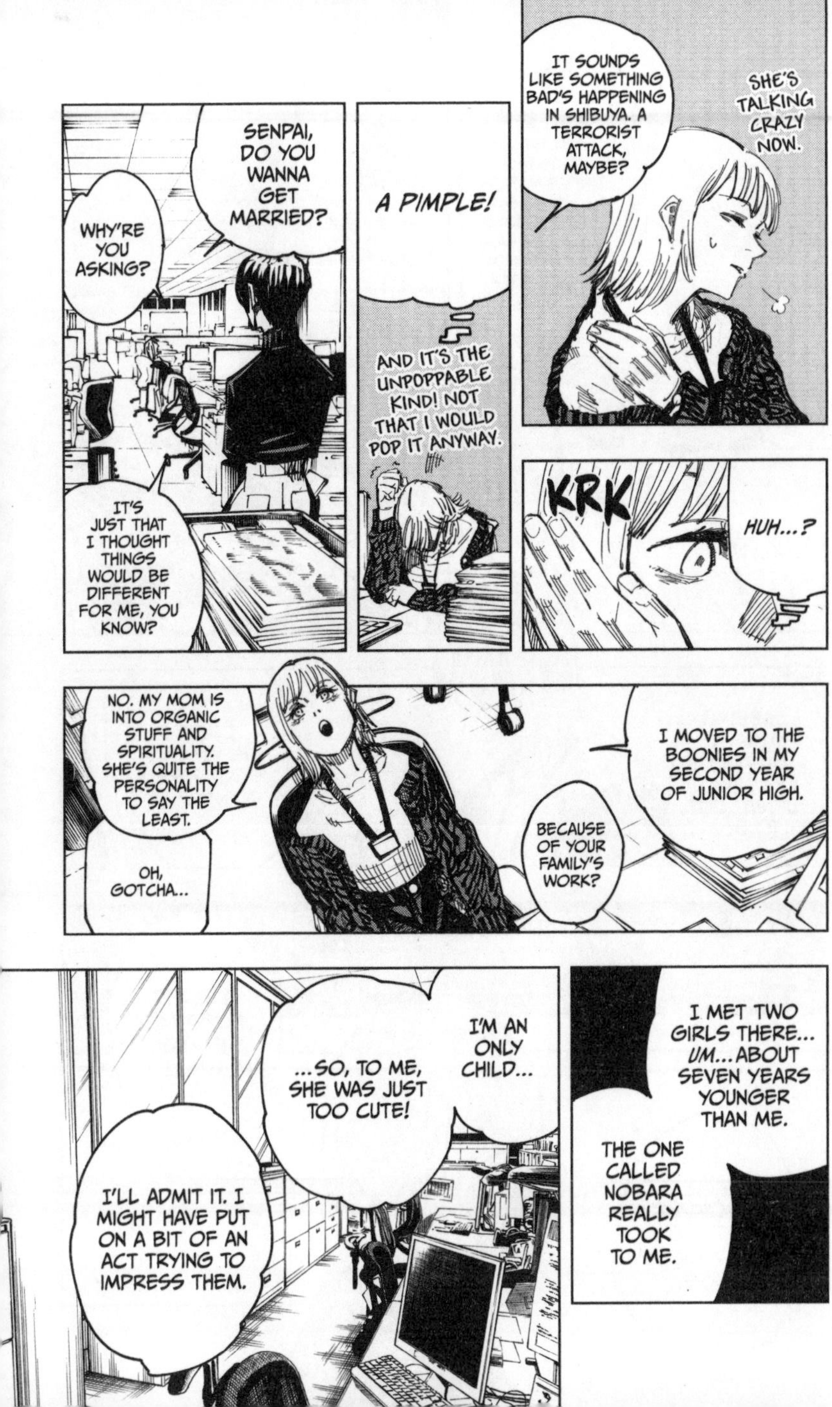
IT SOUNDS LIKE SOMETHING BAD'S HAPPENING IN SHIBUYA. A TERRORIST ATTACK, MAYBE?
SHE'S TALKING CRAZY NOW.
KRK
HUH...?
A PIMPLE!
AND IT'S THE UNPOPPABLE KIND! NOT THAT I WOULD POP IT ANYWAY.
SENPAI, DO YOU WANNA GET MARRIED?
WHY'RE YOU ASKING?
IT'S JUST THAT I THOUGHT THINGS WOULD BE DIFFERENT FOR ME, YOU KNOW?
I MOVED TO THE BOONIES IN MY SECOND YEAR OF JUNIOR HIGH.
BECAUSE OF YOUR FAMILY'S WORK?
NO. MY MOM IS INTO ORGANIC STUFF AND SPIRITUALITY. SHE'S QUITE THE PERSONALITY TO SAY THE LEAST.
OH, GOTCHA...
I MET TWO GIRLS THERE... *UM*... ABOUT SEVEN YEARS YOUNGER THAN ME.
THE ONE CALLED NOBARA REALLY TOOK TO ME.
I'M AN ONLY CHILD...
...SO, TO ME, SHE WAS JUST TOO CUTE!
I'LL ADMIT IT. I MIGHT HAVE PUT ON A BIT OF AN ACT TRYING TO IMPRESS THEM.

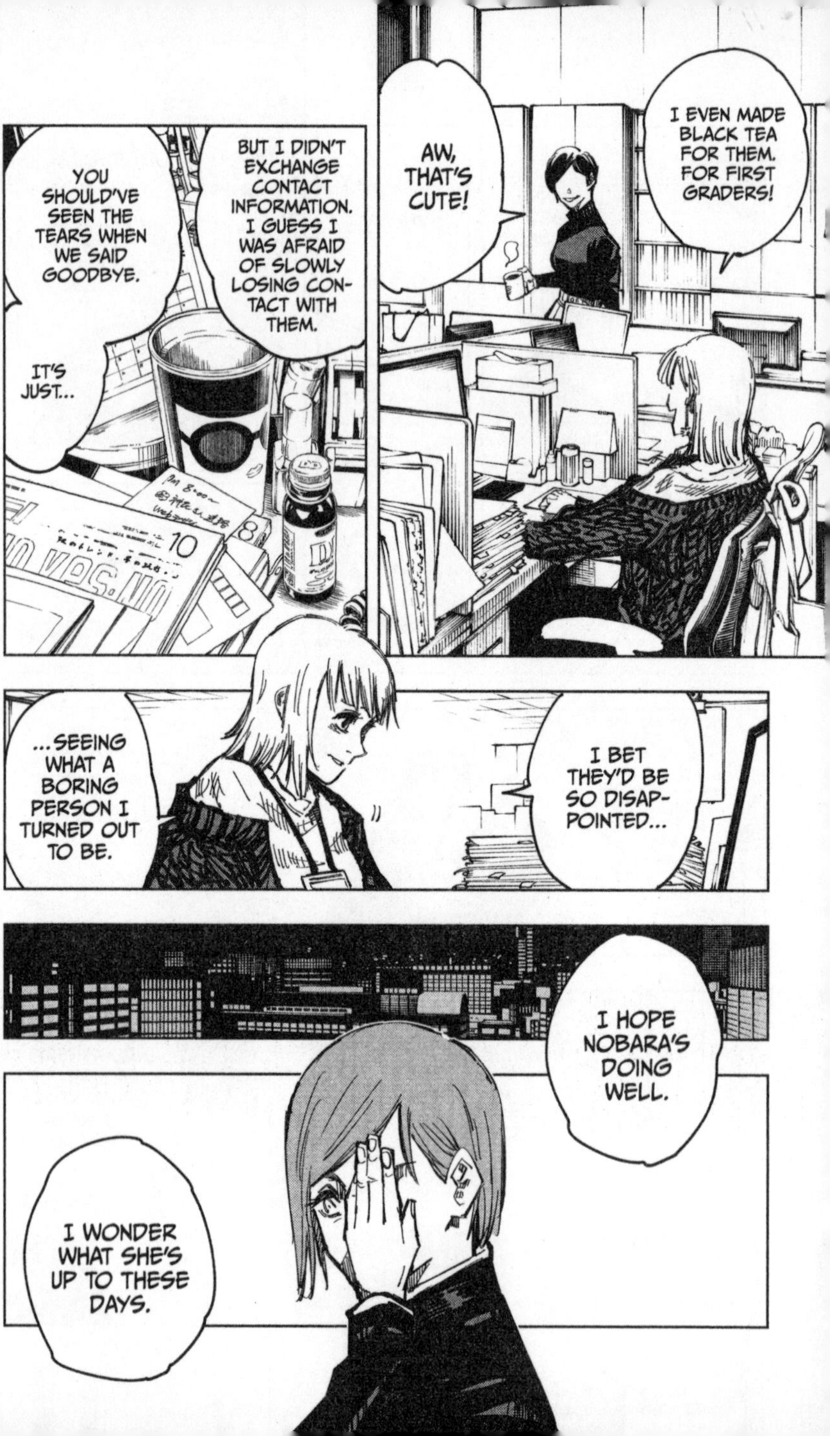
I EVEN MADE BLACK TEA FOR THEM. FOR FIRST GRADERS!
AW, THAT'S CUTE!
BUT I DIDN'T EXCHANGE CONTACT INFORMATION. I GUESS I WAS AFRAID OF SLOWLY LOSING CONTACT WITH THEM.
YOU SHOULD'VE SEEN THE TEARS WHEN WE SAID GOODBYE.
IT'S JUST...
I BET THEY'D BE SO DISAPPOINTED...
...SEEING WHAT A BORING PERSON I TURNED OUT TO BE.
I HOPE NOBARA'S DOING WELL.
I WONDER WHAT SHE'S UP TO THESE DAYS.

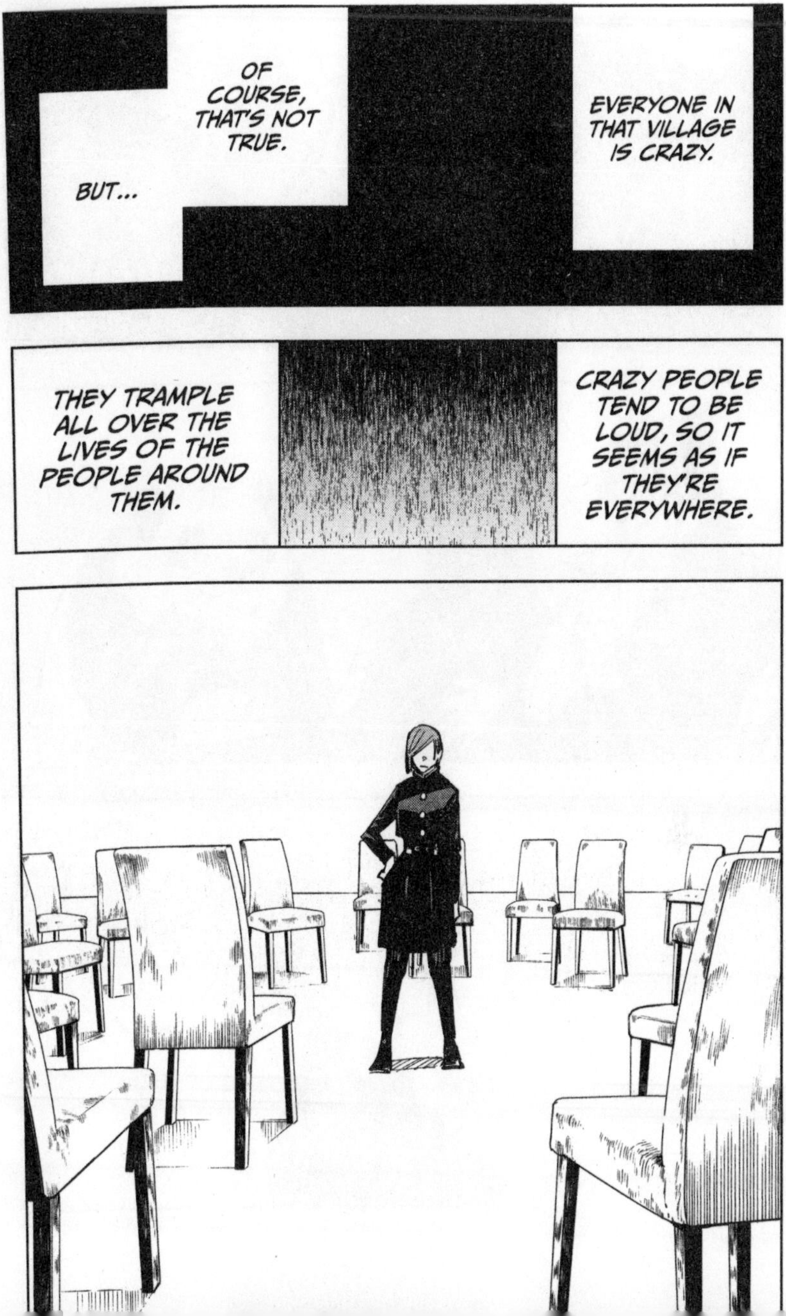
EVERYONE IN THAT VILLAGE IS CRAZY.
OF COURSE, THAT'S NOT TRUE.
BUT...
CRAZY PEOPLE TEND TO BE LOUD, SO IT SEEMS AS IF THEY'RE EVERYWHERE.
THEY TRAMPLE ALL OVER THE LIVES OF THE PEOPLE AROUND THEM.

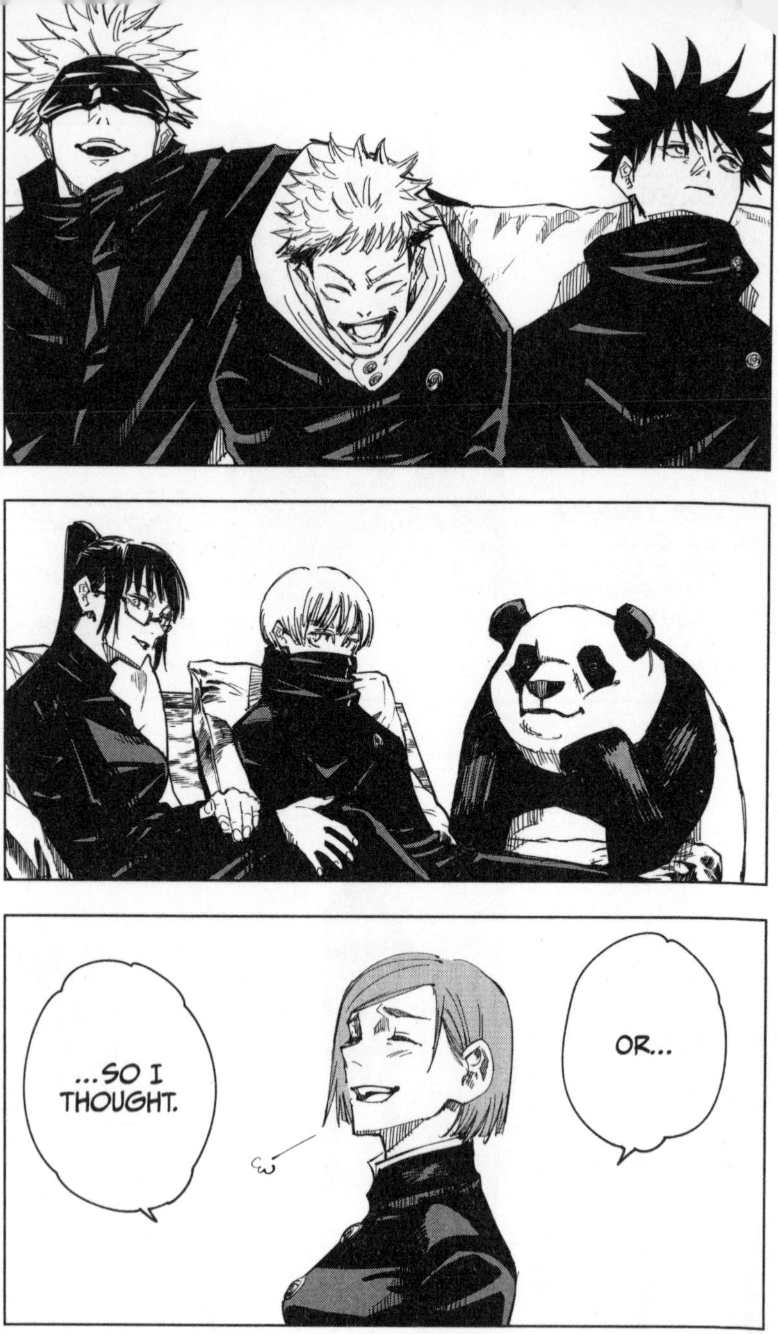
OR...
...SO I THOUGHT.

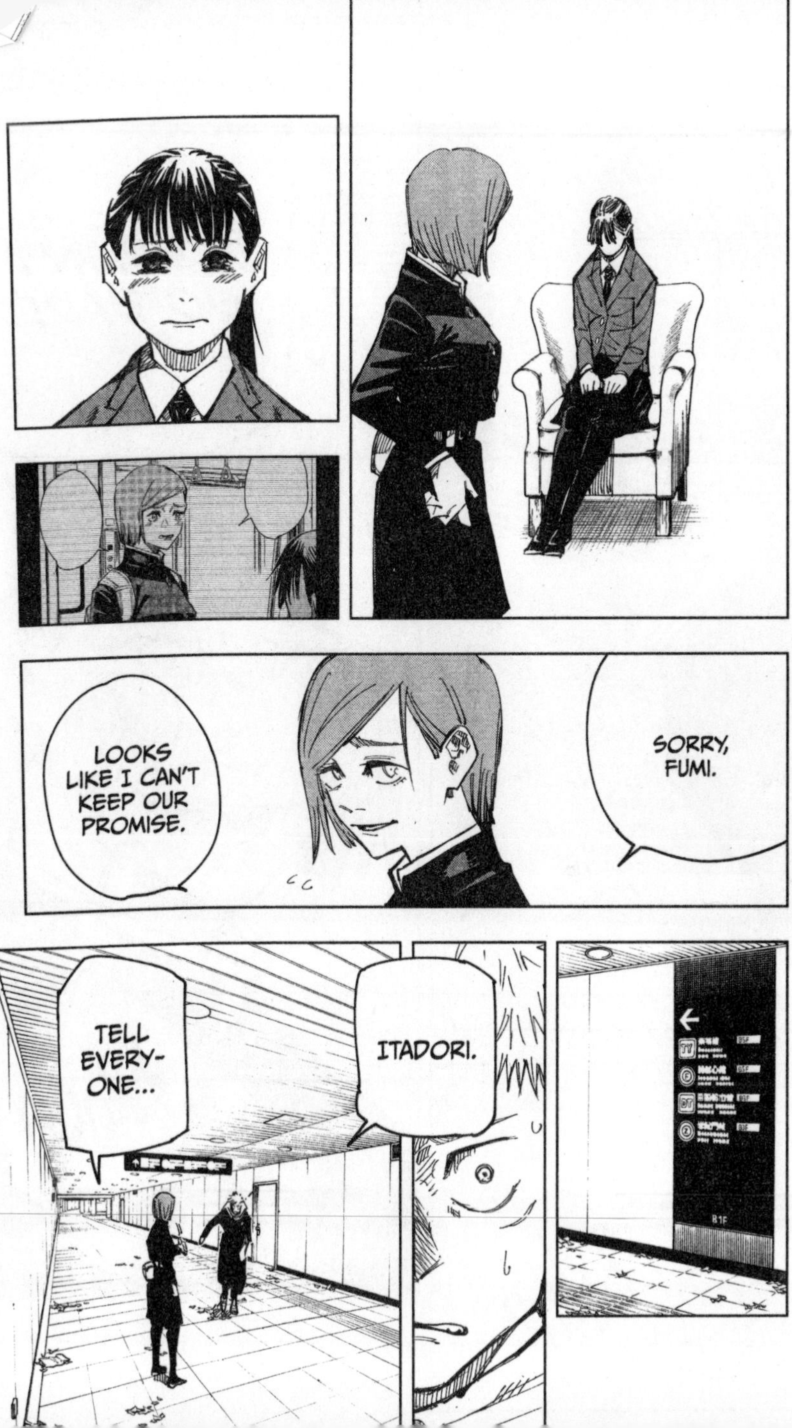
SORRY, FUMI.
LOOKS LIKE I CAN'T KEEP OUR PROMISE.
ITADORI.
TELL EVERY-ONE...

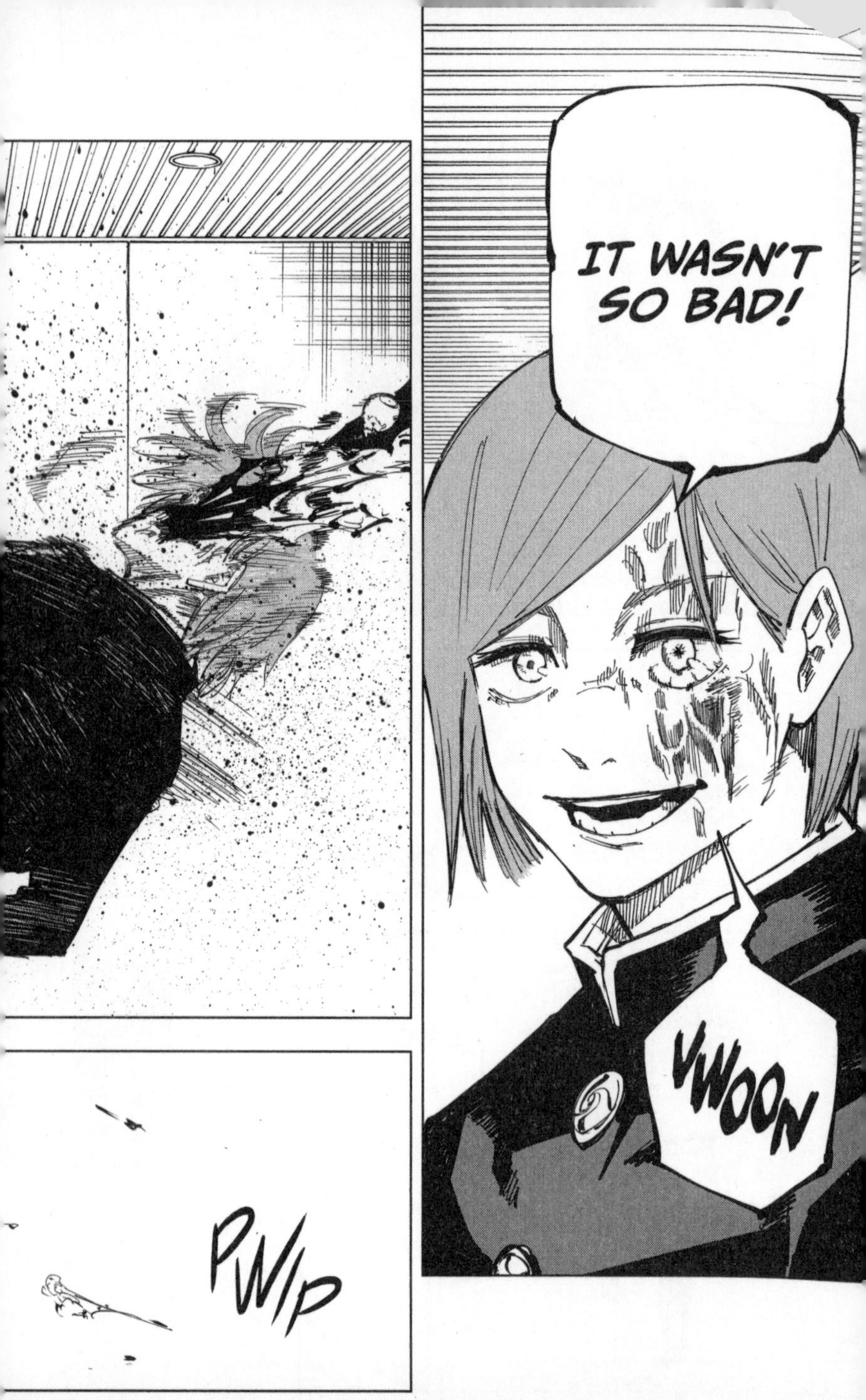
IT WASN'T SO BAD!
VWOON
PWIP

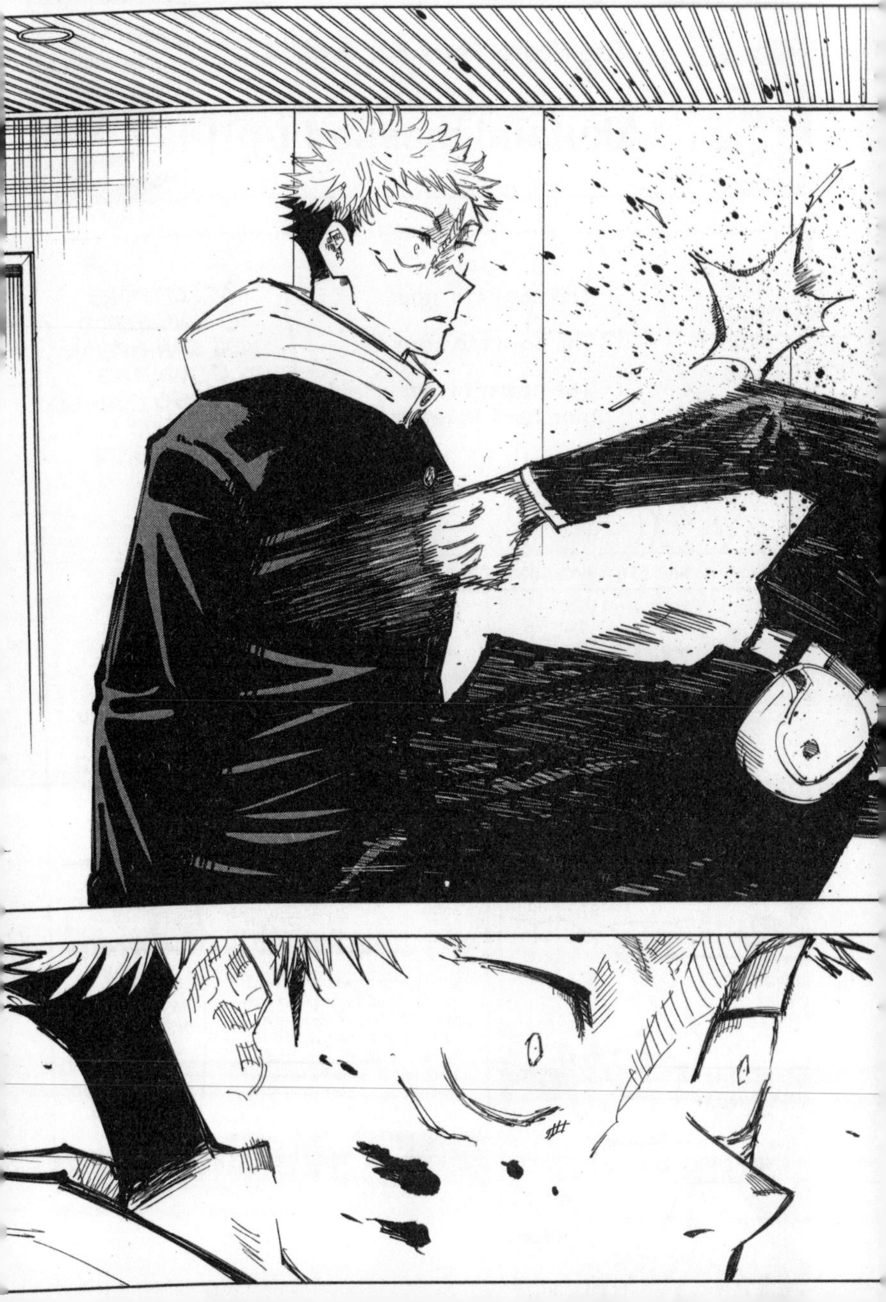

Getting It Right!!
Limitless Cursed Technique, Part 1

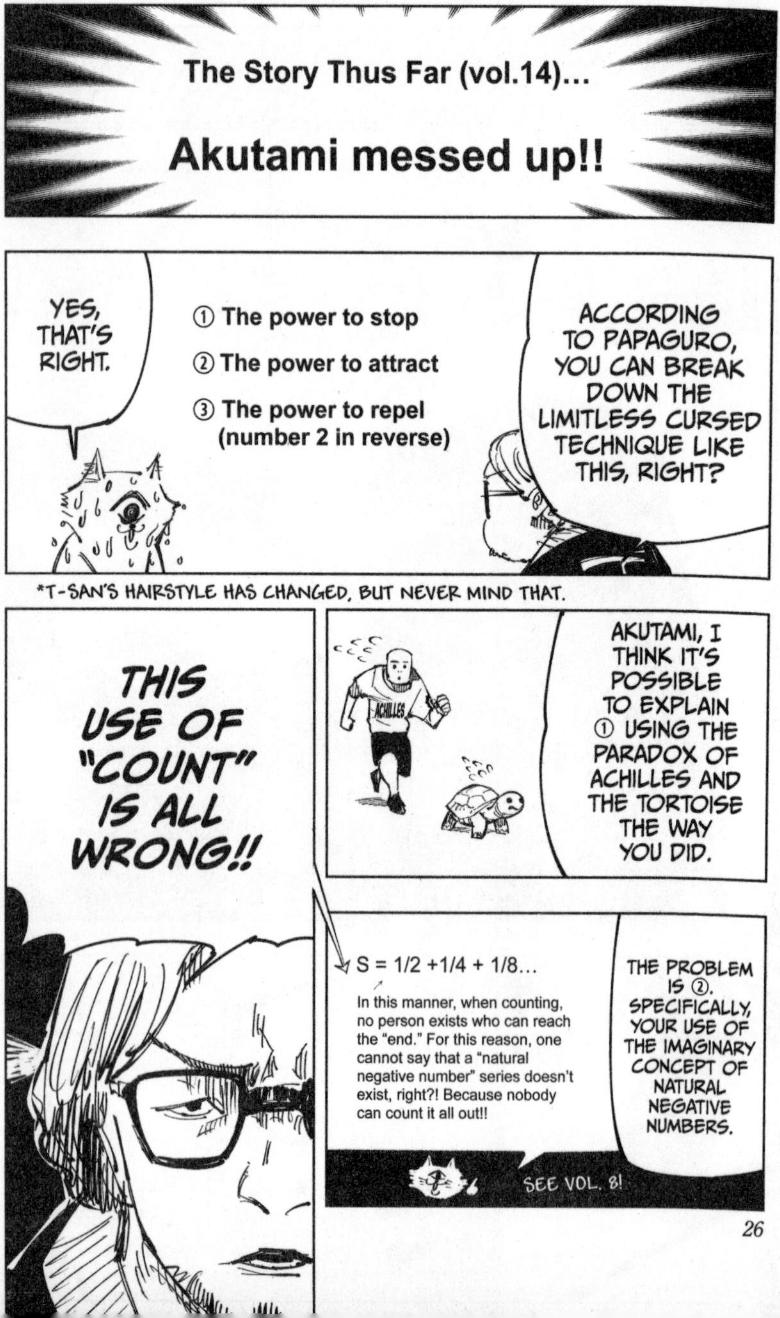

The Story Thus Far (vol.14)...
Akutami messed up!!
ACCORDING TO PAPAGURO, YOU CAN BREAK DOWN THE LIMITLESS CURSED TECHNIQUE LIKE THIS, RIGHT?
① The power to stop
② The power to attract
③ The power to repel (number 2 in reverse)
YES, THAT'S RIGHT.
*T-SAN'S HAIRSTYLE HAS CHANGED, BUT NEVER MIND THAT.
AKUTAMI, I THINK IT'S POSSIBLE TO EXPLAIN ① USING THE PARADOX OF ACHILLES AND THE TORTOISE THE WAY YOU DID.
ACHILLES
THE PROBLEM IS ②. SPECIFICALLY, YOUR USE OF THE IMAGINARY CONCEPT OF NATURAL NEGATIVE NUMBERS.
S = 1/2 +1/4 + 1/8...
In this manner, when counting, no person exists who can reach the "end." For this reason, one cannot say that a "natural negative number" series doesn't exist, right?! Because nobody can count it all out!!
SEE VOL. 8!
THIS USE OF "COUNT" IS ALL WRONG!!

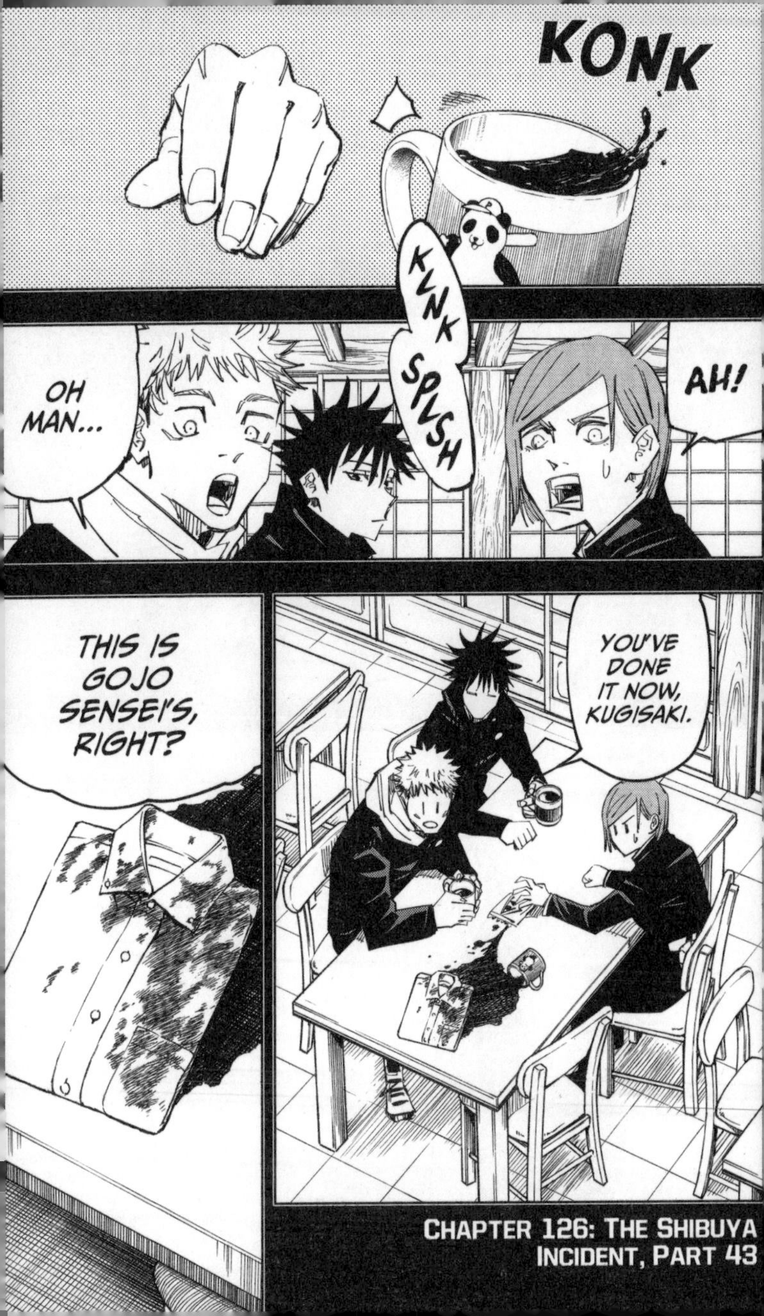
KONK
AH!
KUNK SPLSH
OH MAN...
YOU'VE DONE IT NOW, KUGISAKI.
THIS IS GOJO SENSEI'S, RIGHT?
CHAPTER 126: THE SHIBUYA INCIDENT, PART 43

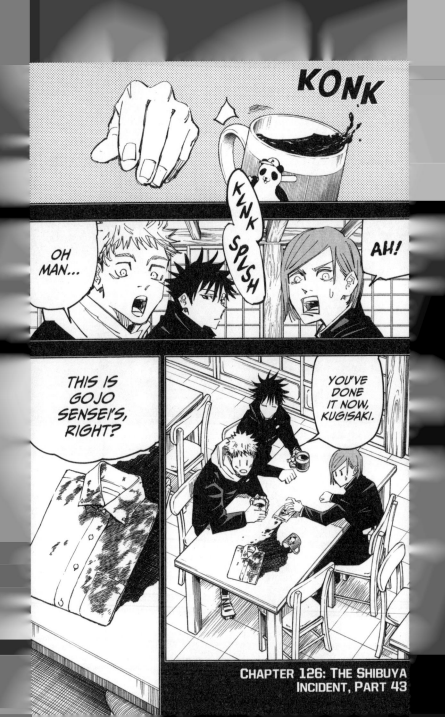

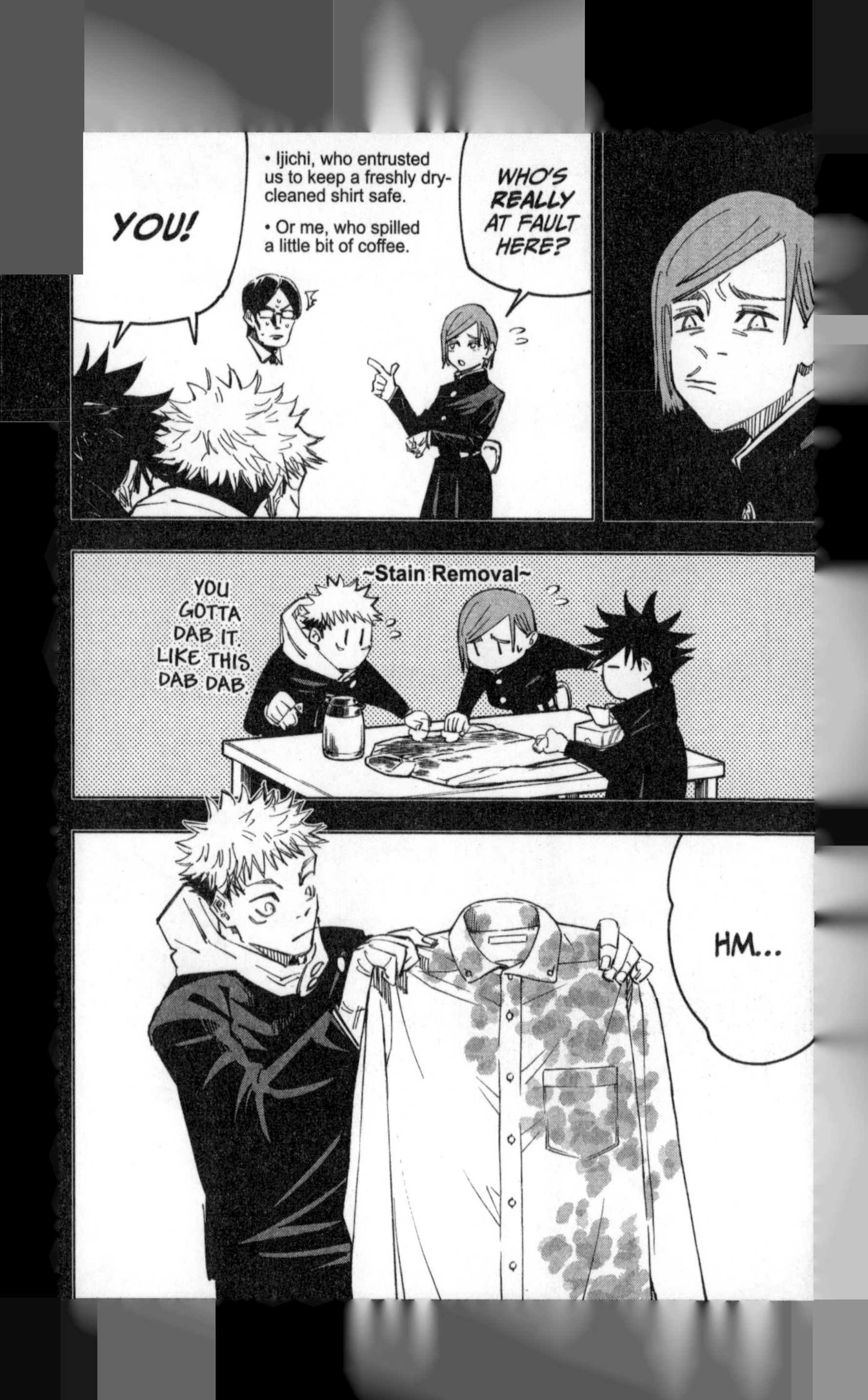
WHO'S REALLY AT FAULT HERE?
• Ijichi, who entrusted us to keep a freshly dry-cleaned shirt safe.
• Or me, who spilled a little bit of coffee.
YOU!
~Stain Removal~
YOU GOTTA DAB IT LIKE THIS. DAB DAB.
HM...

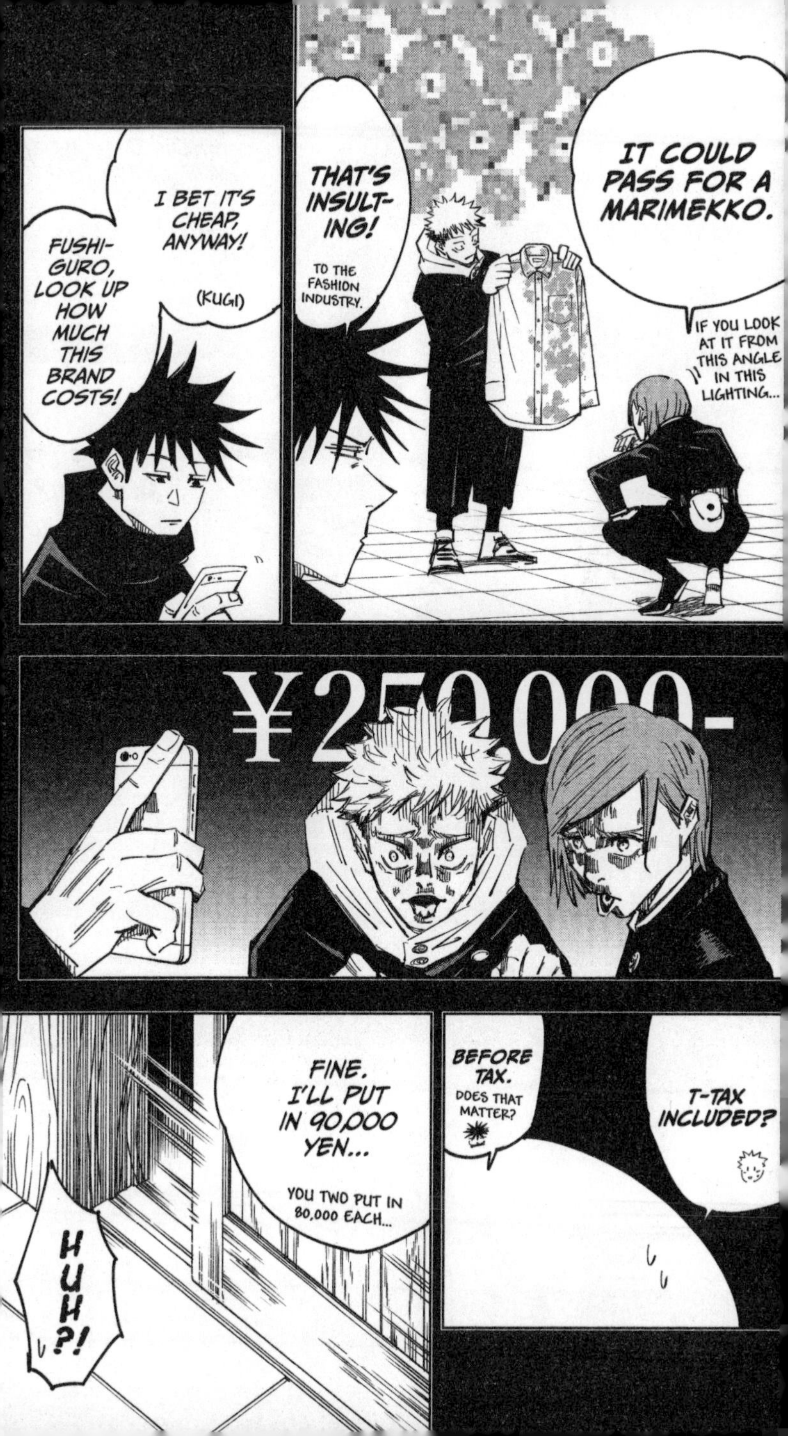
IT COULD PASS FOR A MARIMEKKO.
IF YOU LOOK AT IT FROM THIS ANGLE IN THIS LIGHTING...
THAT'S INSULTING! TO THE FASHION INDUSTRY.
I BET IT'S CHEAP, ANYWAY! (KUGI)
FUSHIGURO, LOOK UP HOW MUCH THIS BRAND COSTS!
¥250000-
T-TAX INCLUDED?
BEFORE TAX. DOES THAT MATTER?
FINE. I'LL PUT IN 90,000 YEN... YOU TWO PUT IN 80,000 EACH...
HUH?!

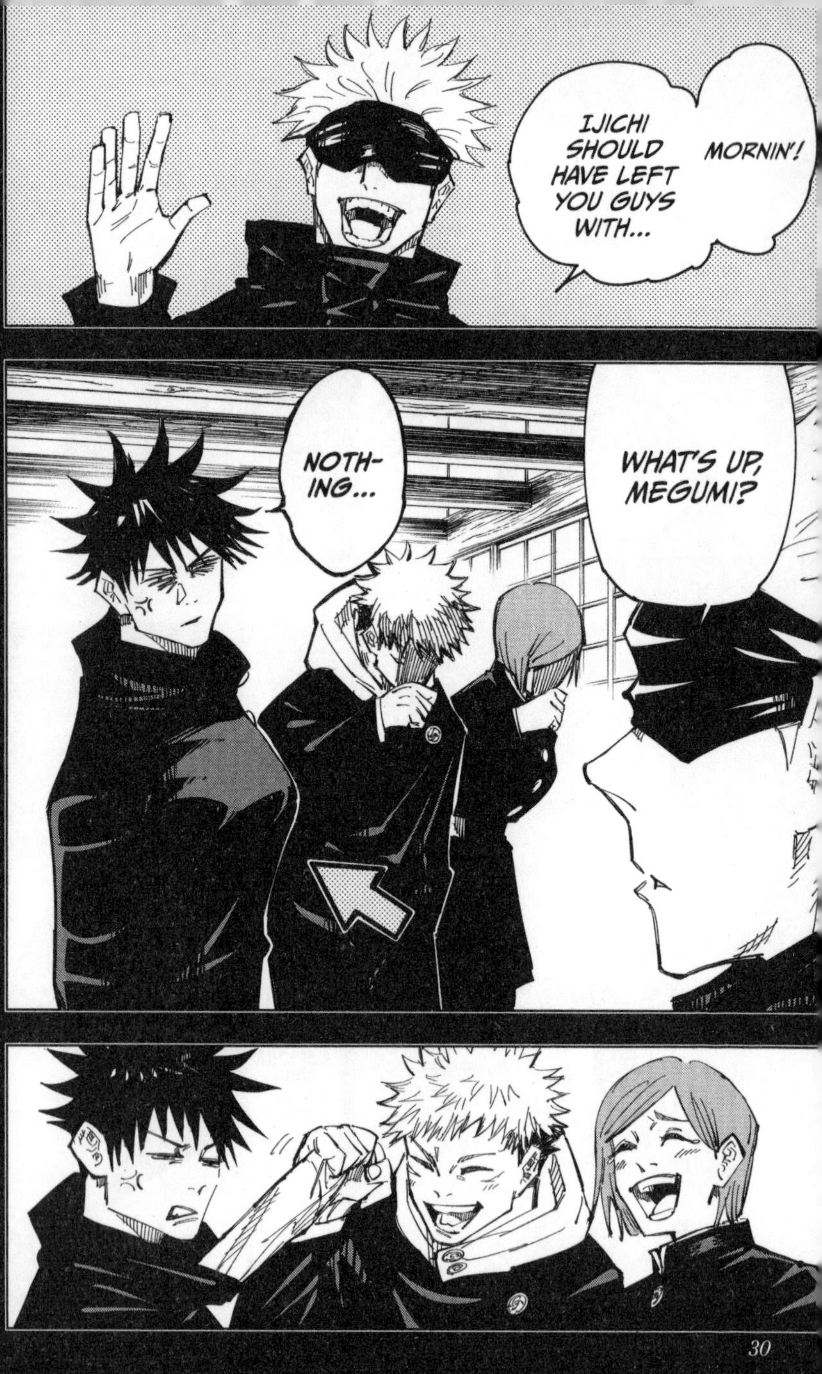
MORNIN'!
IJICHI SHOULD HAVE LEFT YOU GUYS WITH...
WHAT'S UP, MEGUMI?
NOTH-ING...

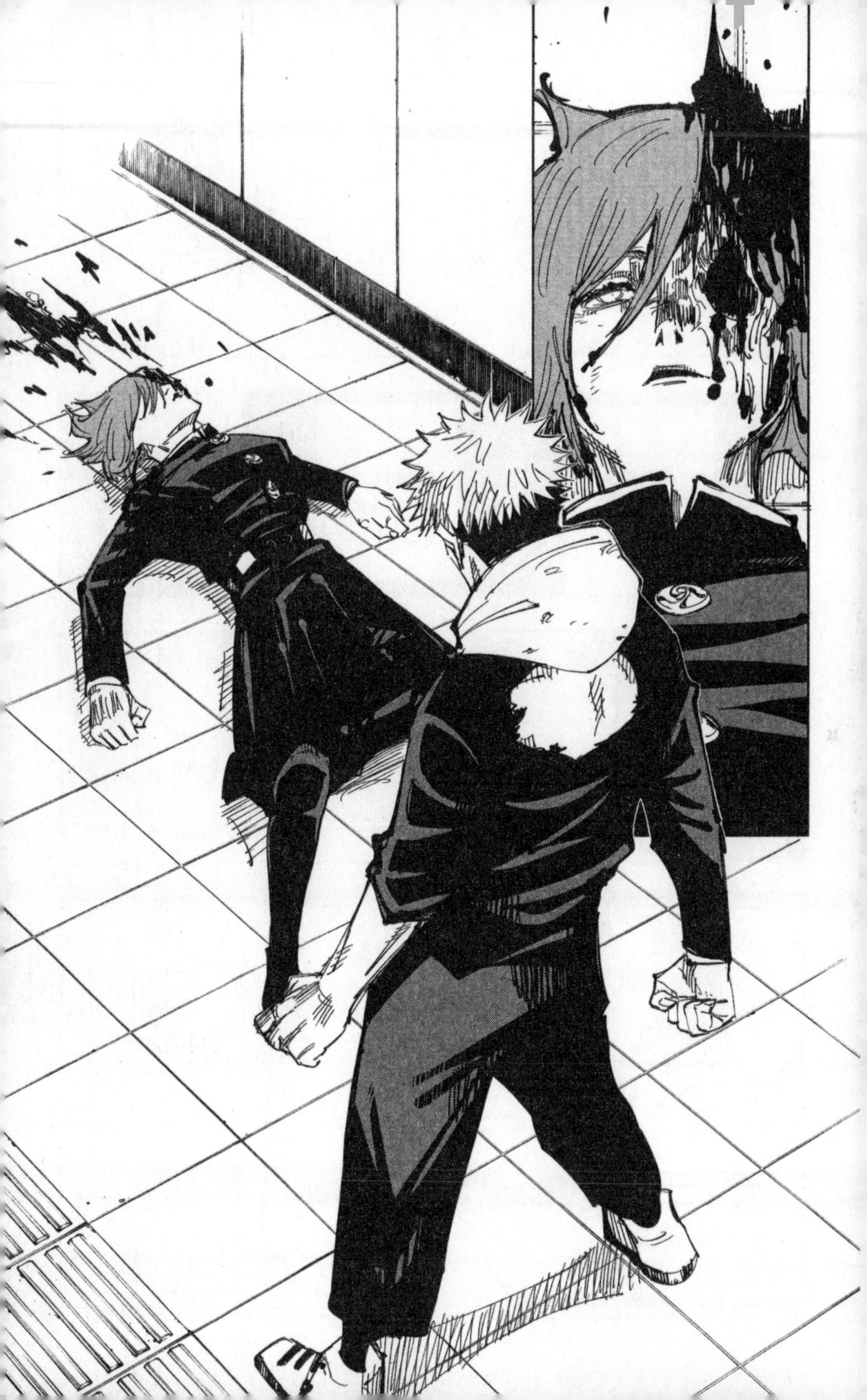

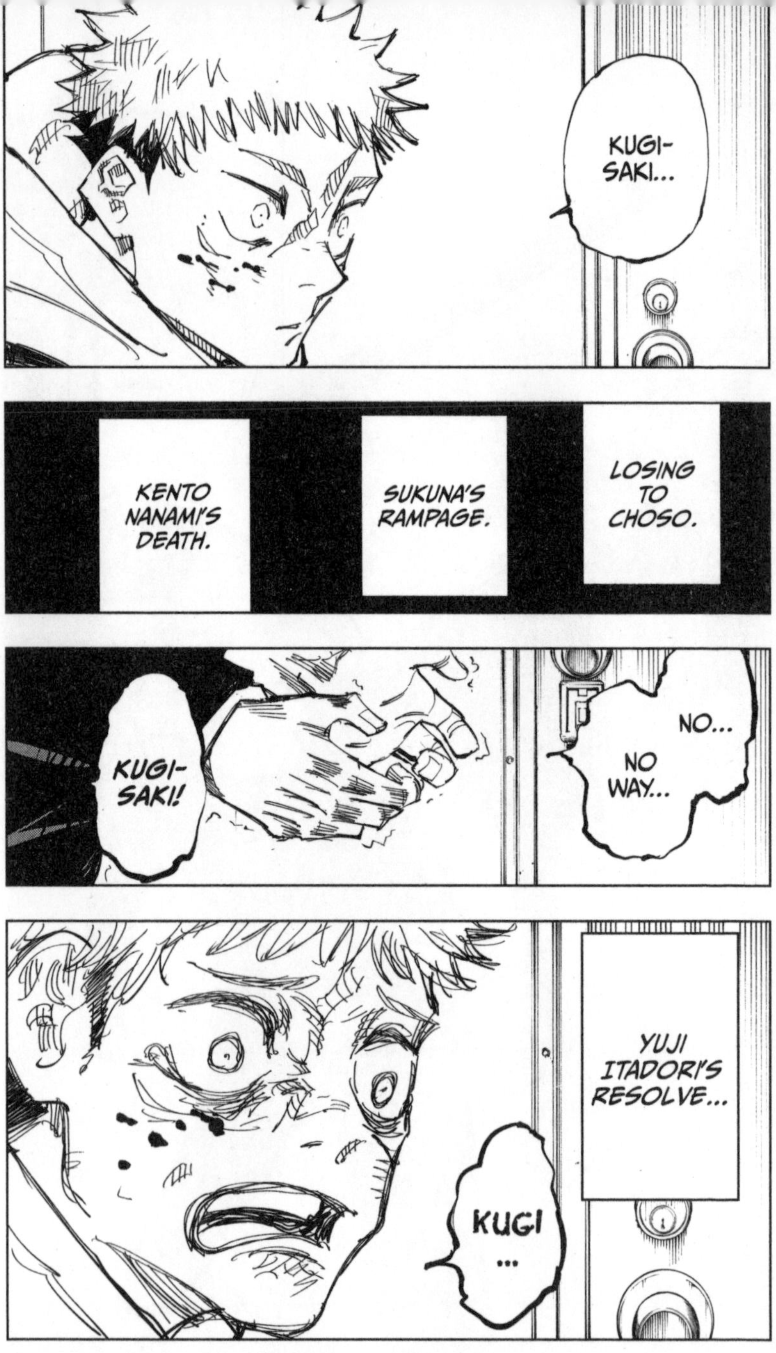
KUGI-SAKI...
LOSING TO CHOSO.
SUKUNA'S RAMPAGE.
KENTO NANAMI'S DEATH.
NO...
NO WAY...
KUGI-SAKI!
YUJI ITADORI'S RESOLVE...
KUGI ...

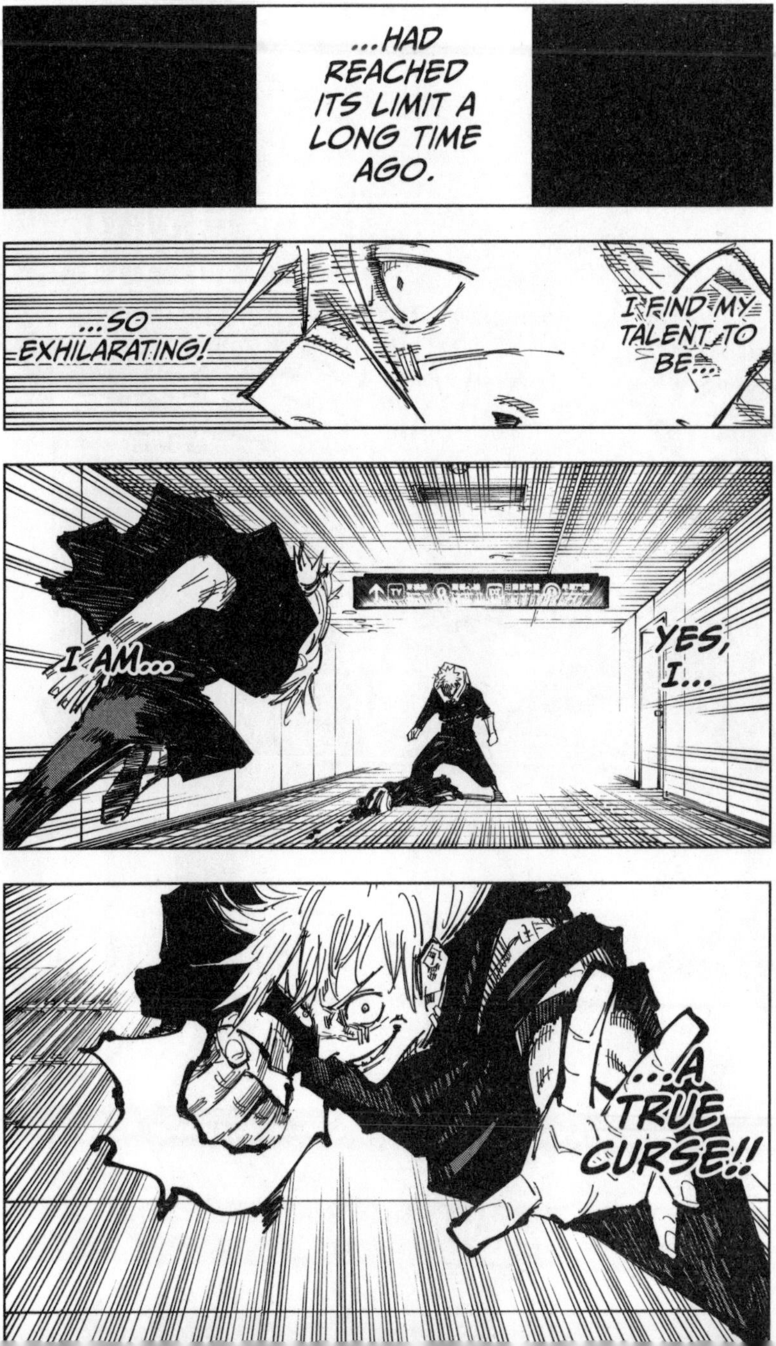
...HAD REACHED ITS LIMIT A LONG TIME AGO.
I FIND MY TALENT TO BE...
...SO EXHILARATING!
YES, I...
I AM...
...A TRUE CURSE!!

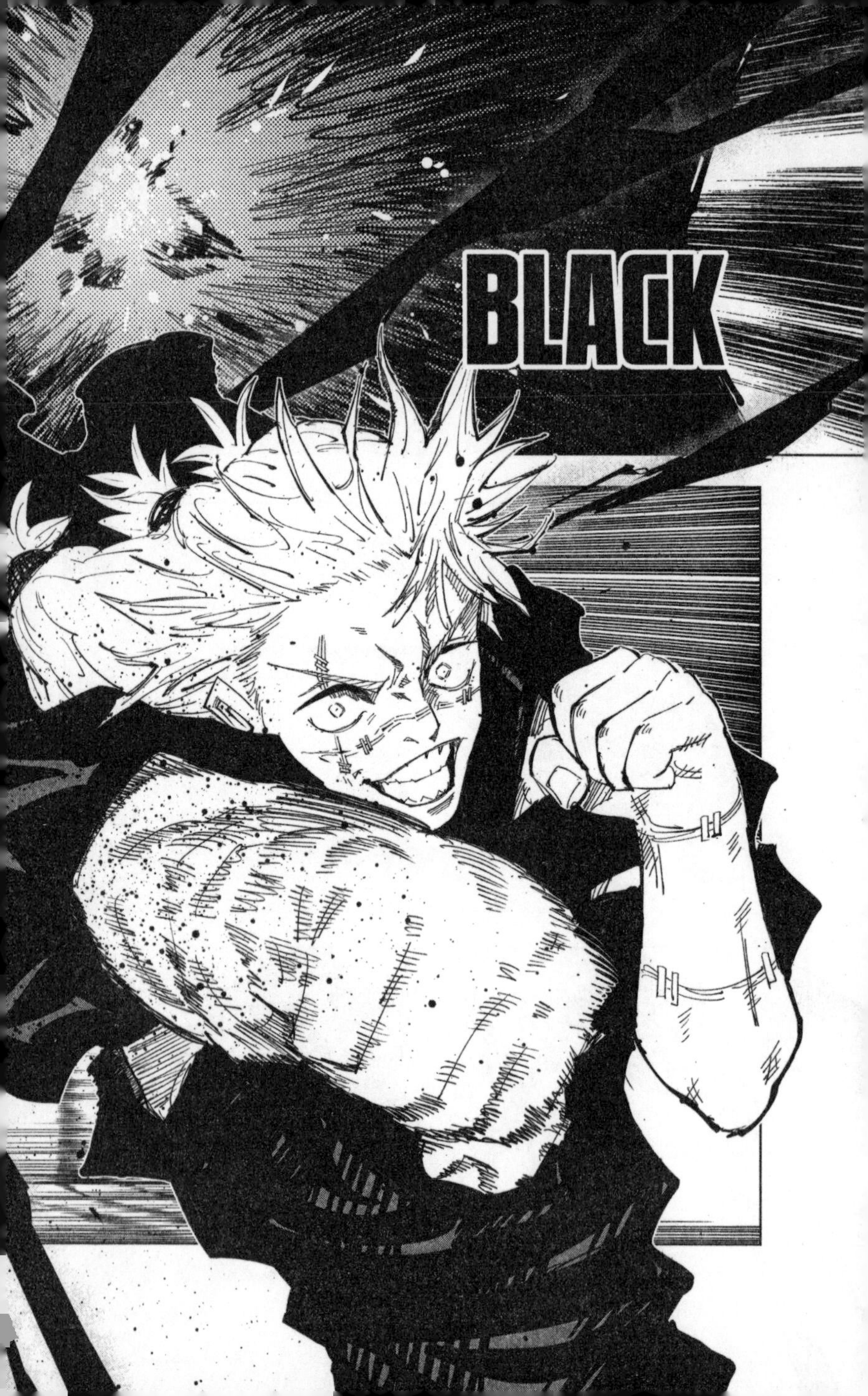
BLACK

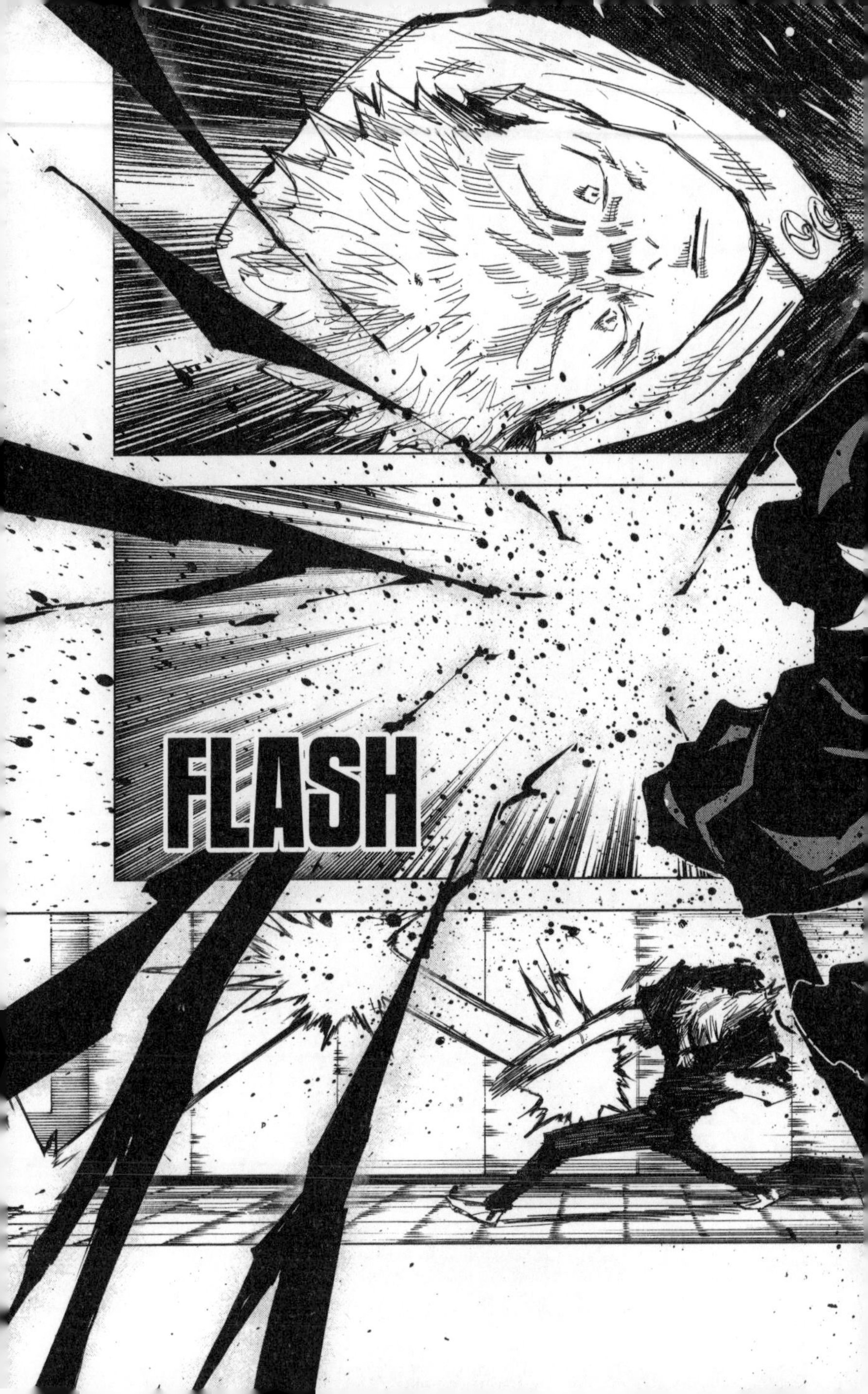
FLASH

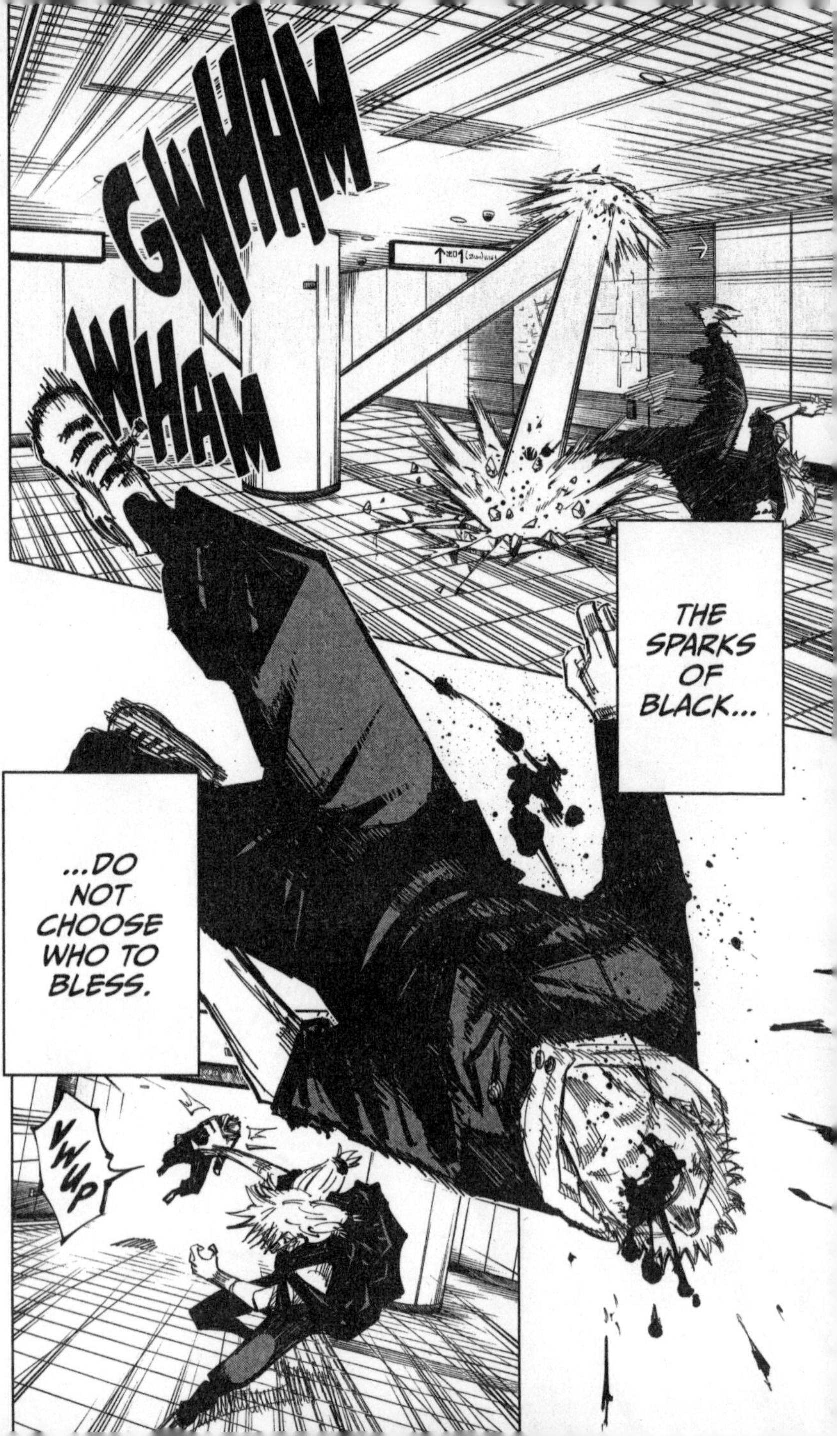
GWHAM
WHAM
THE SPARKS OF BLACK...
...DO NOT CHOOSE WHO TO BLESS.
VWUP

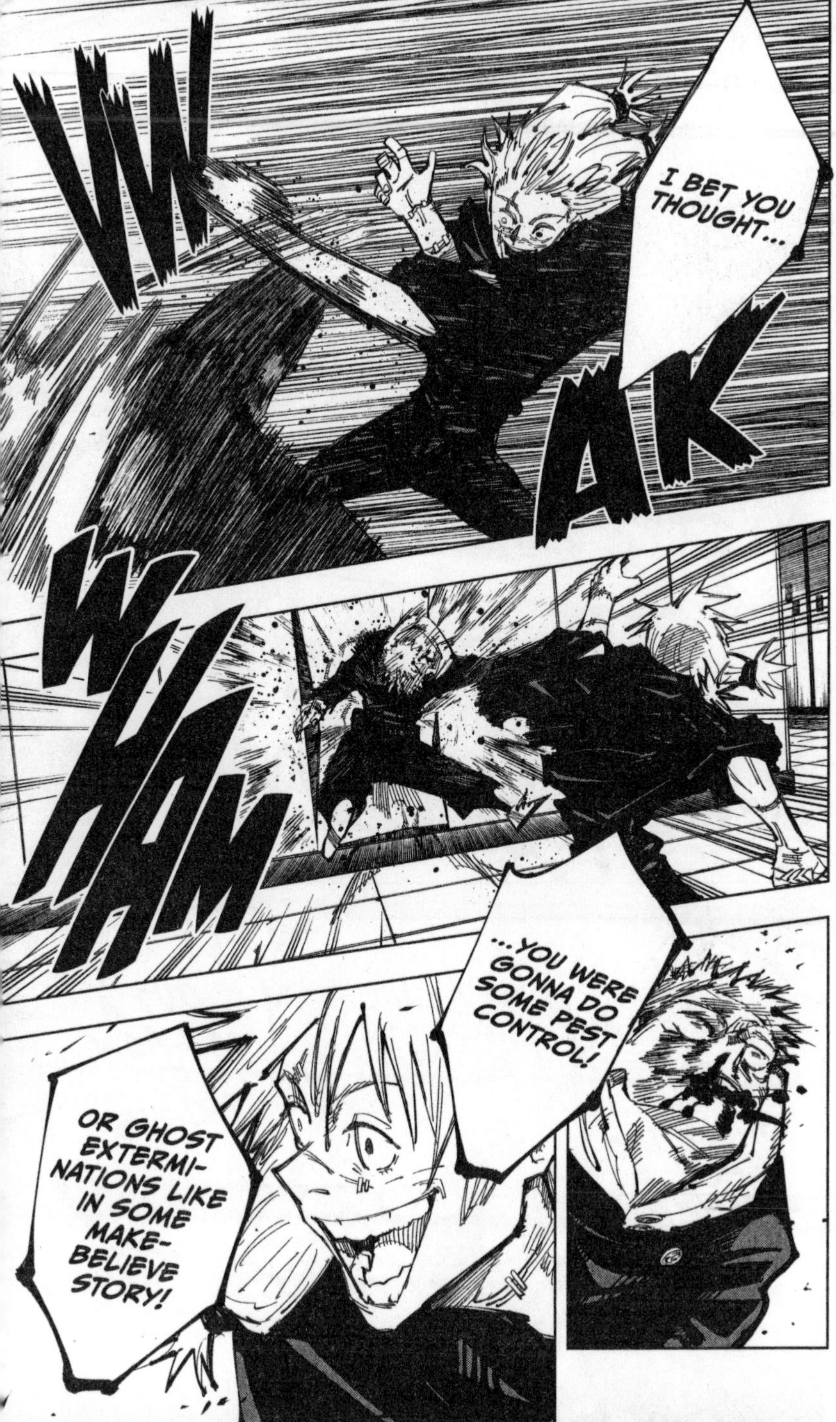
I BET YOU THOUGHT...
WW
AK
WHAM
...YOU WERE GONNA DO SOME PEST CONTROL!
OR GHOST EXTERMI-NATIONS LIKE IN SOME MAKE-BELIEVE STORY!

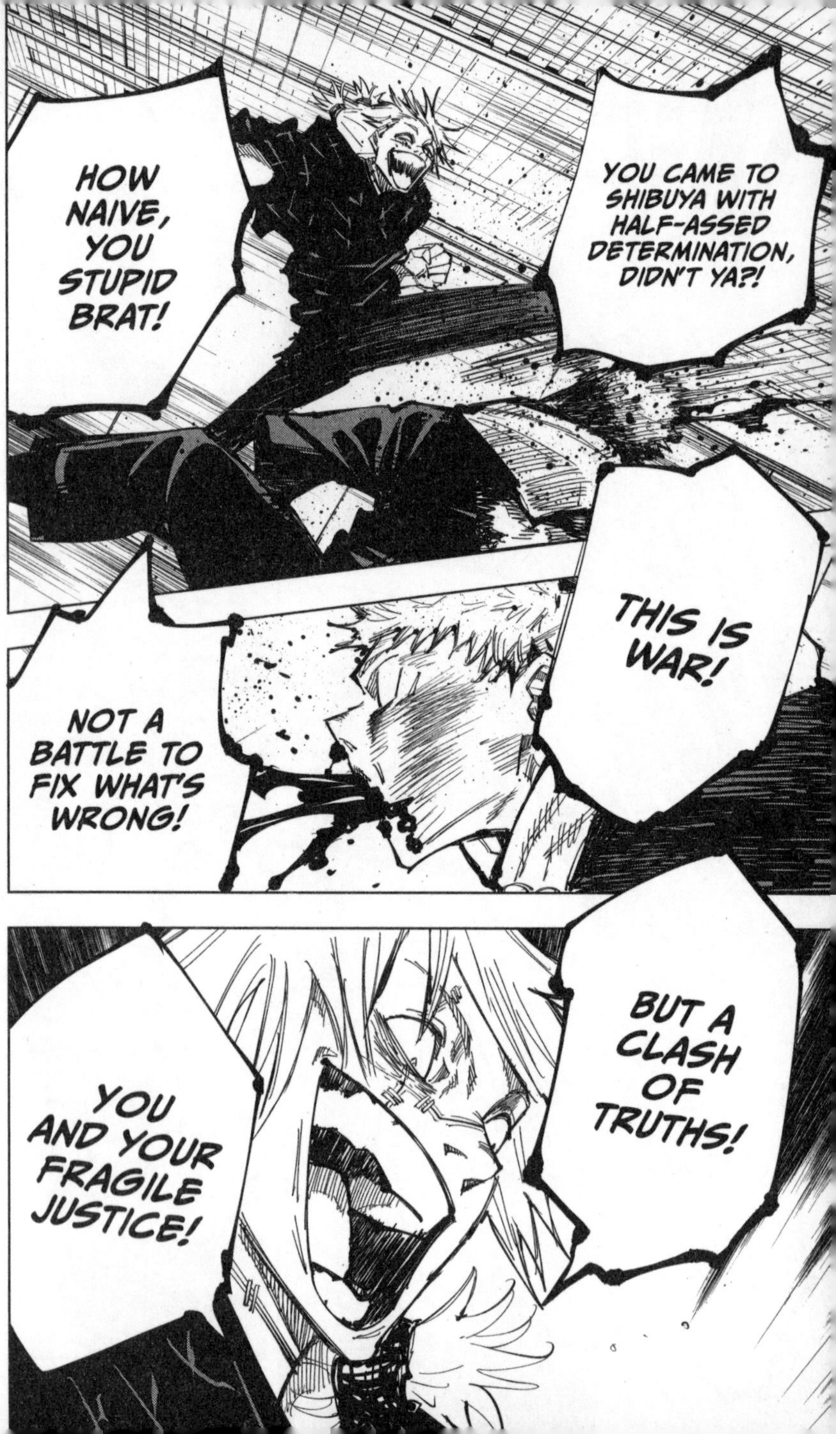
YOU CAME TO SHIBUYA WITH HALF-ASSED DETERMINATION, DIDN'T YA?!
HOW NAIVE, YOU STUPID BRAT!
THIS IS WAR!
NOT A BATTLE TO FIX WHAT'S WRONG!
BUT A CLASH OF TRUTHS!
YOU AND YOUR FRAGILE JUSTICE!

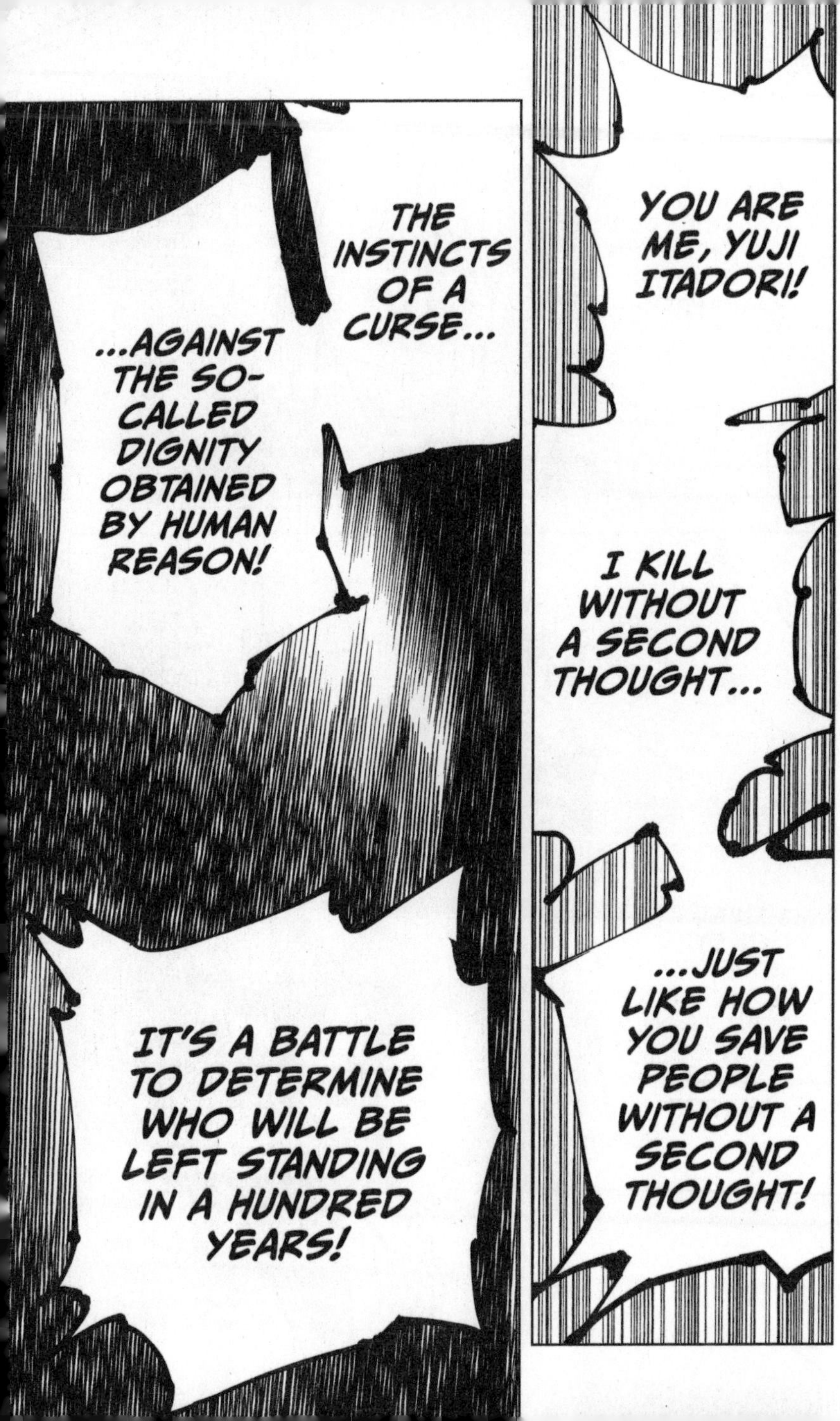
YOU ARE ME, YUJI ITADORI!
I KILL WITHOUT A SECOND THOUGHT...
...JUST LIKE HOW YOU SAVE PEOPLE WITHOUT A SECOND THOUGHT!
THE INSTINCTS OF A CURSE...
...AGAINST THE SO-CALLED DIGNITY OBTAINED BY HUMAN REASON!
IT'S A BATTLE TO DETERMINE WHO WILL BE LEFT STANDING IN A HUNDRED YEARS!

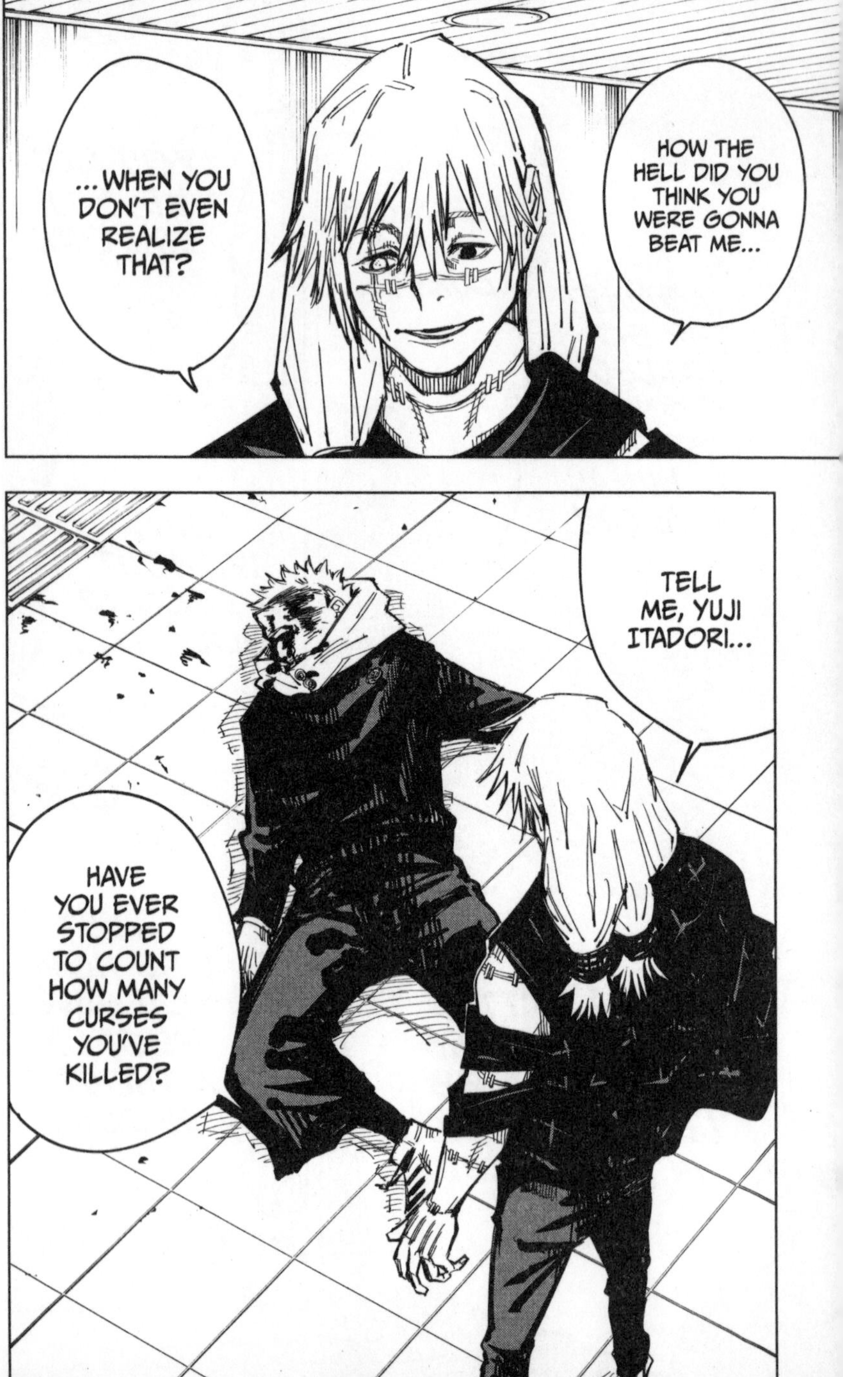
HOW THE HELL DID YOU THINK YOU WERE GONNA BEAT ME...
...WHEN YOU DON'T EVEN REALIZE THAT?
TELL ME, YUJI ITADORI...
HAVE YOU EVER STOPPED TO COUNT HOW MANY CURSES YOU'VE KILLED?

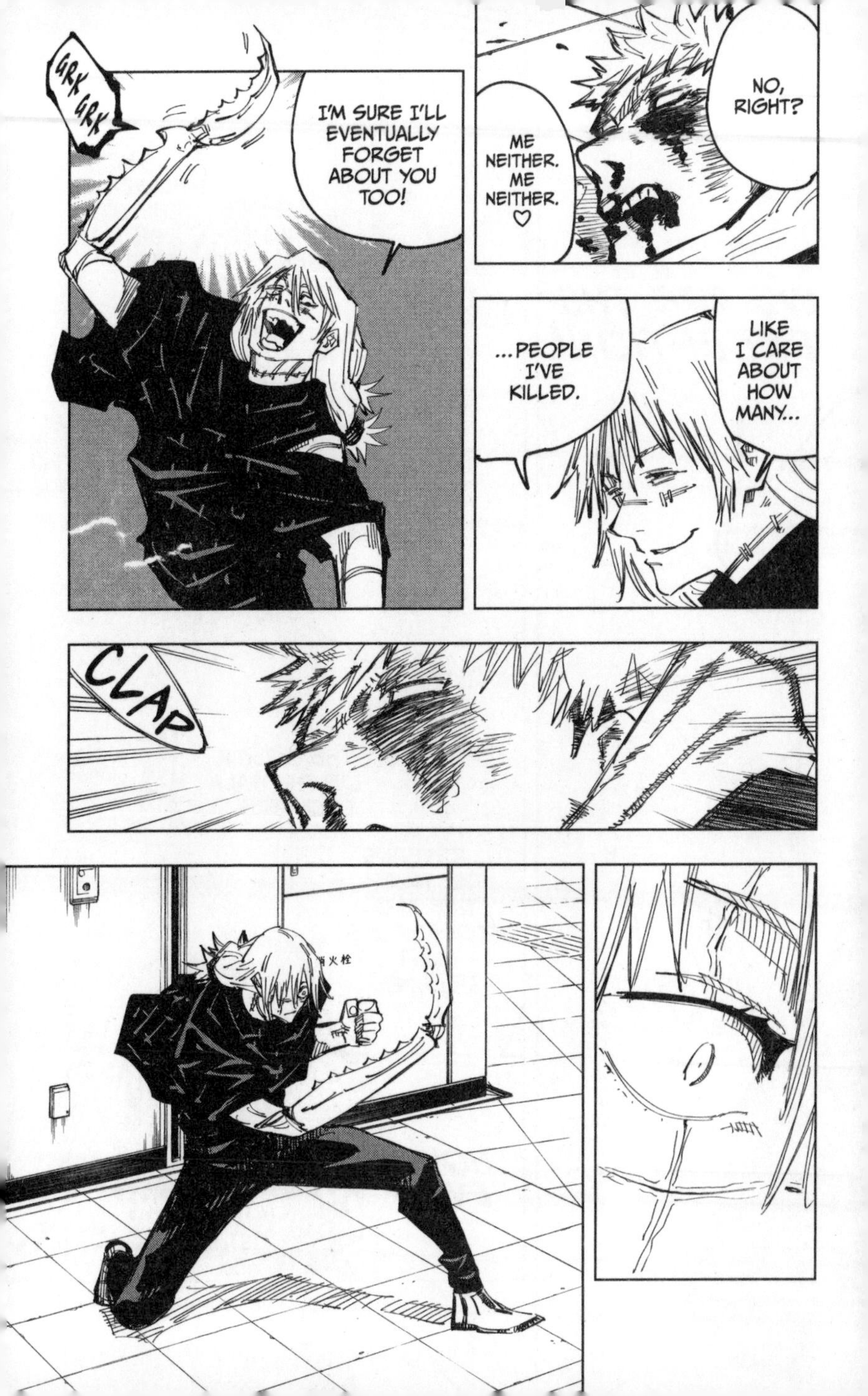
NO, RIGHT?
ME NEITHER. ME NEITHER. ♡
LIKE I CARE ABOUT HOW MANY...
...PEOPLE I'VE KILLED.
GRK GRK
I'M SURE I'LL EVENTUALLY FORGET ABOUT YOU TOO!
CLAP

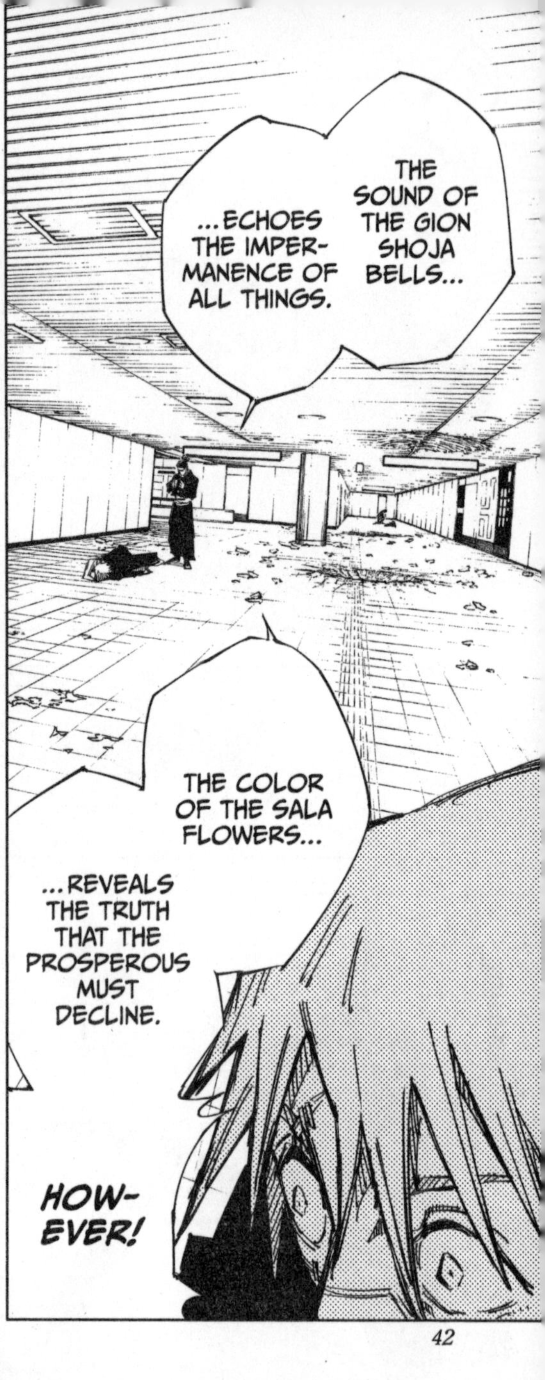
THE SOUND OF THE GION SHOJA BELLS...
...ECHOES THE IMPERMANENCE OF ALL THINGS.
THE COLOR OF THE SALA FLOWERS...
...REVEALS THE TRUTH THAT THE PROSPEROUS MUST DECLINE.
HOW-EVER!

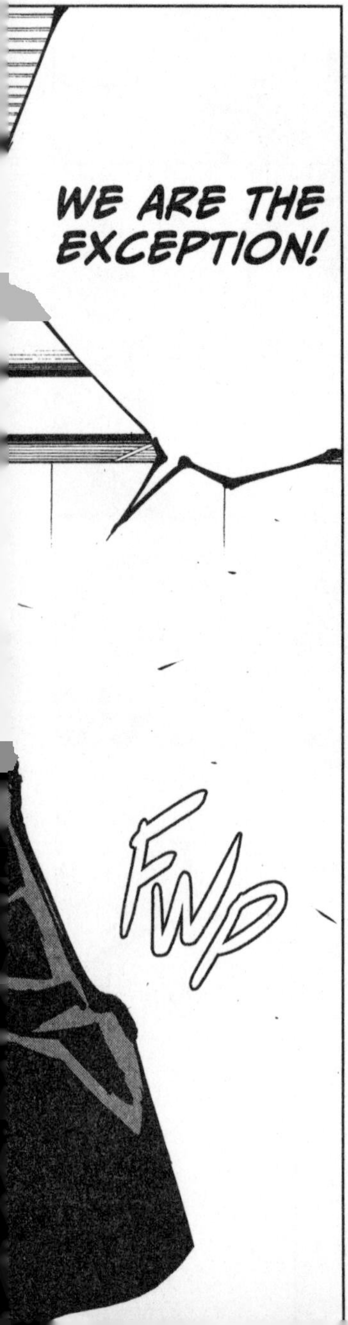
WE ARE THE EXCEPTION!
FWP

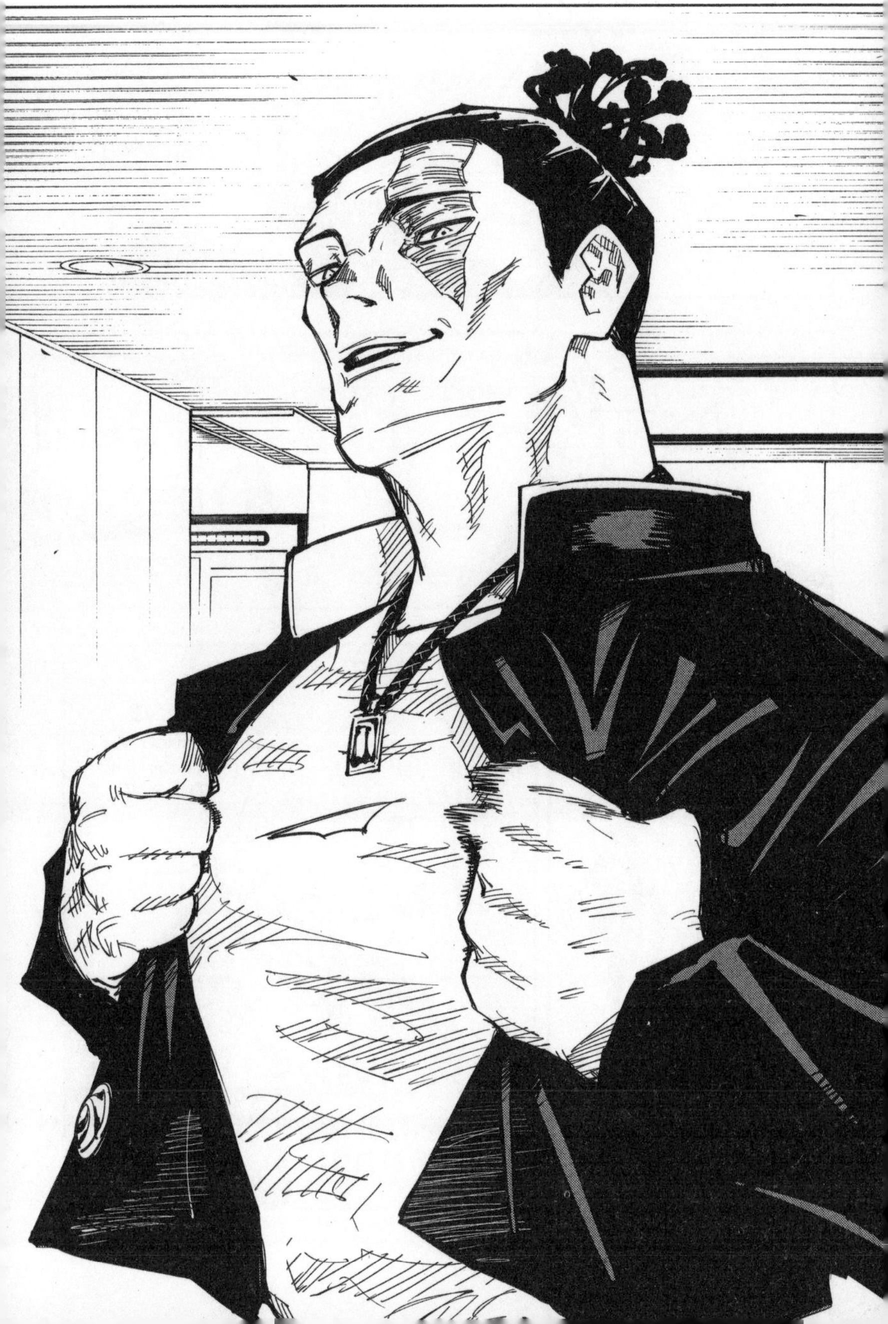

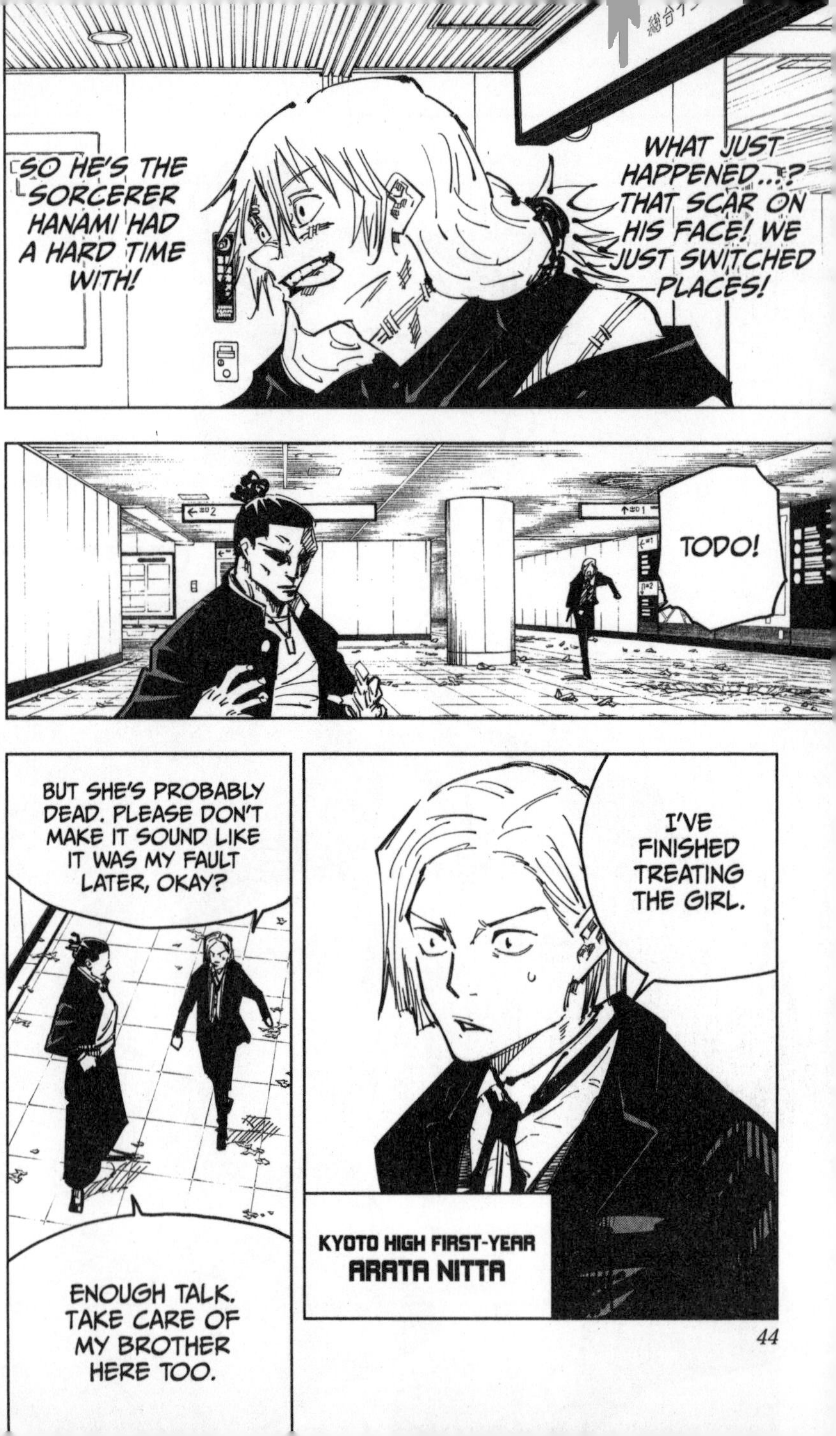
WHAT JUST HAPPENED...? THAT SCAR ON HIS FACE! WE JUST SWITCHED PLACES!
SO HE'S THE SORCERER HANAMI HAD A HARD TIME WITH!
TODO!
I'VE FINISHED TREATING THE GIRL.
KYOTO HIGH FIRST-YEAR
ARATA NITTA
BUT SHE'S PROBABLY DEAD. PLEASE DON'T MAKE IT SOUND LIKE IT WAS MY FAULT LATER, OKAY?
ENOUGH TALK. TAKE CARE OF MY BROTHER HERE TOO.

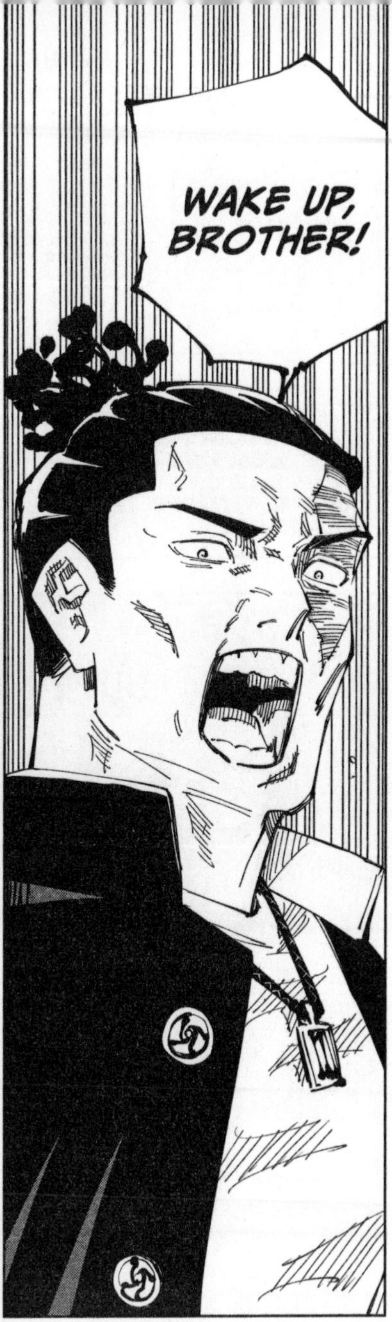
WAKE UP, BROTHER!
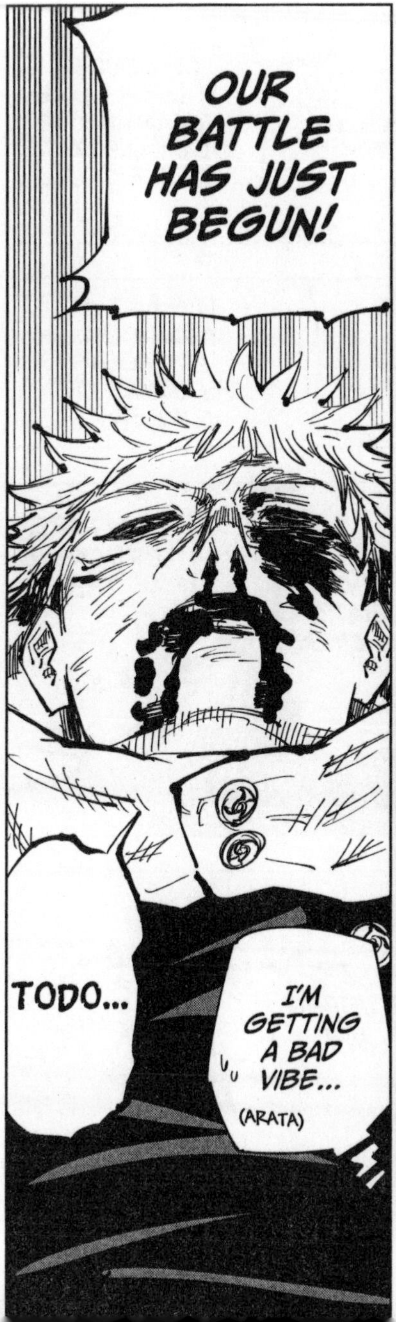
OUR BATTLE HAS JUST BEGUN!
I'M GETTING A BAD VIBE...
(ARATA)
TODO...

Getting It Right!!
Limitless Cursed Technique, Part 2

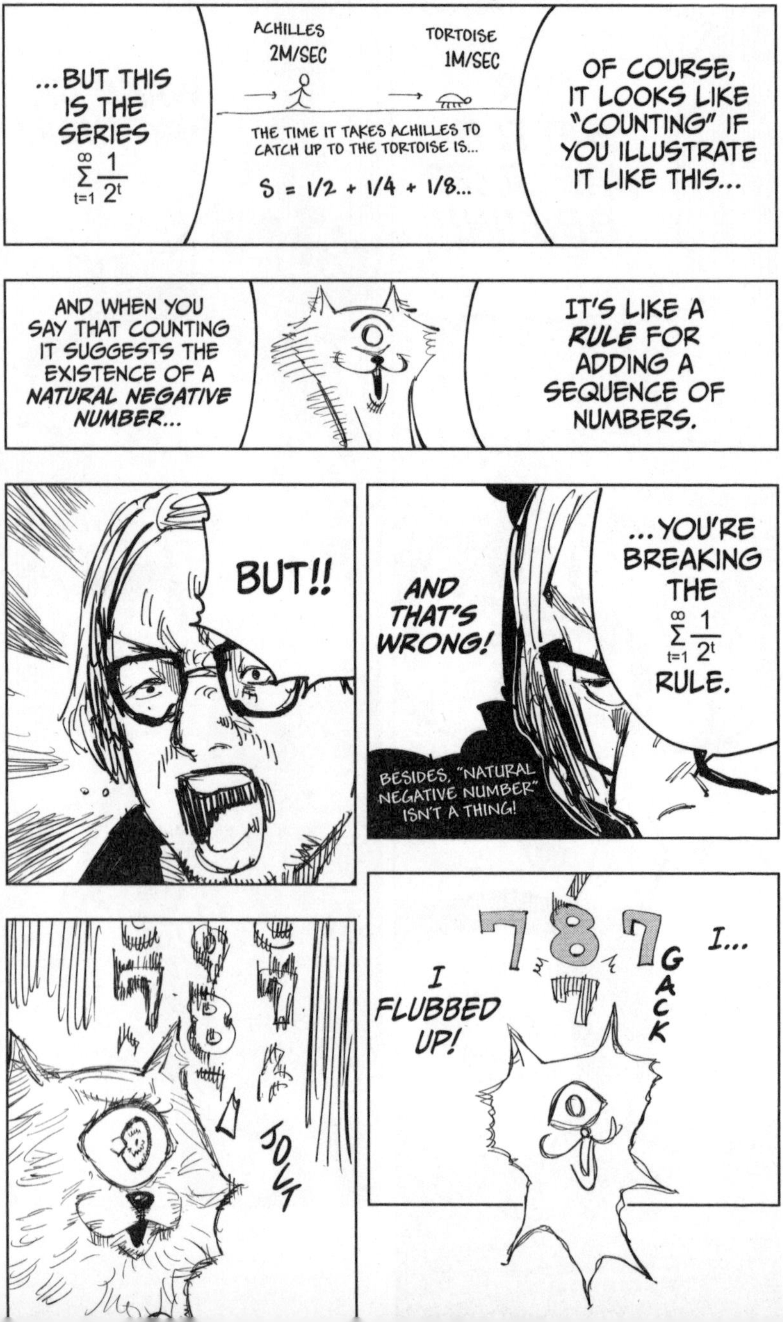
OF COURSE, IT LOOKS LIKE "COUNTING" IF YOU ILLUSTRATE IT LIKE THIS...
ACHILLES 2M/SEC
TORTOISE 1M/SEC
THE TIME IT TAKES ACHILLES TO CATCH UP TO THE TORTOISE IS...
S = 1/2 + 1/4 + 1/8...
...BUT THIS IS THE SERIES $\sum_{t=1}^{\infty} \frac{1}{2^t}$
IT'S LIKE A *RULE* FOR ADDING A SEQUENCE OF NUMBERS.
AND WHEN YOU SAY THAT COUNTING IT SUGGESTS THE EXISTENCE OF A *NATURAL NEGATIVE NUMBER*...
...YOU'RE BREAKING THE $\sum_{t=1}^{\infty} \frac{1}{2^t}$ RULE.
AND THAT'S WRONG!
BESIDES, "NATURAL NEGATIVE NUMBER" ISN'T A THING!
BUT!!
I...
GACK
787
I FLUBBED UP!
787
JOLT

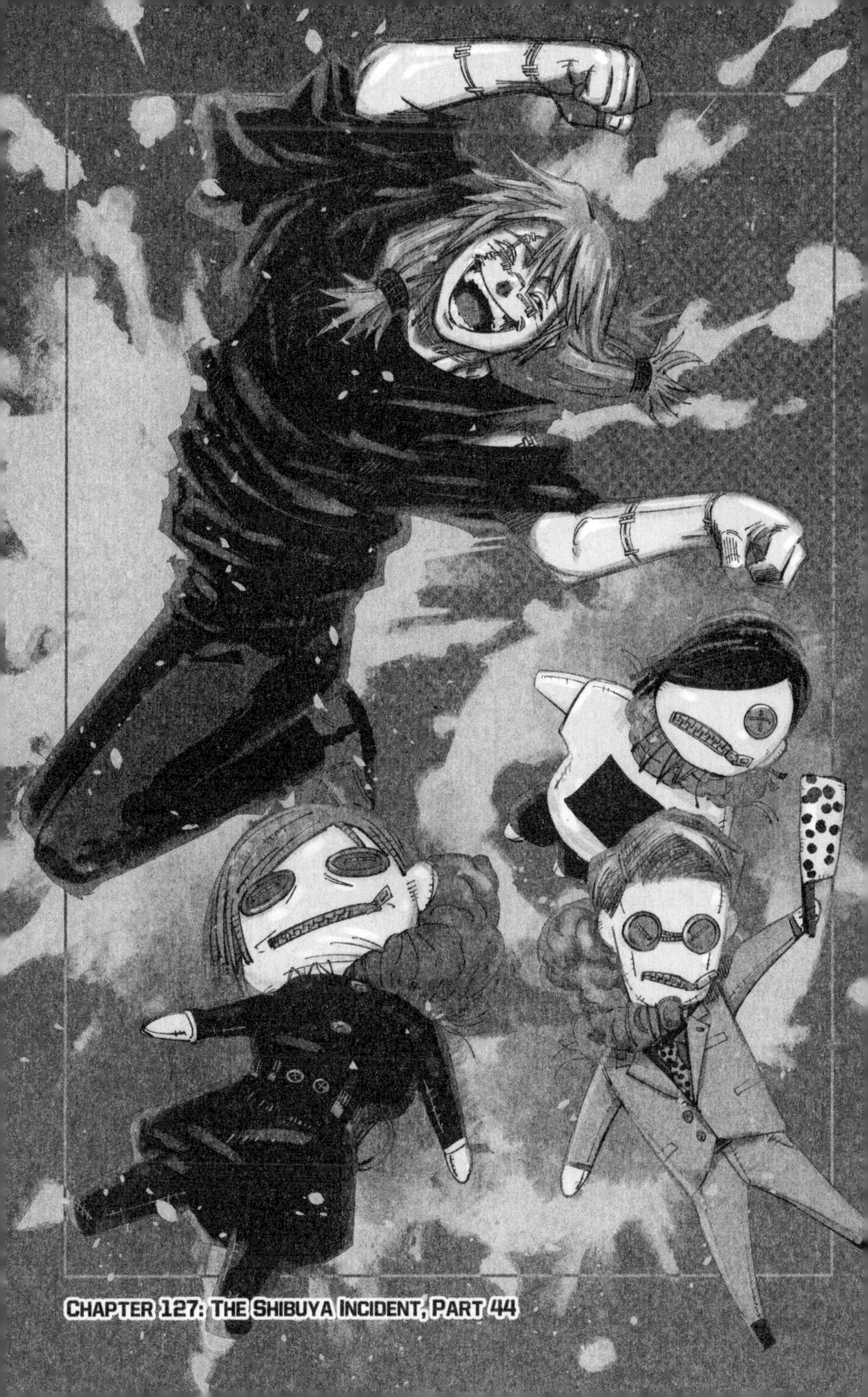

Chapter 127: The Shibuya Incident, Part 44

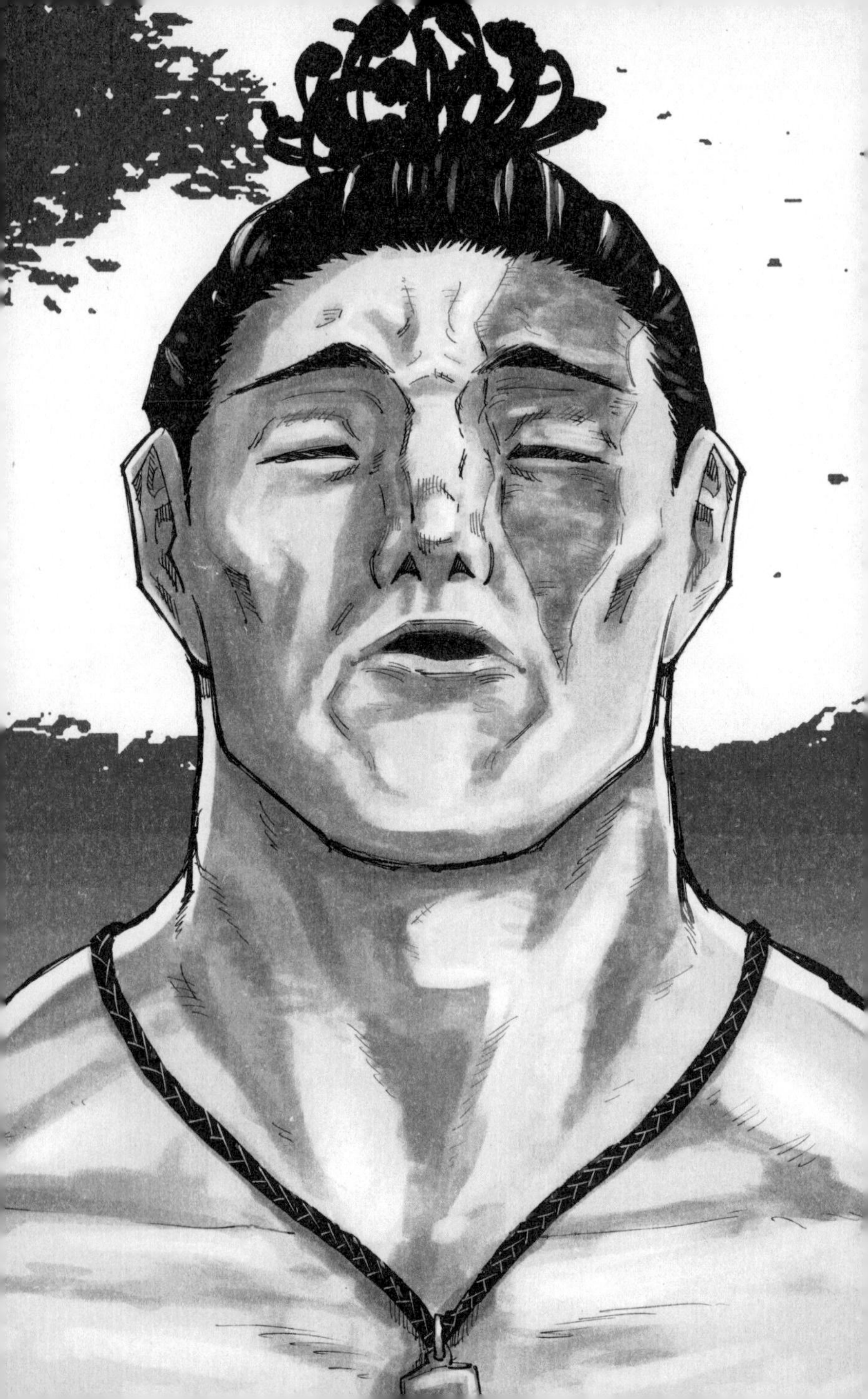

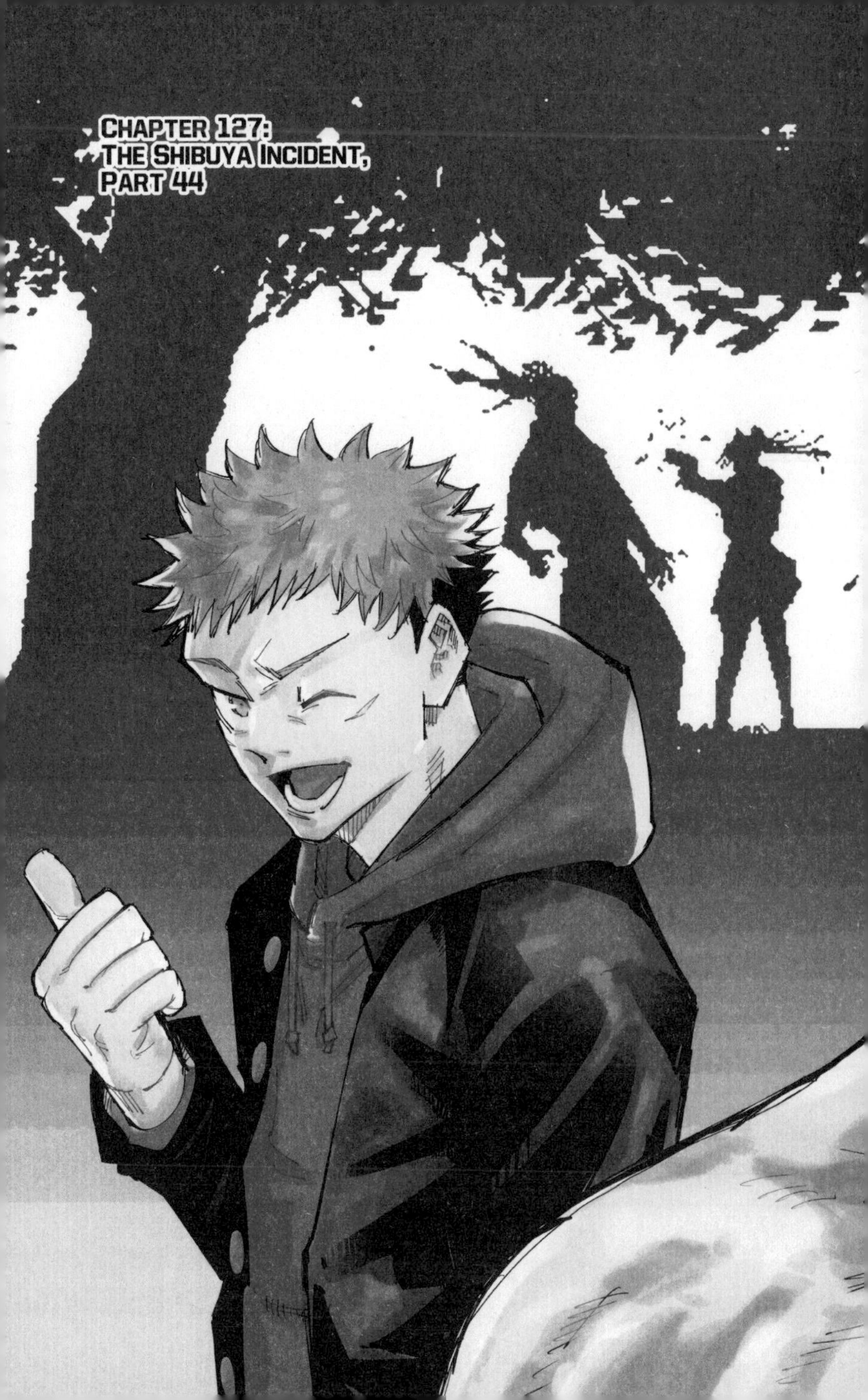
CHAPTER 127:
THE SHIBUYA INCIDENT,
PART 44

JUJUTSU KAISEN

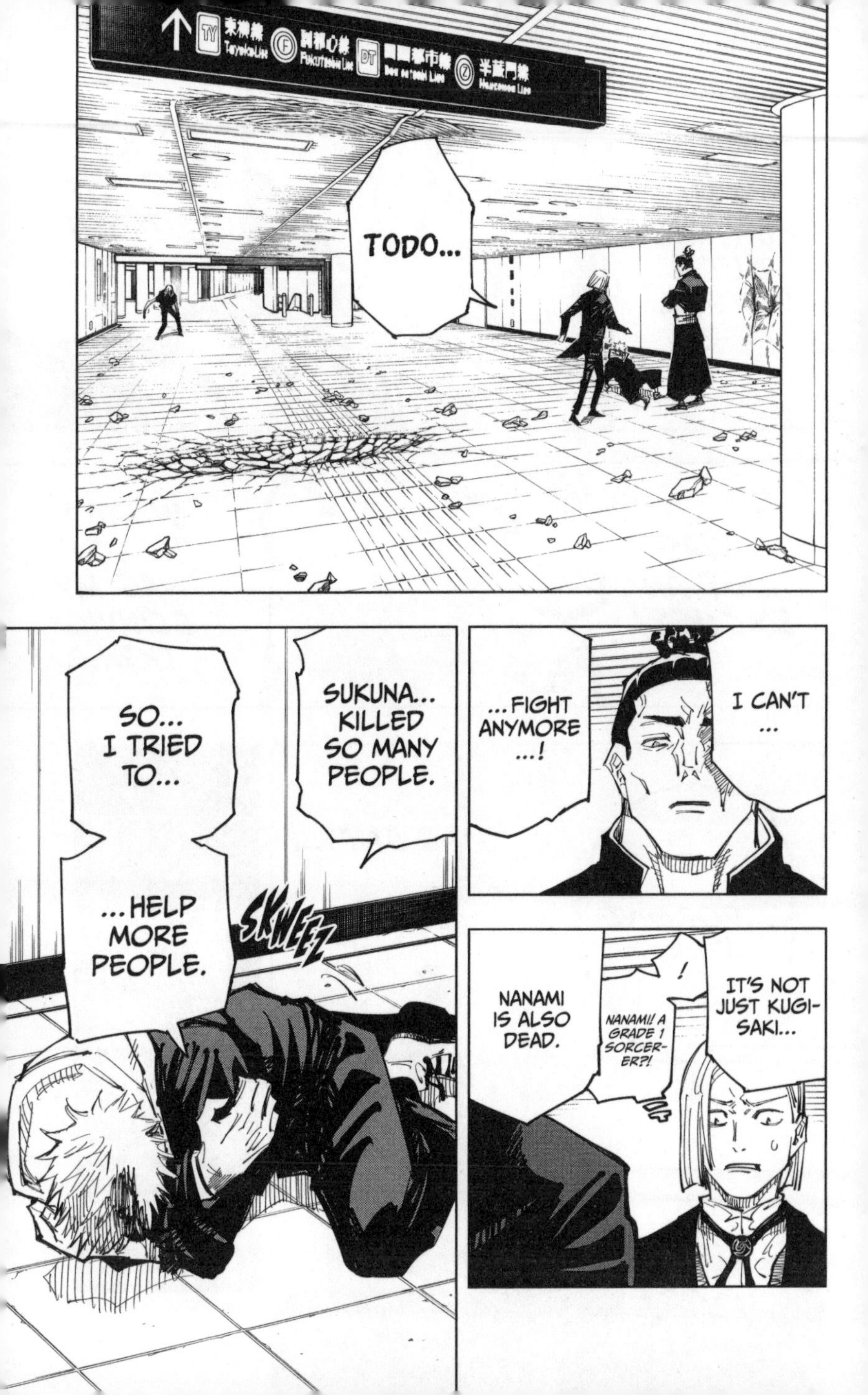
TODO...
I CAN'T ...
...FIGHT ANYMORE ...!
IT'S NOT JUST KUGI-SAKI...
!
NANAMI! A GRADE 1 SORCERER?!
NANAMI IS ALSO DEAD.
SUKUNA... KILLED SO MANY PEOPLE.
SO... I TRIED TO...
...HELP MORE PEOPLE.
SKWEEZ

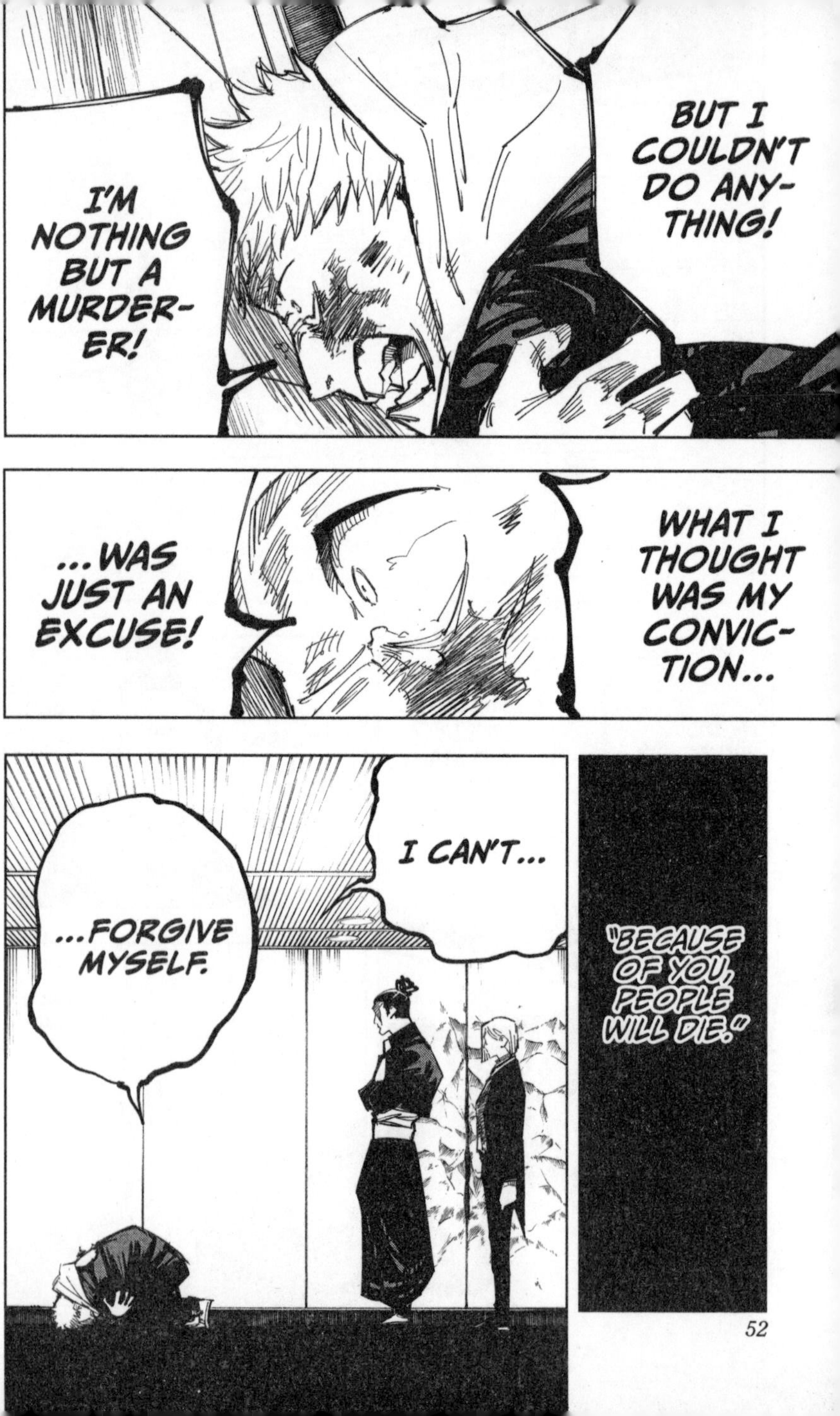
BUT I COULDN'T DO ANYTHING!
I'M NOTHING BUT A MURDERER!
WHAT I THOUGHT WAS MY CONVICTION...
...WAS JUST AN EXCUSE!
"BECAUSE OF YOU, PEOPLE WILL DIE."
I CAN'T...
...FORGIVE MYSELF.

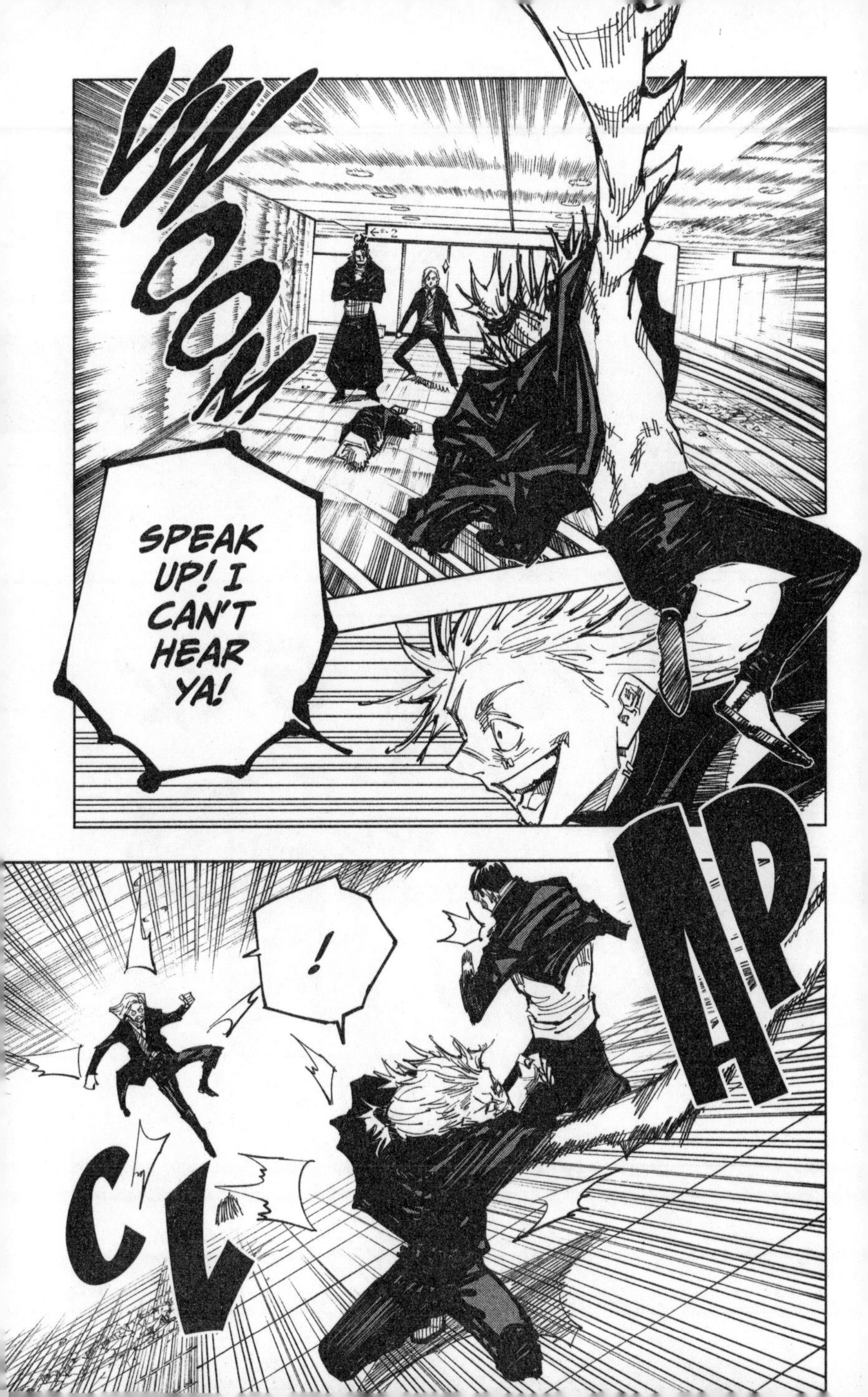
WOOM
SPEAK UP! I CAN'T HEAR YA!
!
CLAP

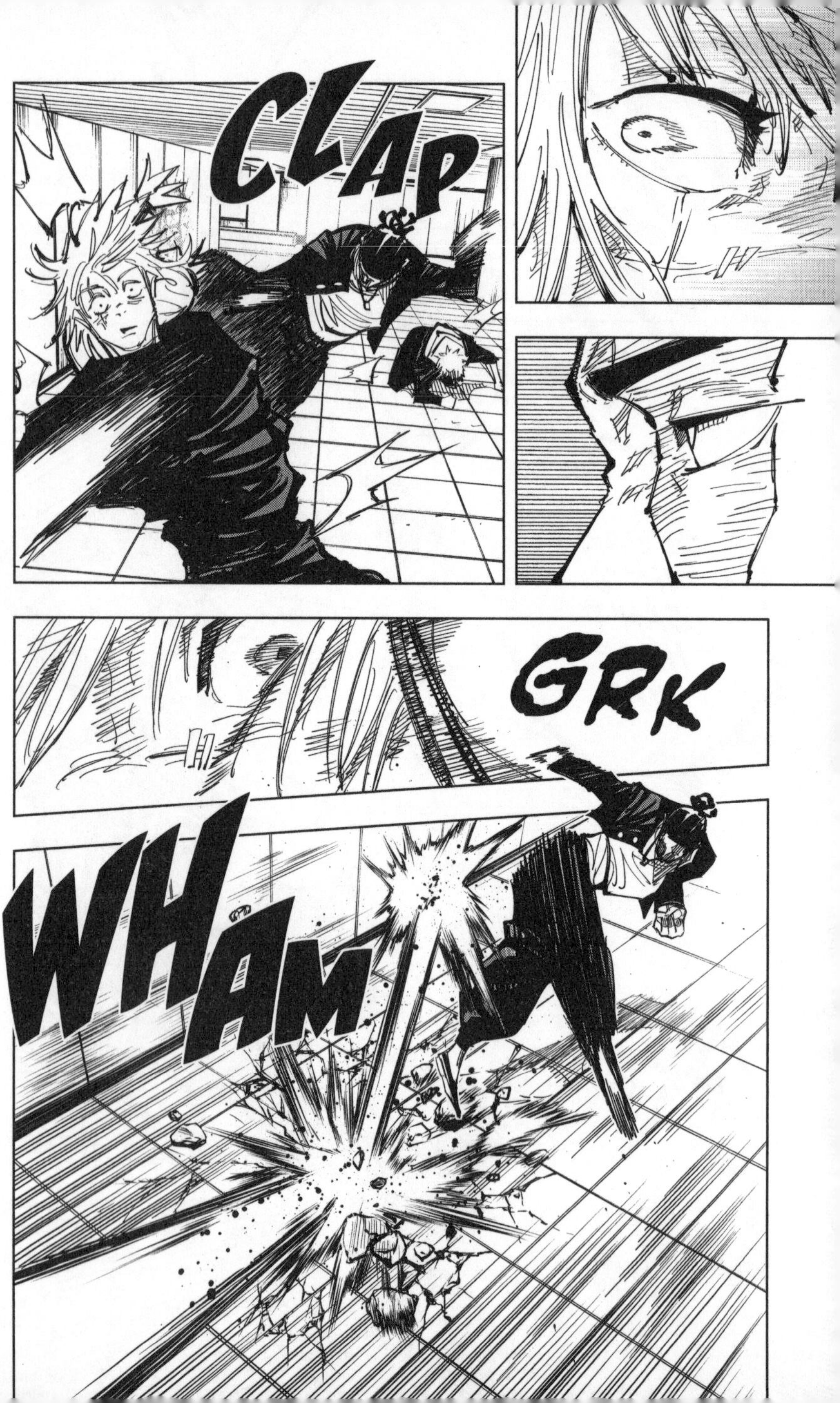
CLAP
GRK
WHAM

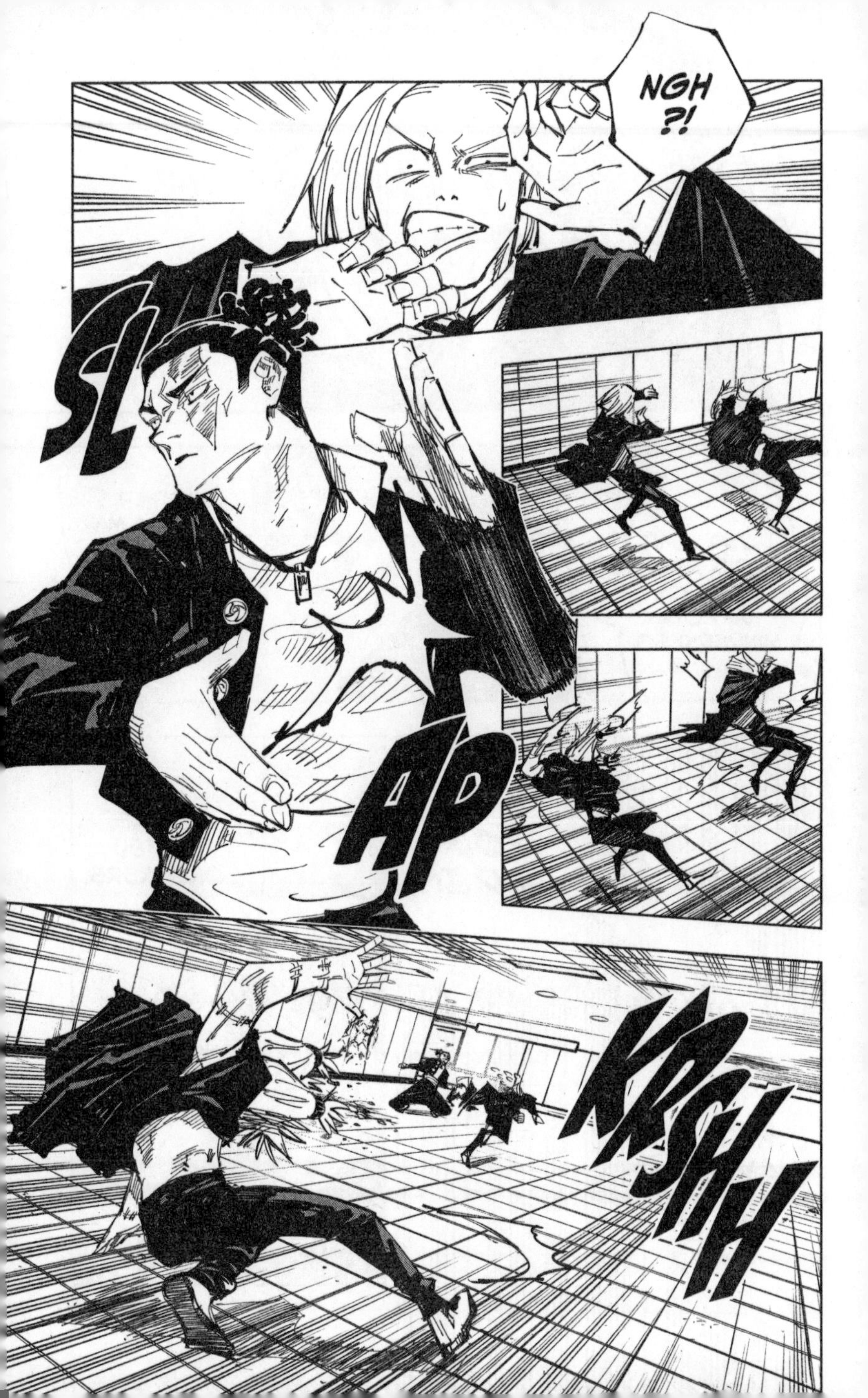
NGH ?!
SLAP
KRSH

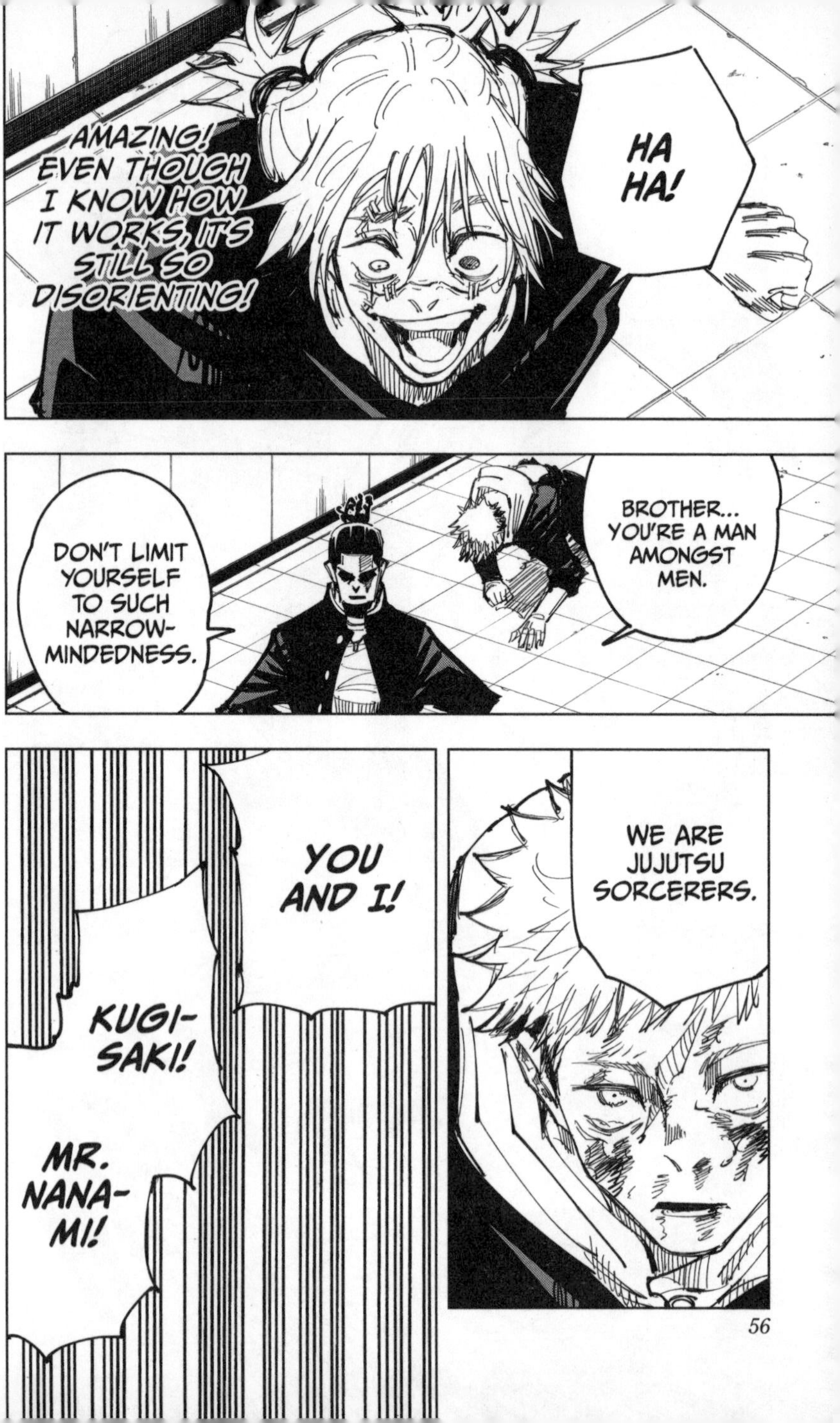
HA HA!
AMAZING! EVEN THOUGH I KNOW HOW IT WORKS, IT'S STILL SO DISORIENTING!
BROTHER... YOU'RE A MAN AMONGST MEN.
DON'T LIMIT YOURSELF TO SUCH NARROW-MINDEDNESS.
WE ARE JUJUTSU SORCERERS.
YOU AND I!
KUGI-SAKI!
MR. NANA-MI!

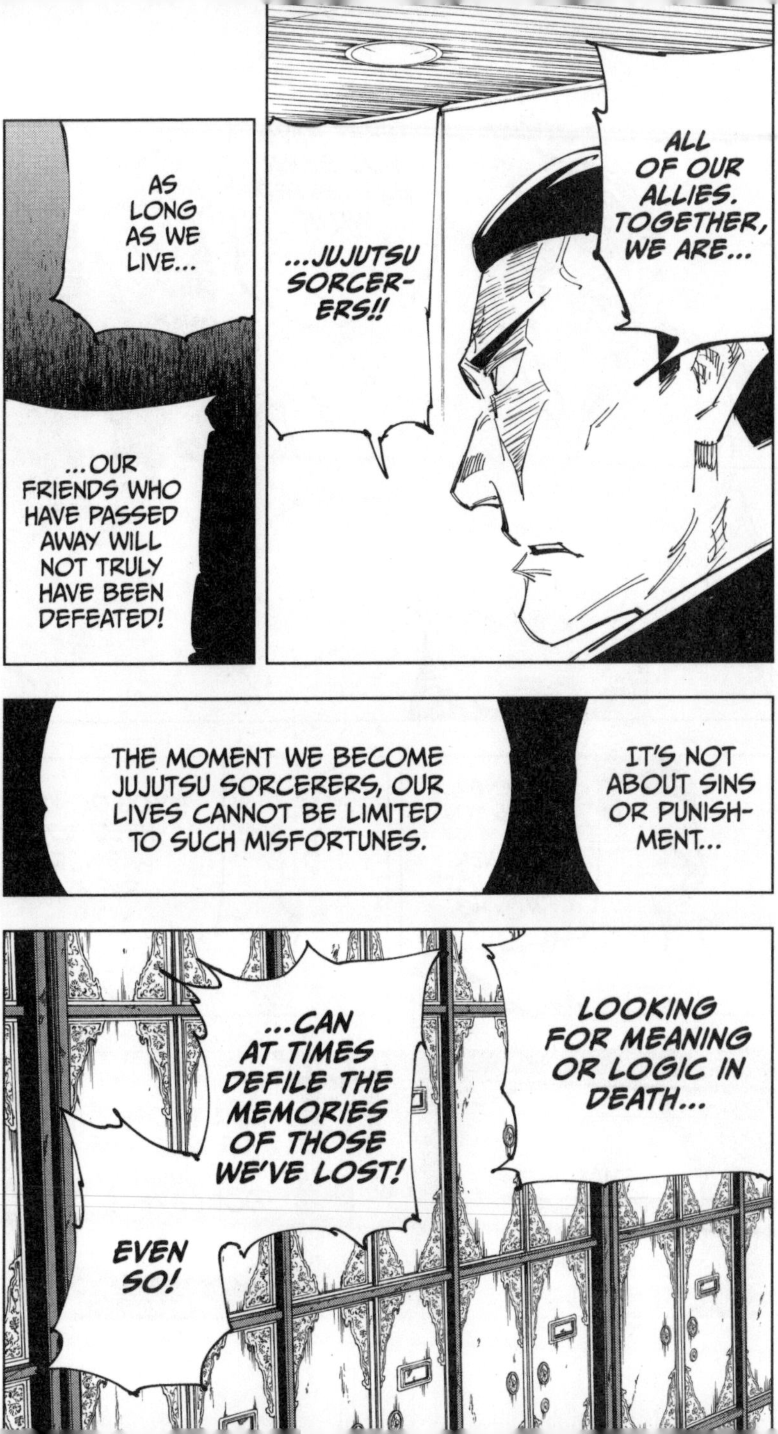
ALL OF OUR ALLIES. TOGETHER, WE ARE...
...JUJUTSU SORCERERS!!
AS LONG AS WE LIVE...
...OUR FRIENDS WHO HAVE PASSED AWAY WILL NOT TRULY HAVE BEEN DEFEATED!
IT'S NOT ABOUT SINS OR PUNISHMENT...
THE MOMENT WE BECOME JUJUTSU SORCERERS, OUR LIVES CANNOT BE LIMITED TO SUCH MISFORTUNES.
LOOKING FOR MEANING OR LOGIC IN DEATH...
...CAN AT TIMES DEFILE THE MEMORIES OF THOSE WE'VE LOST!
EVEN SO!

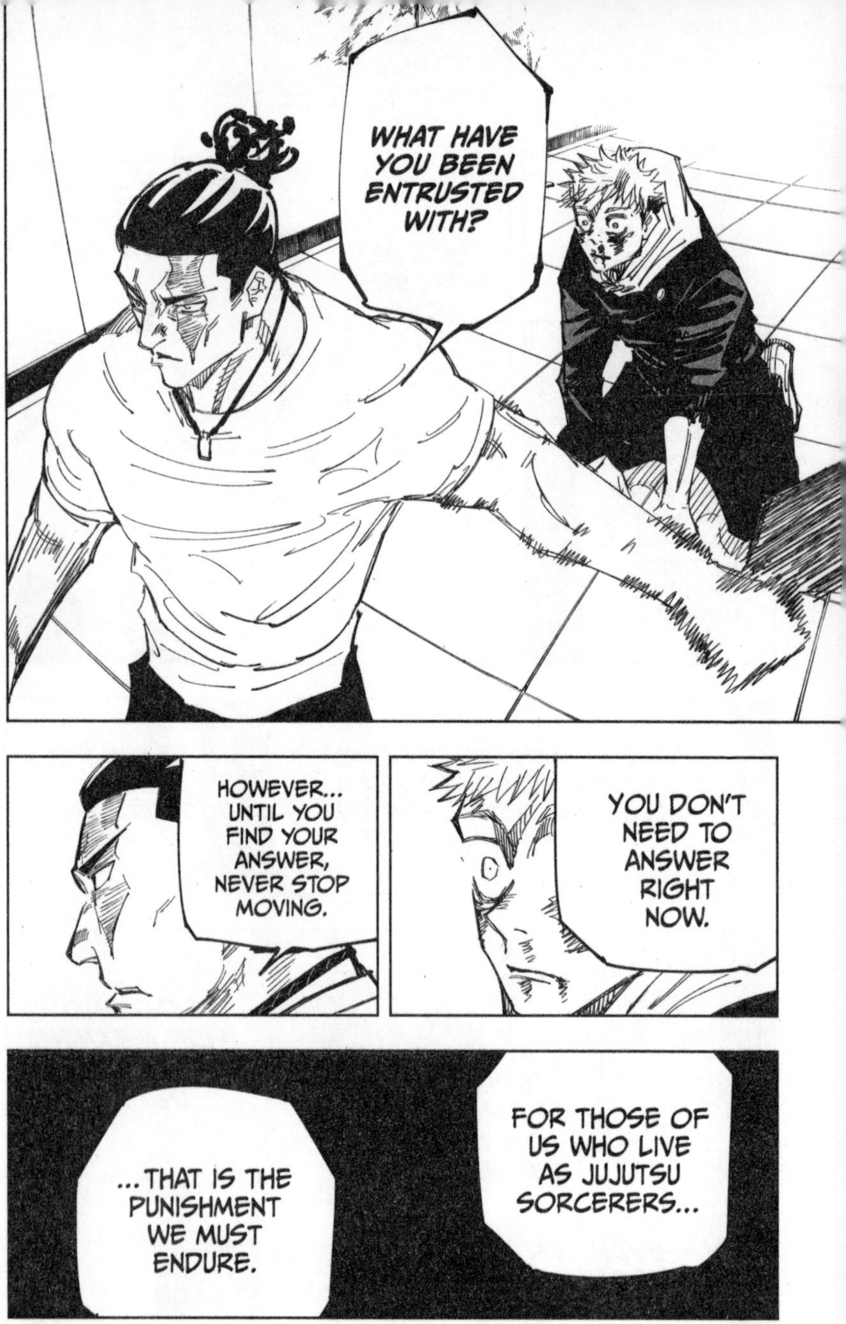
WHAT HAVE YOU BEEN ENTRUSTED WITH?
YOU DON'T NEED TO ANSWER RIGHT NOW.
HOWEVER... UNTIL YOU FIND YOUR ANSWER, NEVER STOP MOVING.
FOR THOSE OF US WHO LIVE AS JUJUTSU SORCERERS...
...THAT IS THE PUNISHMENT WE MUST ENDURE.

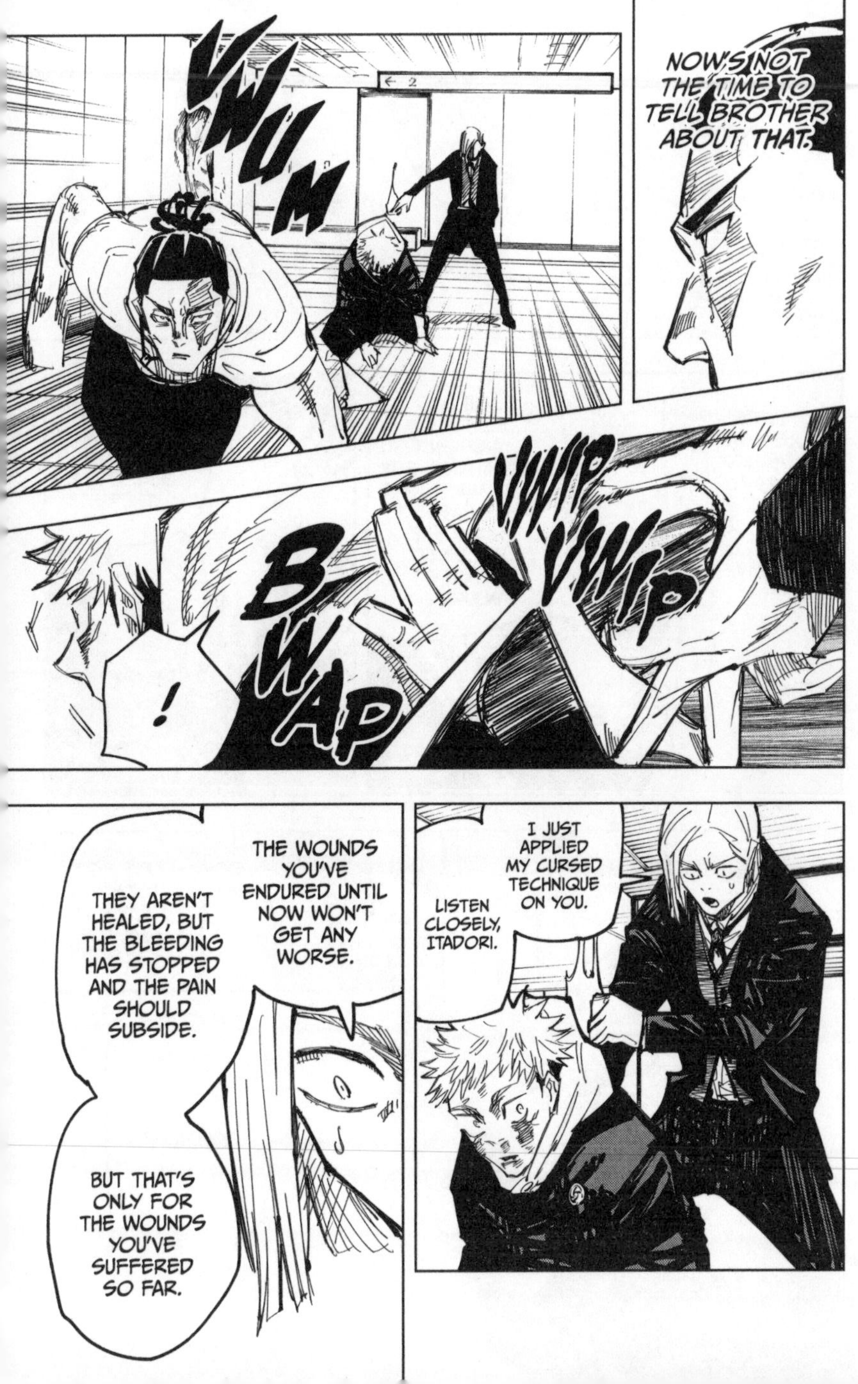
NOW'S NOT THE TIME TO TELL BROTHER ABOUT THAT.
VWUM
VWIP
VWIP
BWAP
!
I JUST APPLIED MY CURSED TECHNIQUE ON YOU.
LISTEN CLOSELY, ITADORI.
THE WOUNDS YOU'VE ENDURED UNTIL NOW WON'T GET ANY WORSE.
THEY AREN'T HEALED, BUT THE BLEEDING HAS STOPPED AND THE PAIN SHOULD SUBSIDE.
BUT THAT'S ONLY FOR THE WOUNDS YOU'VE SUFFERED SO FAR.

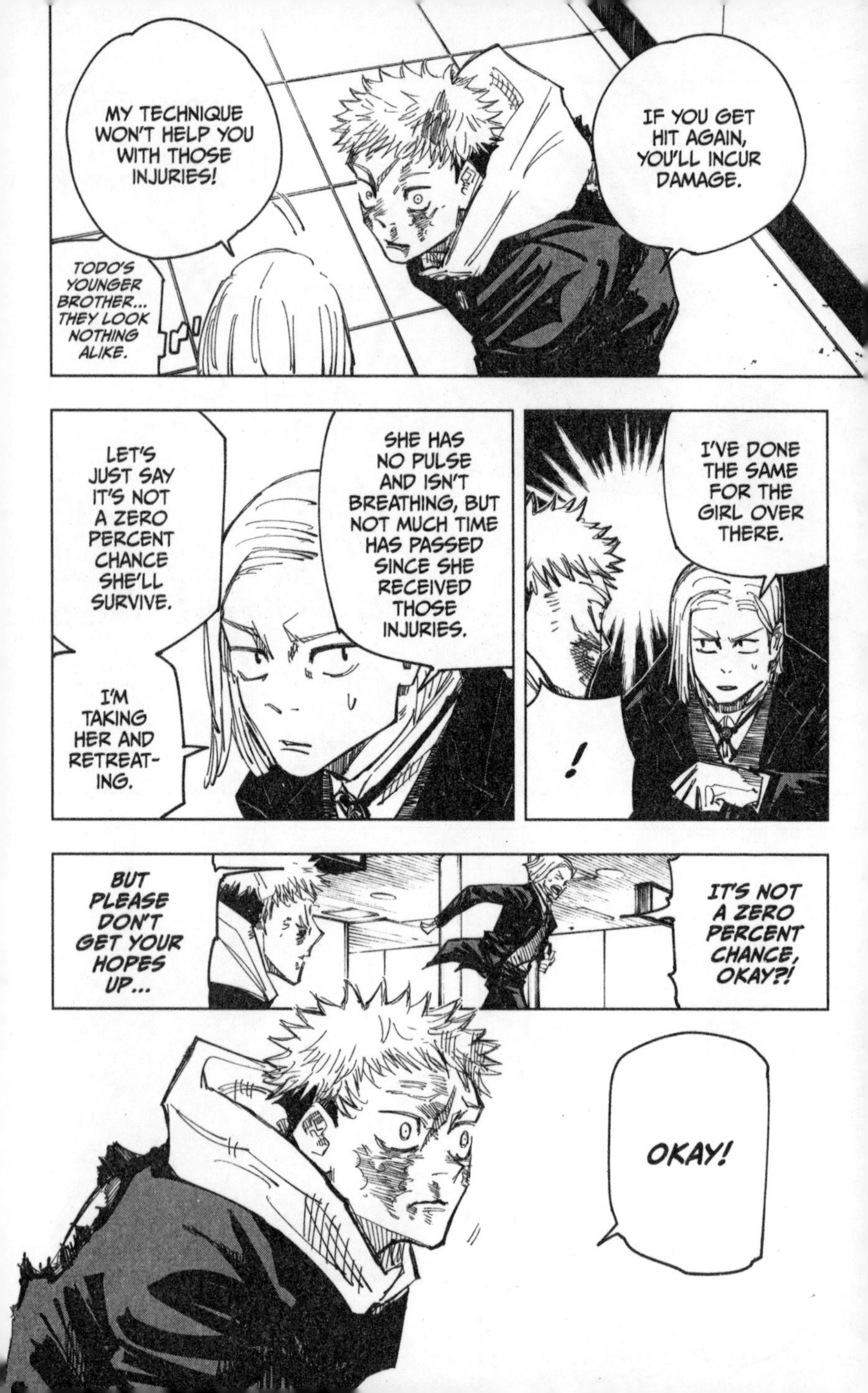
IF YOU GET HIT AGAIN, YOU'LL INCUR DAMAGE.
MY TECHNIQUE WON'T HELP YOU WITH THOSE INJURIES!
TODO'S YOUNGER BROTHER... THEY LOOK NOTHING ALIKE.
I'VE DONE THE SAME FOR THE GIRL OVER THERE.
!
SHE HAS NO PULSE AND ISN'T BREATHING, BUT NOT MUCH TIME HAS PASSED SINCE SHE RECEIVED THOSE INJURIES.
LET'S JUST SAY IT'S NOT A ZERO PERCENT CHANCE SHE'LL SURVIVE.
I'M TAKING HER AND RETREAT-ING.
IT'S NOT A ZERO PERCENT CHANCE, OKAY?!
BUT PLEASE DON'T GET YOUR HOPES UP...
OKAY!

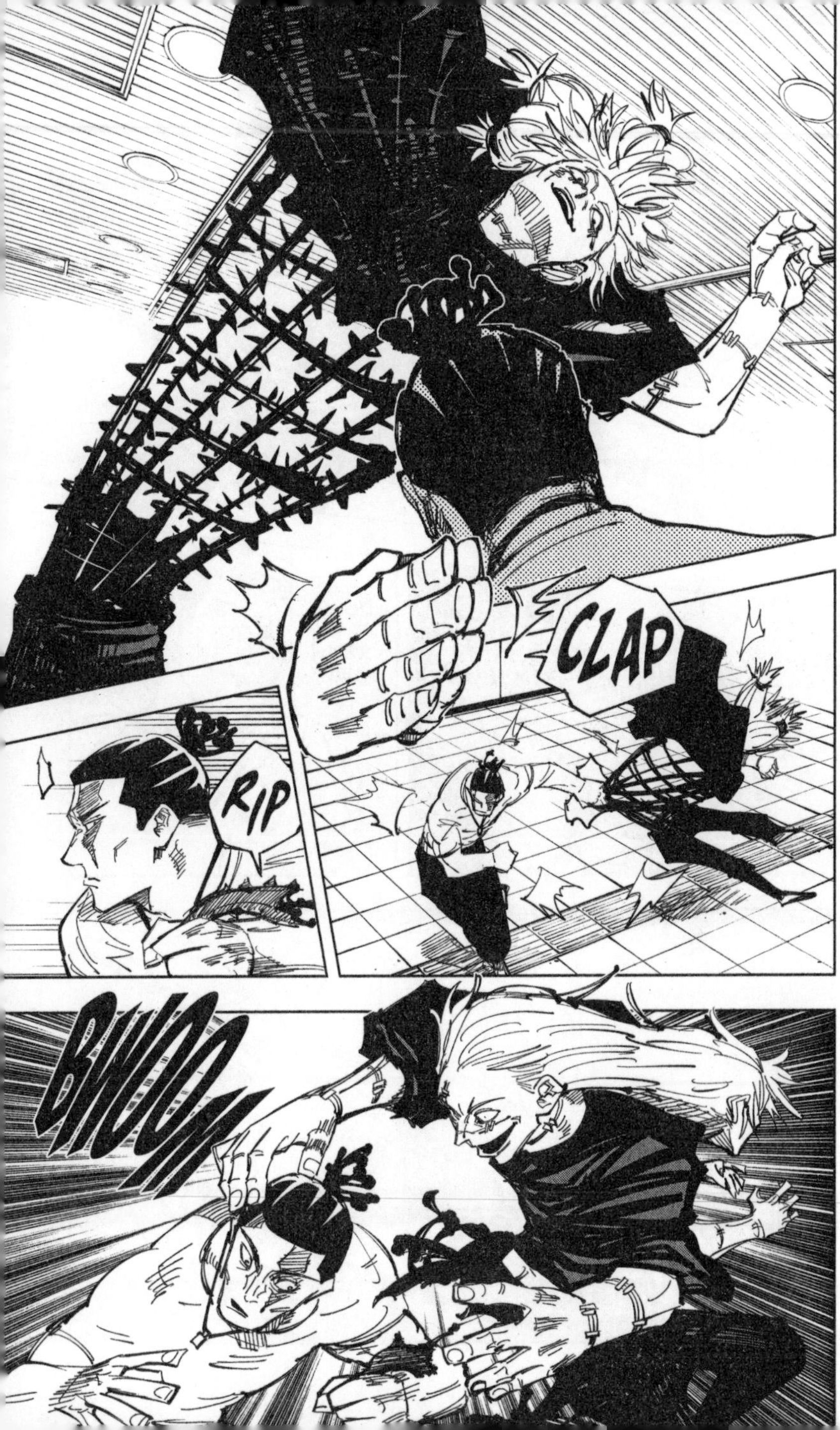
CLAP
RIP
BWOOM

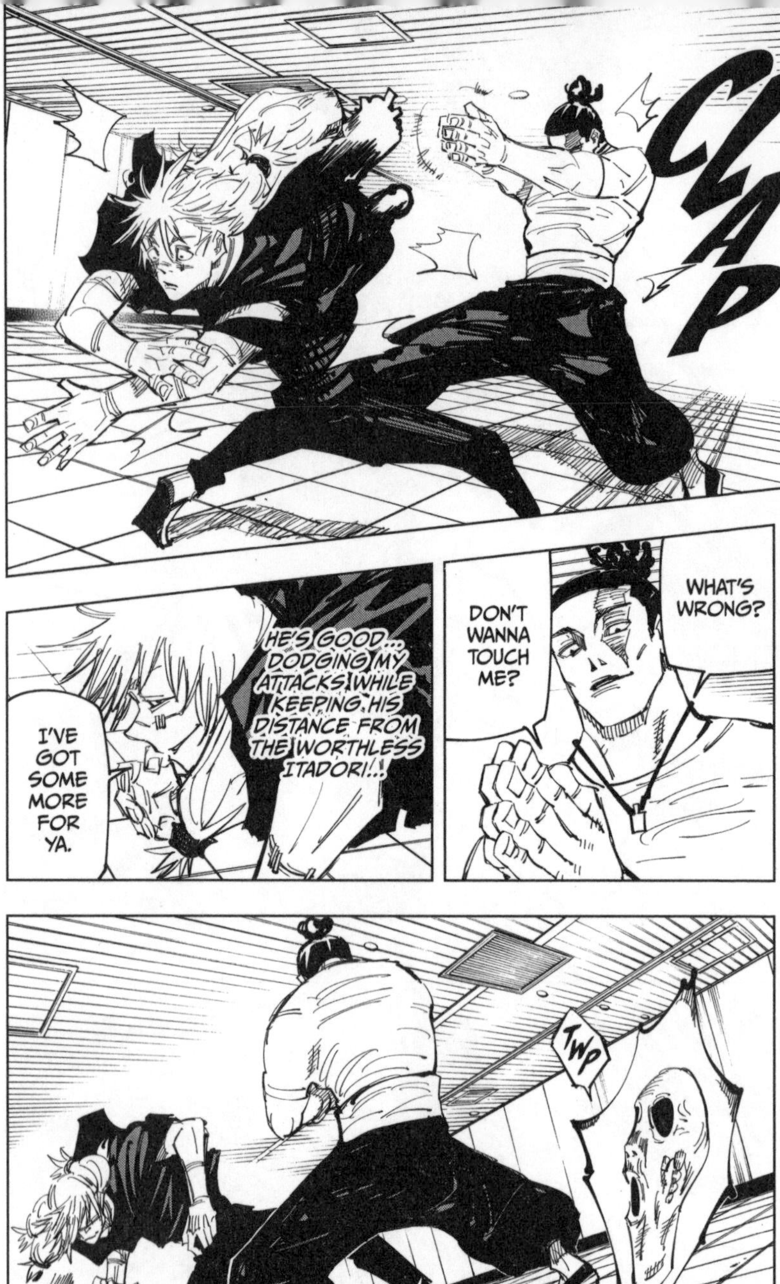
CLAP
WHAT'S WRONG?
DON'T WANNA TOUCH ME?
HE'S GOOD... DODGING MY ATTACKS WHILE KEEPING HIS DISTANCE FROM THE WORTHLESS ITADORI!..!
I'VE GOT SOME MORE FOR YA.
TWP

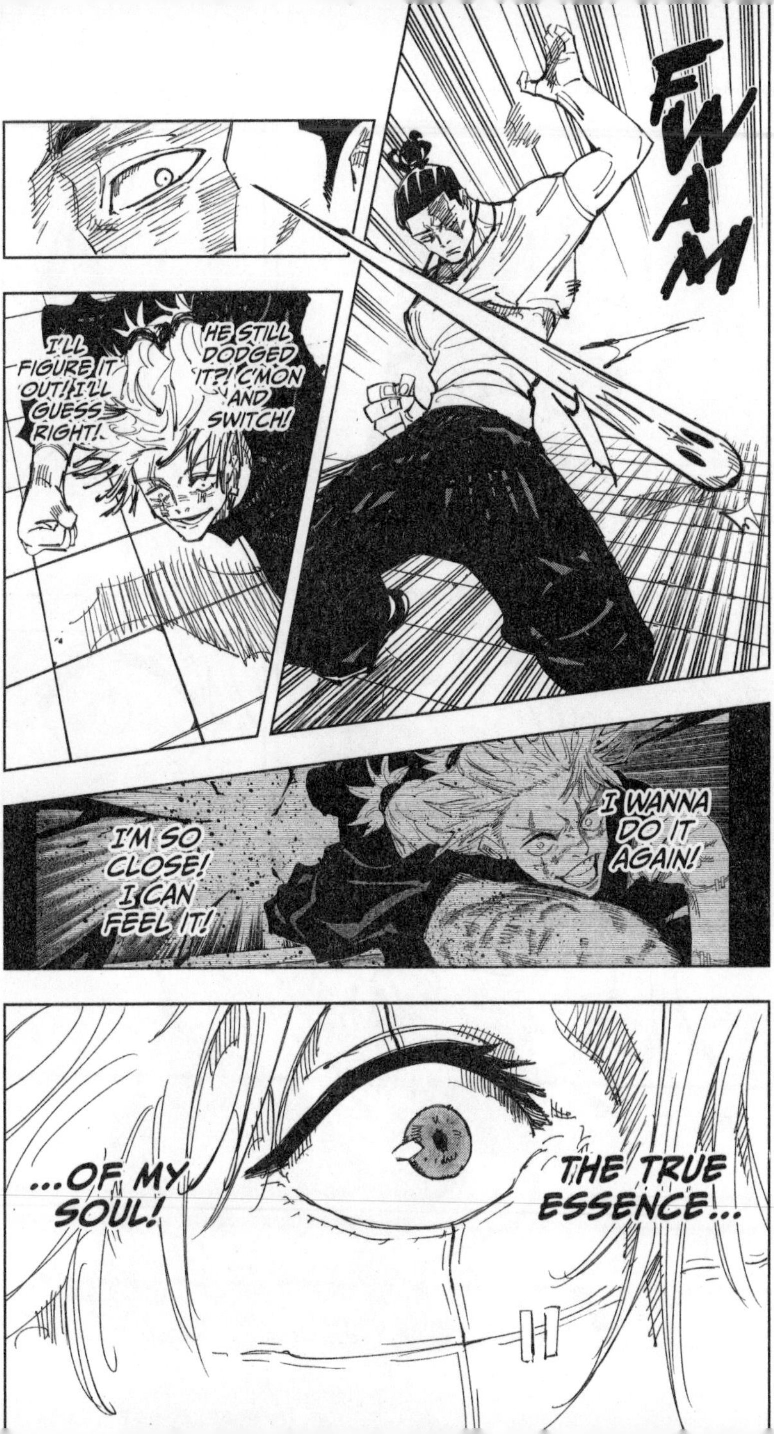
FWAM
HE STILL DODGED IT?! C'MON AND SWITCH!
I'LL FIGURE IT OUT! I'LL GUESS RIGHT!
I WANNA DO IT AGAIN!
I'M SO CLOSE! I CAN FEEL IT!
THE TRUE ESSENCE...
...OF MY SOUL!

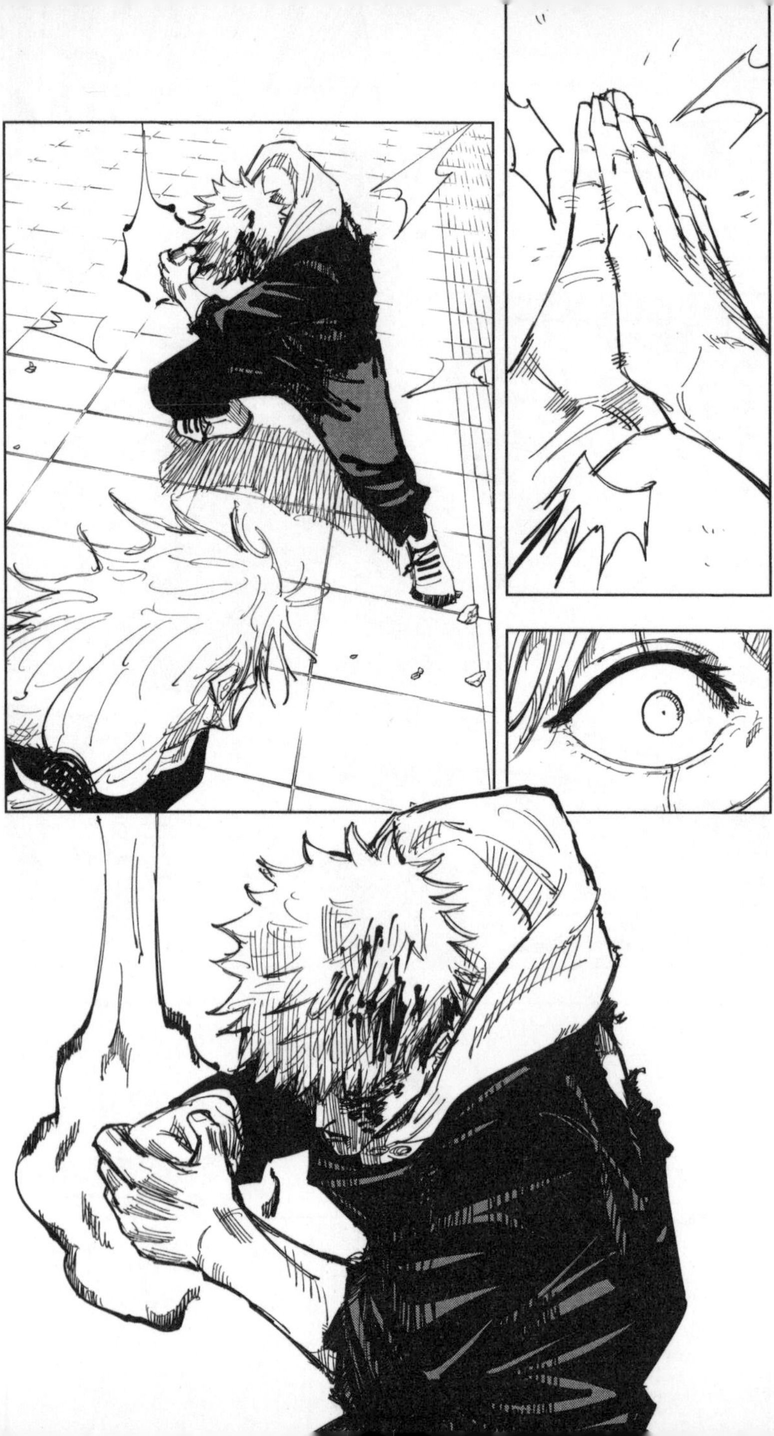

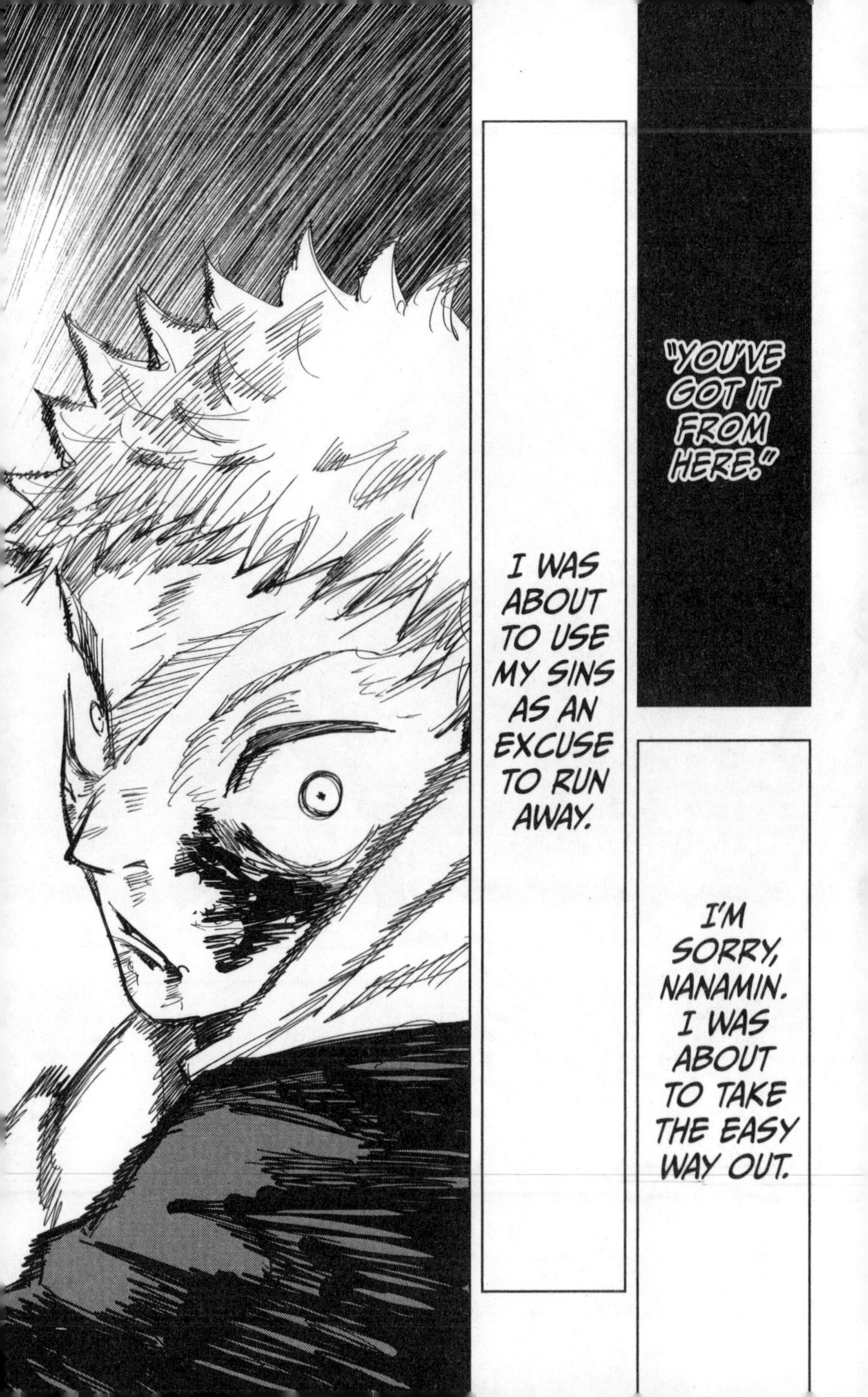
"YOU'VE GOT IT FROM HERE."
I'M SORRY, NANAMIN. I WAS ABOUT TO TAKE THE EASY WAY OUT.
I WAS ABOUT TO USE MY SINS AS AN EXCUSE TO RUN AWAY.

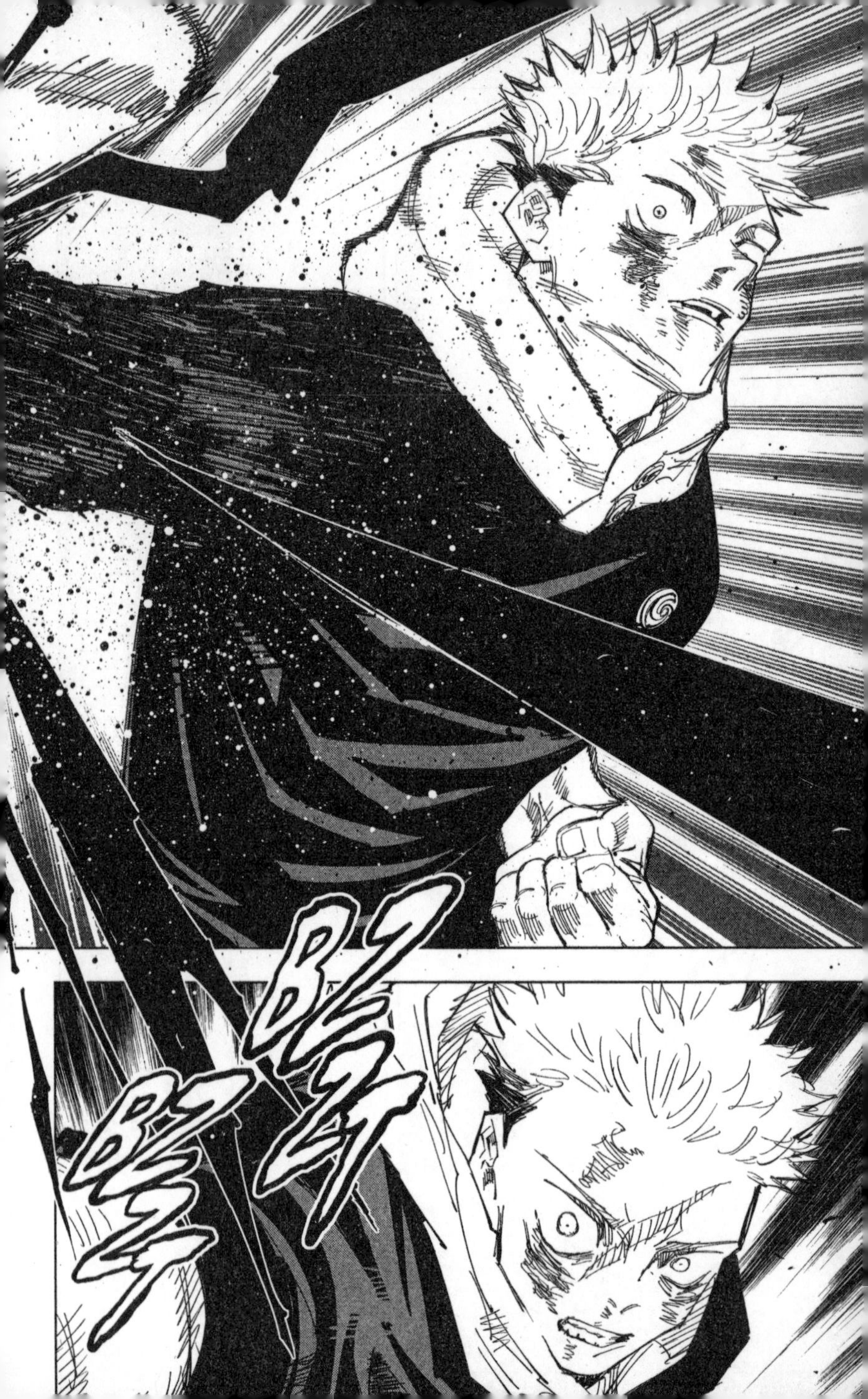
BZZT
BZZT

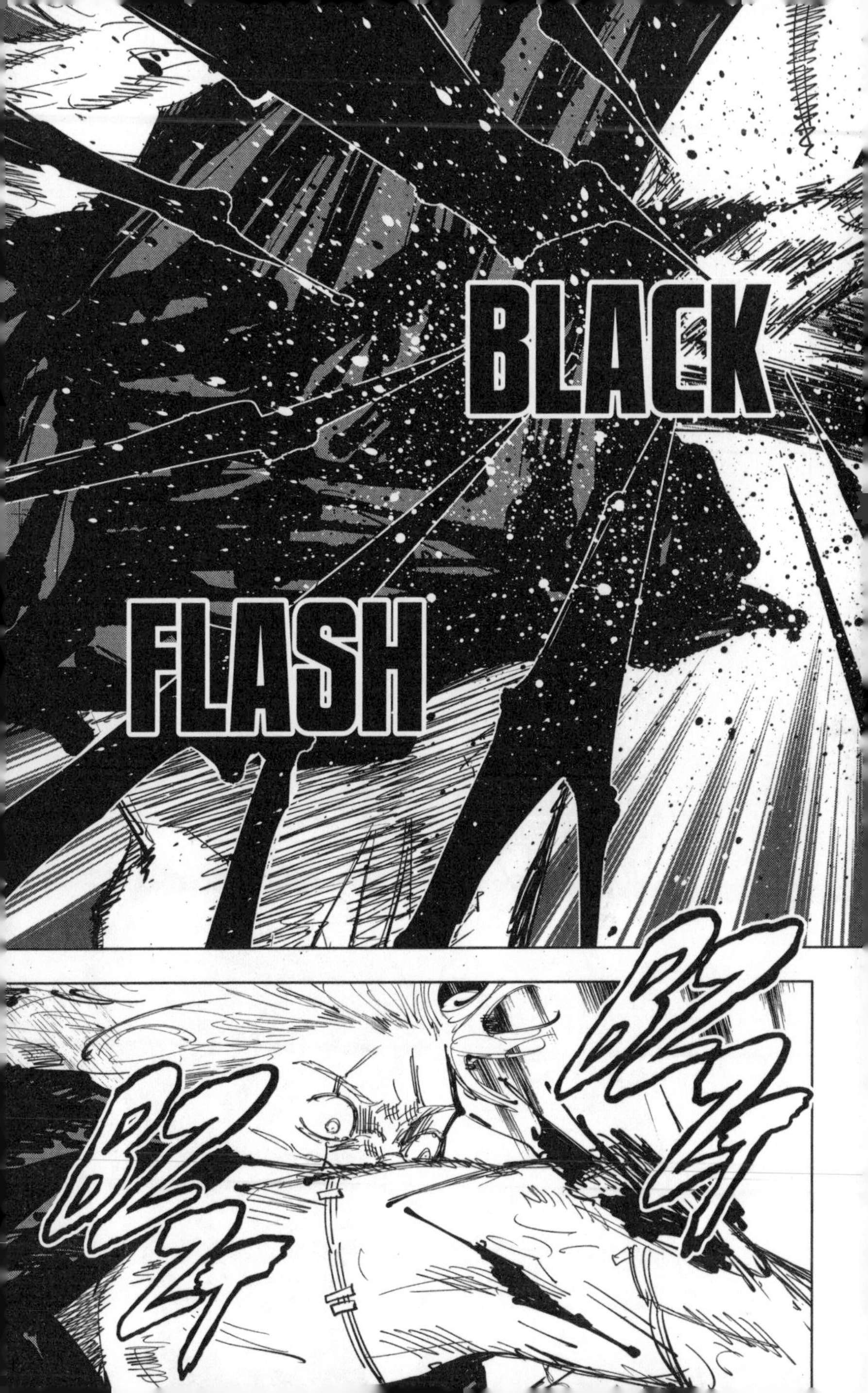
BLACK
FLASH
BZZT
BZZT

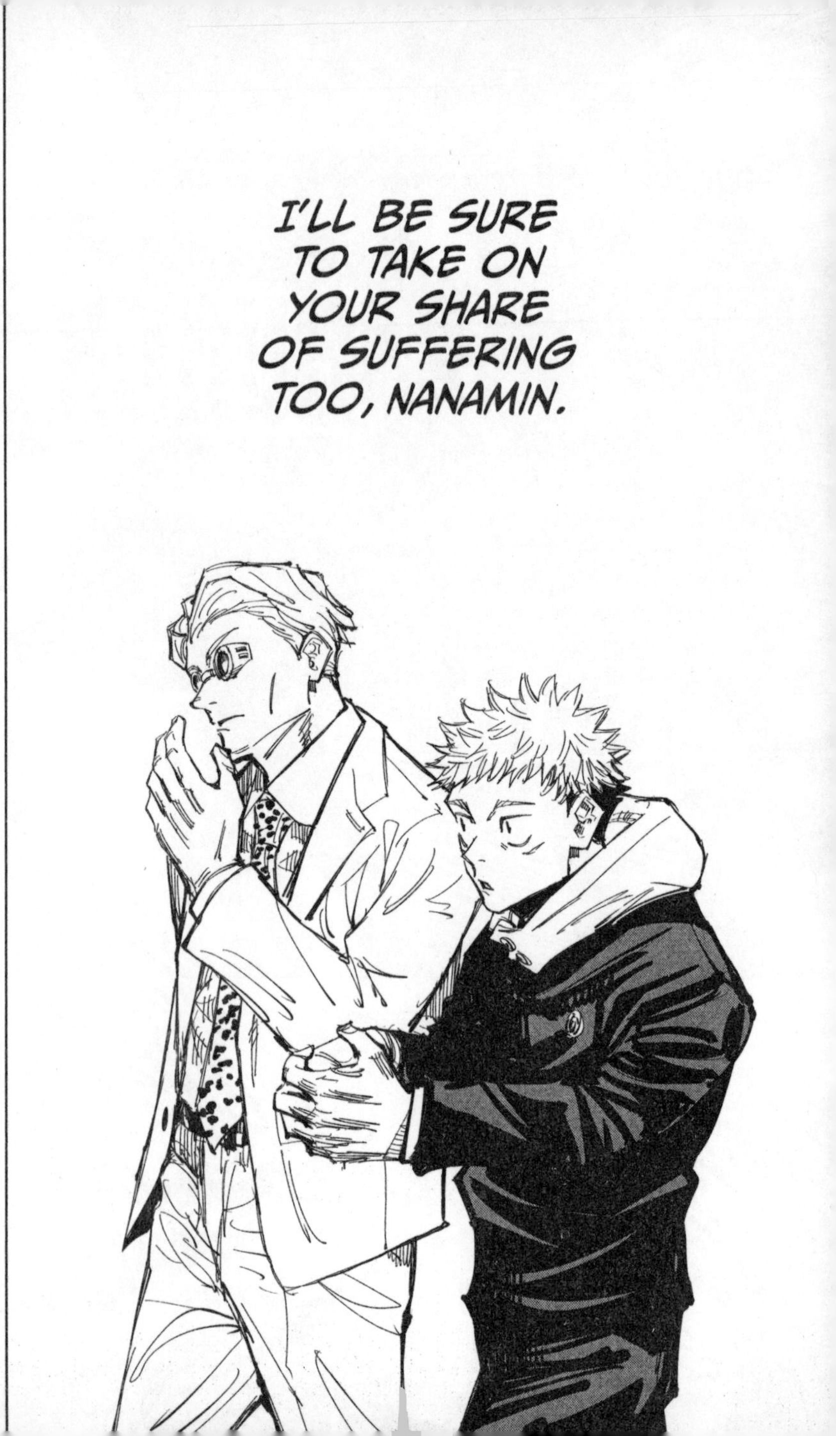
I'LL BE SURE TO TAKE ON YOUR SHARE OF SUFFERING TOO, NANAMIN.

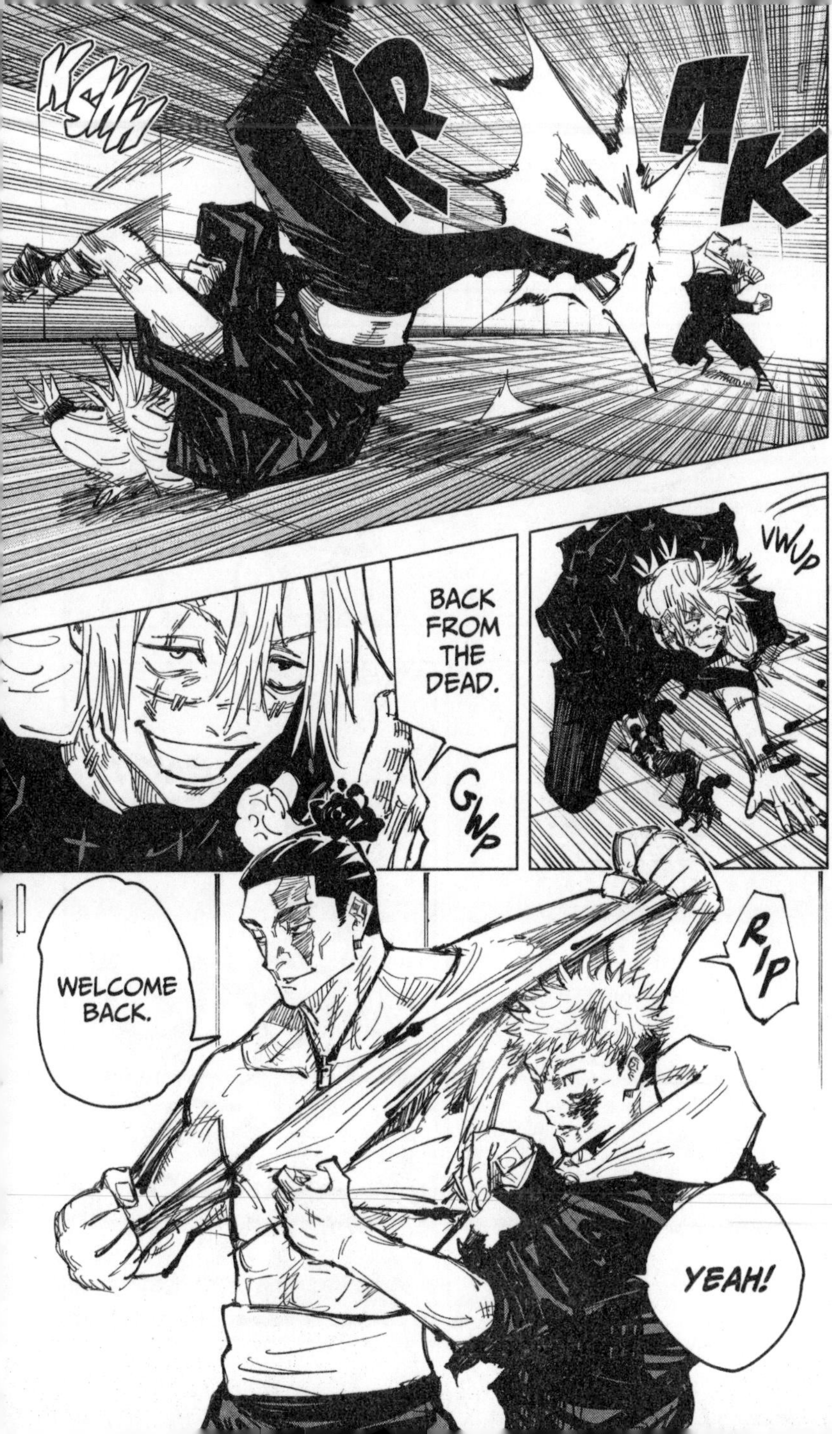
KRAK
KSHH
VWUP
BACK FROM THE DEAD.
GWP
RIP
WELCOME BACK.
YEAH!

Getting It Right!!
Limitless Cursed Technique, Part 3

The Story Thus Far…

But!!

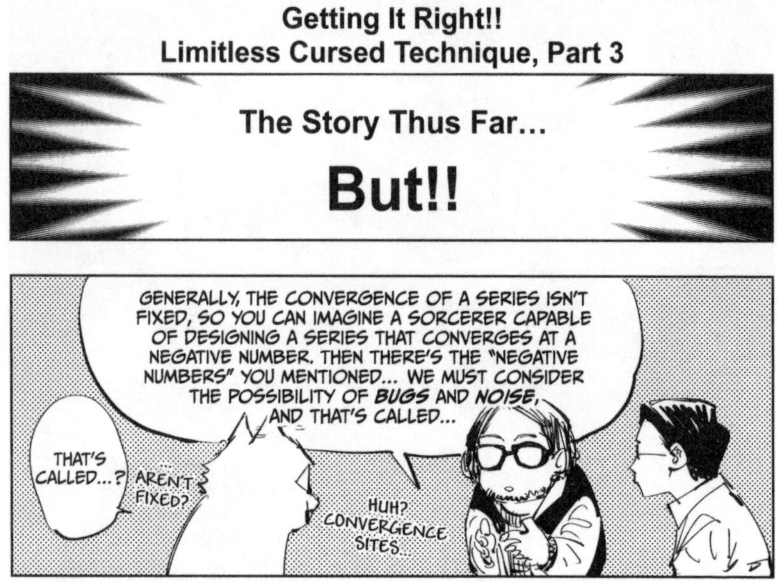
GENERALLY, THE CONVERGENCE OF A SERIES ISN'T FIXED, SO YOU CAN IMAGINE A SORCERER CAPABLE OF DESIGNING A SERIES THAT CONVERGES AT A NEGATIVE NUMBER. THEN THERE'S THE "NEGATIVE NUMBERS" YOU MENTIONED… WE MUST CONSIDER THE POSSIBILITY OF *BUGS* AND *NOISE*, AND THAT'S CALLED…
HUH? CONVERGENCE SITES…
AREN'T FIXED?
THAT'S CALLED…?

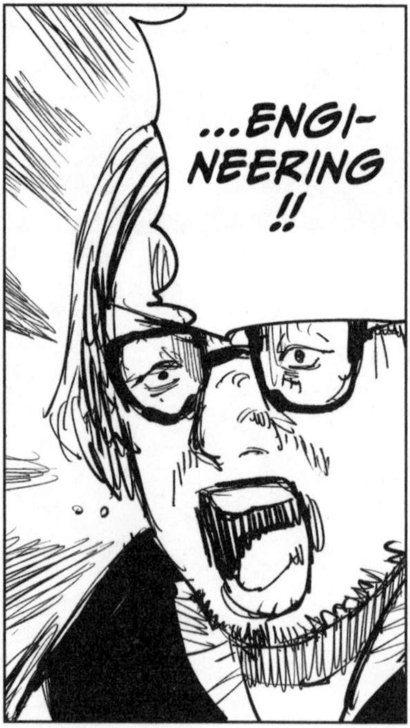
…ENGI-NEERING !!

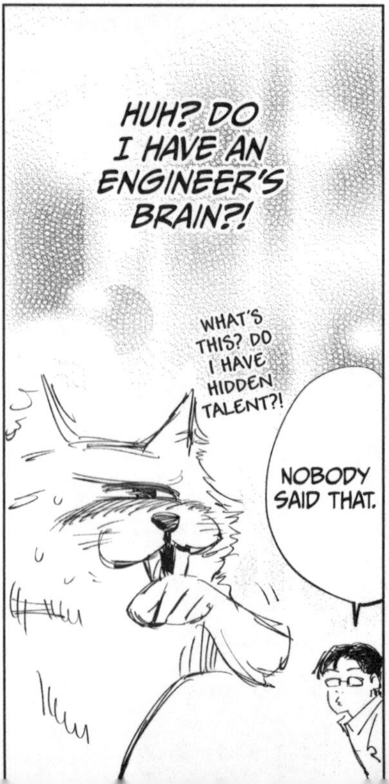
HUH? DO I HAVE AN ENGINEER'S BRAIN?!
WHAT'S THIS? DO I HAVE HIDDEN TALENT?!
NOBODY SAID THAT.

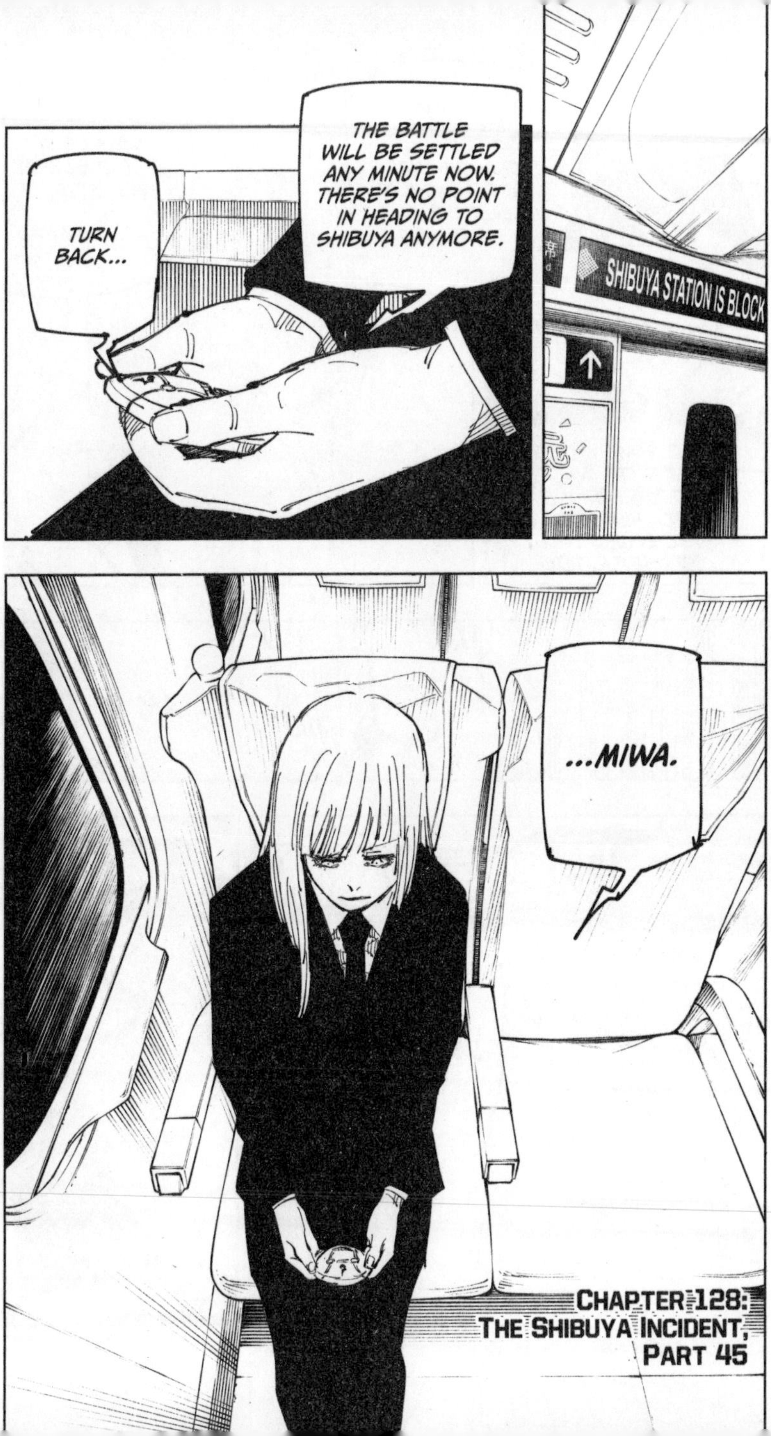
SHIBUYA STATION IS BLOCK
THE BATTLE WILL BE SETTLED ANY MINUTE NOW. THERE'S NO POINT IN HEADING TO SHIBUYA ANYMORE.
TURN BACK...
...MIWA.
CHAPTER 128: THE SHIBUYA INCIDENT, PART 45

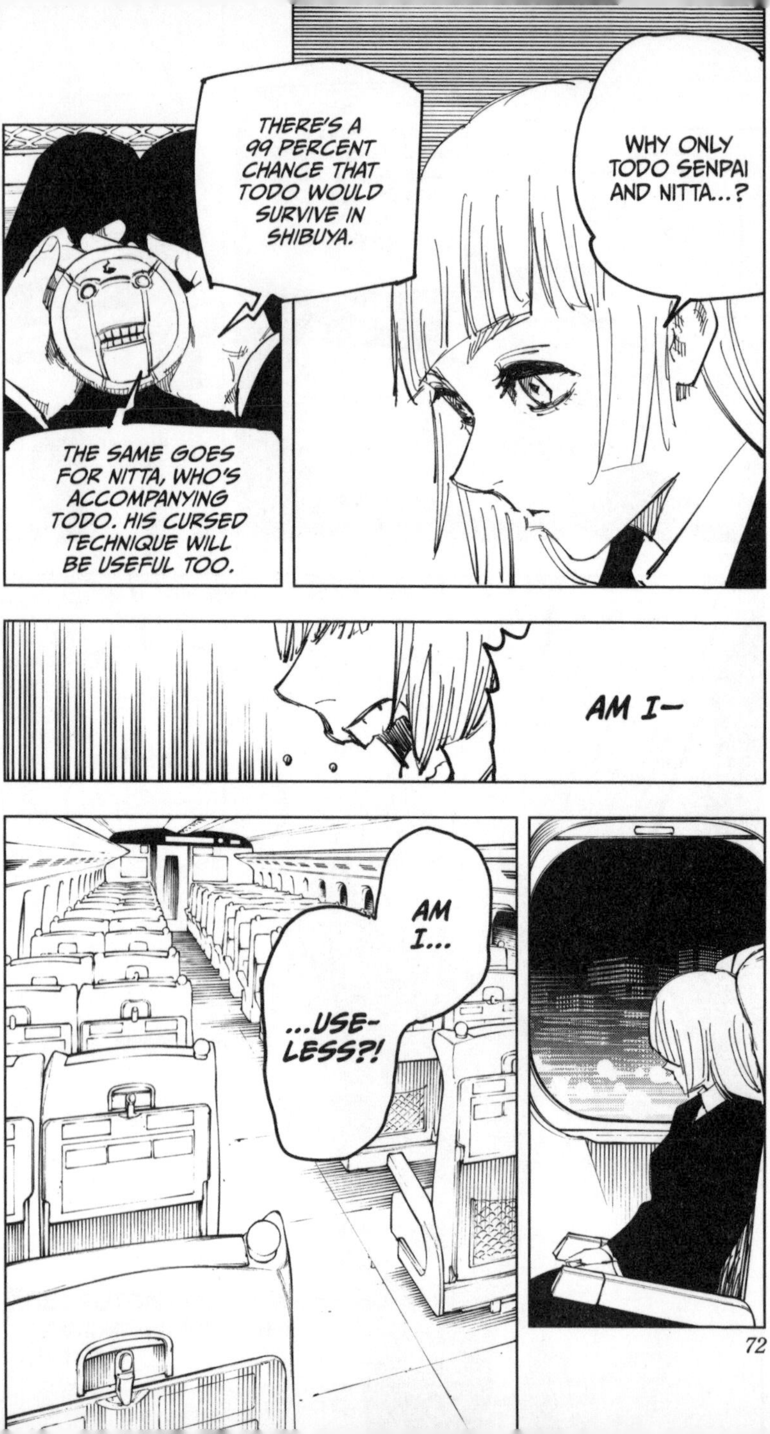
WHY ONLY TODO SENPAI AND NITTA...?
THERE'S A 99 PERCENT CHANCE THAT TODO WOULD SURVIVE IN SHIBUYA.
THE SAME GOES FOR NITTA, WHO'S ACCOMPANYING TODO. HIS CURSED TECHNIQUE WILL BE USEFUL TOO.
AM I—
AM I...
...USELESS?!

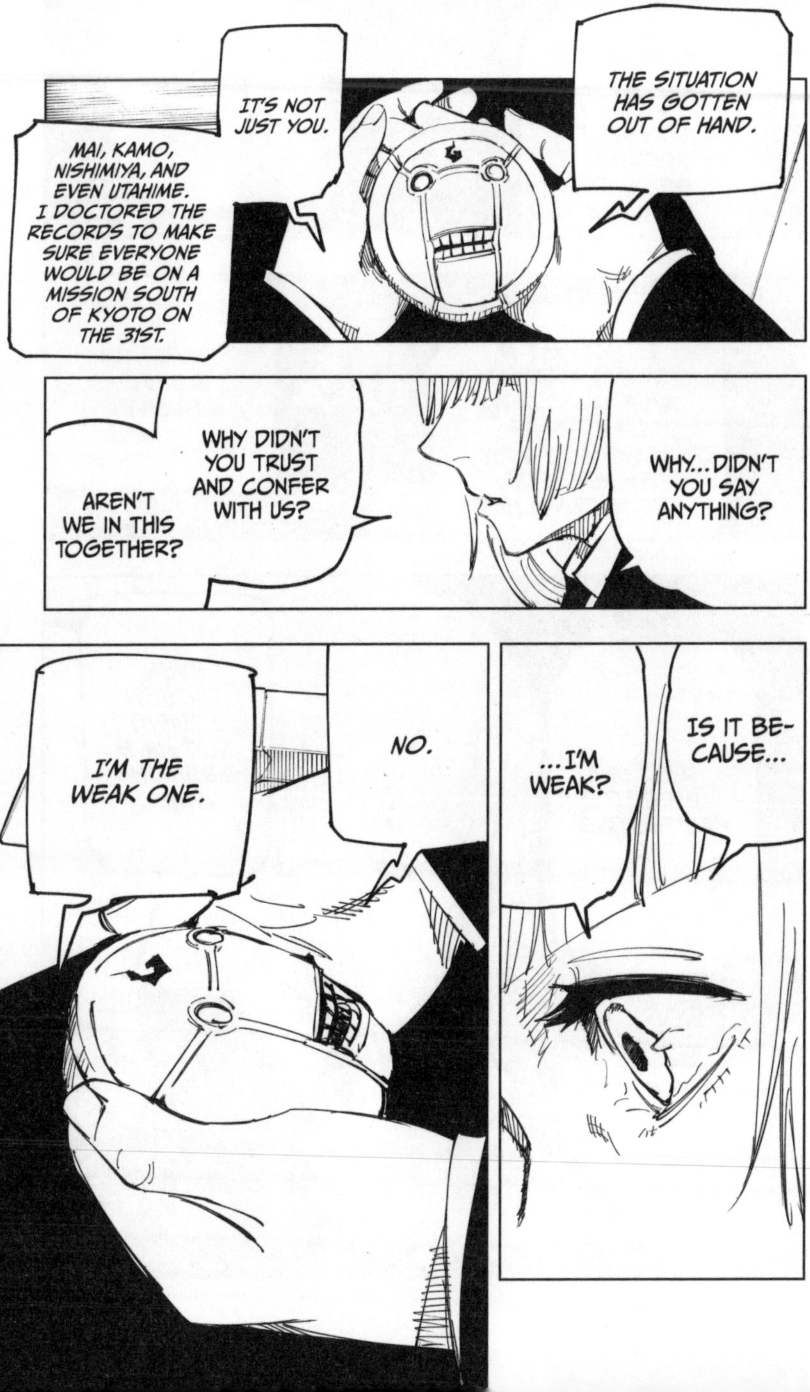
THE SITUATION HAS GOTTEN OUT OF HAND.
IT'S NOT JUST YOU.
MAI, KAMO, NISHIMIYA, AND EVEN UTAHIME. I DOCTORED THE RECORDS TO MAKE SURE EVERYONE WOULD BE ON A MISSION SOUTH OF KYOTO ON THE 31ST.
WHY...DIDN'T YOU SAY ANYTHING?
WHY DIDN'T YOU TRUST AND CONFER WITH US?
AREN'T WE IN THIS TOGETHER?
IS IT BE- CAUSE...
...I'M WEAK?
NO.
I'M THE WEAK ONE.

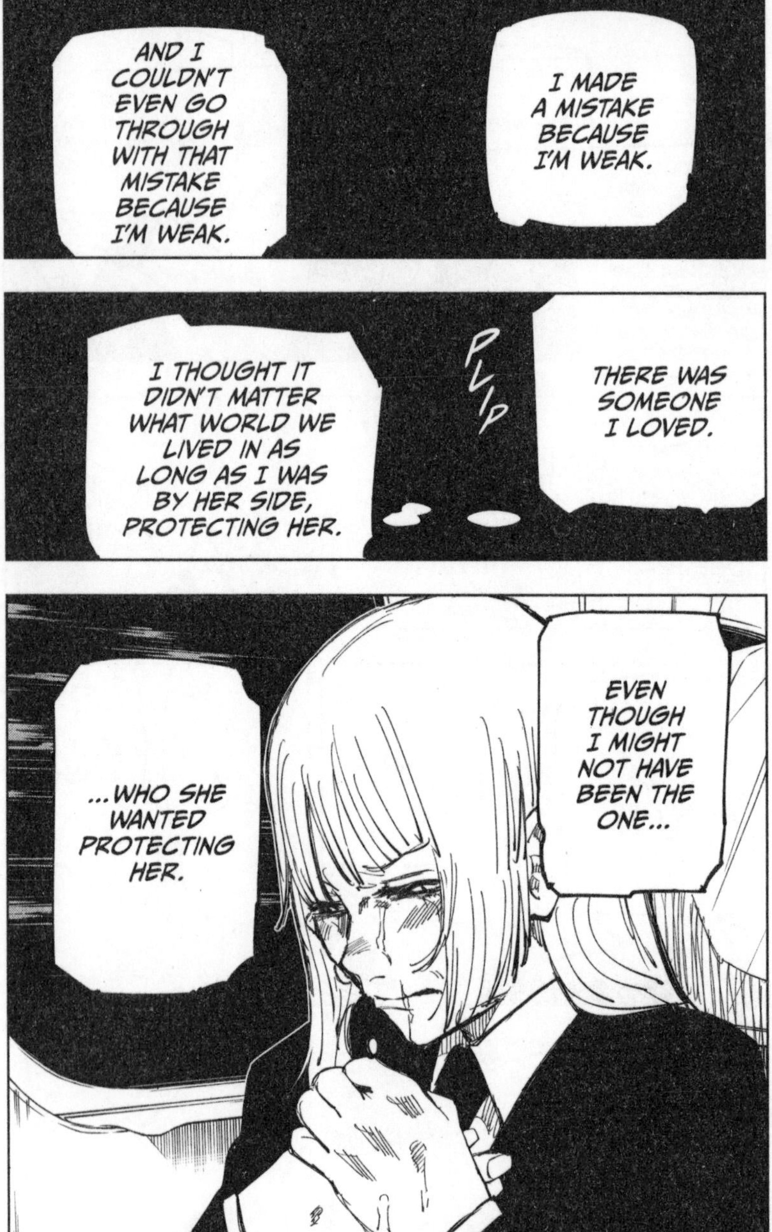
I MADE A MISTAKE BECAUSE I'M WEAK.
AND I COULDN'T EVEN GO THROUGH WITH THAT MISTAKE BECAUSE I'M WEAK.
THERE WAS SOMEONE I LOVED.
PLIP
I THOUGHT IT DIDN'T MATTER WHAT WORLD WE LIVED IN AS LONG AS I WAS BY HER SIDE, PROTECTING HER.
EVEN THOUGH I MIGHT NOT HAVE BEEN THE ONE...
...WHO SHE WANTED PROTECTING HER.

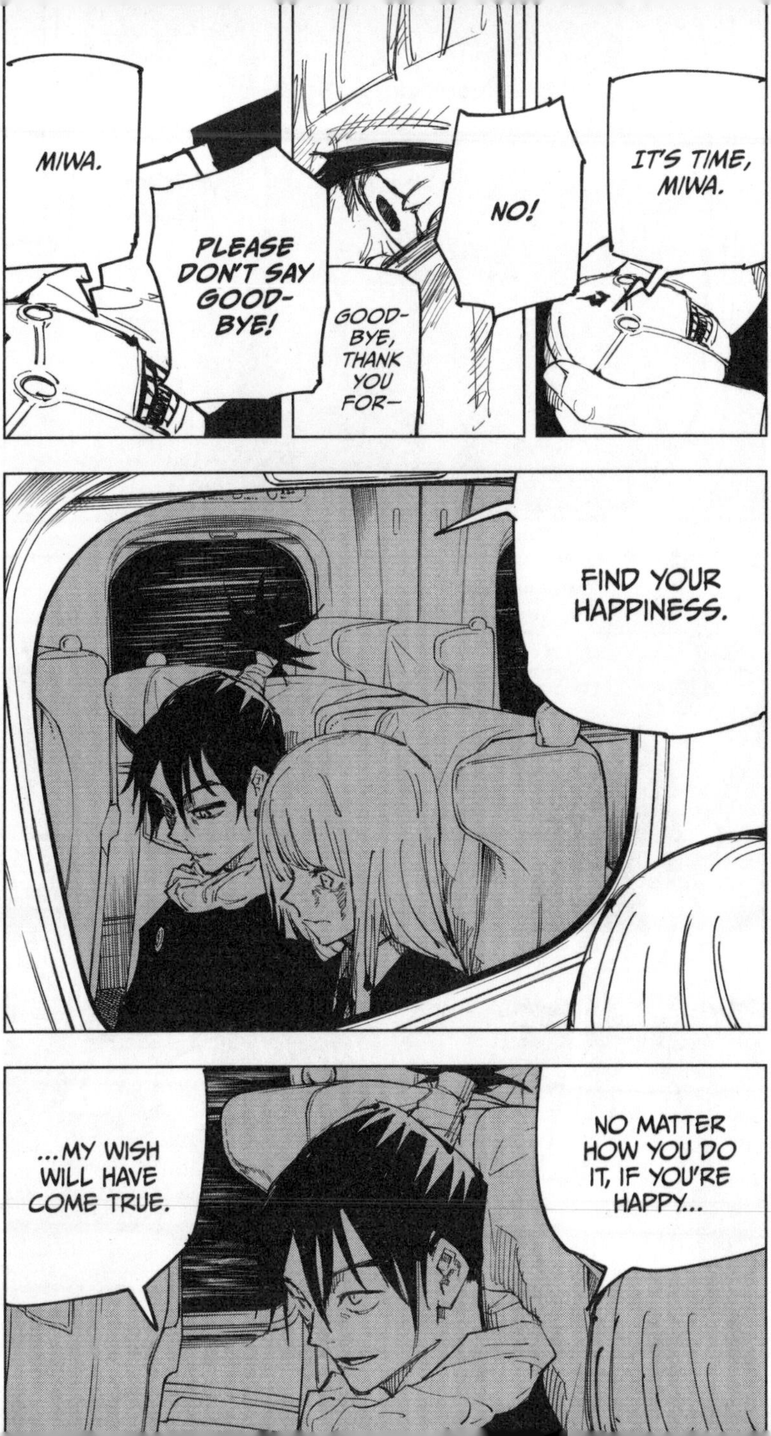
IT'S TIME, MIWA.
NO!
GOOD-BYE, THANK YOU FOR—
MIWA.
PLEASE DON'T SAY GOOD-BYE!
FIND YOUR HAPPINESS.
NO MATTER HOW YOU DO IT, IF YOU'RE HAPPY...
...MY WISH WILL HAVE COME TRUE.

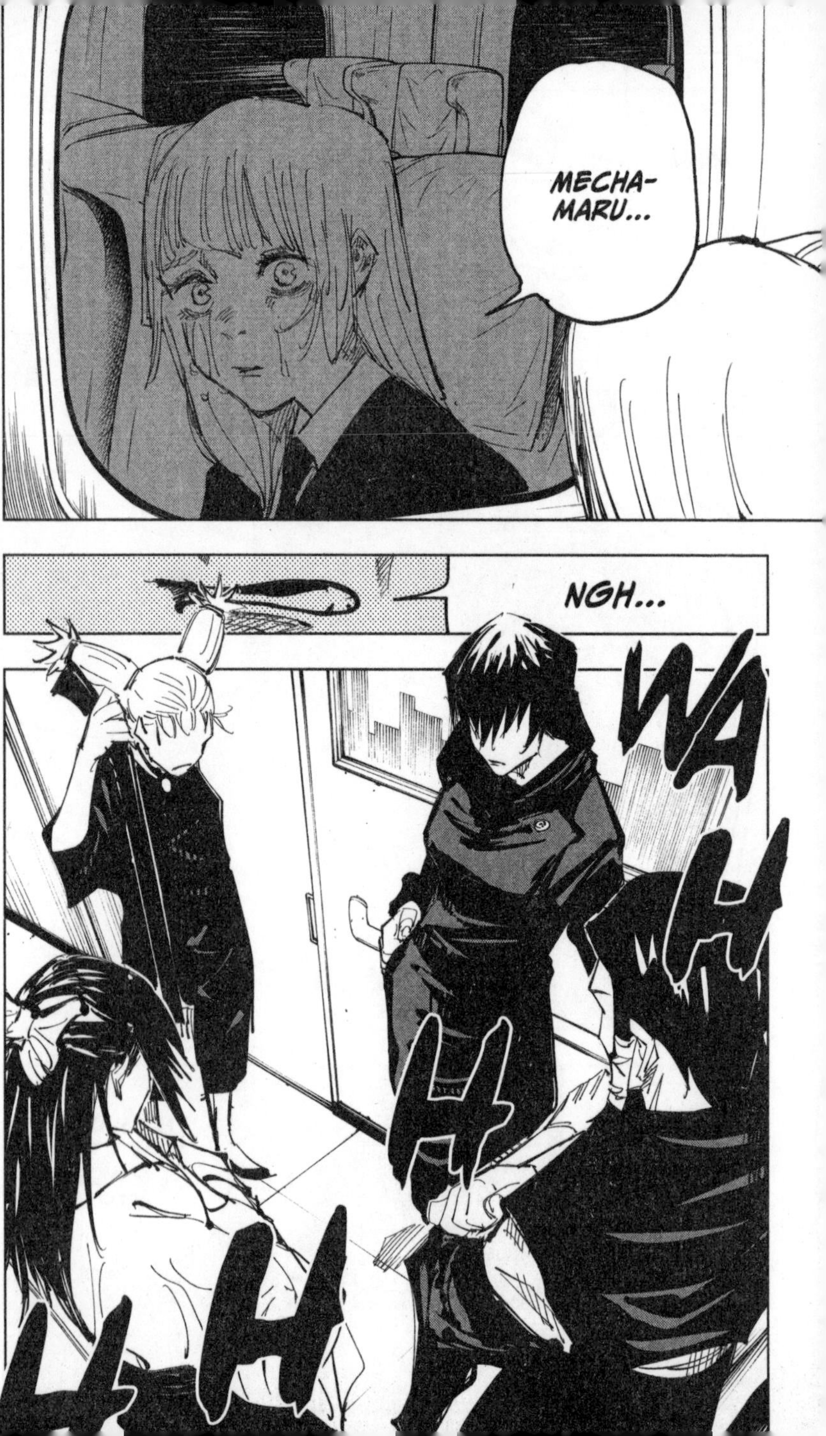
MECHA-
MARU...
NGH...
WAAHHH

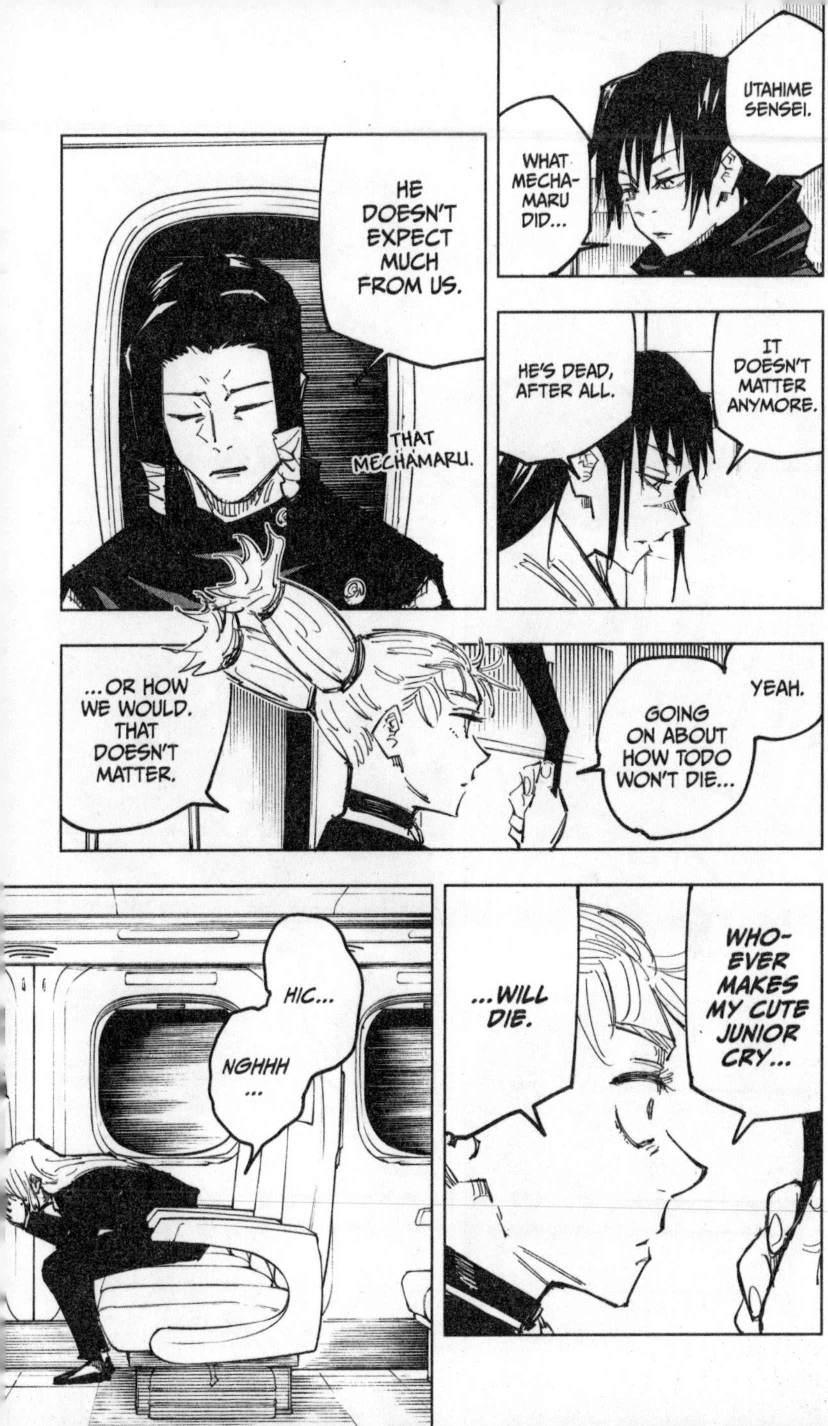
UTAHIME SENSEI.
WHAT MECHAMARU DID...
IT DOESN'T MATTER ANYMORE.
HE'S DEAD, AFTER ALL.
HE DOESN'T EXPECT MUCH FROM US.
THAT MECHAMARU.
YEAH.
GOING ON ABOUT HOW TODO WON'T DIE...
...OR HOW WE WOULD. THAT DOESN'T MATTER.
WHO-EVER MAKES MY CUTE JUNIOR CRY...
...WILL DIE.
HIC...
NGHHH...

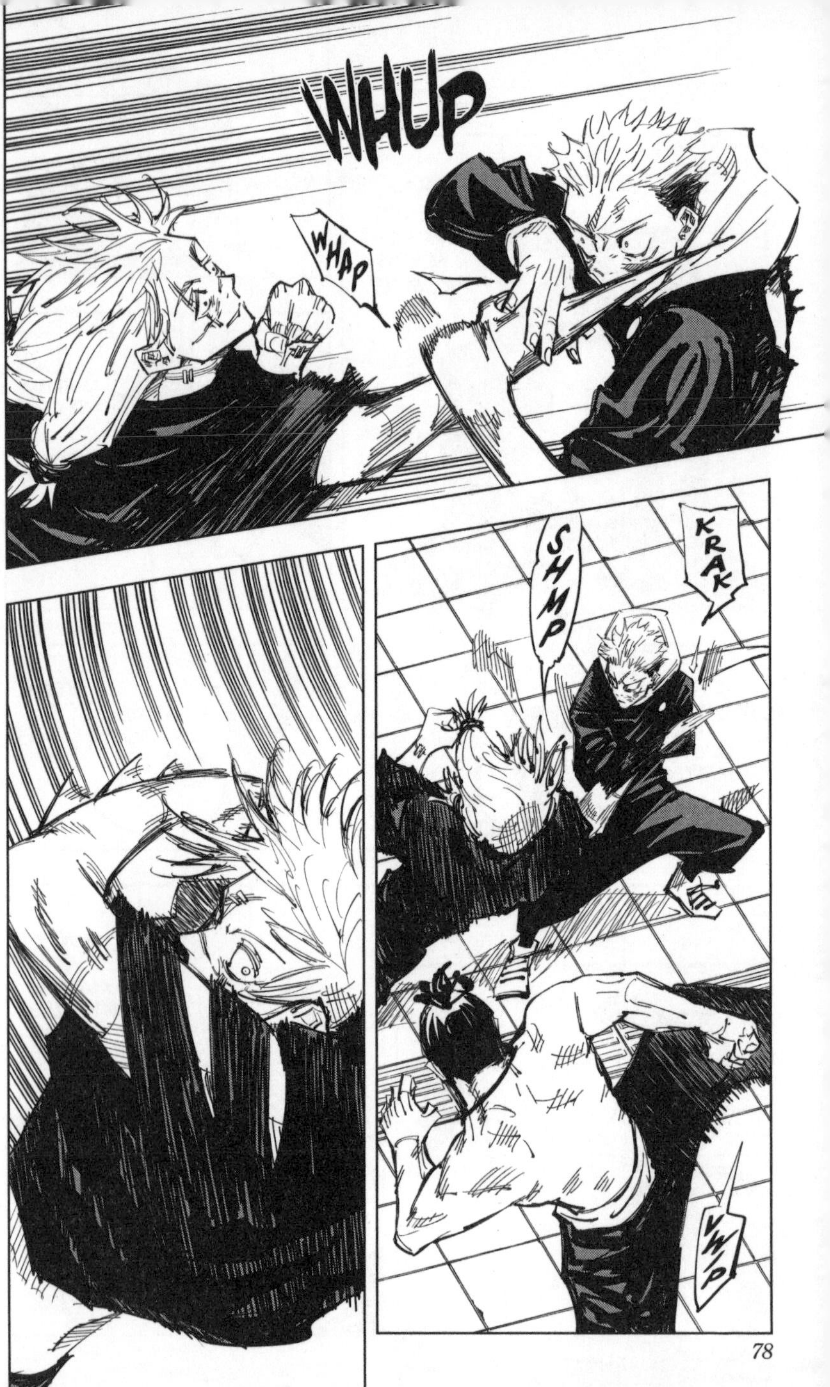
WHUP
WHAP
KRAK
SHMP
VWIP

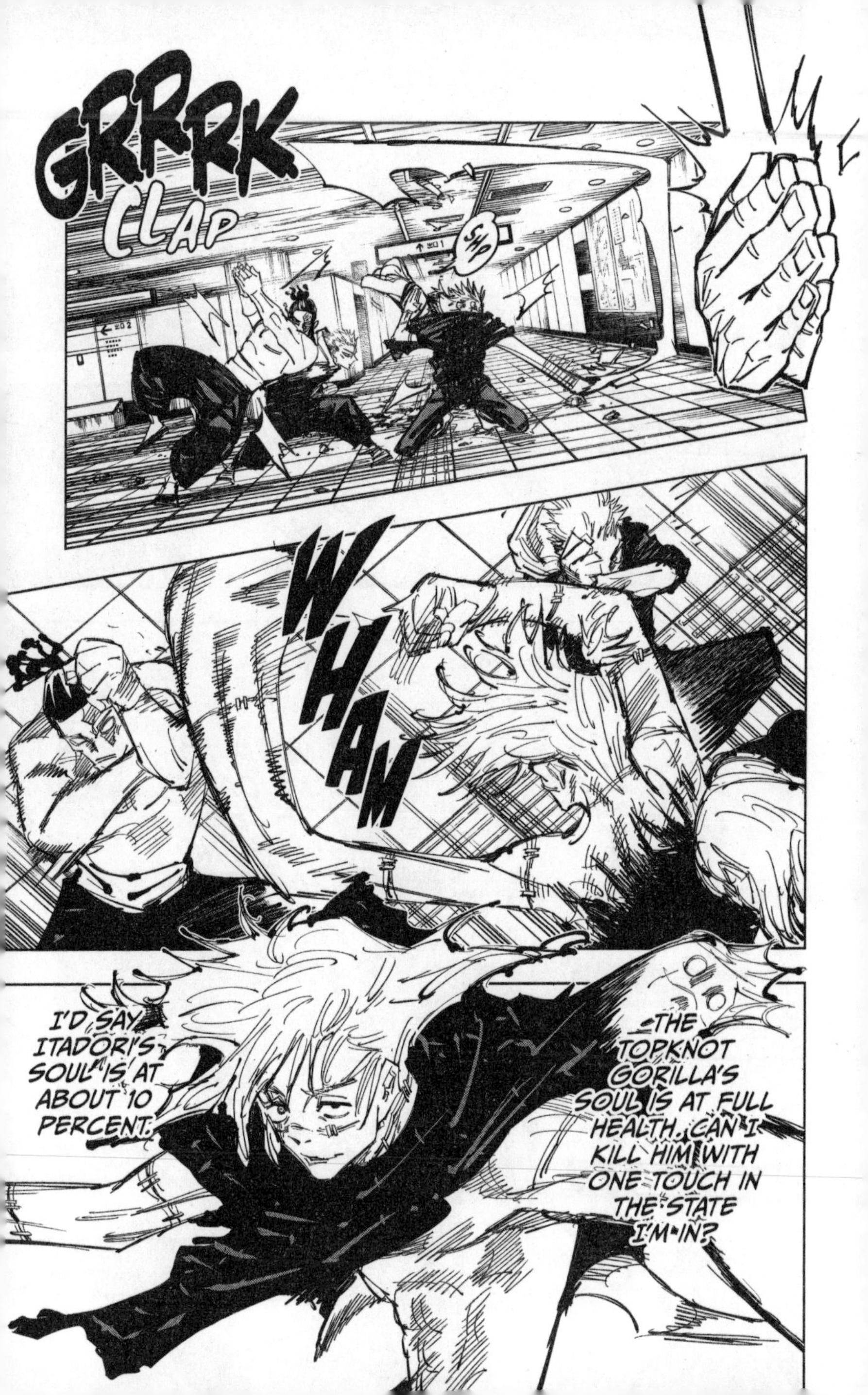

SHP
GRRRK
CLAP
WHAM
THE TOPKNOT GORILLA'S SOUL IS AT FULL HEALTH. CAN I KILL HIM WITH ONE TOUCH IN THE STATE I'M IN?
I'D SAY ITADORI'S SOUL IS AT ABOUT 10 PERCENT.

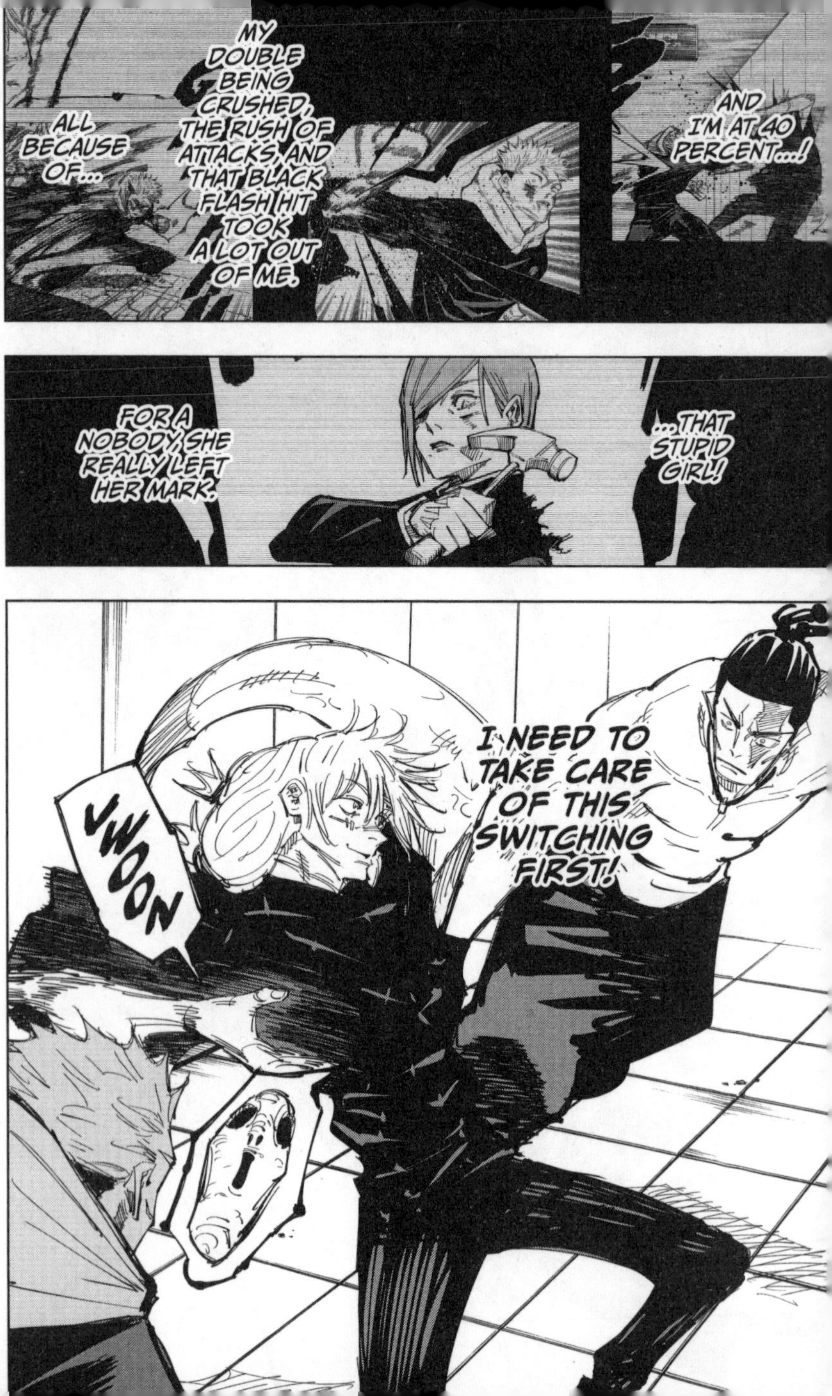
AND I'M AT 40 PERCENT...!
MY DOUBLE BEING CRUSHED, THE RUSH OF ATTACKS, AND THAT BLACK FLASH HIT TOOK A LOT OUT OF ME.
ALL BECAUSE OF...
...THAT STUPID GIRL!
FOR A NOBODY, SHE REALLY LEFT HER MARK.
I NEED TO TAKE CARE OF THIS SWITCHING FIRST!
JWOON

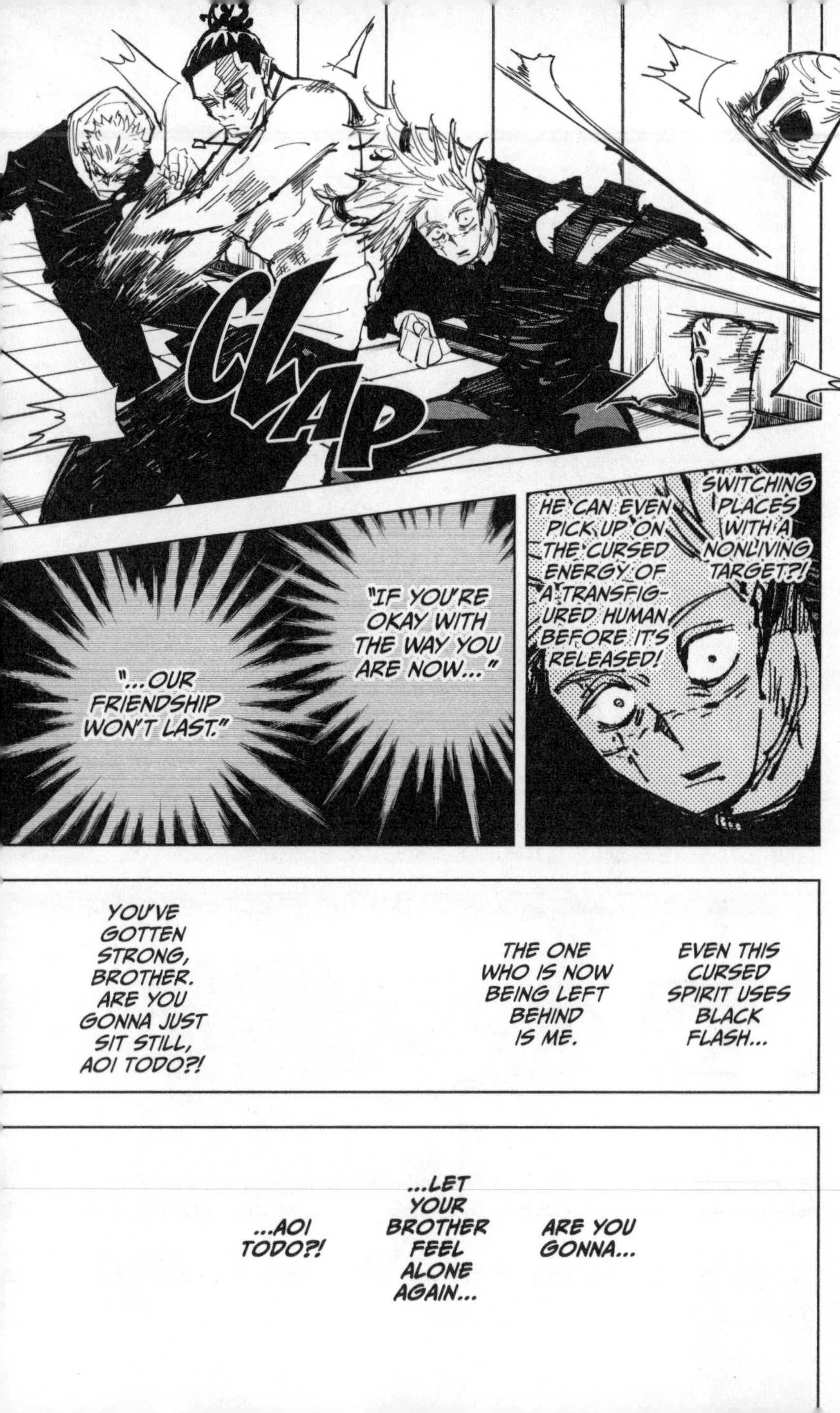
CLAP
SWITCHING PLACES WITH A NONLIVING TARGET?!
HE CAN EVEN PICK UP ON THE CURSED ENERGY OF A TRANSFIGURED HUMAN BEFORE IT'S RELEASED!
"IF YOU'RE OKAY WITH THE WAY YOU ARE NOW..."
"...OUR FRIENDSHIP WON'T LAST."
EVEN THIS CURSED SPIRIT USES BLACK FLASH...
THE ONE WHO IS NOW BEING LEFT BEHIND IS ME.
YOU'VE GOTTEN STRONG, BROTHER. ARE YOU GONNA JUST SIT STILL, AOI TODO?!
ARE YOU GONNA...
...LET YOUR BROTHER FEEL ALONE AGAIN...
...AOI TODO?!

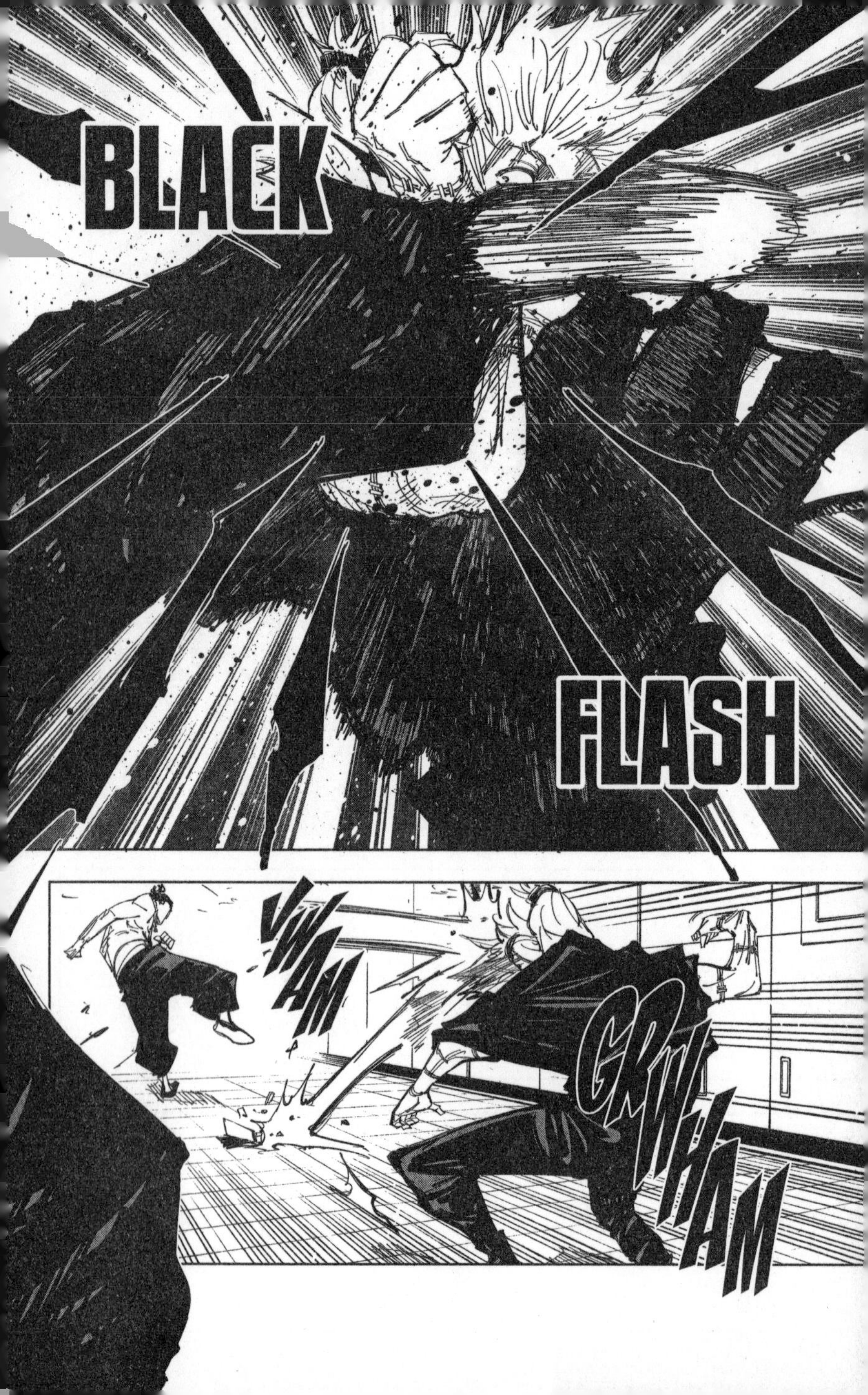
BLACK
FLASH
GRWHAM
VWAM

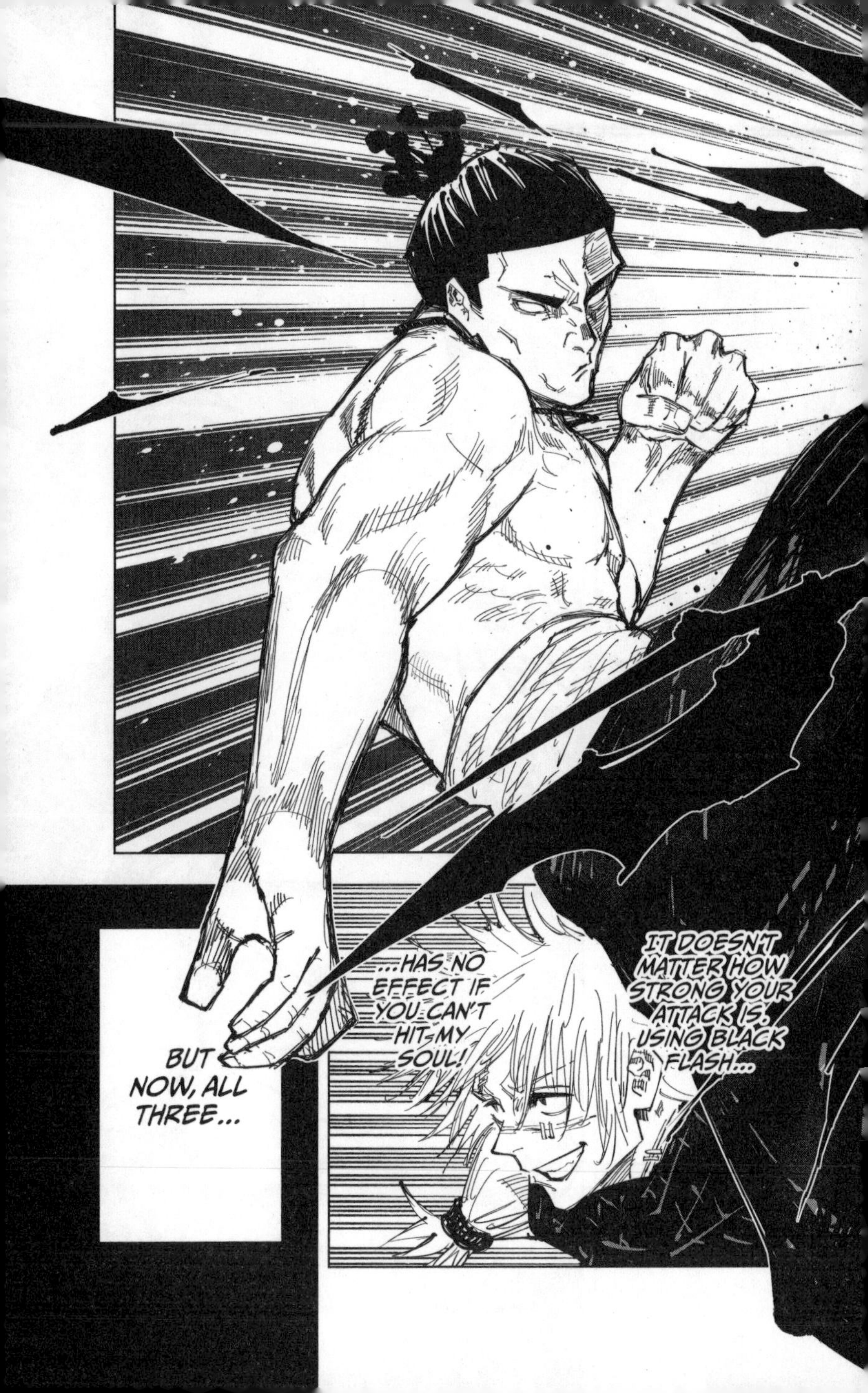
IT DOESN'T MATTER HOW STRONG YOUR ATTACK IS. USING BLACK FLASH...
...HAS NO EFFECT IF YOU CAN'T HIT MY SOUL!
BUT NOW, ALL THREE...

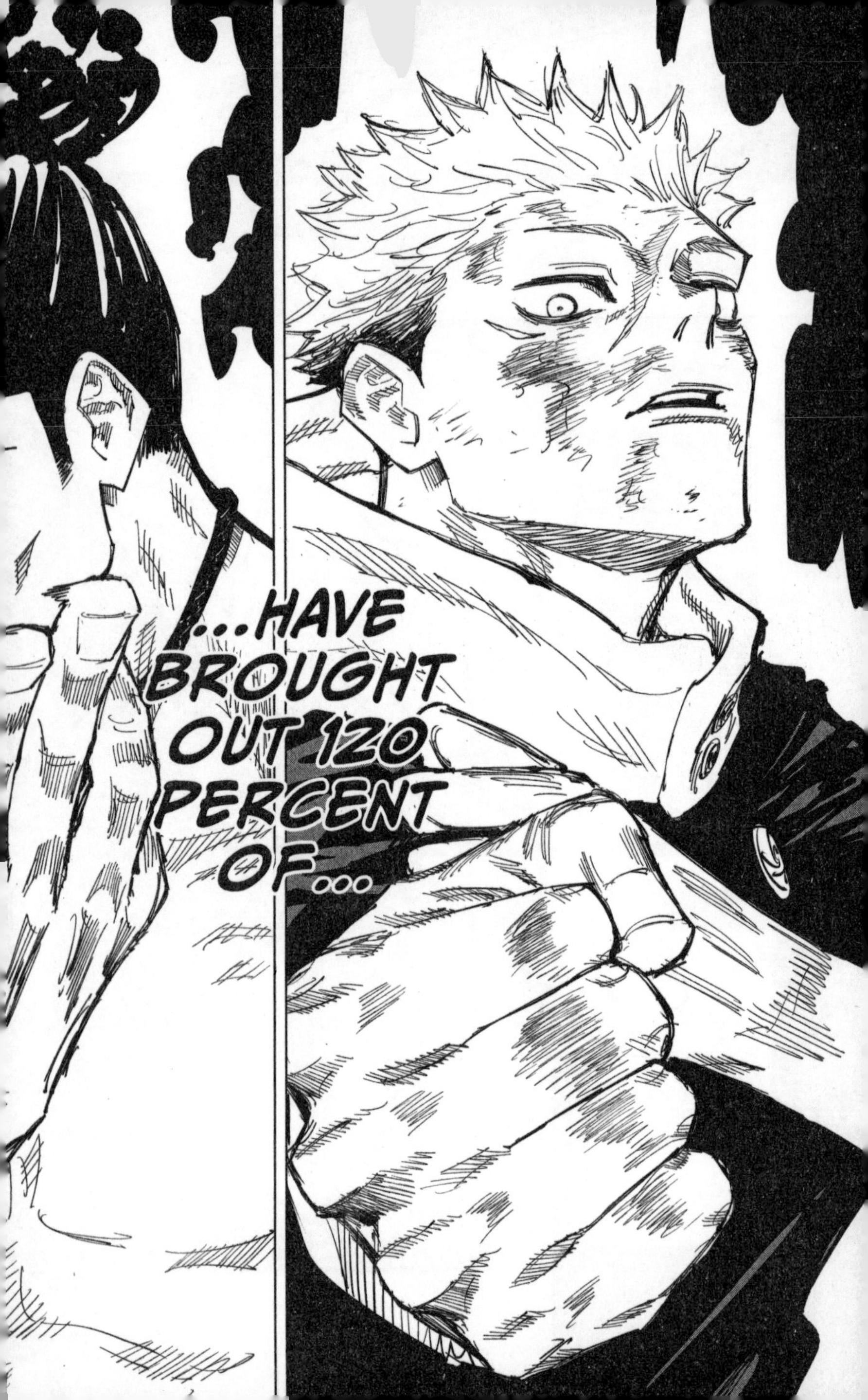
...HAVE BROUGHT OUT 120 PERCENT OF...

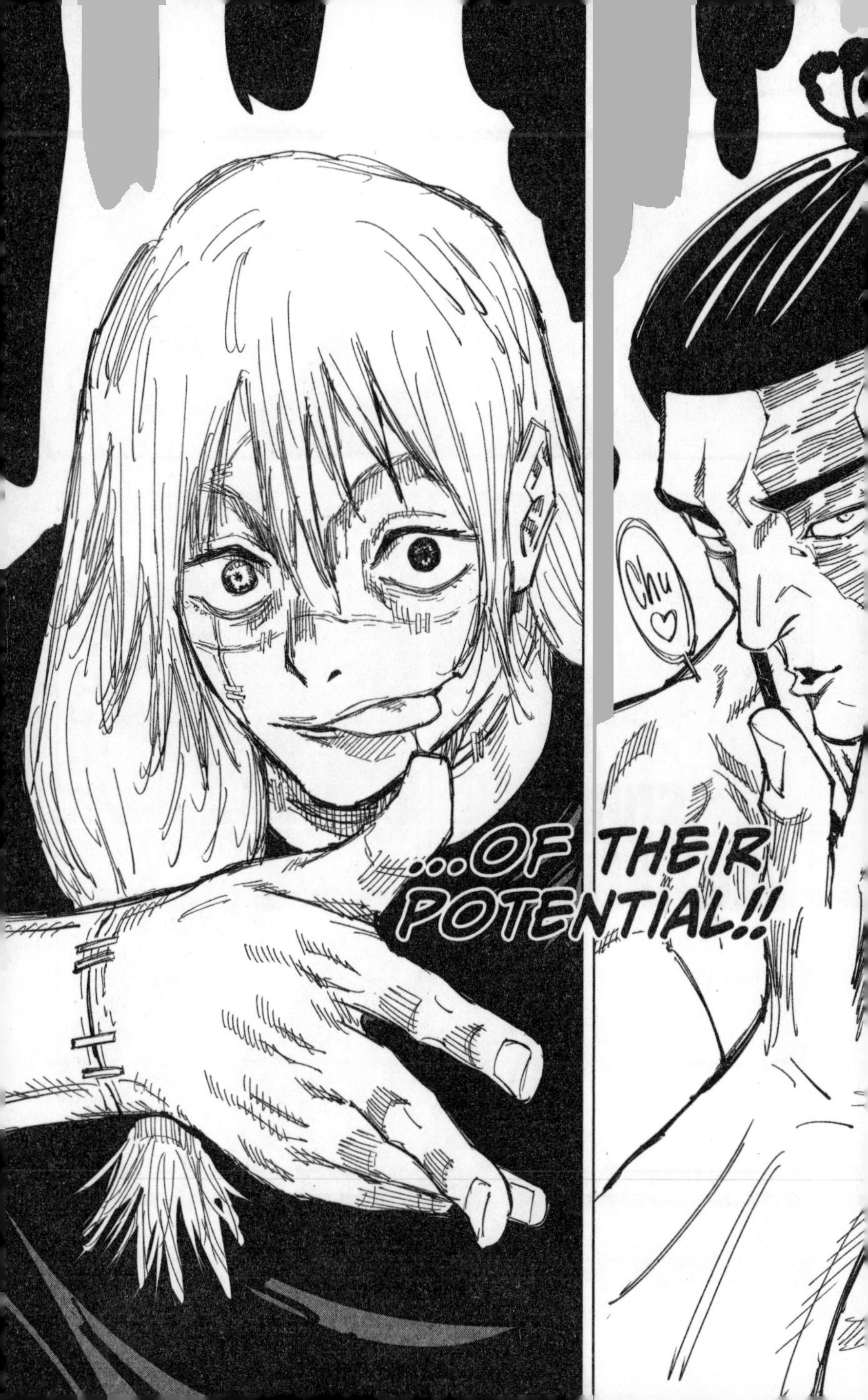
Chu ♡
...OF THEIR POTENTIAL!!

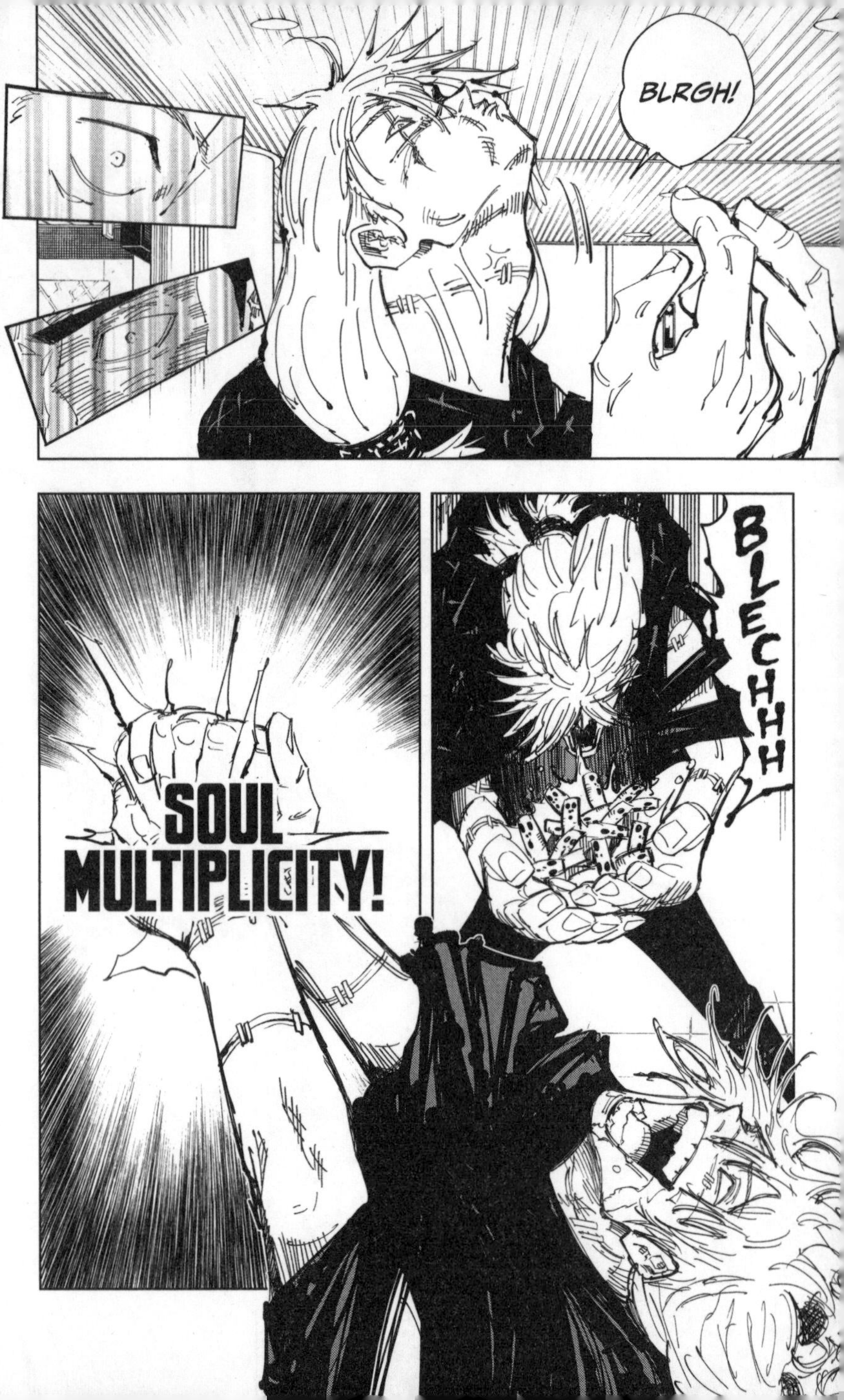
BLRGH!
BLECHHH
SOUL MULTIPLICITY!

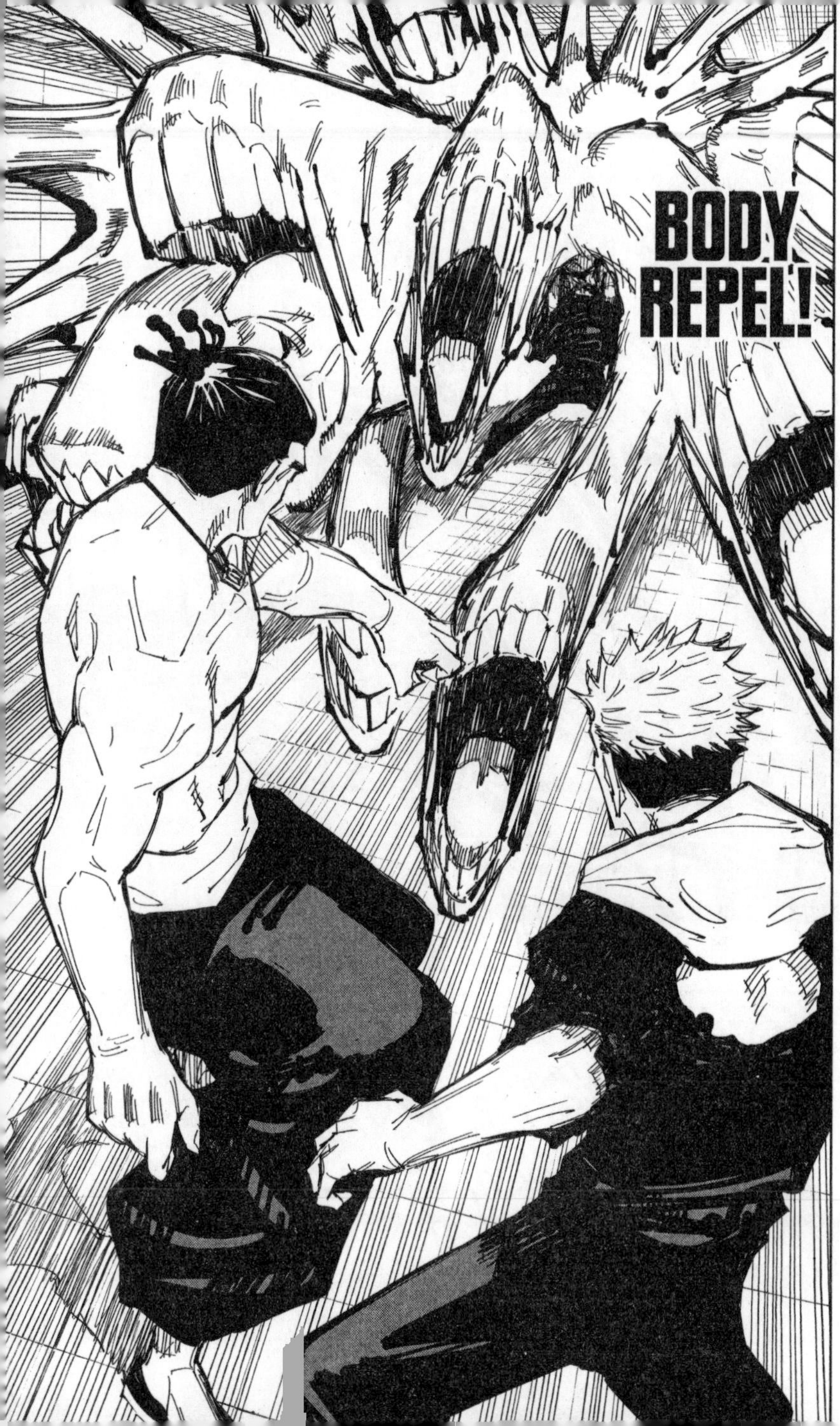
BODY REPEL!

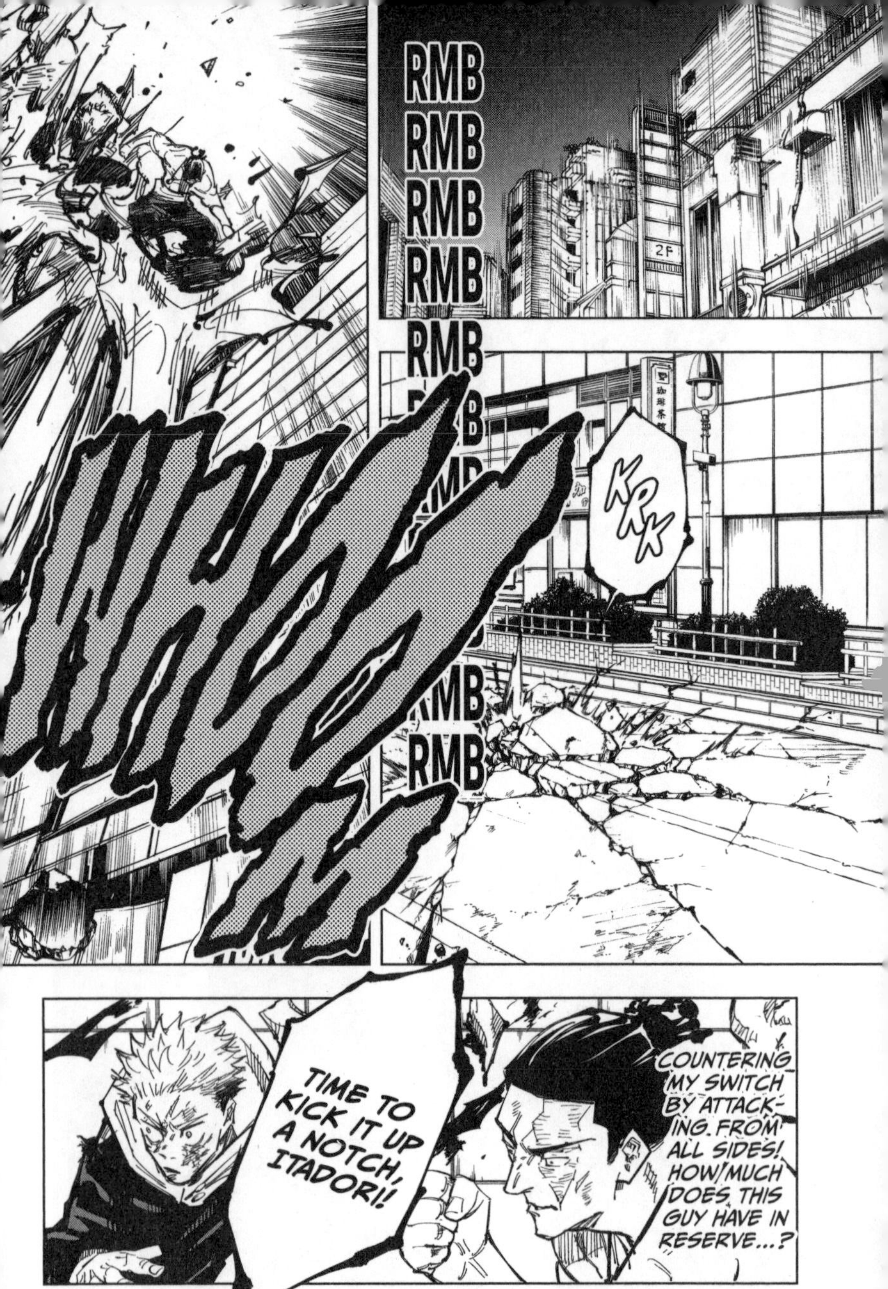
RMB
RMB
RMB
RMB
RMB
RMB
RMB
KRK
COUNTERING MY SWITCH BY ATTACKING FROM ALL SIDES! HOW MUCH DOES THIS GUY HAVE IN RESERVE...?
TIME TO KICK IT UP A NOTCH, ITADORI!

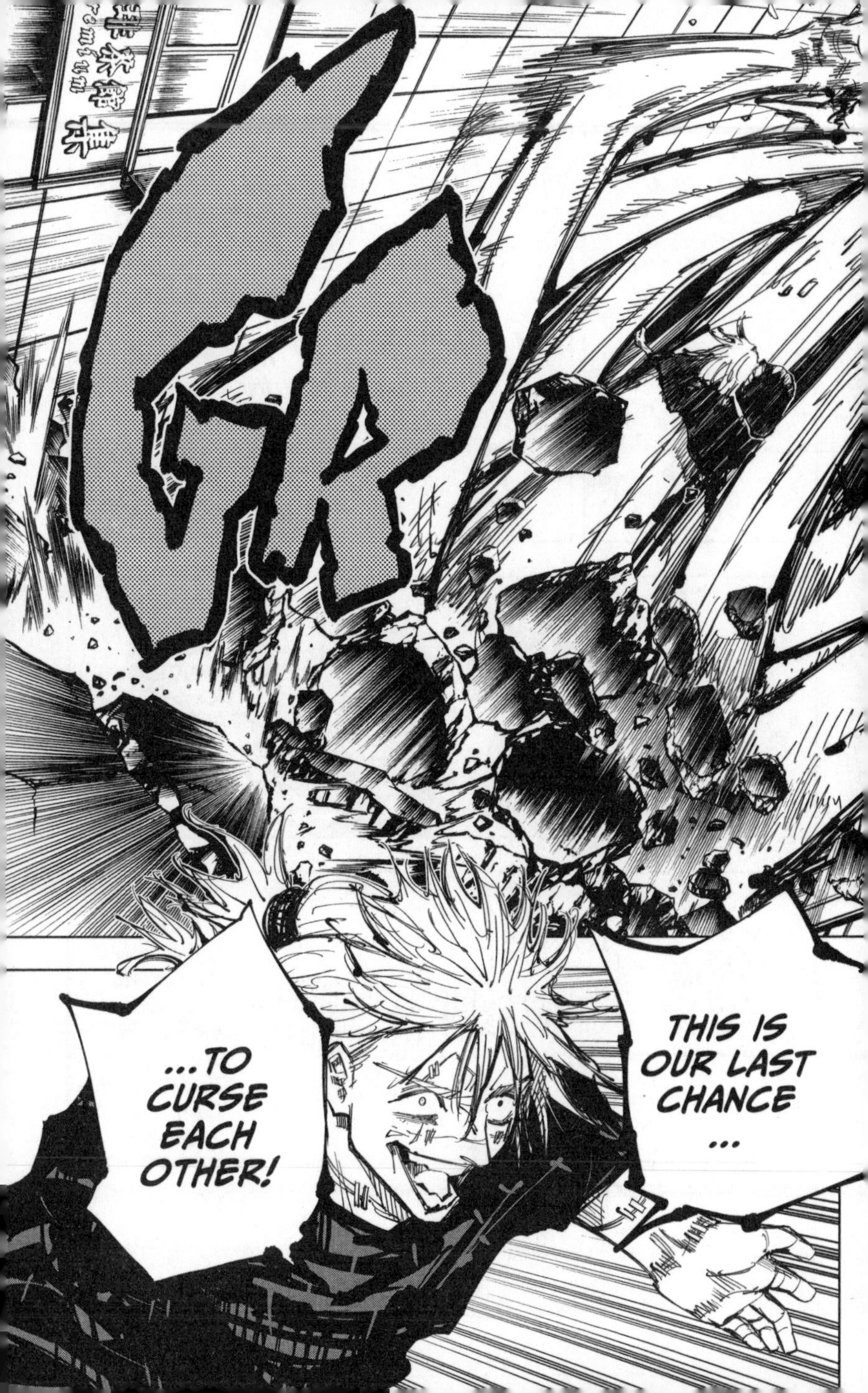
THIS IS OUR LAST CHANCE ...
...TO CURSE EACH OTHER!

Getting It Right!!
Limitless Cursed Technique, Part 4

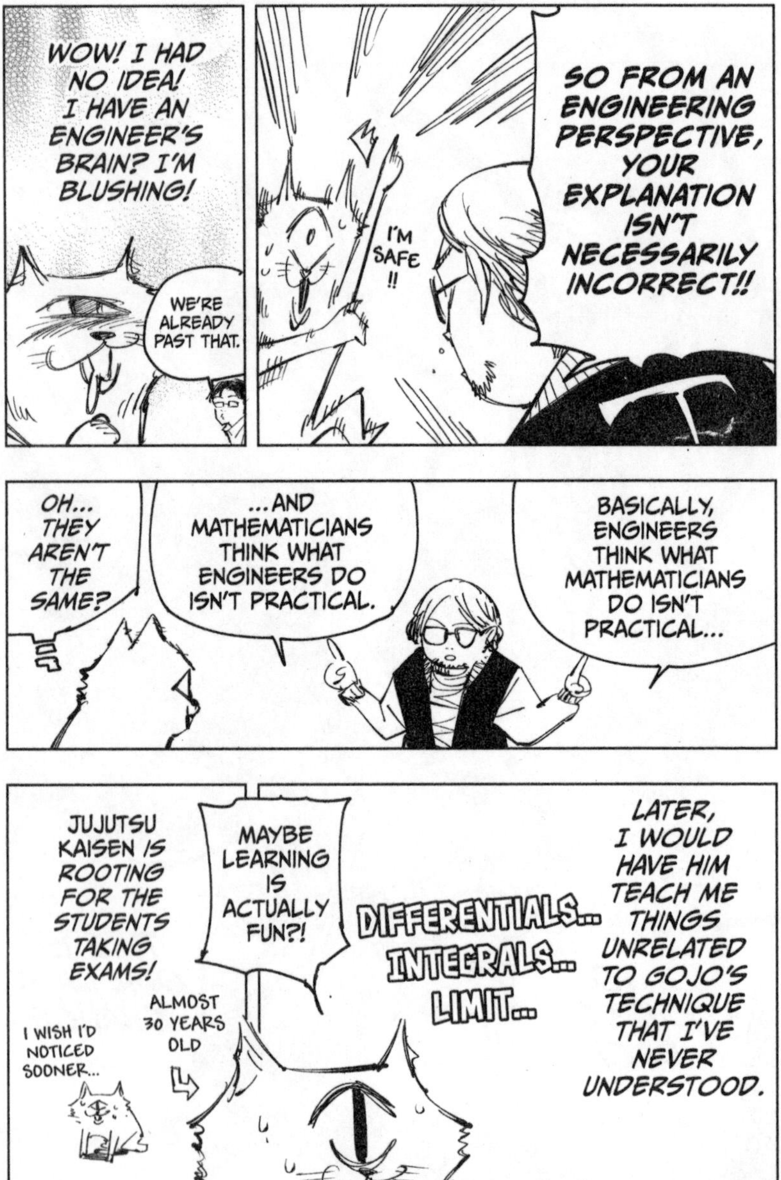
SO FROM AN ENGINEERING PERSPECTIVE, YOUR EXPLANATION ISN'T NECESSARILY INCORRECT!!
I'M SAFE!!
WOW! I HAD NO IDEA! I HAVE AN ENGINEER'S BRAIN? I'M BLUSHING!
WE'RE ALREADY PAST THAT.
BASICALLY, ENGINEERS THINK WHAT MATHEMATICIANS DO ISN'T PRACTICAL...
...AND MATHEMATICIANS THINK WHAT ENGINEERS DO ISN'T PRACTICAL.
OH... THEY AREN'T THE SAME?
LATER, I WOULD HAVE HIM TEACH ME THINGS UNRELATED TO GOJO'S TECHNIQUE THAT I'VE NEVER UNDERSTOOD.
DIFFERENTIALS... INTEGRALS... LIMIT...
MAYBE LEARNING IS ACTUALLY FUN?!
JUJUTSU KAISEN IS ROOTING FOR THE STUDENTS TAKING EXAMS!
ALMOST 30 YEARS OLD
I WISH I'D NOTICED SOONER...

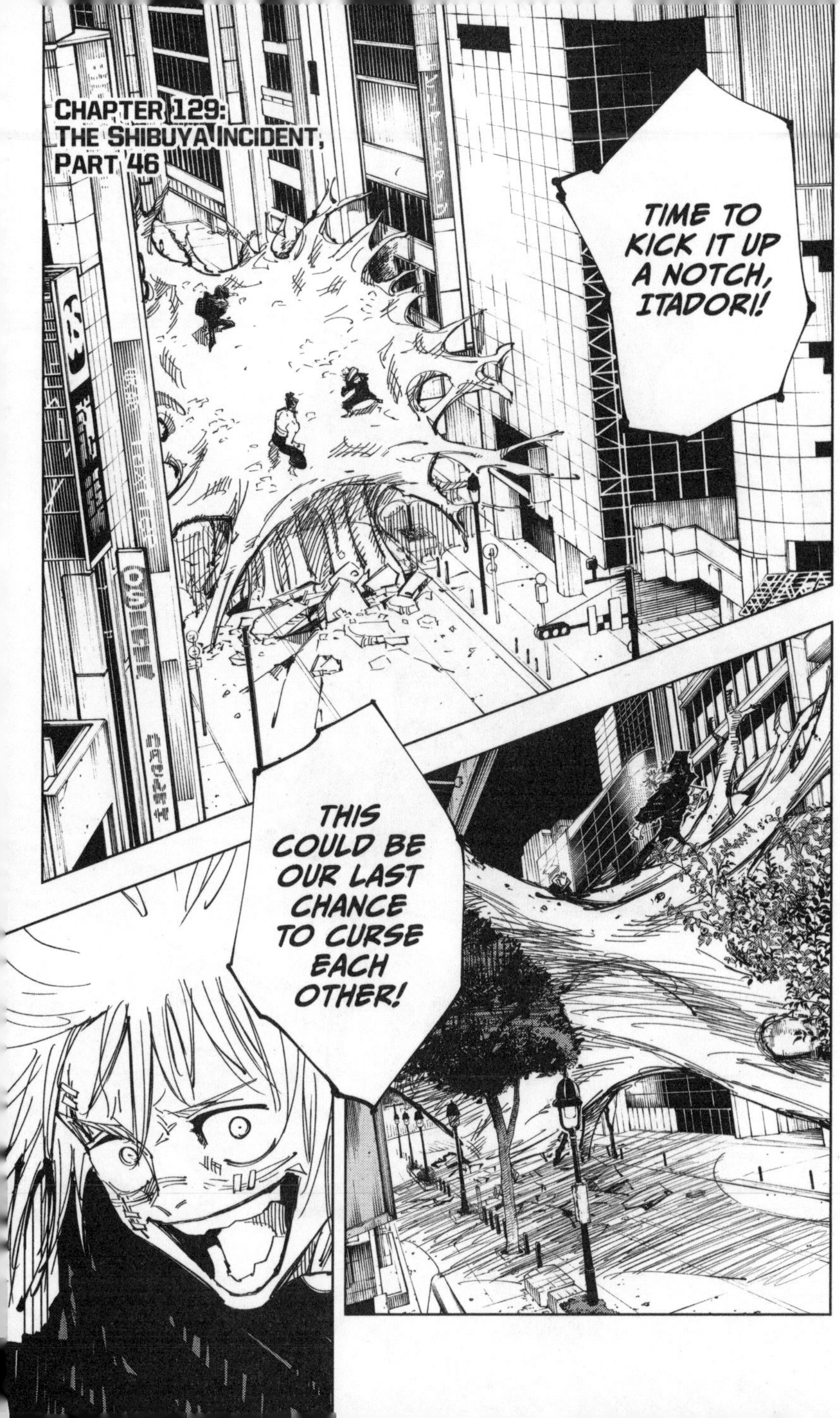

CHAPTER 129: THE SHIBUYA INCIDENT, PART 46
TIME TO KICK IT UP A NOTCH, ITADORI!
THIS COULD BE OUR LAST CHANCE TO CURSE EACH OTHER!

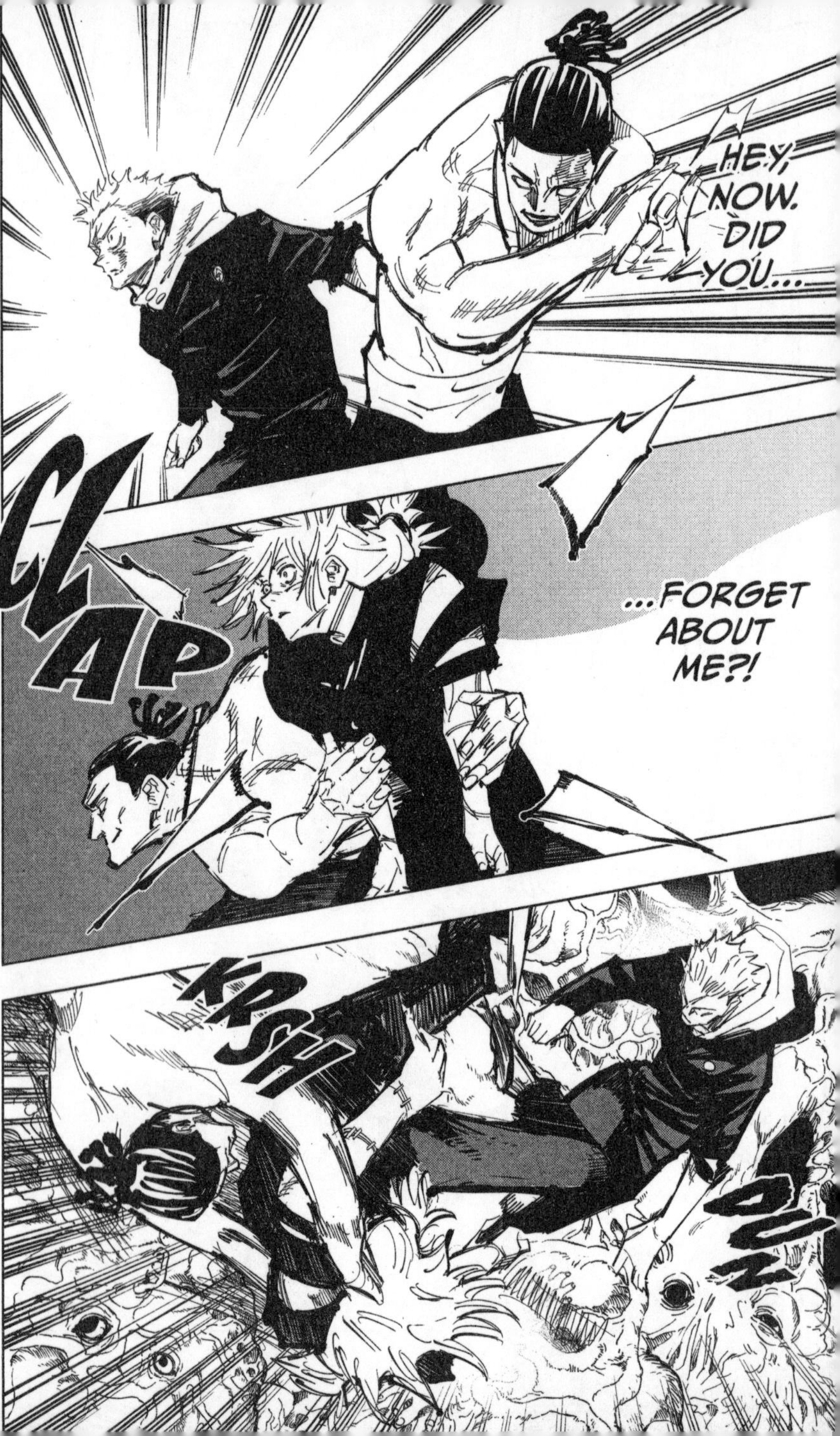
HEY, NOW. DID YOU...
CLAP
...FORGET ABOUT ME?!
KRSH

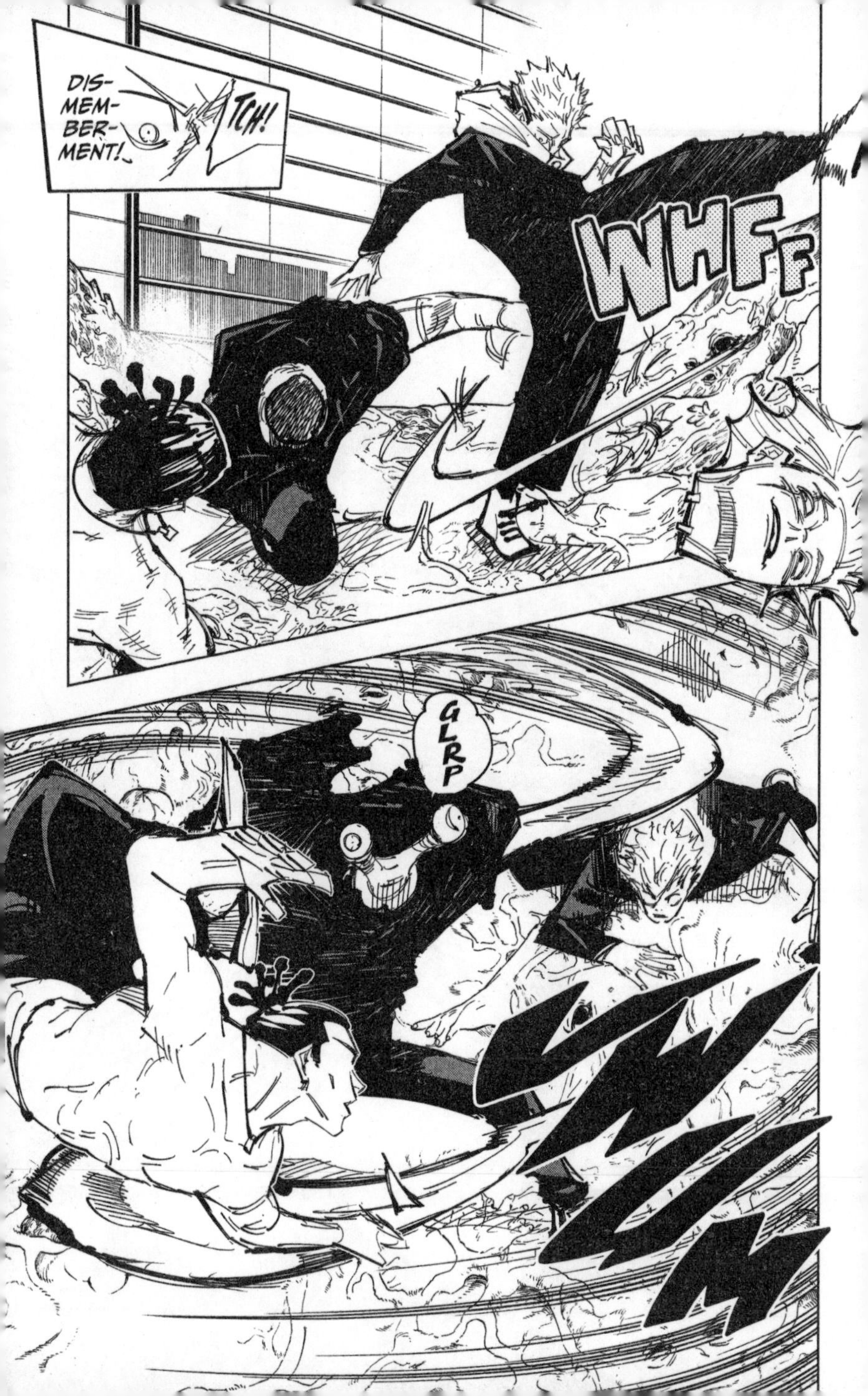
TCH!
DIS-MEM-BER-MENT!
WHFF
GLRP

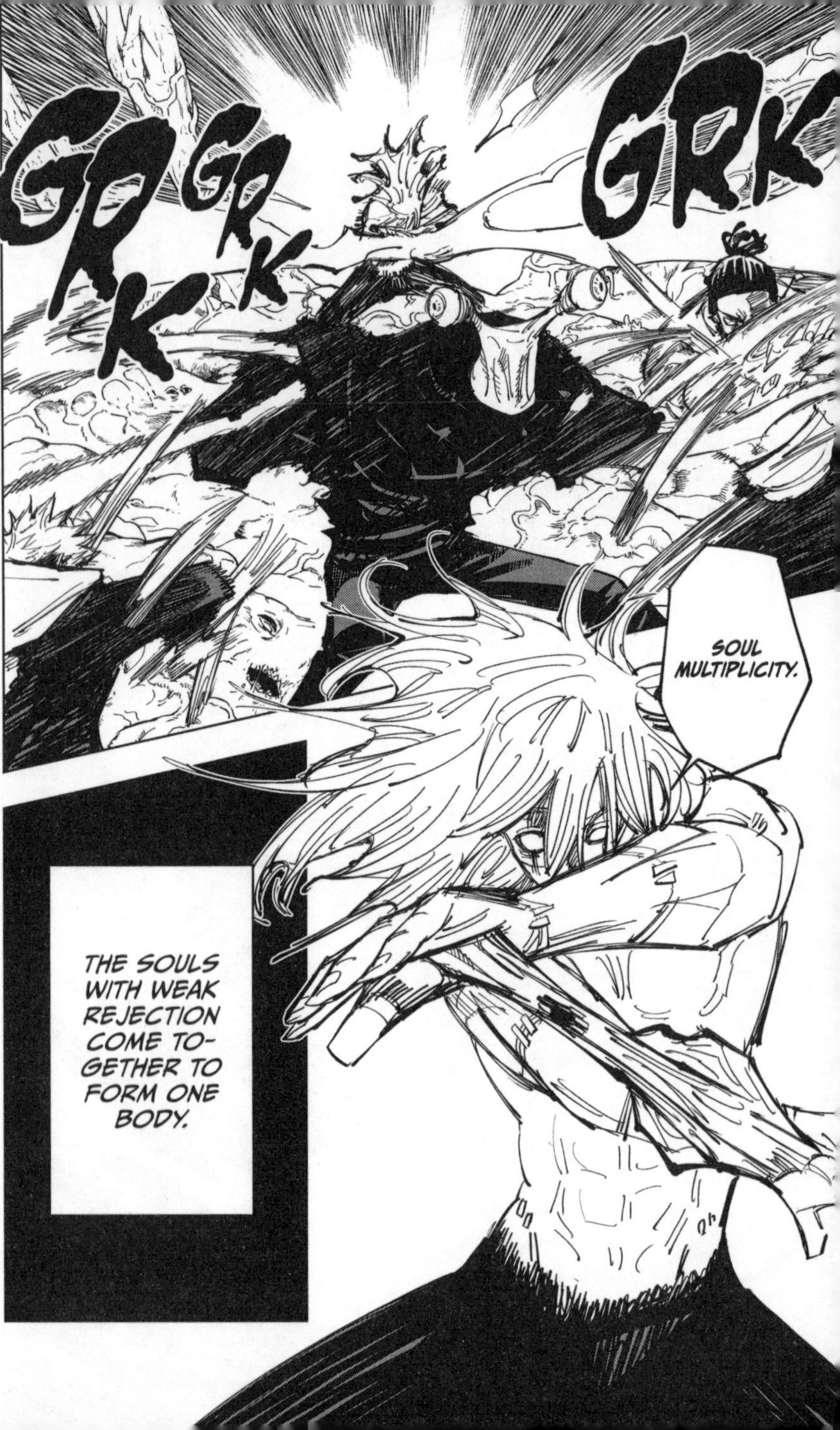
GRK
GRK
GRK
SOUL MULTIPLICITY.
THE SOULS WITH WEAK REJECTION COME TO- GETHER TO FORM ONE BODY.

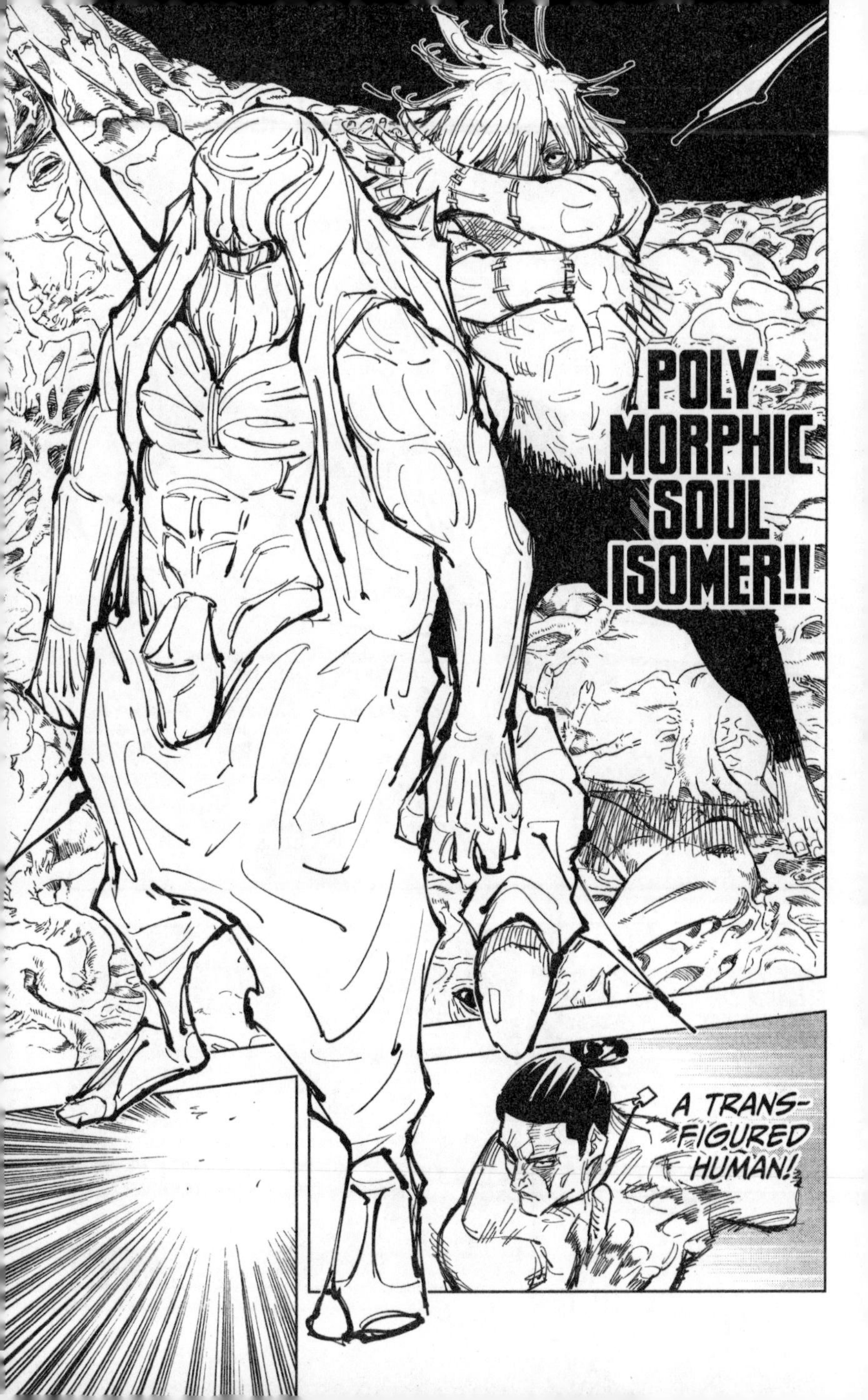
POLY-
MORPHIC
SOUL
ISOMER!!
A TRANS-
FIGURED
HUMAN!

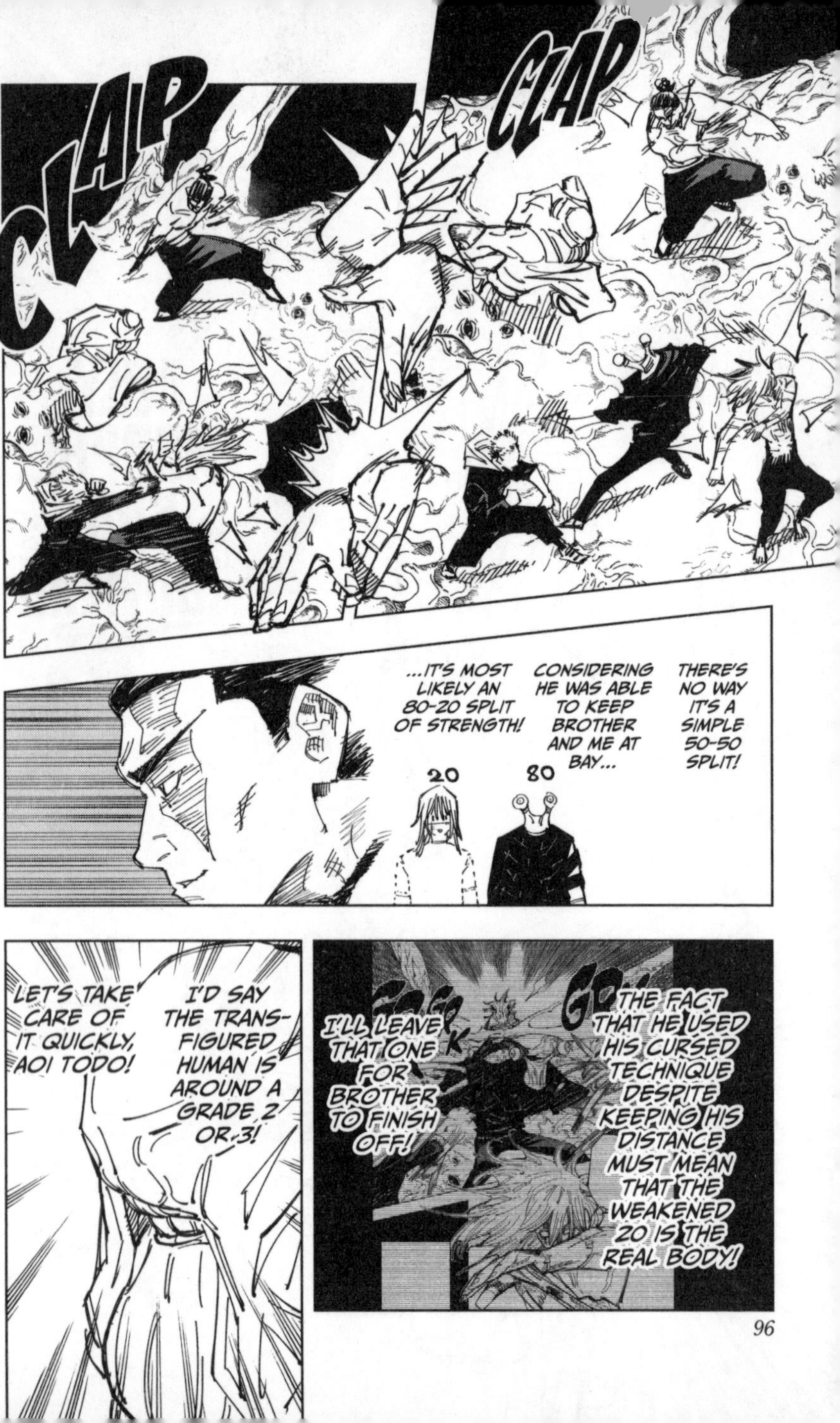
CLAP
CLAP
THERE'S NO WAY IT'S A SIMPLE 50-50 SPLIT!
CONSIDERING HE WAS ABLE TO KEEP BROTHER AND ME AT BAY...
...IT'S MOST LIKELY AN 80-20 SPLIT OF STRENGTH!
80
20
THE FACT THAT HE USED HIS CURSED TECHNIQUE DESPITE KEEPING HIS DISTANCE MUST MEAN THAT THE WEAKENED 20 IS THE REAL BODY!
I'LL LEAVE THAT ONE FOR BROTHER TO FINISH OFF!
I'D SAY THE TRANS-FIGURED HUMAN IS AROUND A GRADE 2 OR 3!
LET'S TAKE CARE OF IT QUICKLY, AOI TODO!

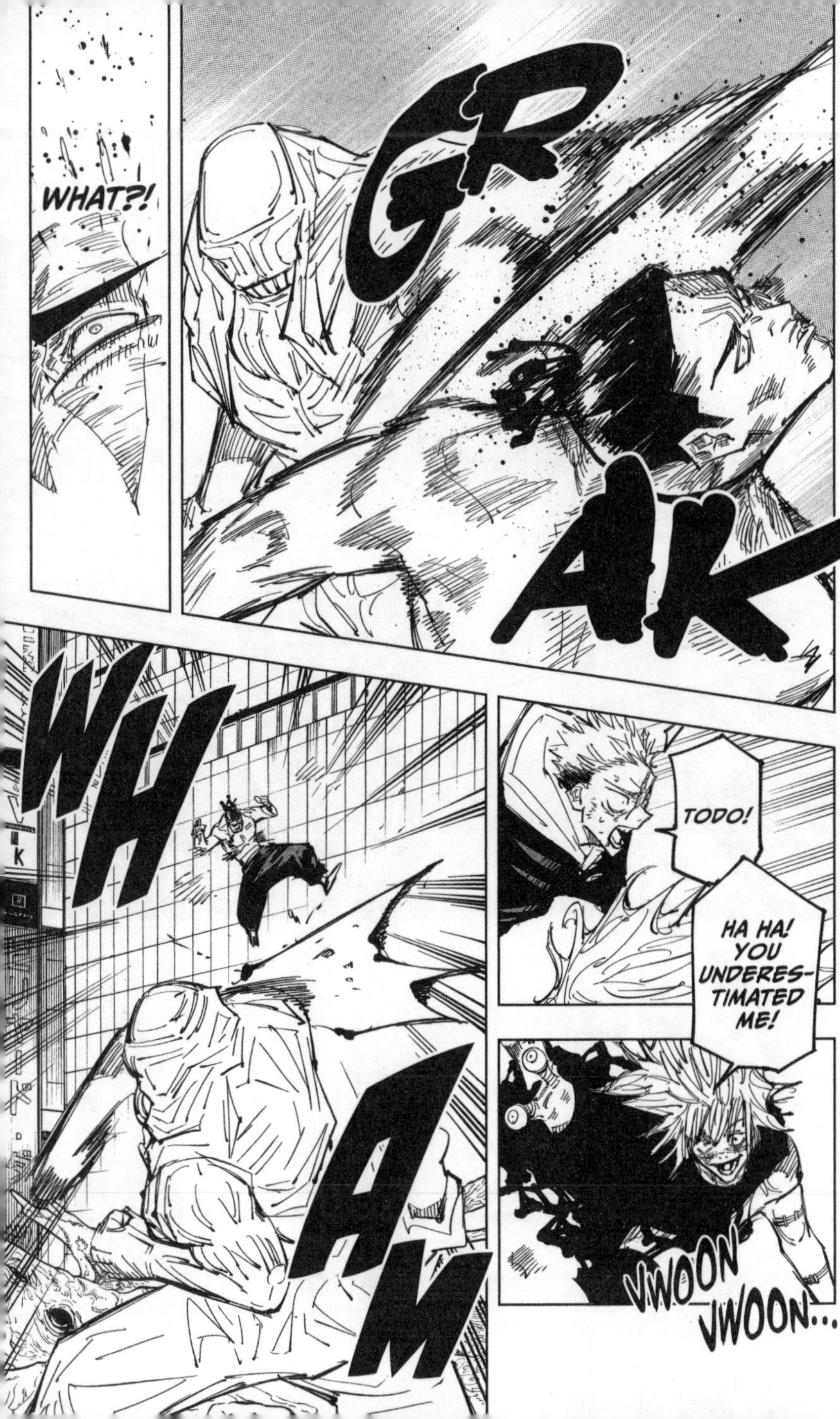
GRAK
WHAT?!
TODO!
HA HA! YOU UNDERES-TIMATED ME!
VWOON VWOON...
WHAM

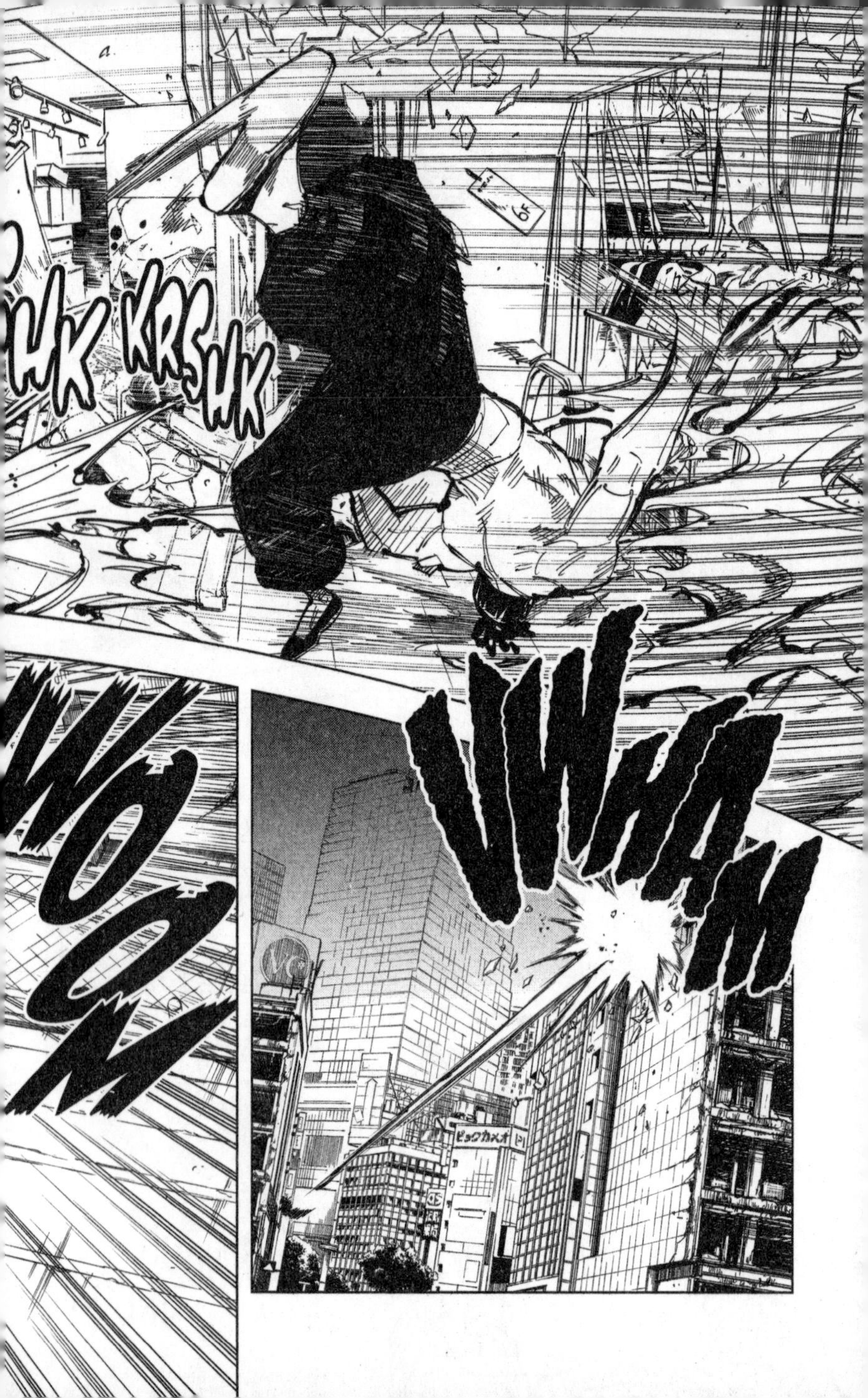
KRSHK
6F
WHAM
ビックカメラ
WOOM

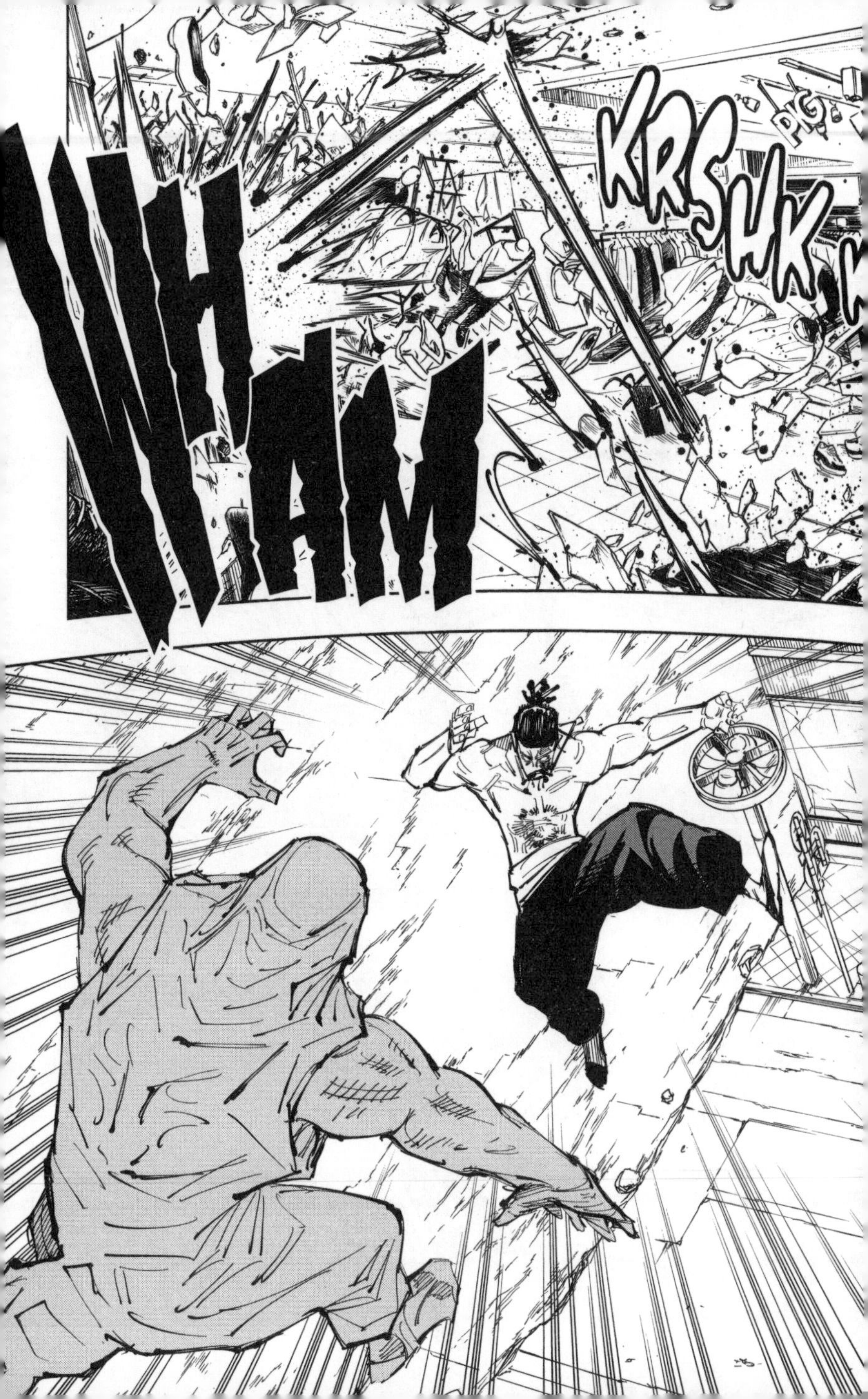

PIG
KRSHK
WHAM

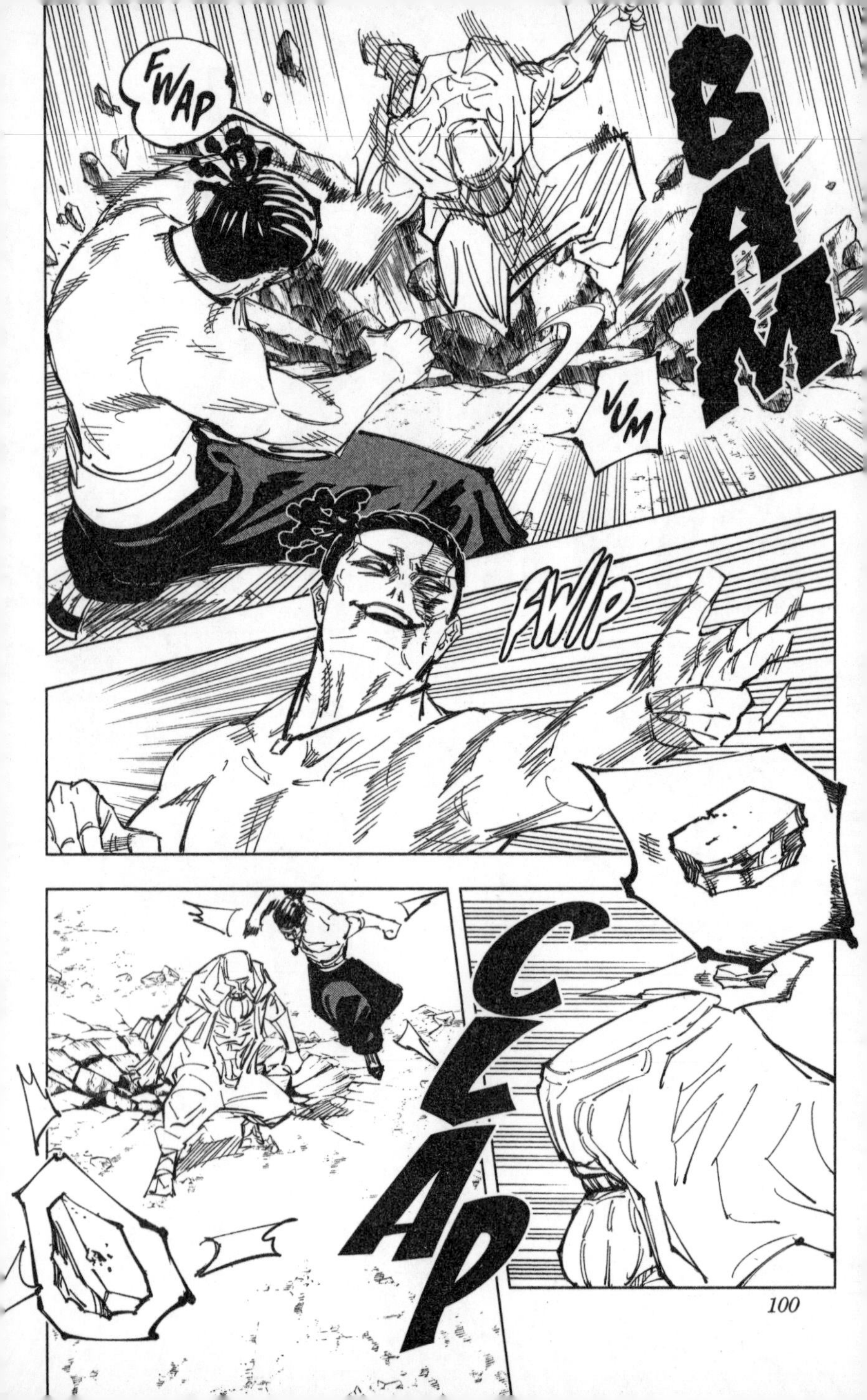
BAM
FWAP
VUM
FWIP
CLAP

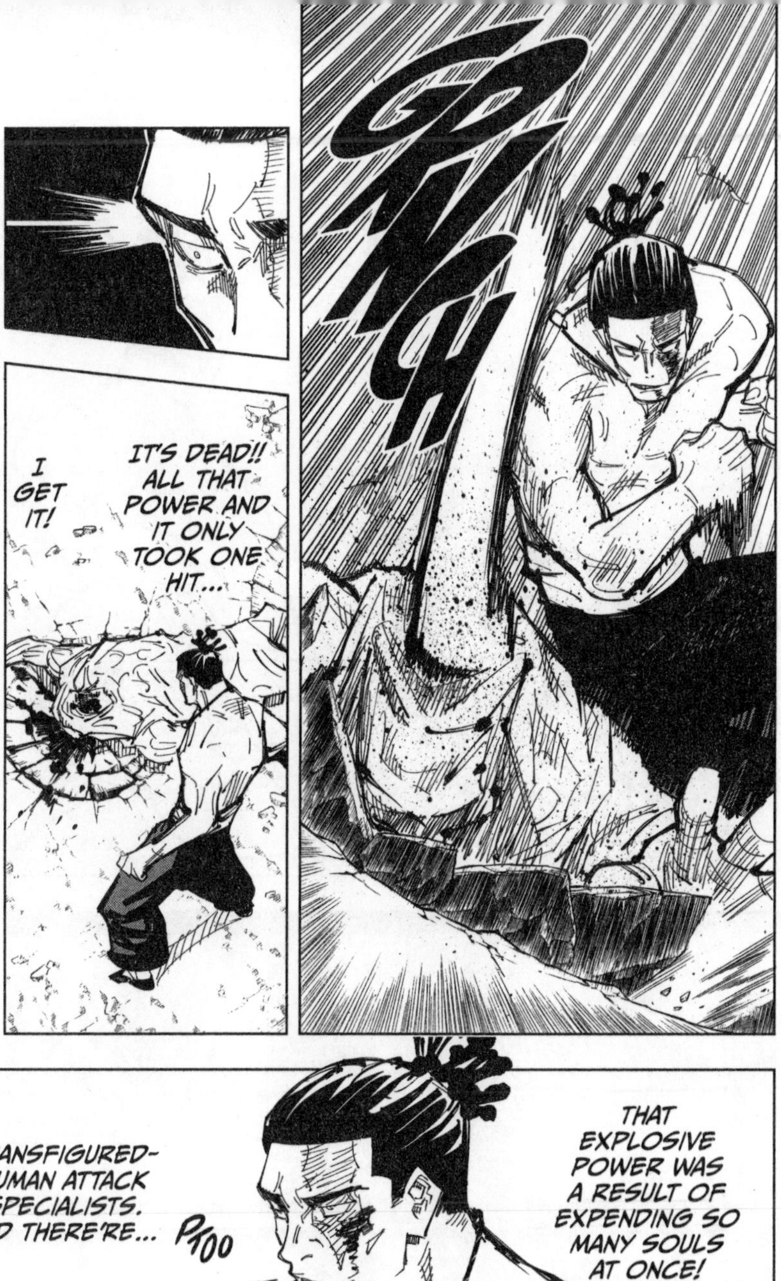
I GET IT!
IT'S DEAD!! ALL THAT POWER AND IT ONLY TOOK ONE HIT...
THAT EXPLOSIVE POWER WAS A RESULT OF EXPENDING SO MANY SOULS AT ONCE!
PTOO
TRANSFIGURED-HUMAN ATTACK SPECIALISTS. AND THERE'RE...

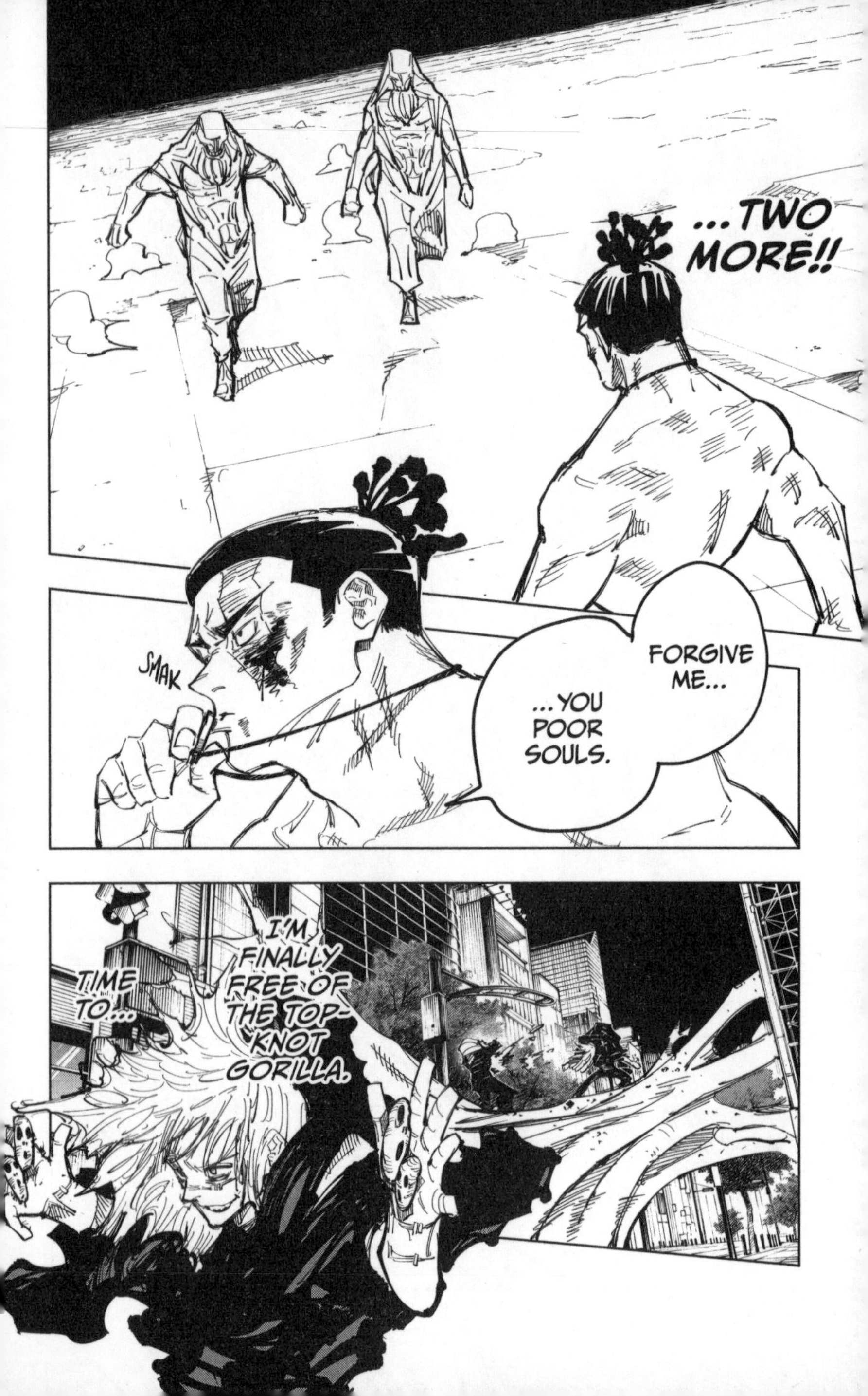
...TWO MORE!!
FORGIVE ME...
...YOU POOR SOULS.
SMAK
I'M FINALLY FREE OF THE TOP-KNOT GORILLA.
TIME TO...

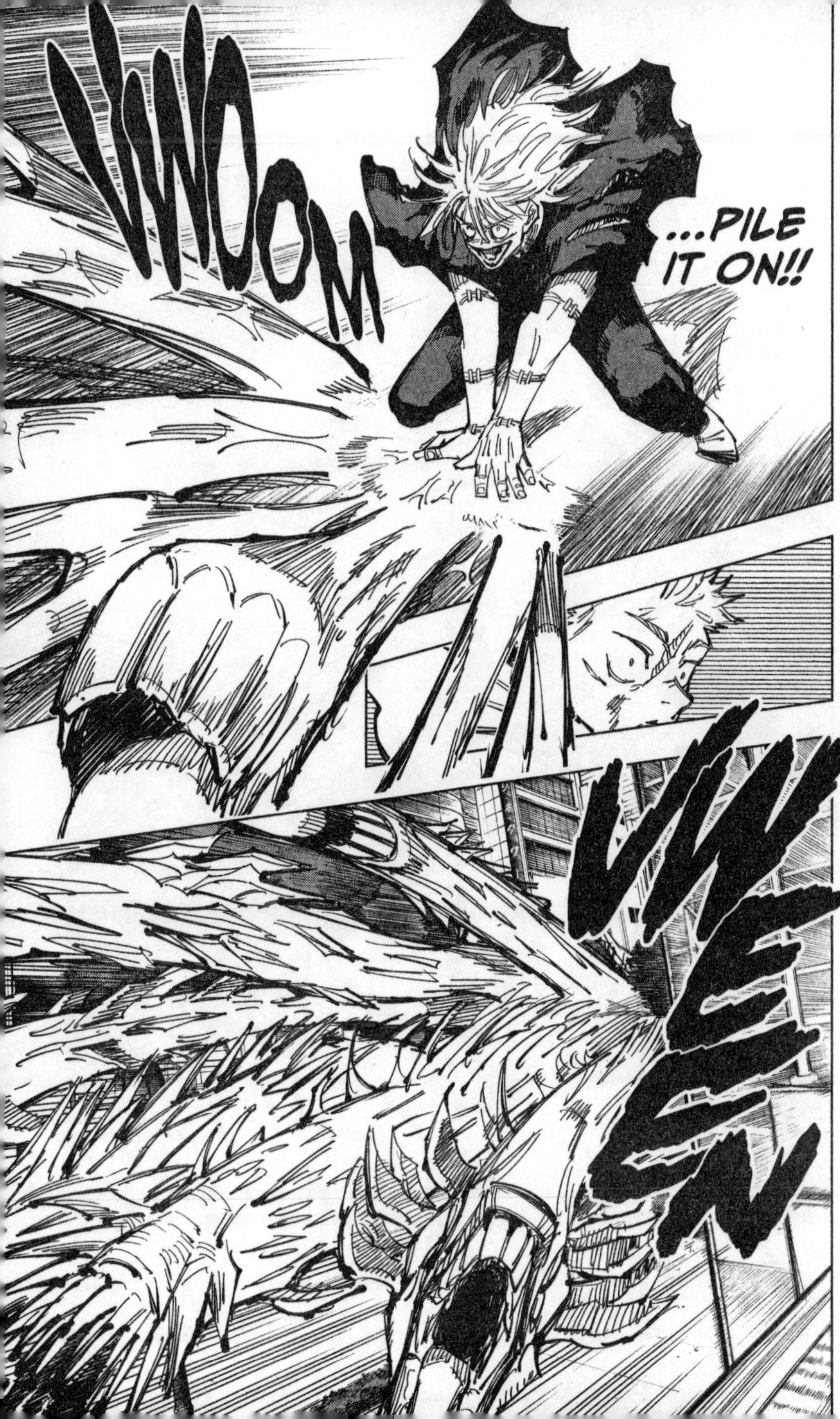
...PILE IT ON!!
VWOOM
VWEEN

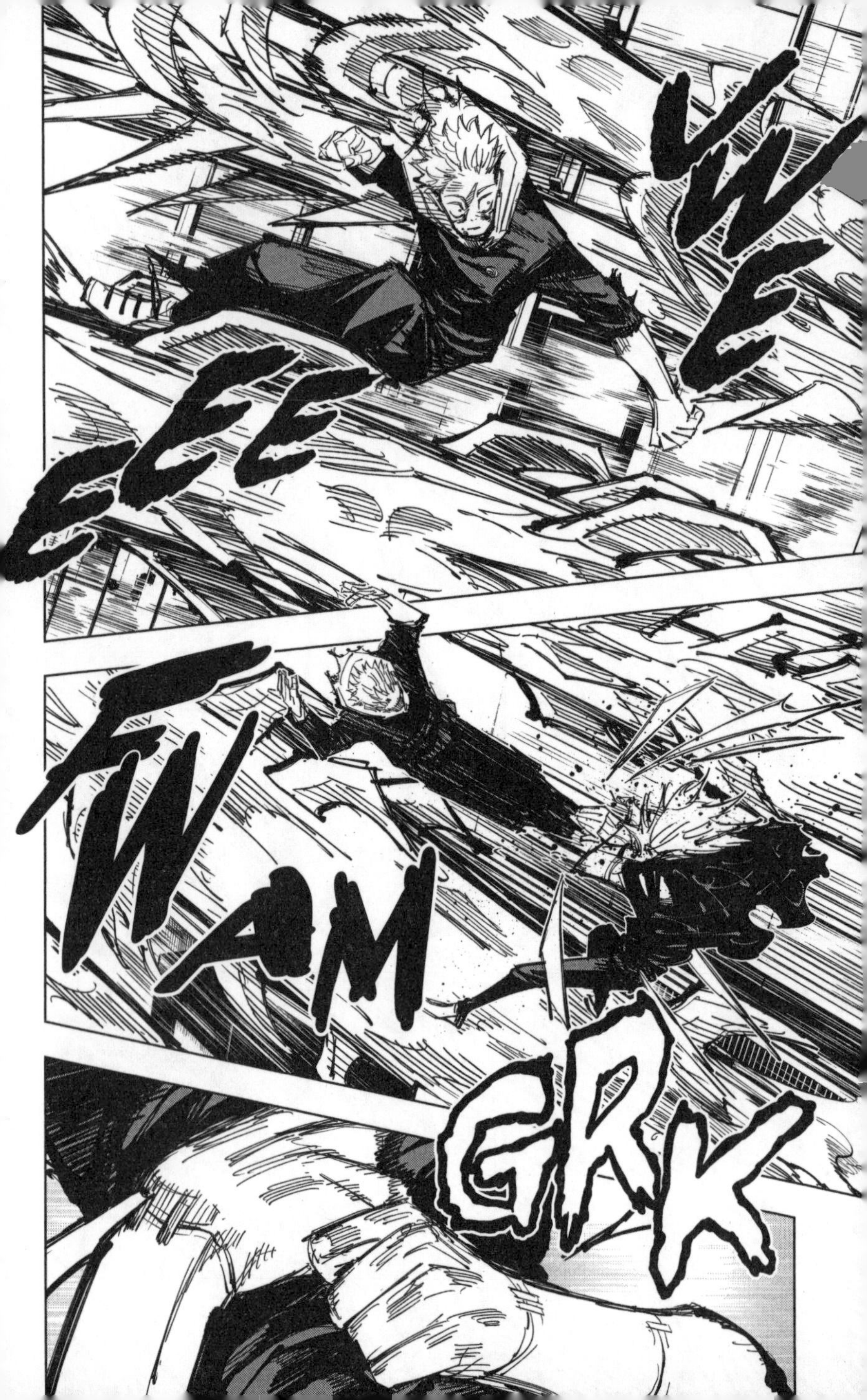

WHEEE
FWAM
GRK

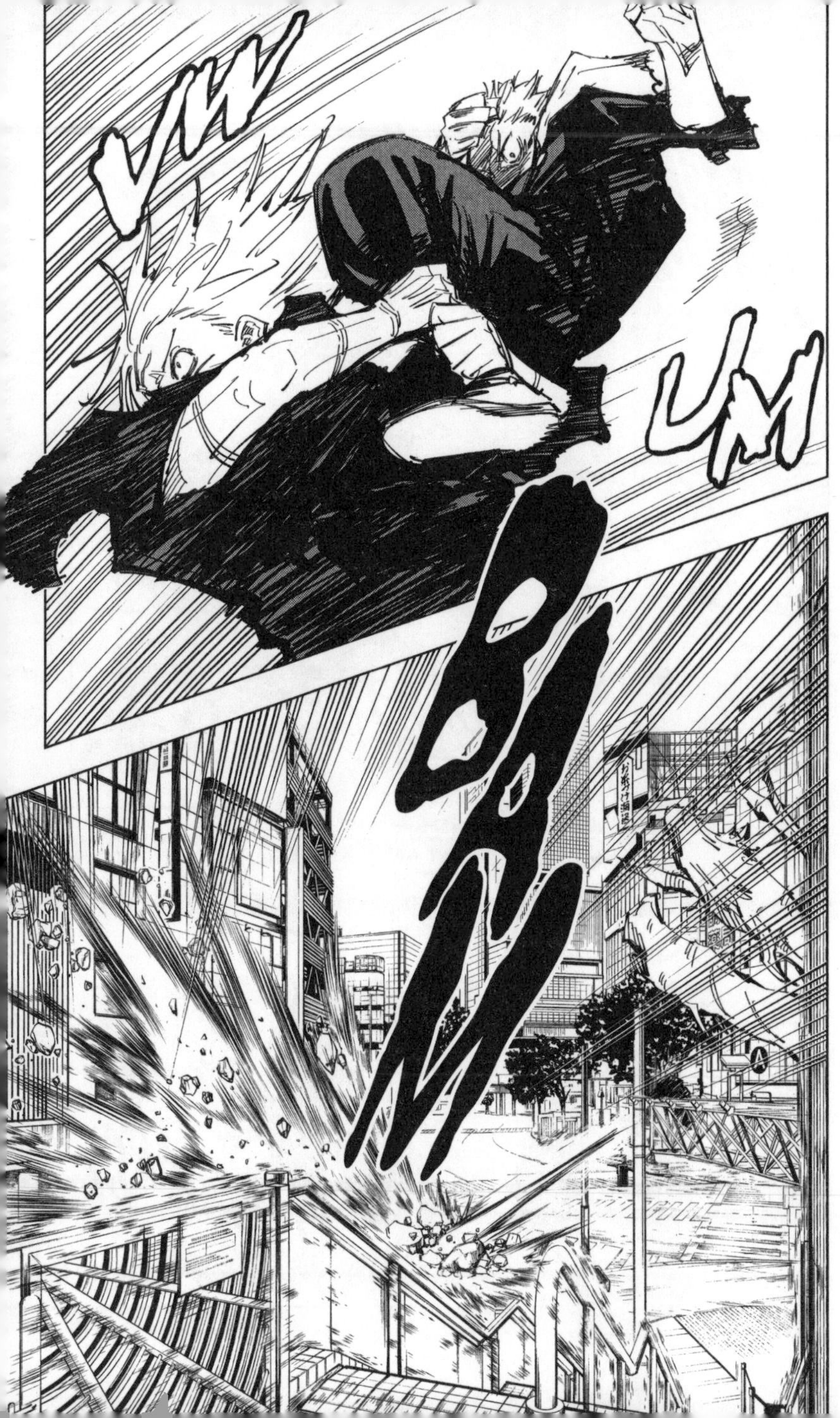
VWV
UM

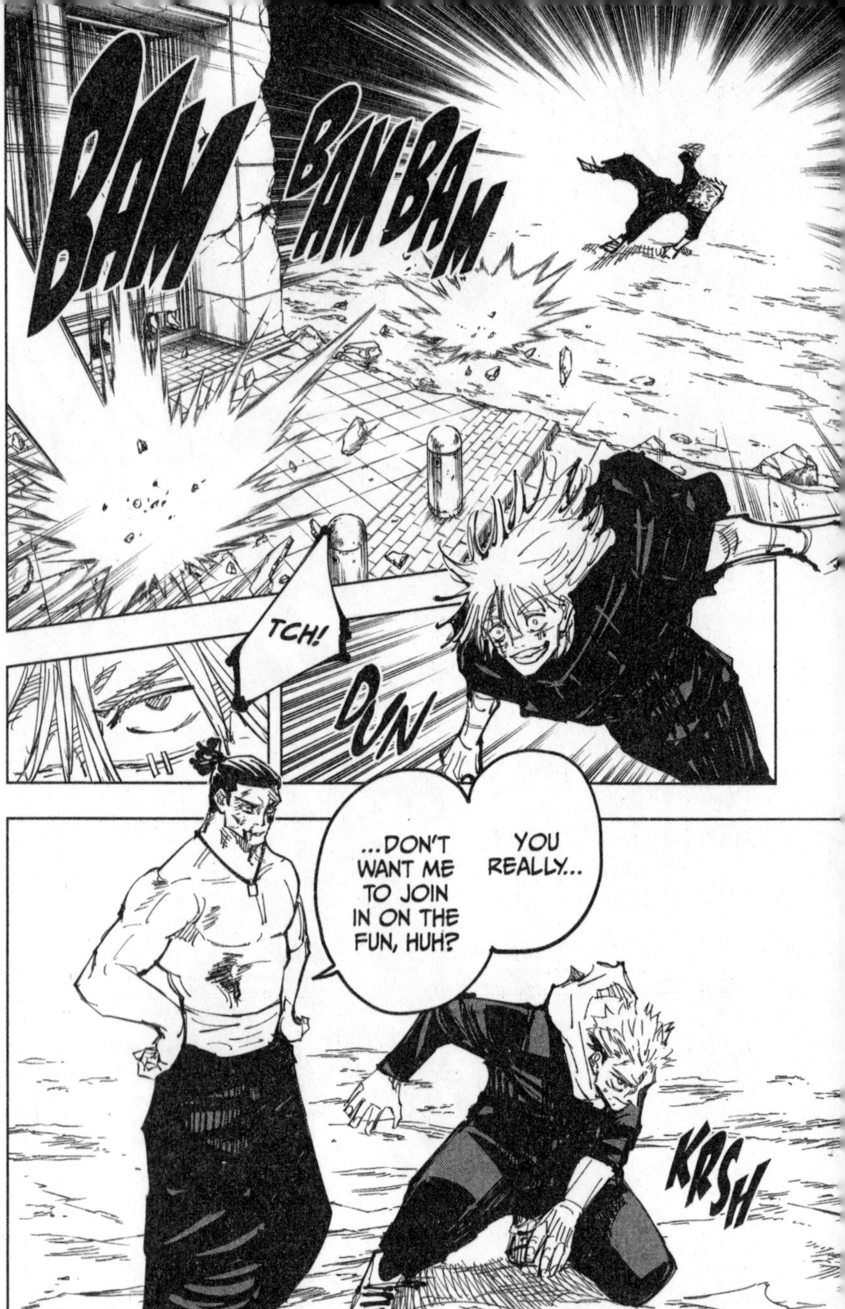
BAM
BAM BAM
BAM BAM
TCH!
DUN
YOU REALLY...
...DON'T WANT ME TO JOIN IN ON THE FUN, HUH?
KRSH

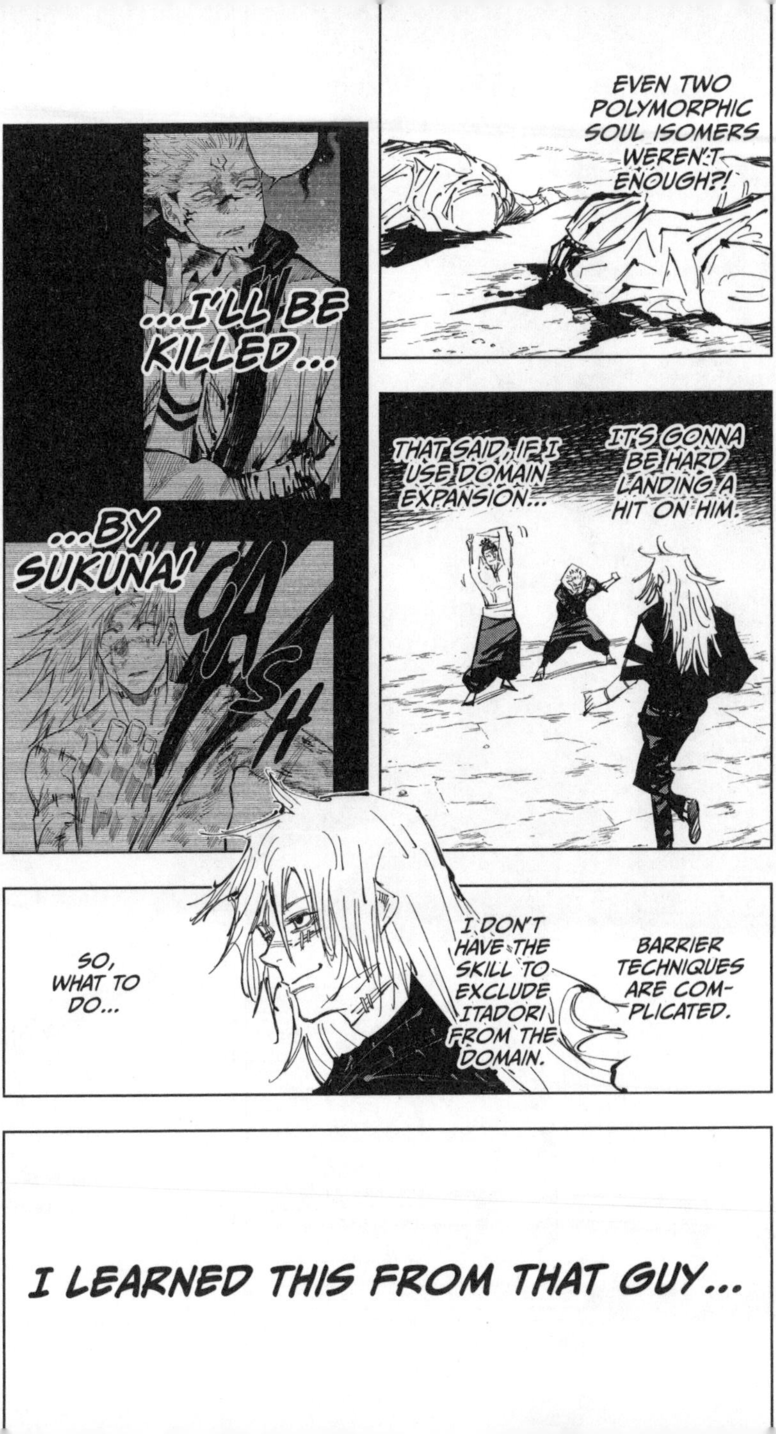
EVEN TWO POLYMORPHIC SOUL ISOMERS WEREN'T ENOUGH?!
...I'LL BE KILLED...
...BY SUKUNA!
GASH
IT'S GONNA BE HARD LANDING A HIT ON HIM.
THAT SAID, IF I USE DOMAIN EXPANSION...
BARRIER TECHNIQUES ARE COM-PLICATED.
I DON'T HAVE THE SKILL TO EXCLUDE ITADORI FROM THE DOMAIN.
SO, WHAT TO DO...
I LEARNED THIS FROM THAT GUY...

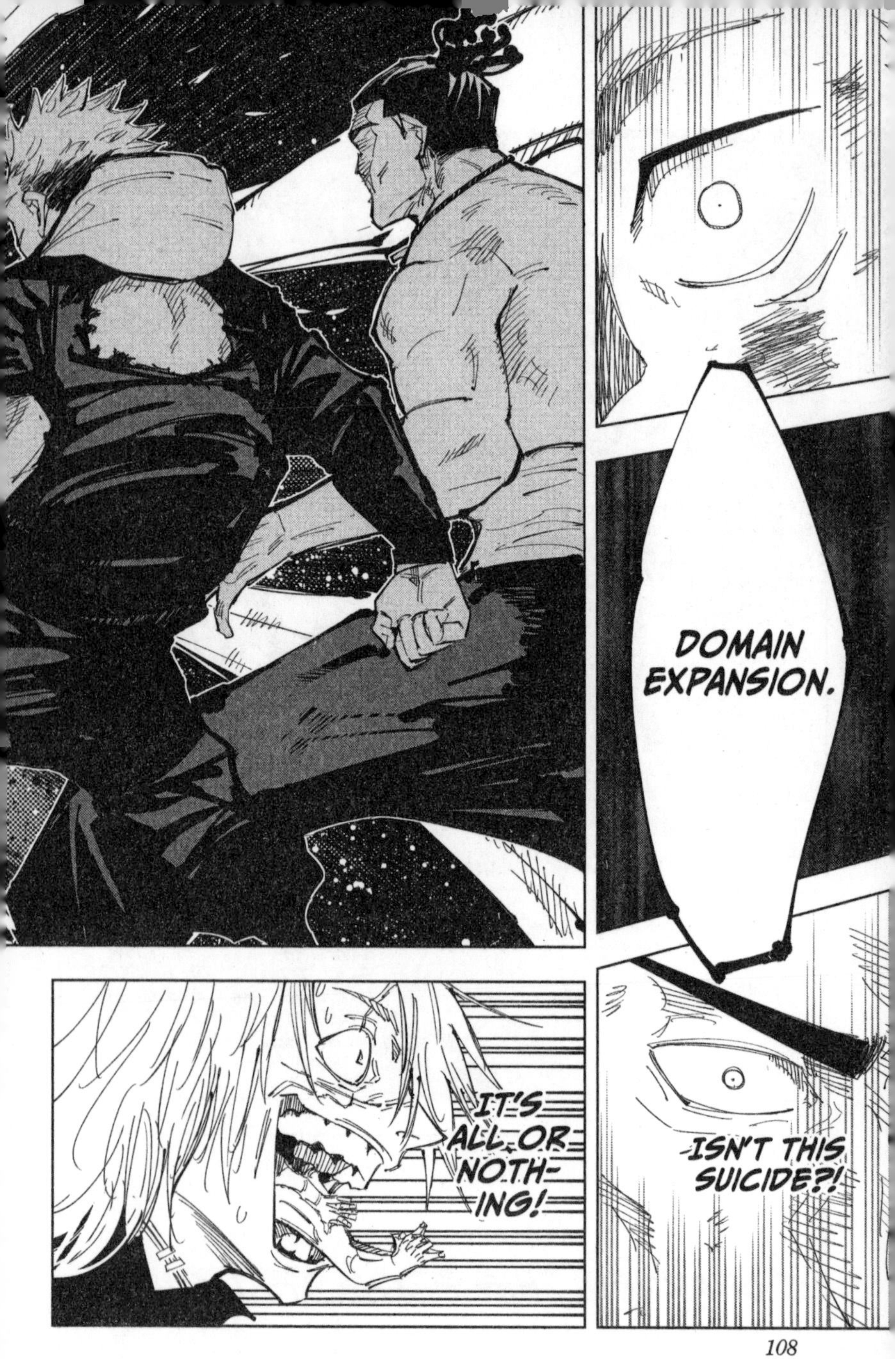
DOMAIN EXPANSION.
ISN'T THIS SUICIDE?!
IT'S ALL OR NOTH-ING!

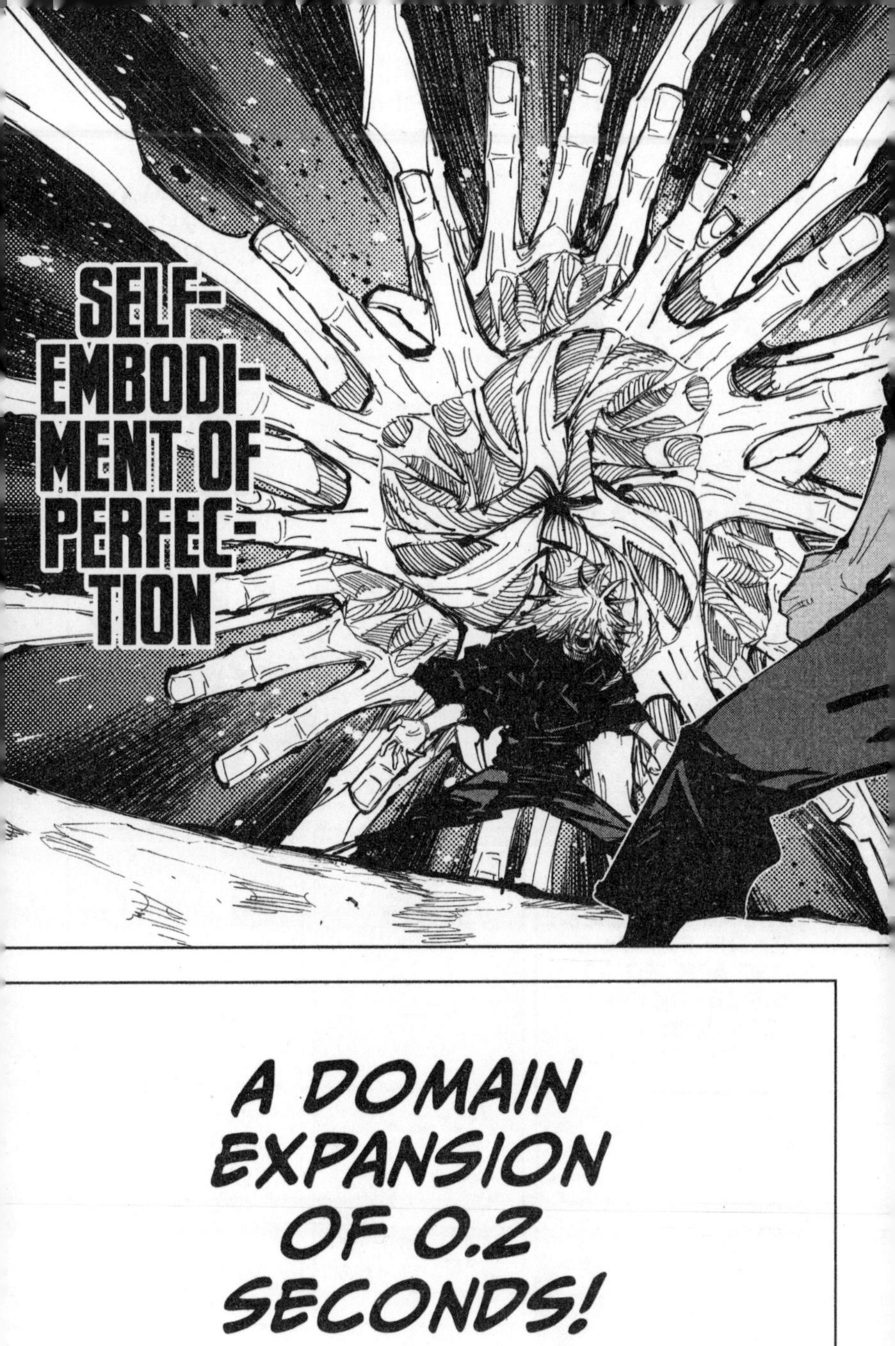
SELF-EMBODIMENT OF PERFECTION

A DOMAIN EXPANSION OF 0.2 SECONDS!

Getting It Right!!
Limitless Cursed Technique, Part 5

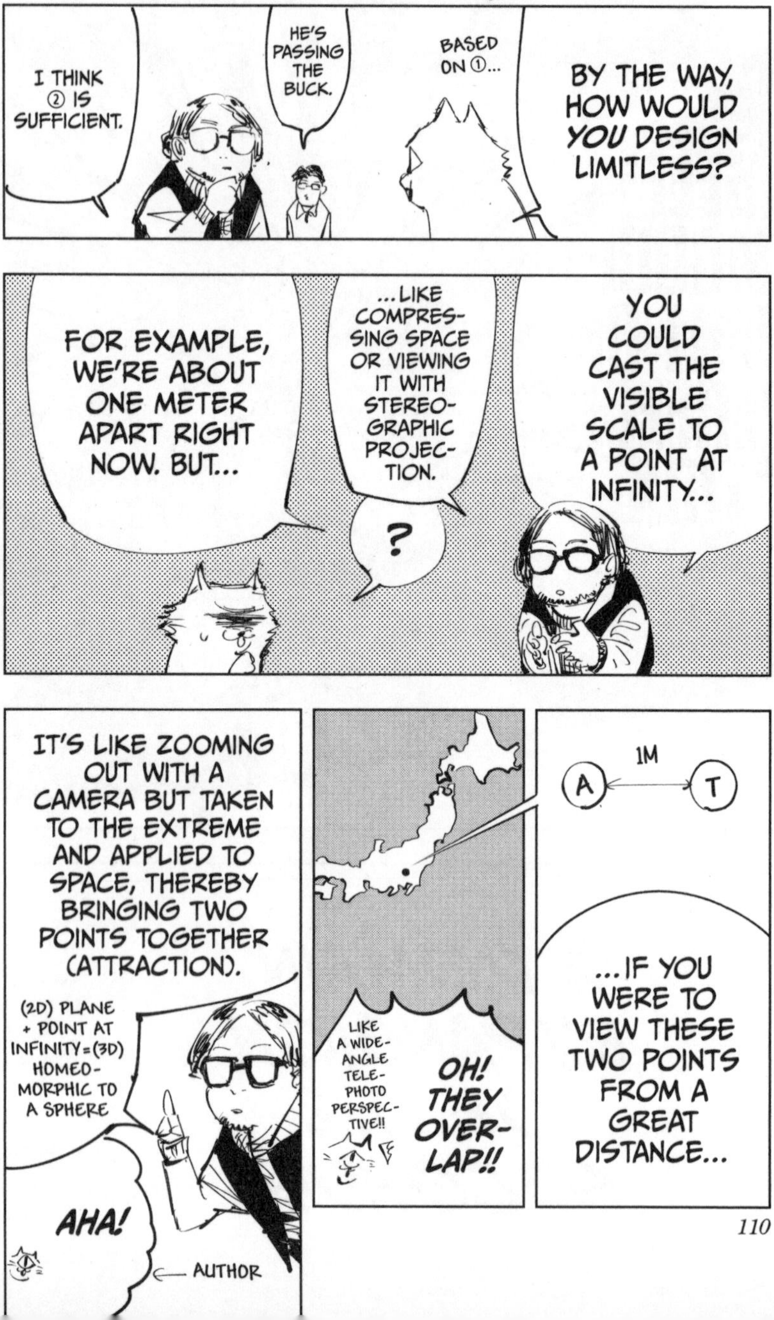

BY THE WAY, HOW WOULD *YOU* DESIGN LIMITLESS?
BASED ON ①...
HE'S PASSING THE BUCK.
I THINK ② IS SUFFICIENT.
YOU COULD CAST THE VISIBLE SCALE TO A POINT AT INFINITY...
...LIKE COMPRESSING SPACE OR VIEWING IT WITH STEREOGRAPHIC PROJECTION.
?
FOR EXAMPLE, WE'RE ABOUT ONE METER APART RIGHT NOW. BUT...
1M
A
T
...IF YOU WERE TO VIEW THESE TWO POINTS FROM A GREAT DISTANCE...
OH! THEY OVERLAP!!
LIKE A WIDE-ANGLE TELEPHOTO PERSPECTIVE!!
IT'S LIKE ZOOMING OUT WITH A CAMERA BUT TAKEN TO THE EXTREME AND APPLIED TO SPACE, THEREBY BRINGING TWO POINTS TOGETHER (ATTRACTION).
(2D) PLANE + POINT AT INFINITY=(3D) HOMEOMORPHIC TO A SPHERE
AHA!
AUTHOR

Chapter 130:
The Shibuya Incident, Part 47

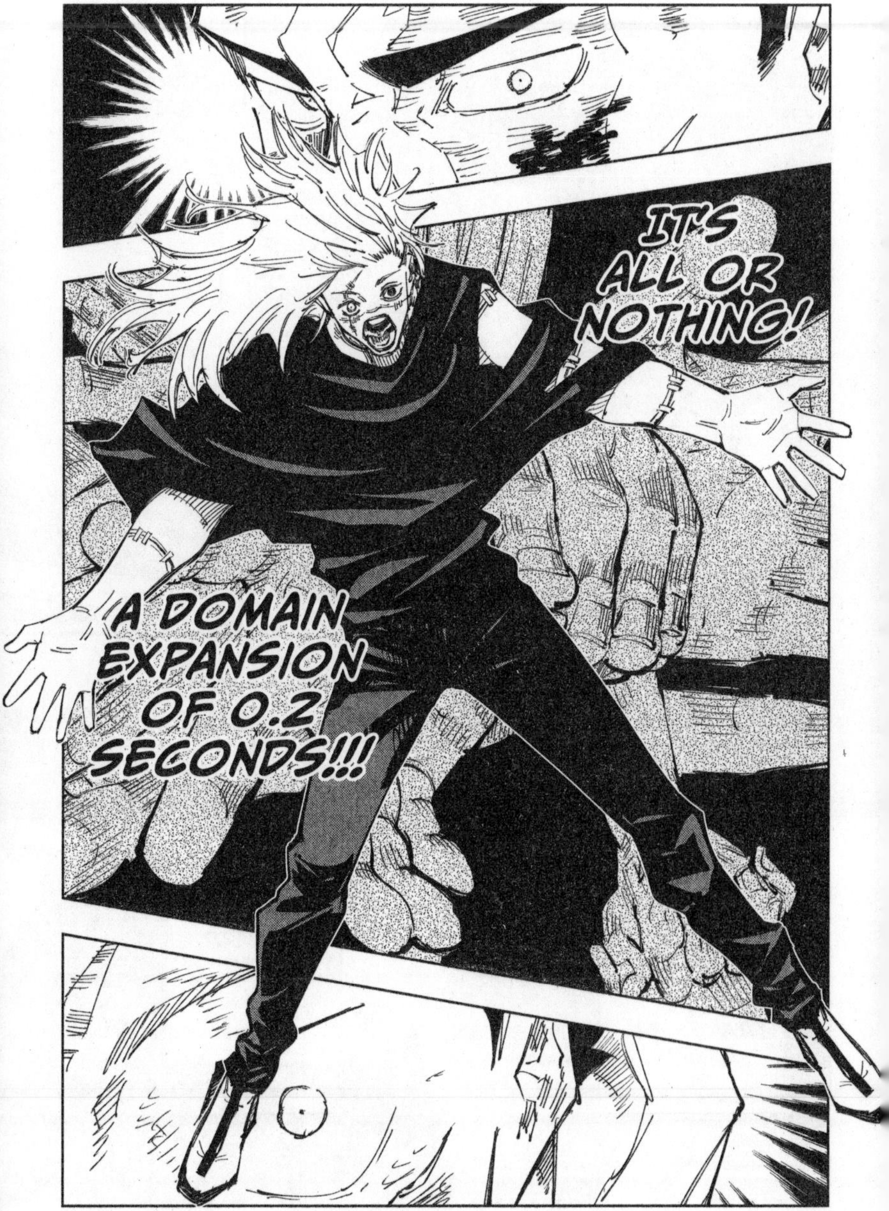
IT'S ALL OR NOTHING!
A DOMAIN EXPANSION OF 0.2 SECONDS!!!

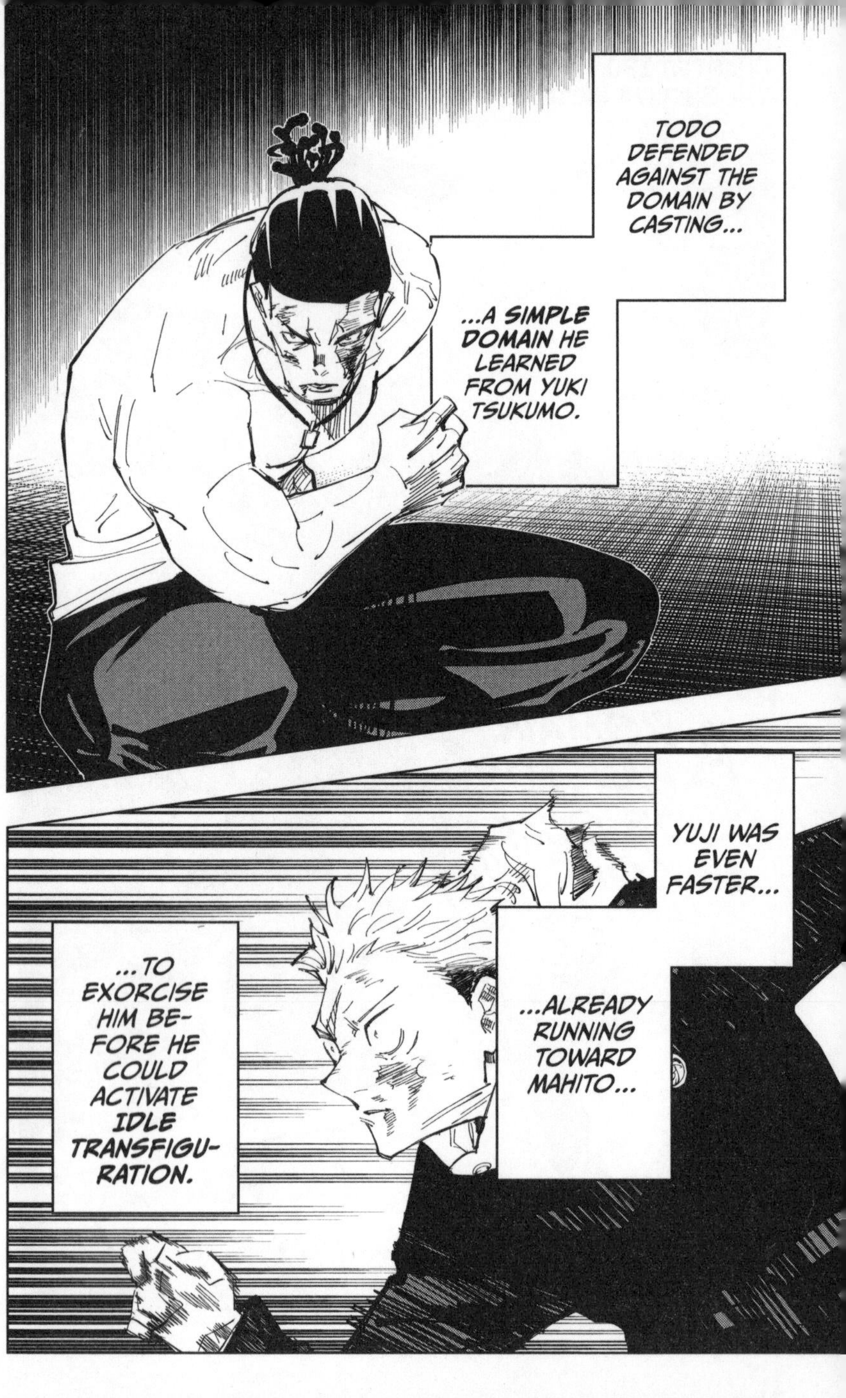
TODO DEFENDED AGAINST THE DOMAIN BY CASTING...
...A SIMPLE DOMAIN HE LEARNED FROM YUKI TSUKUMO.
YUJI WAS EVEN FASTER...
...ALREADY RUNNING TOWARD MAHITO...
...TO EXORCISE HIM BEFORE HE COULD ACTIVATE IDLE TRANSFIGURATION.

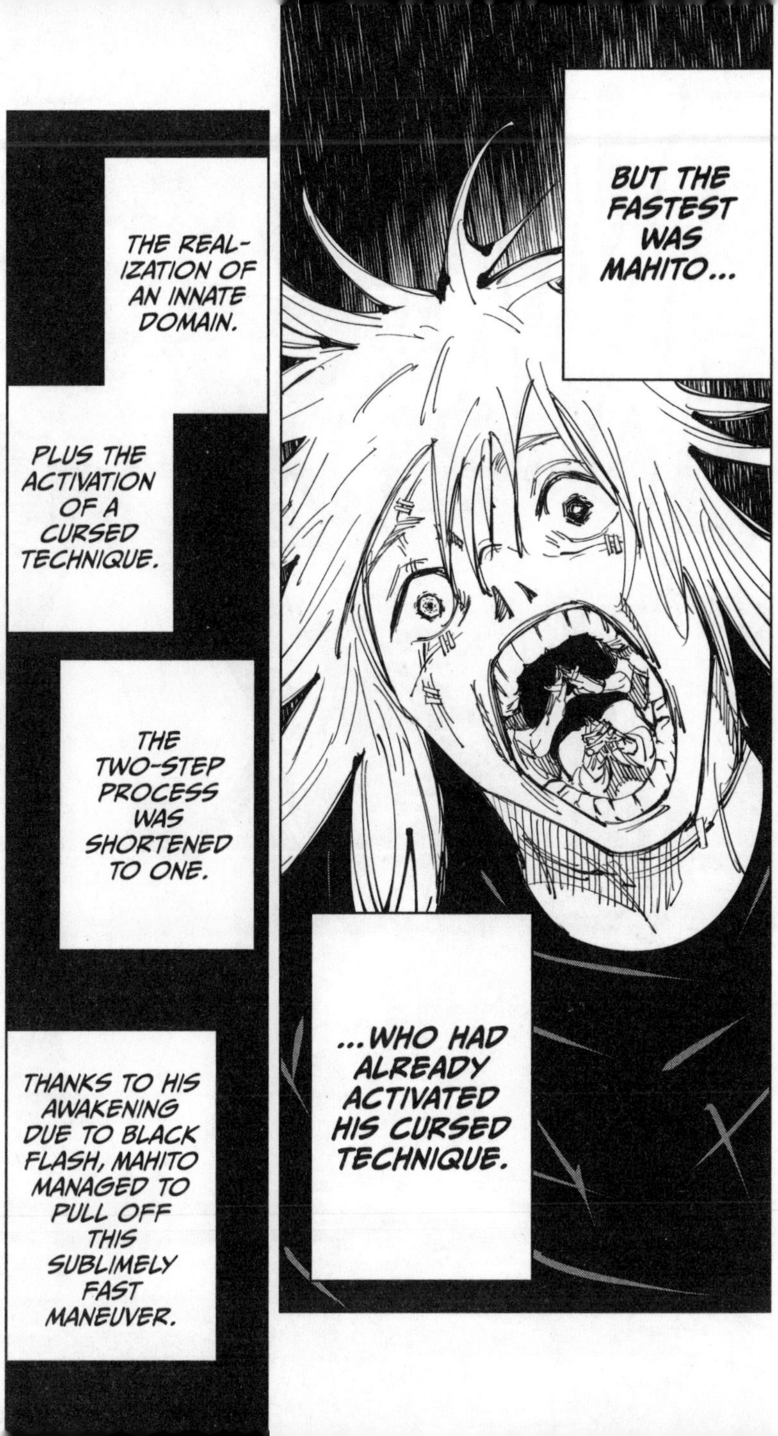
BUT THE FASTEST WAS MAHITO...
...WHO HAD ALREADY ACTIVATED HIS CURSED TECHNIQUE.
THE REAL-IZATION OF AN INNATE DOMAIN.
PLUS THE ACTIVATION OF A CURSED TECHNIQUE.
THE TWO-STEP PROCESS WAS SHORTENED TO ONE.
THANKS TO HIS AWAKENING DUE TO BLACK FLASH, MAHITO MANAGED TO PULL OFF THIS SUBLIMELY FAST MANEUVER.

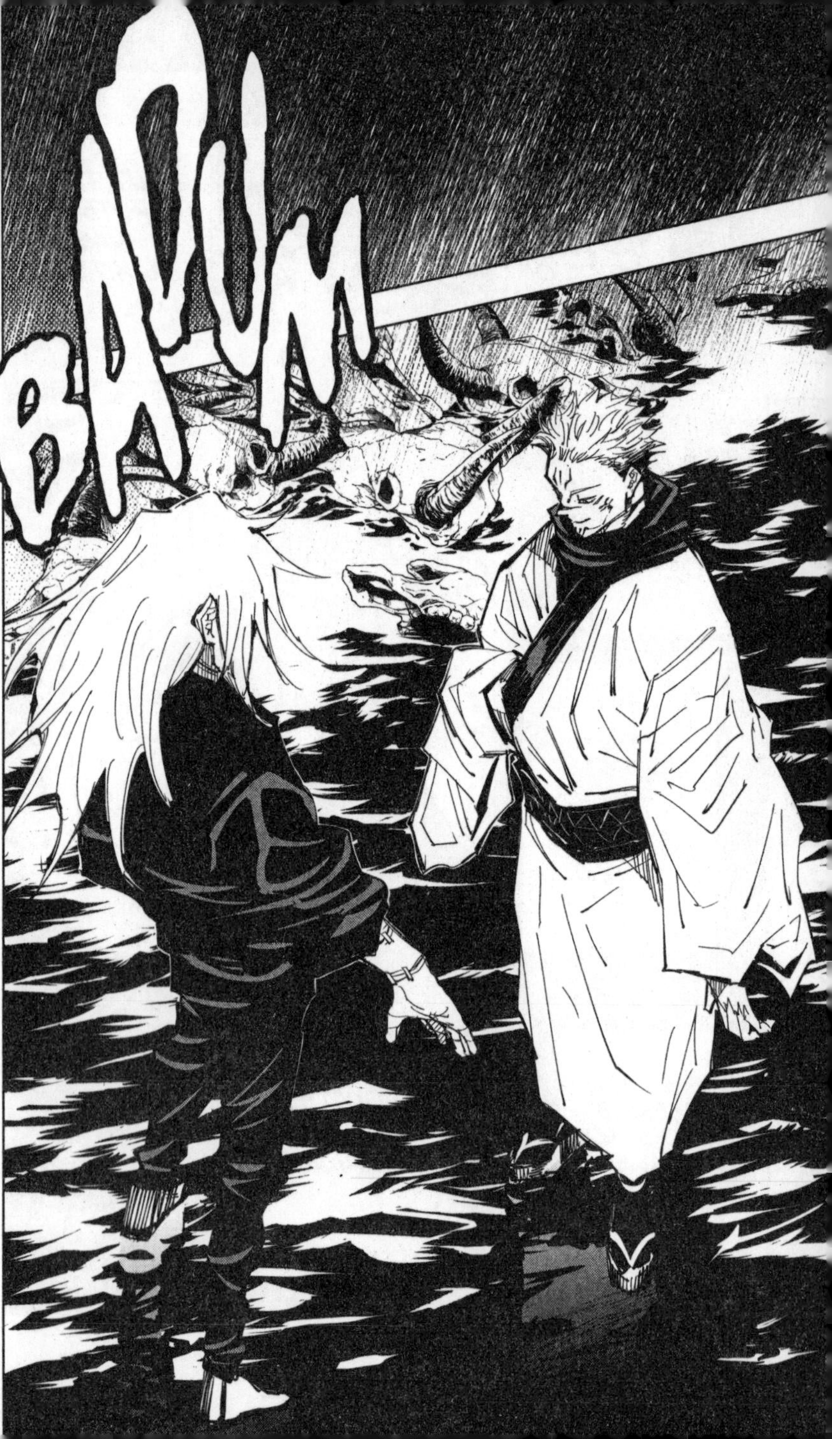
BADUM

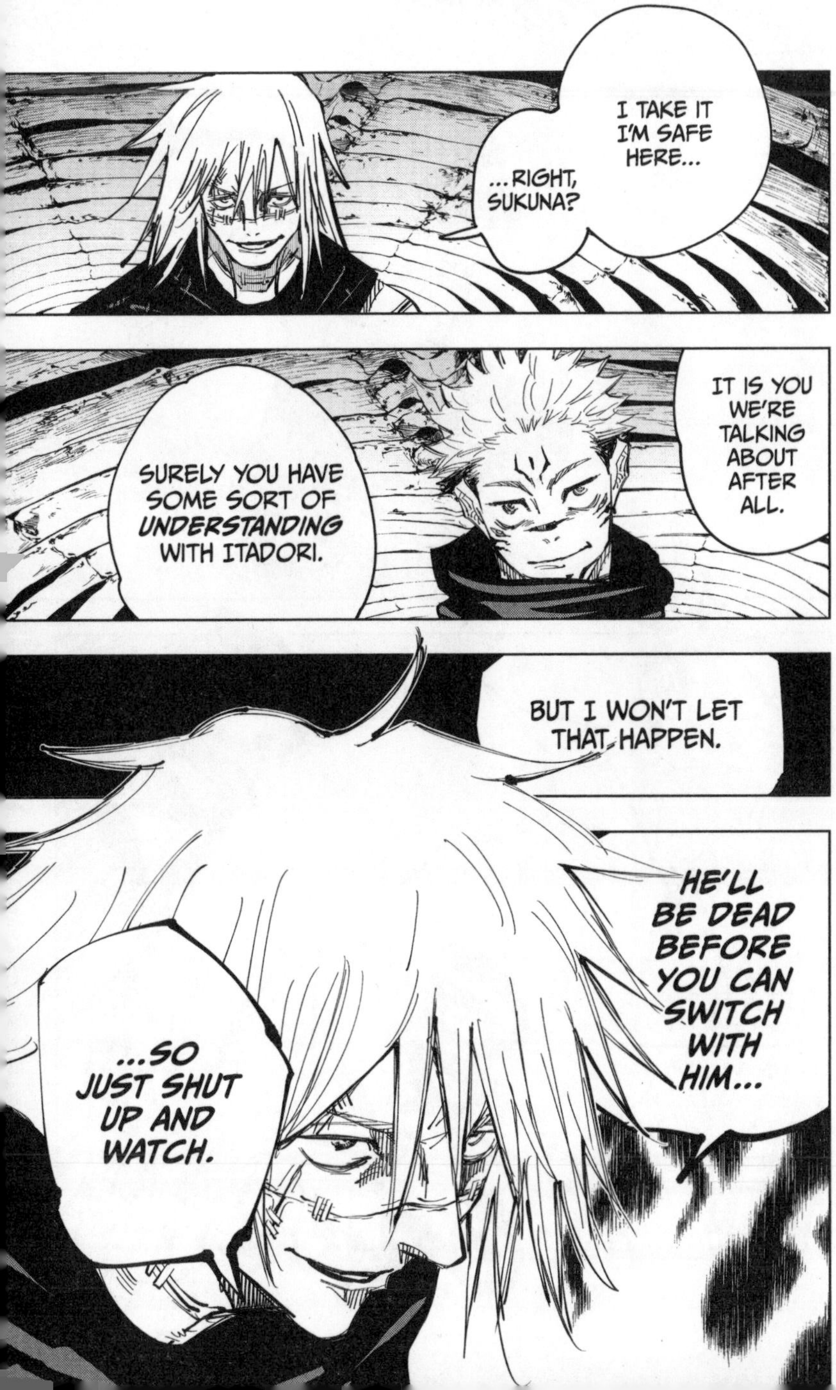
I TAKE IT I'M SAFE HERE...
...RIGHT, SUKUNA?
IT IS YOU WE'RE TALKING ABOUT AFTER ALL.
SURELY YOU HAVE SOME SORT OF UNDERSTANDING WITH ITADORI.
BUT I WON'T LET THAT HAPPEN.
HE'LL BE DEAD BEFORE YOU CAN SWITCH WITH HIM...
...SO JUST SHUT UP AND WATCH.

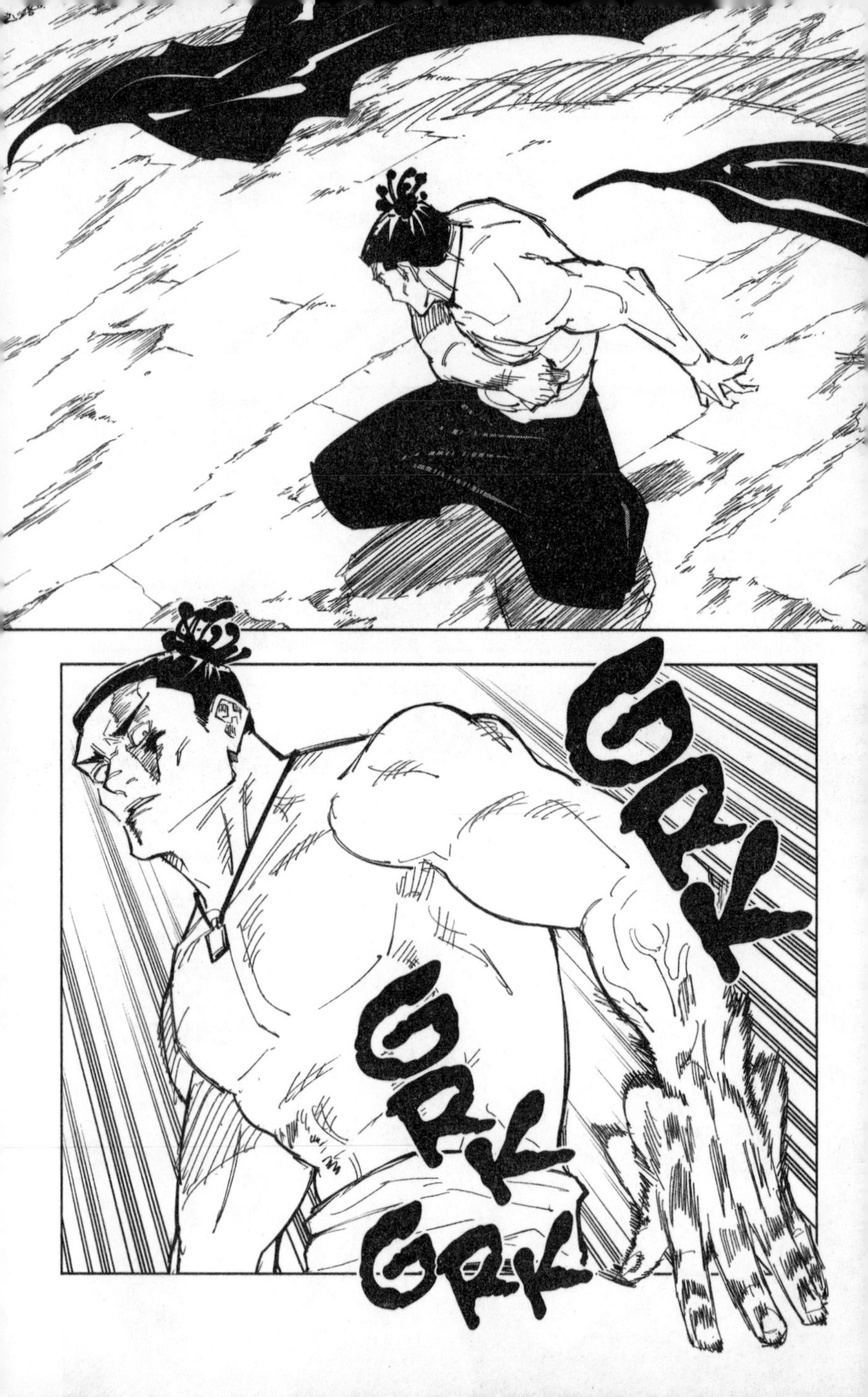
GRK
GRK
GRK

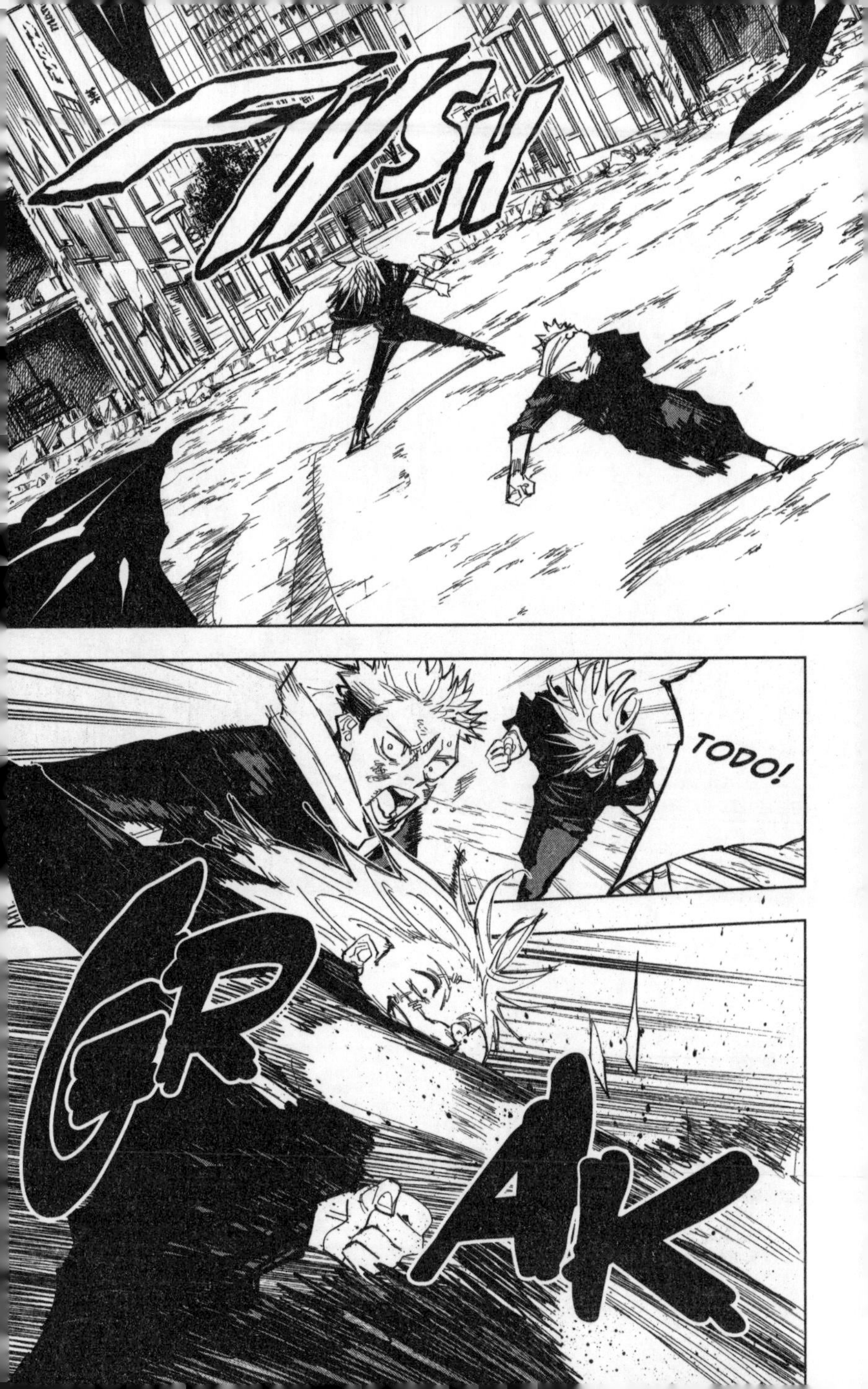
FSH
TODO!
CRAK

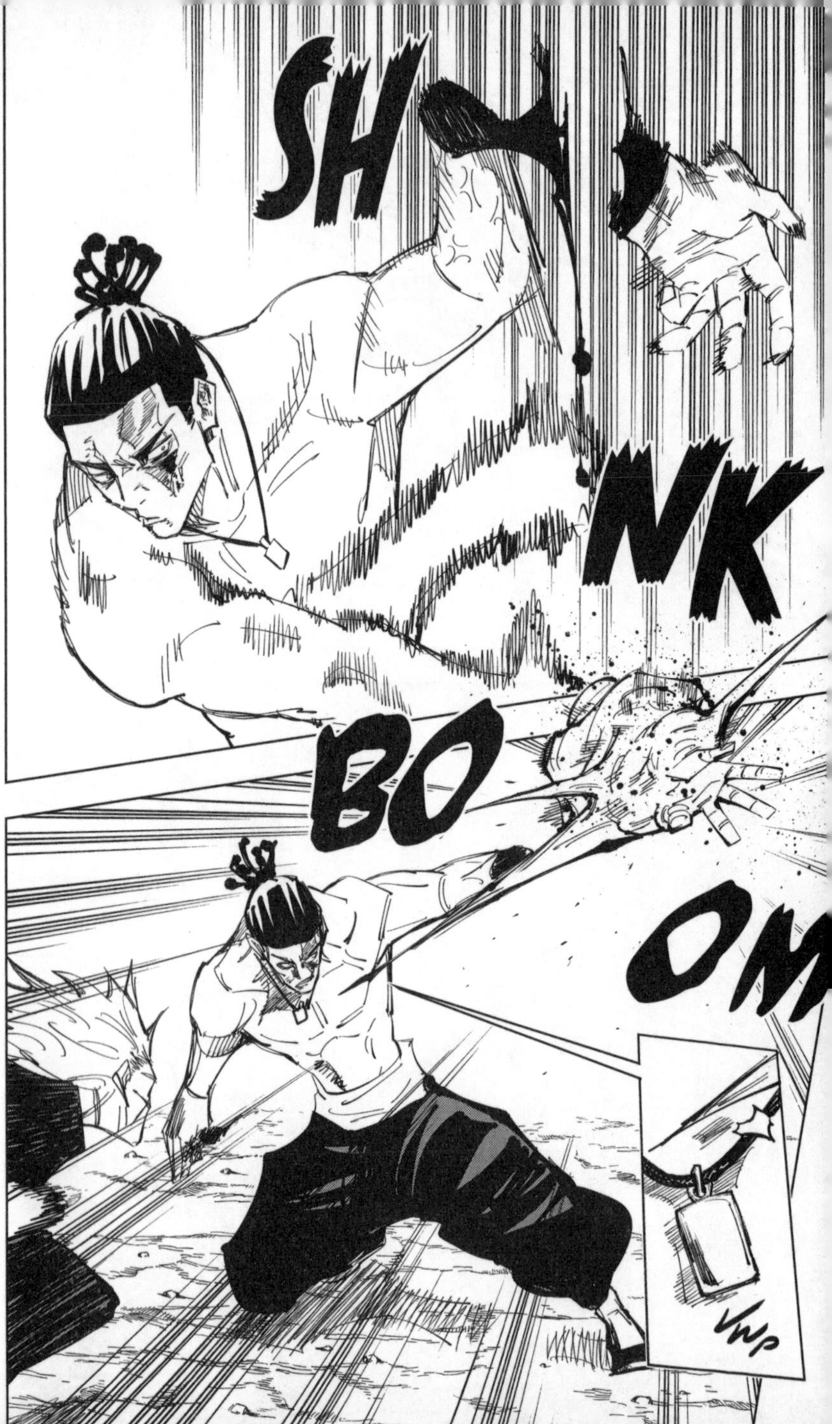
SH
NK
BO
OM
Vwp

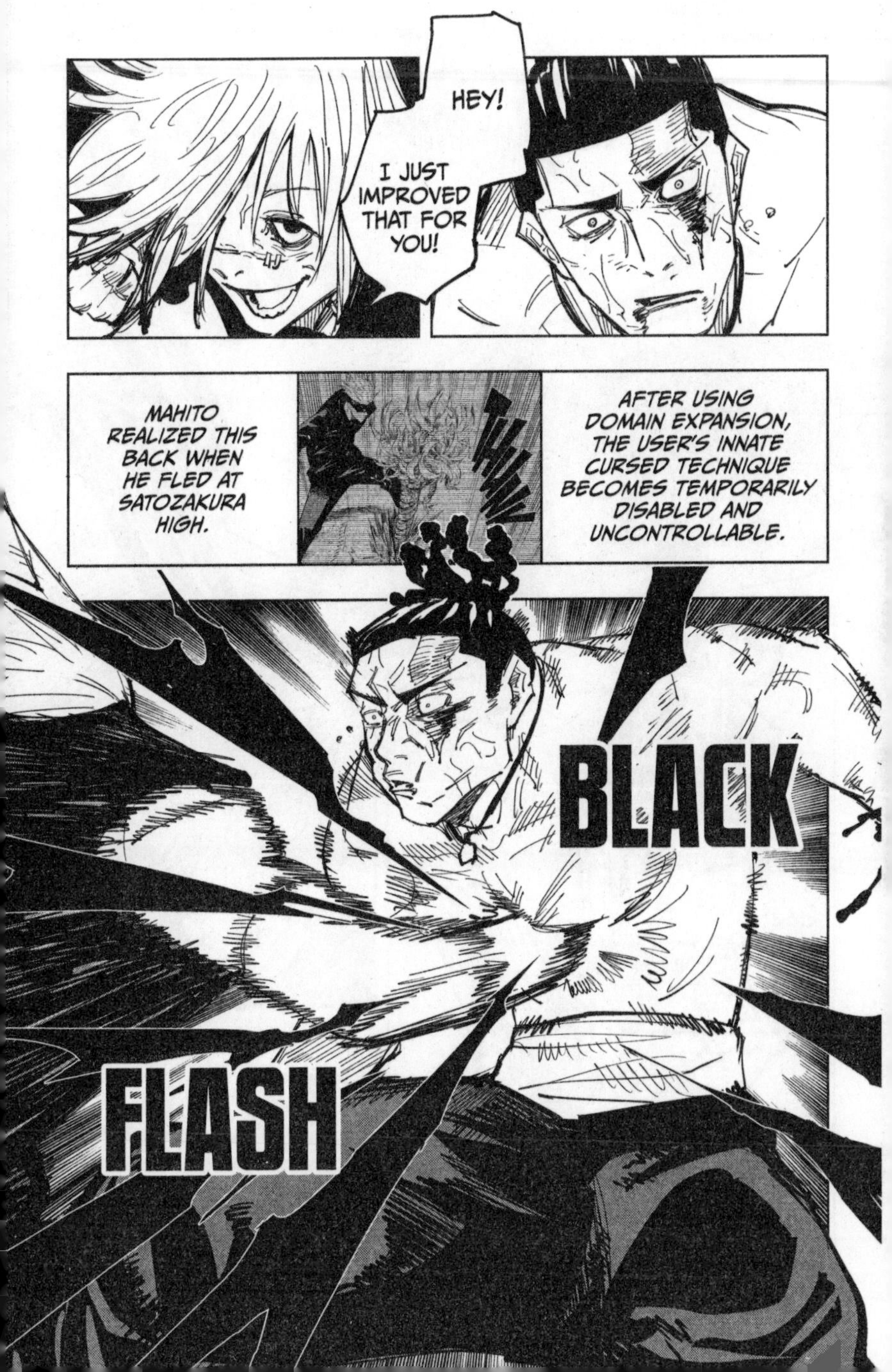
HEY!
I JUST IMPROVED THAT FOR YOU!
AFTER USING DOMAIN EXPANSION, THE USER'S INNATE CURSED TECHNIQUE BECOMES TEMPORARILY DISABLED AND UNCONTROLLABLE.
MAHITO REALIZED THIS BACK WHEN HE FLED AT SATOZAKURA HIGH.
BLACK
FLASH

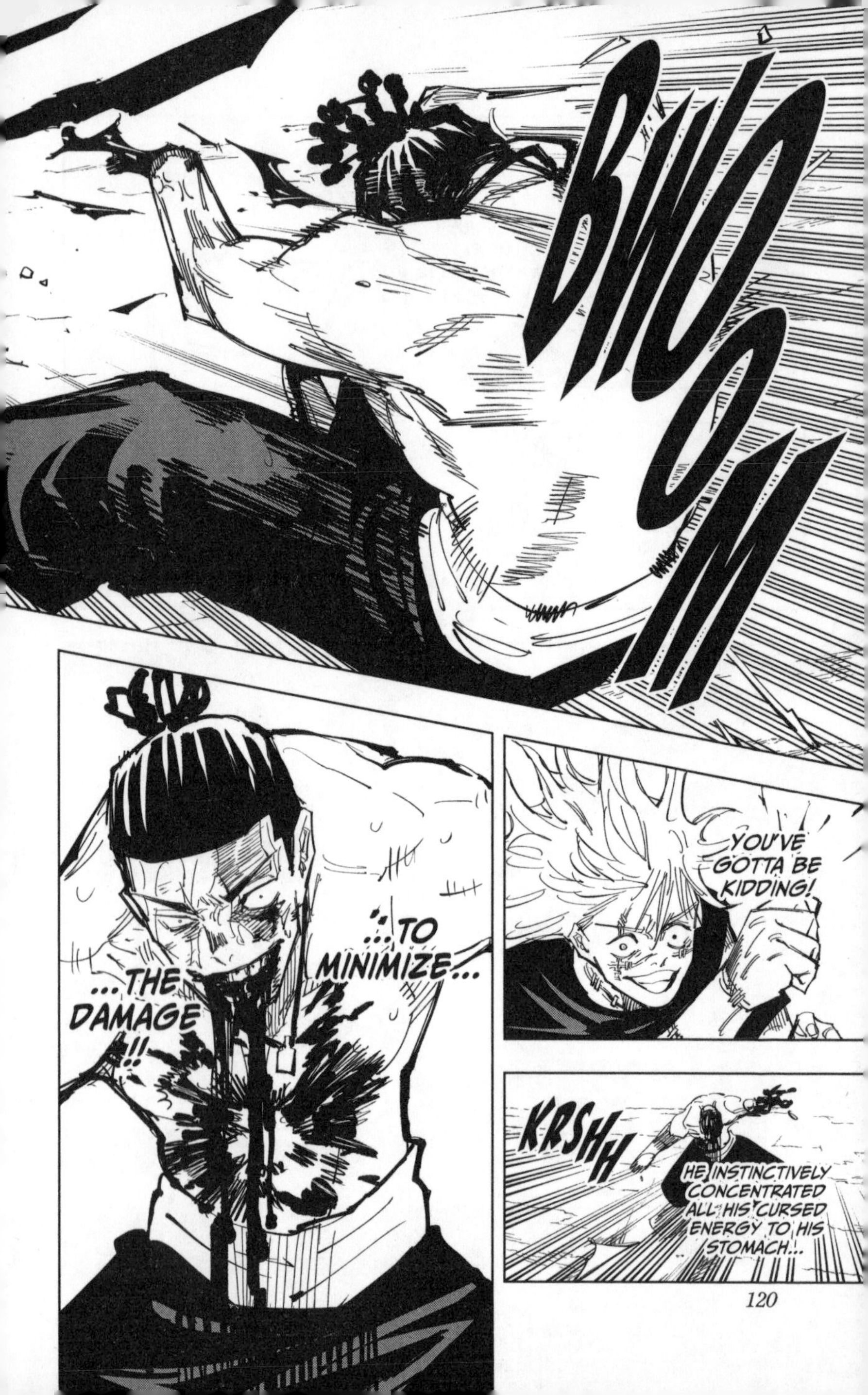
YOU'VE GOTTA BE KIDDING!
KRSHH
HE INSTINCTIVELY CONCENTRATED ALL HIS CURSED ENERGY TO HIS STOMACH...
...TO MINIMIZE...
...THE DAMAGE!!

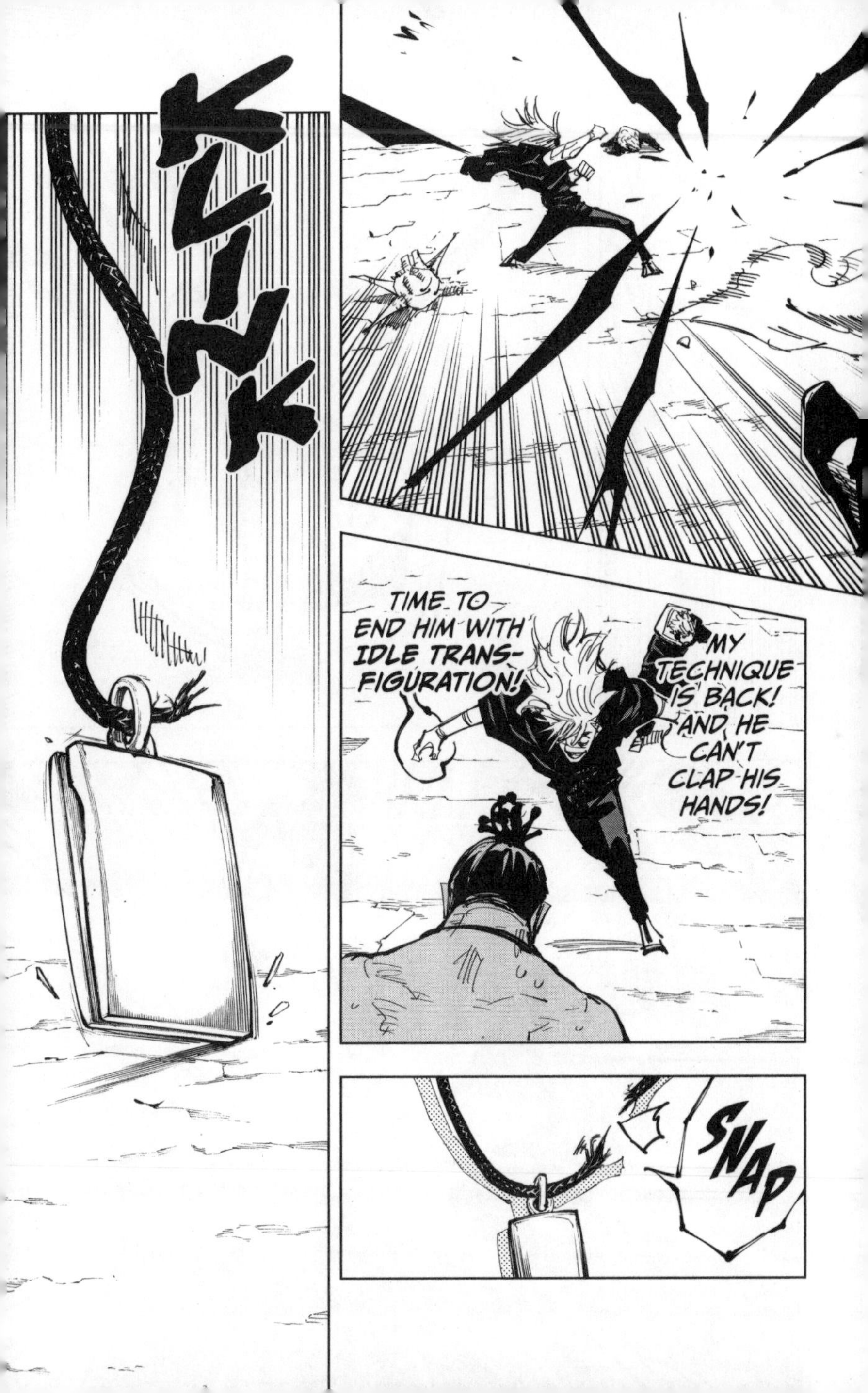
MY TECHNIQUE IS BACK! AND HE CAN'T CLAP HIS HANDS!
TIME TO END HIM WITH IDLE TRANS-FIGURATION!
SNAP
CLINK

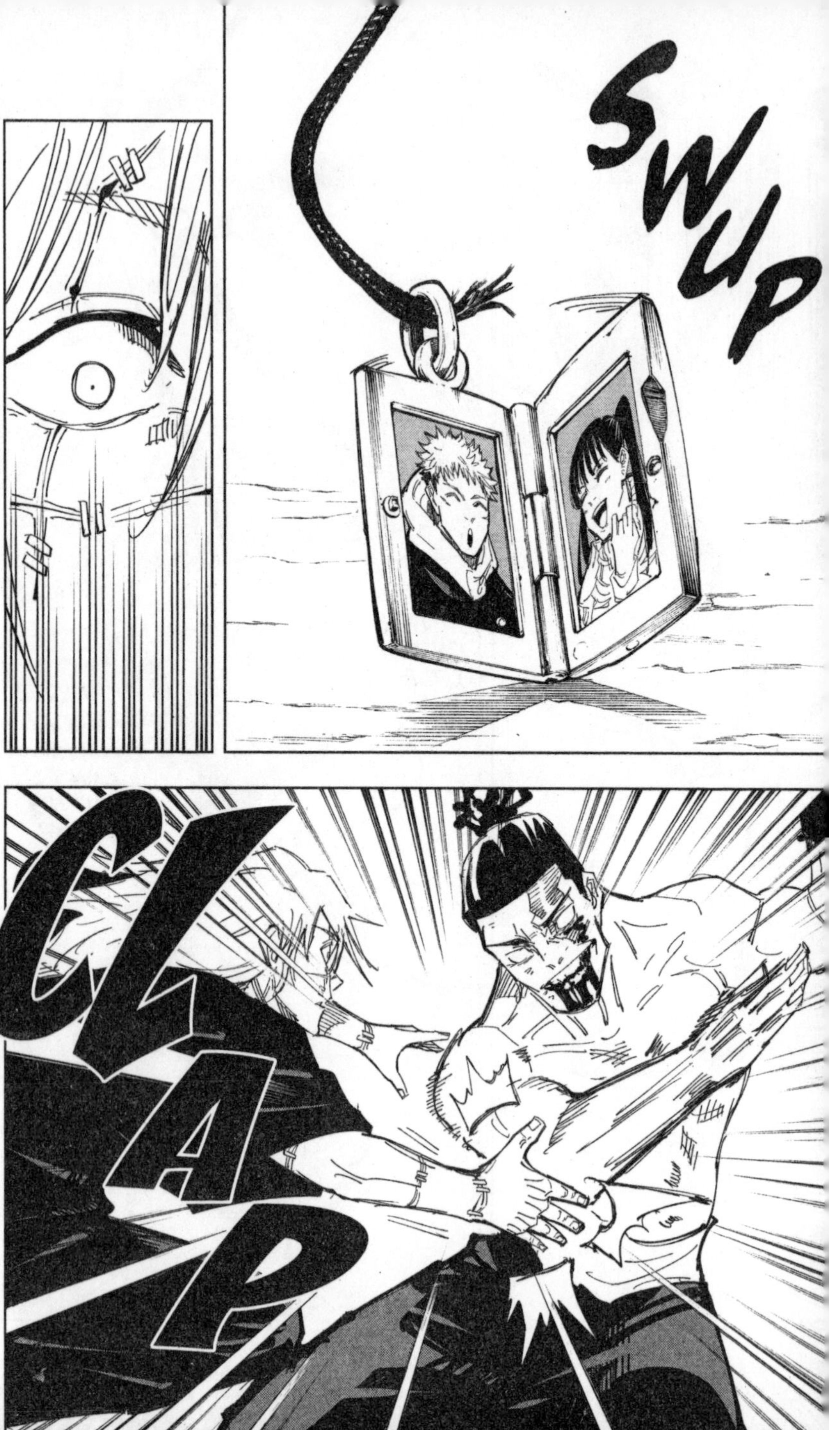
SWUP
CLAP

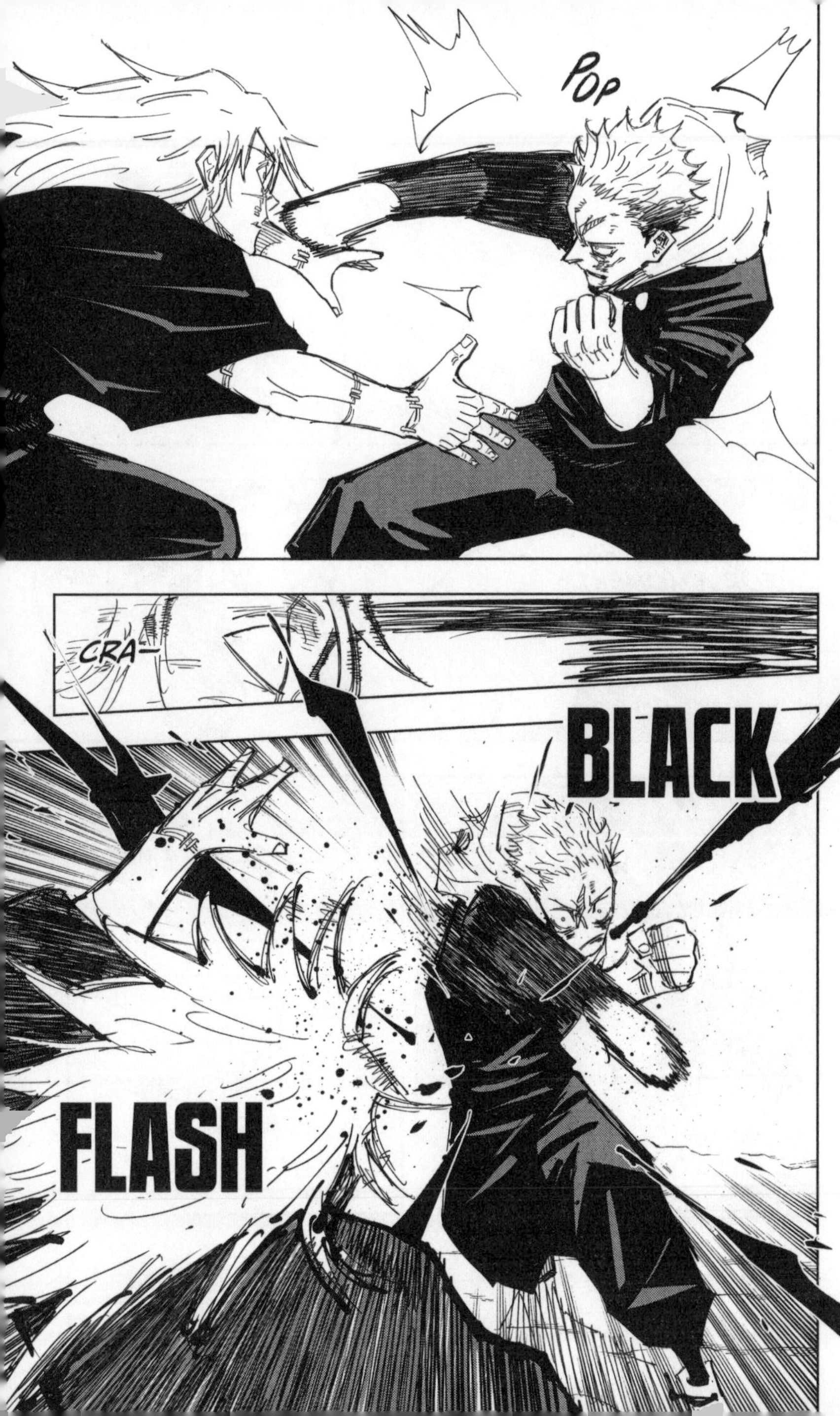
POP
CRA-
BLACK
FLASH

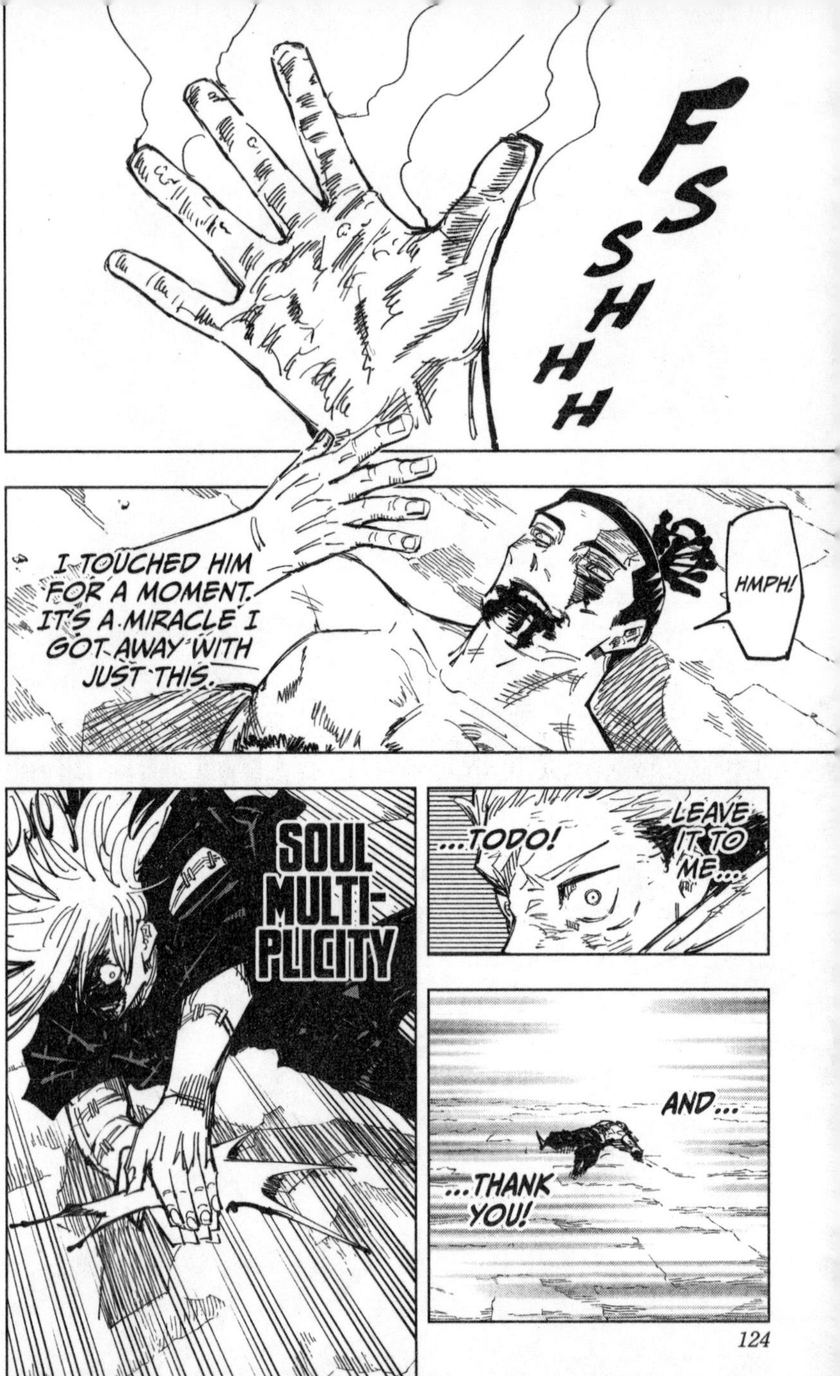
FSSHHH
HMPH!
I TOUCHED HIM FOR A MOMENT. IT'S A MIRACLE I GOT AWAY WITH JUST THIS.
LEAVE IT TO ME...
...TODO!
AND...
...THANK YOU!
SOUL MULTI-PLICITY

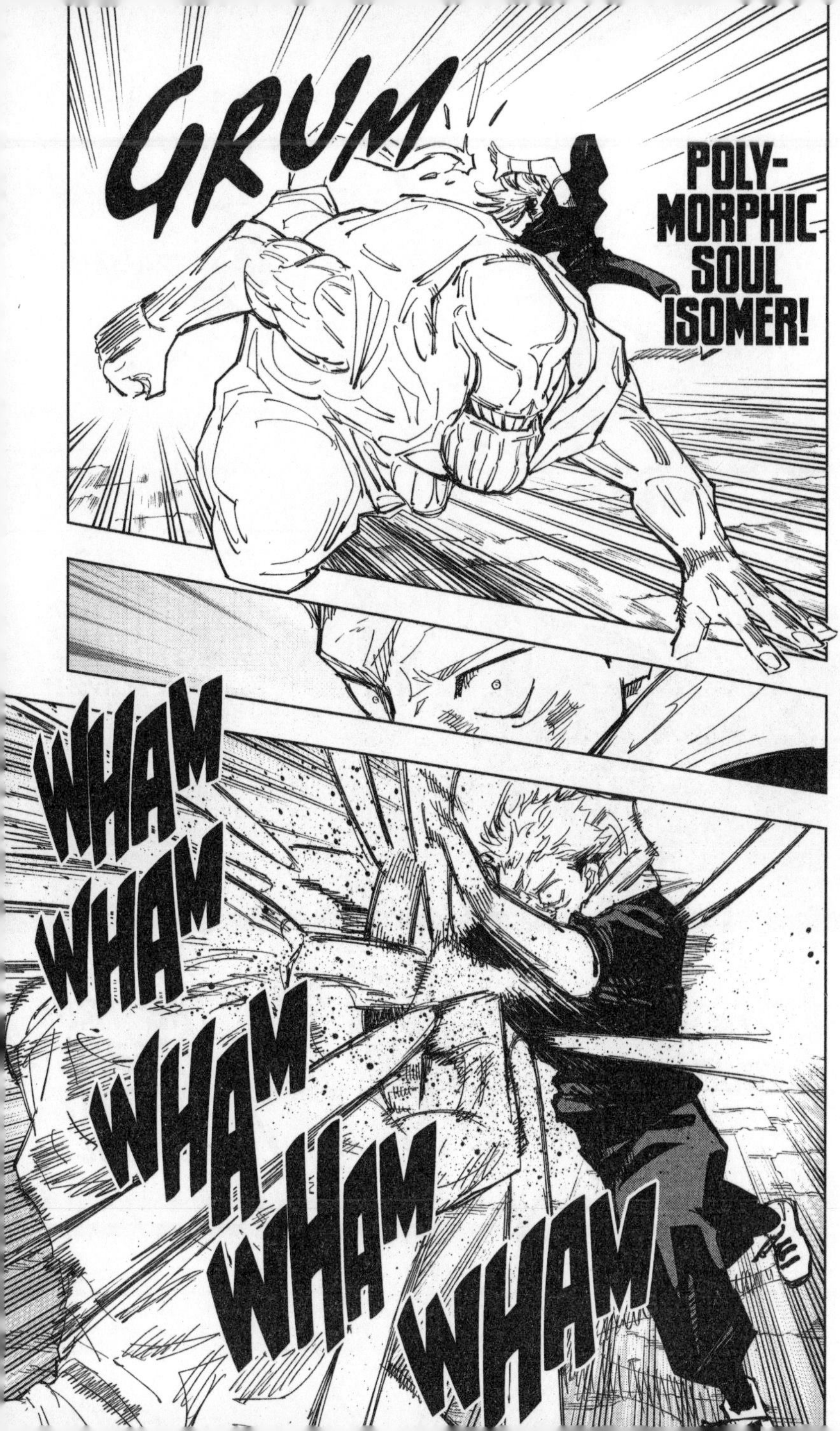
POLY-MORPHIC SOUL ISOMER!
GRUM
WHAM
WHAM
WHAM
WHAM
WHAM

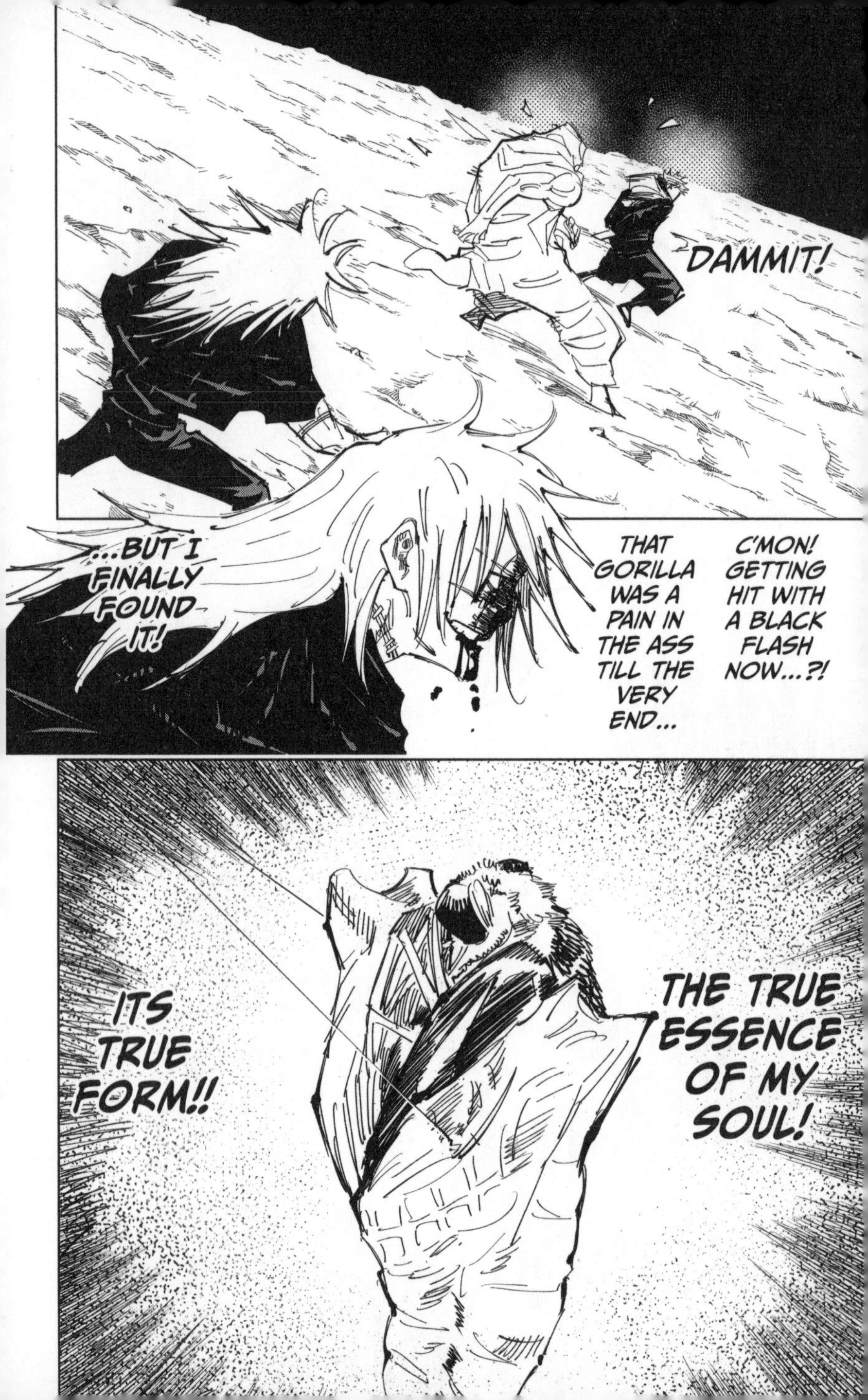
DAMMIT!
C'MON! GETTING HIT WITH A BLACK FLASH NOW...?!
THAT GORILLA WAS A PAIN IN THE ASS TILL THE VERY END...
...BUT I FINALLY FOUND IT!
THE TRUE ESSENCE OF MY SOUL!
ITS TRUE FORM!!

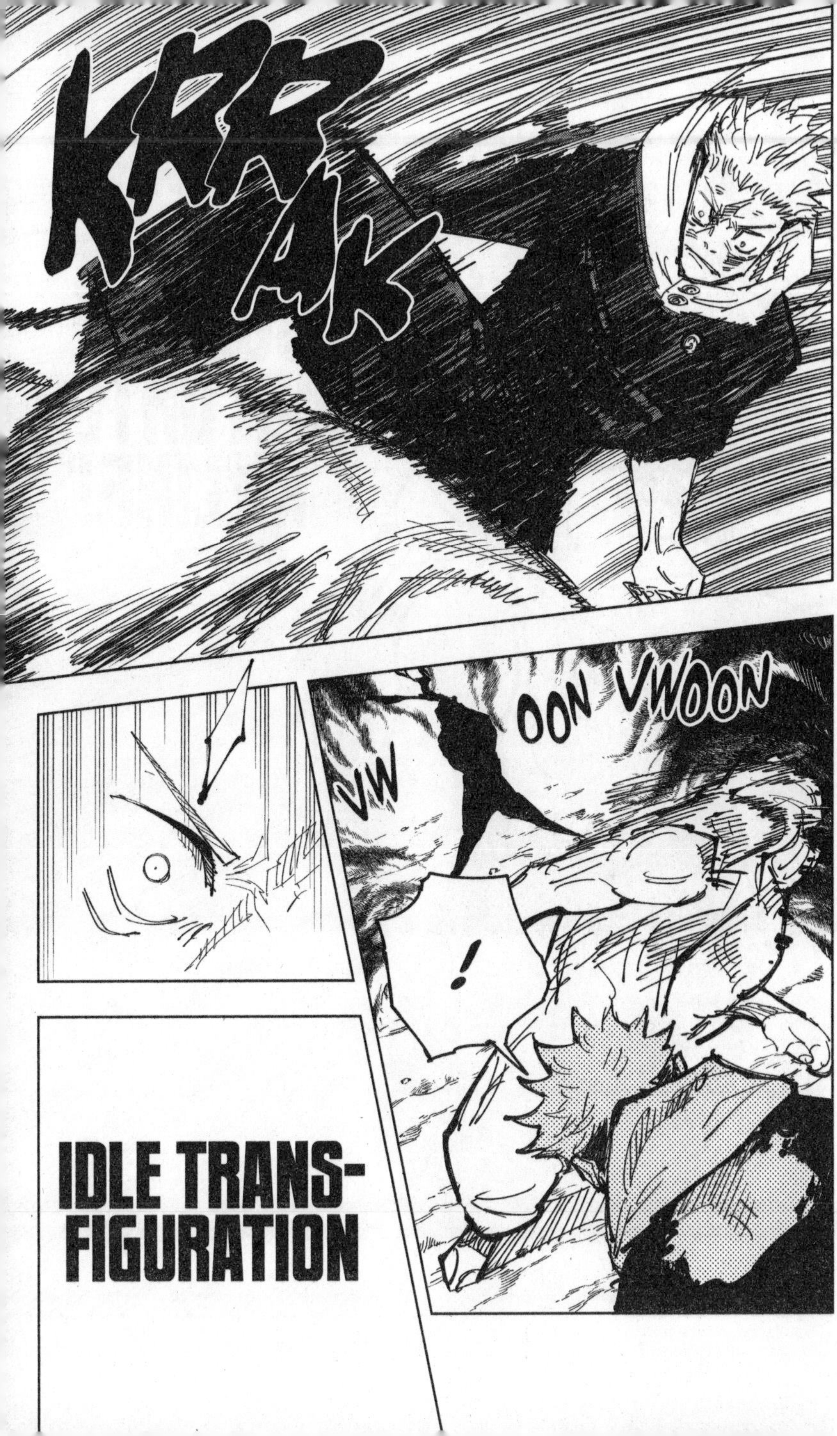
KRRAK
VWOON
VW OON
!
IDLE TRANS-
FIGURATION

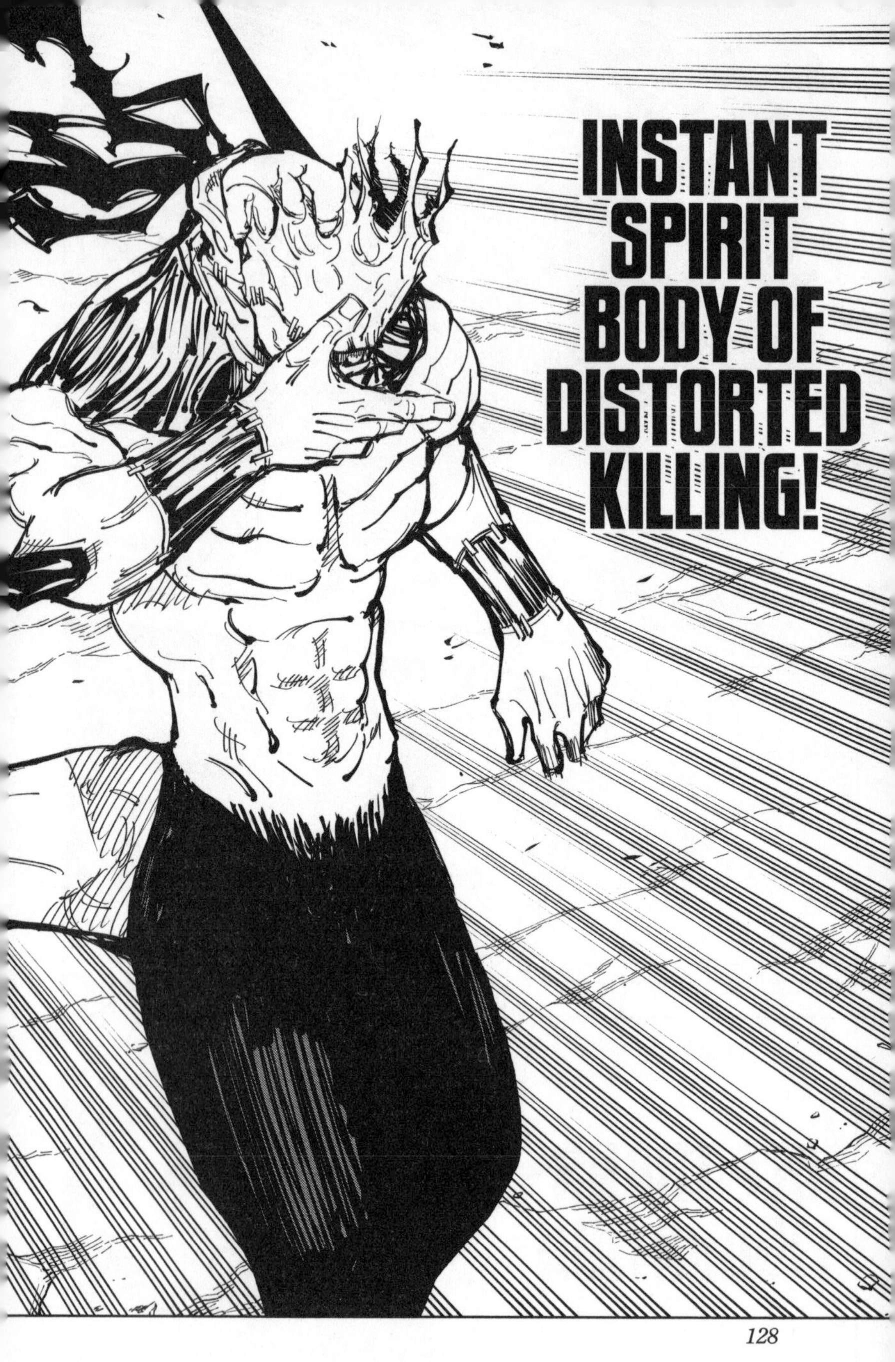
INSTANT SPIRIT BODY OF DISTORTED KILLING!

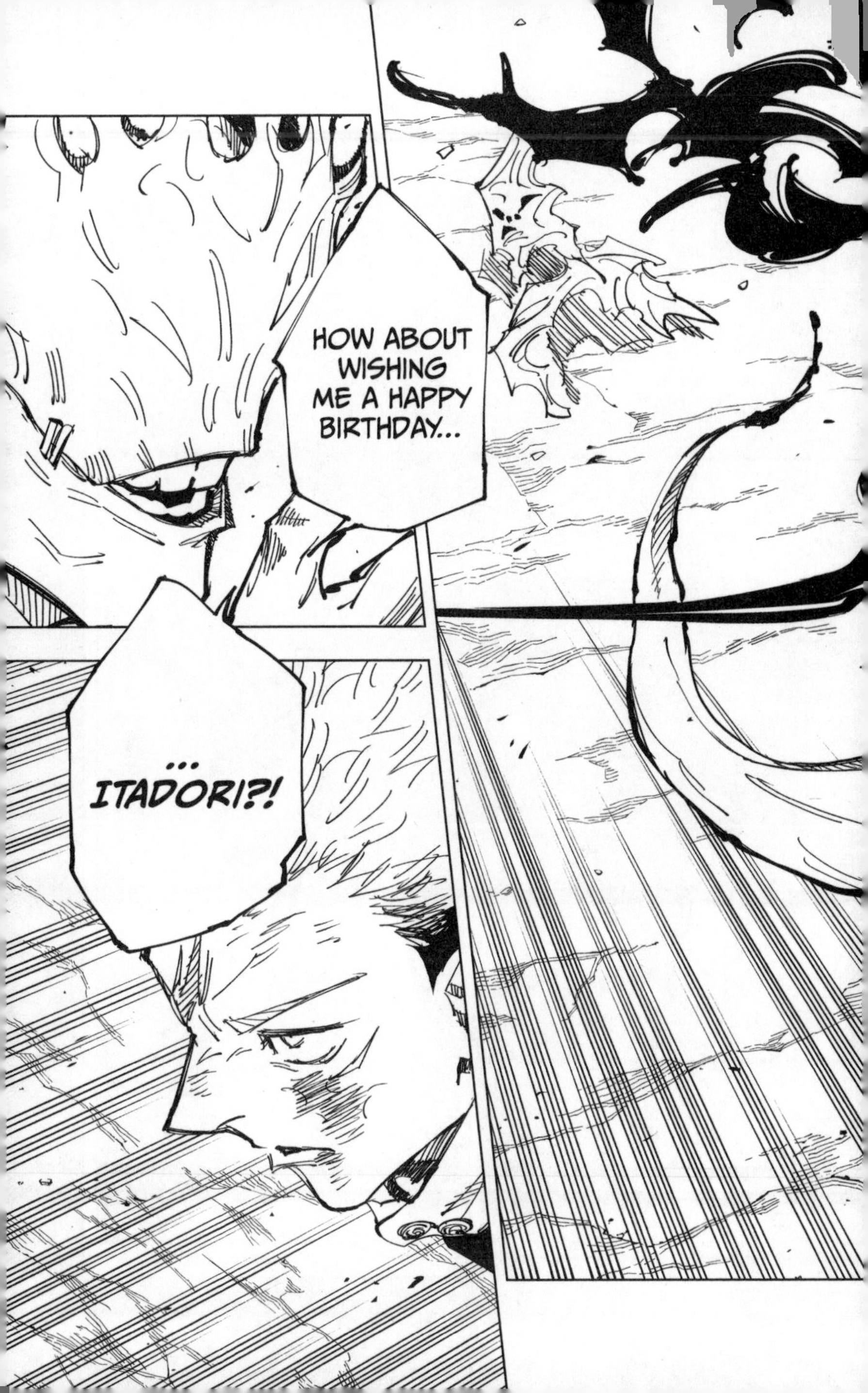
HOW ABOUT WISHING ME A HAPPY BIRTHDAY...
...ITADORI?!

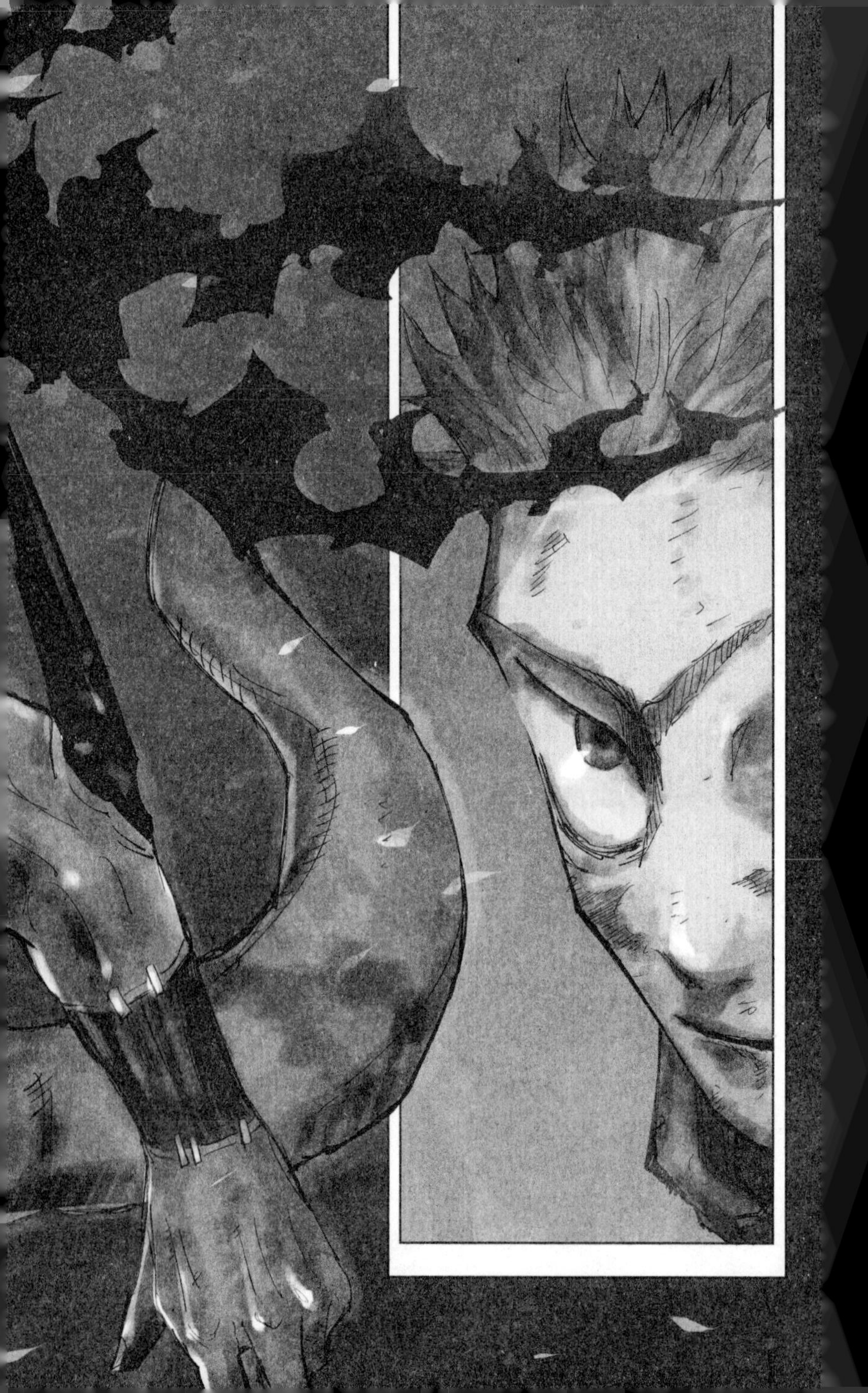

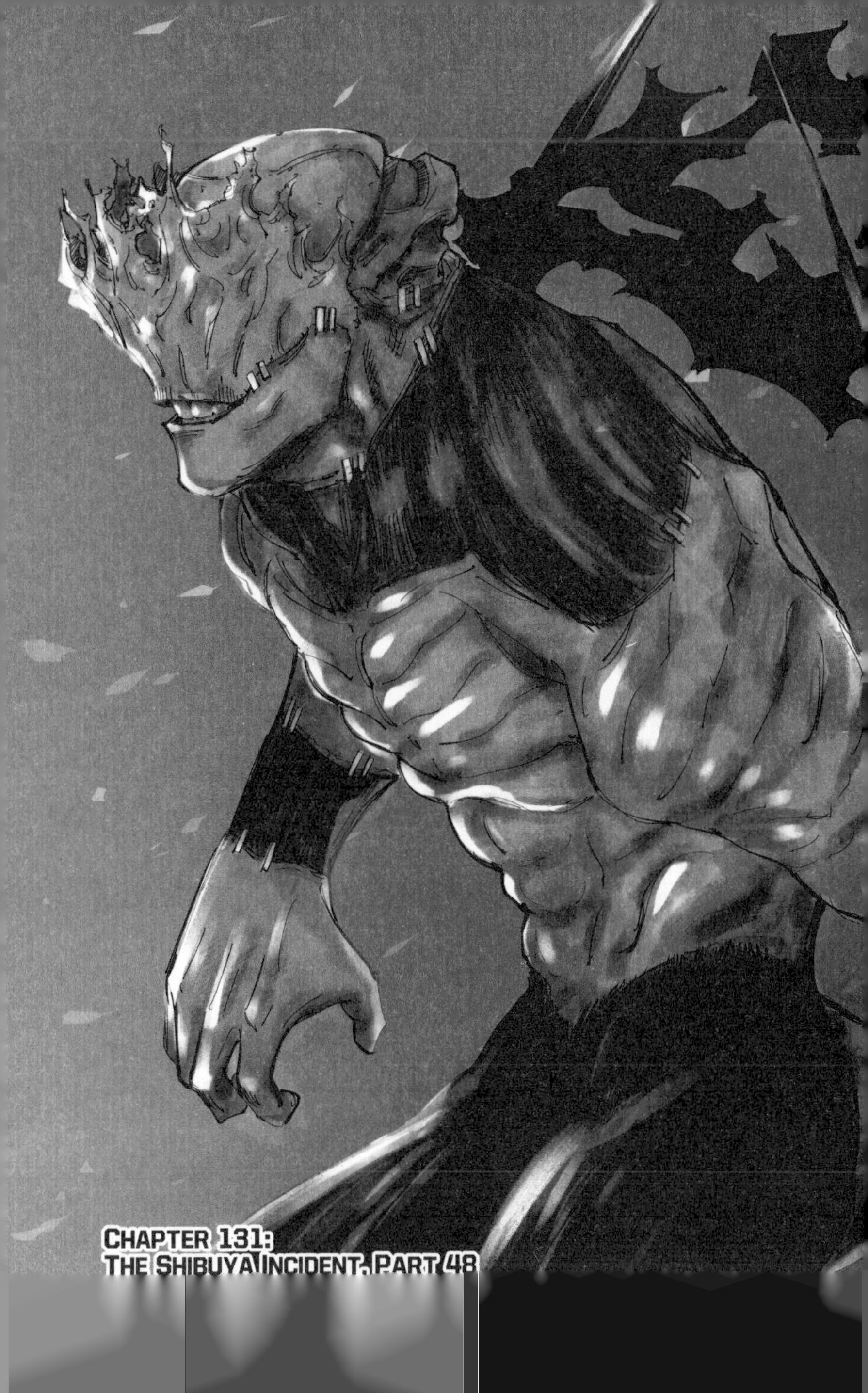
CHAPTER 131:
THE SHIBUYA INCIDENT, PART 48

JUJUTSU KAISEN

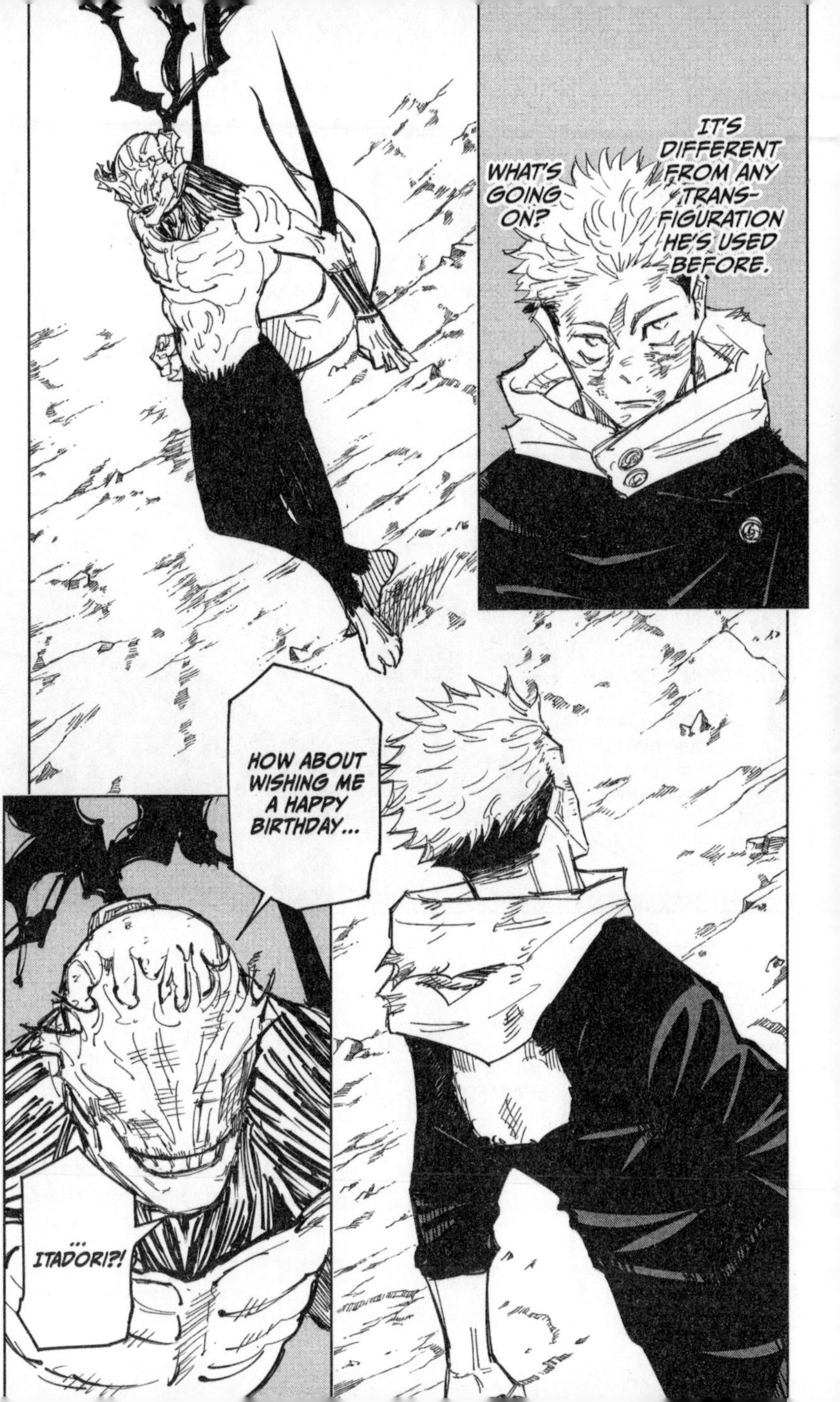
IT'S DIFFERENT FROM ANY TRANS-FIGURATION HE'S USED BEFORE.
WHAT'S GOING ON?
HOW ABOUT WISHING ME A HAPPY BIRTHDAY...
... ITADORI?!

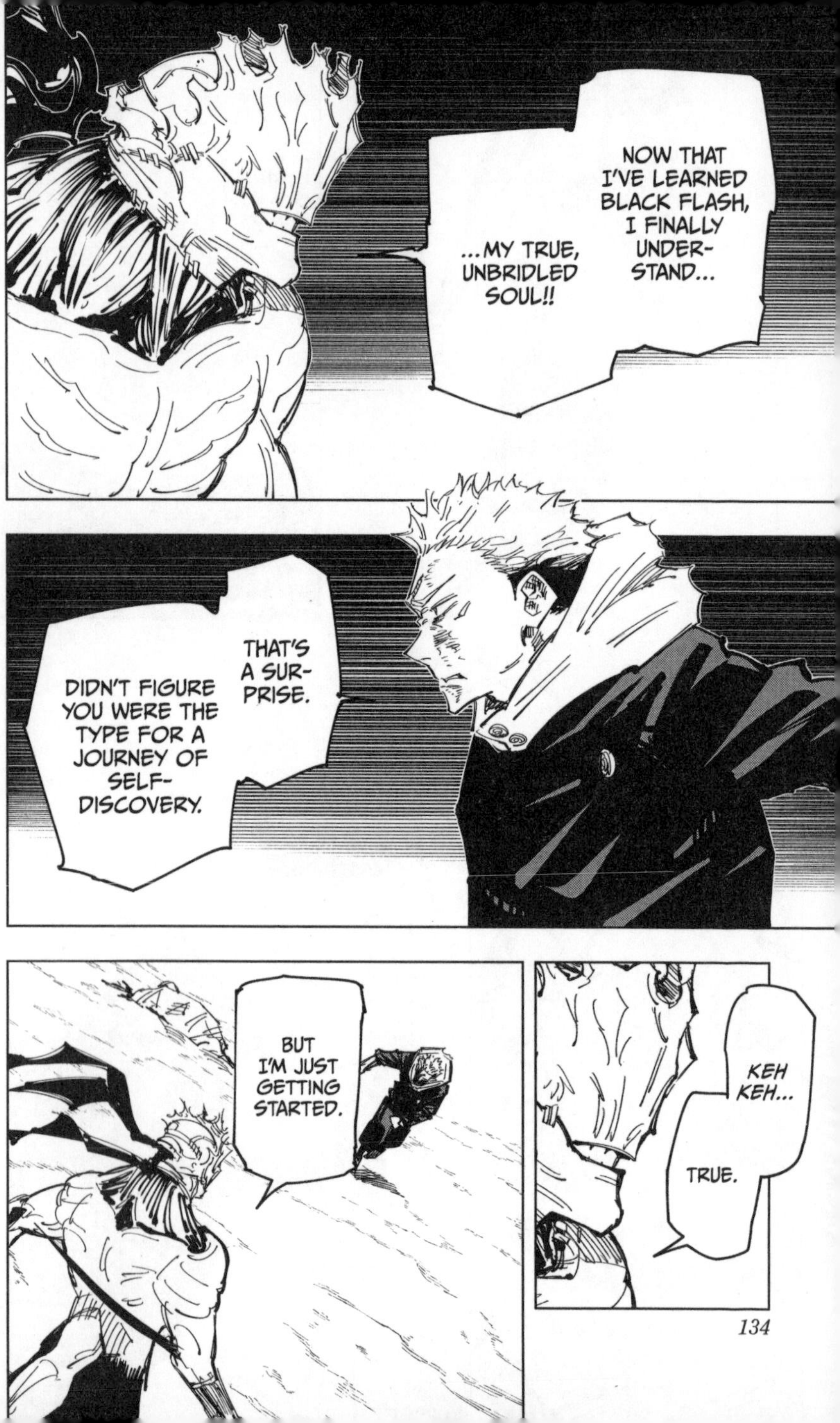
NOW THAT I'VE LEARNED BLACK FLASH, I FINALLY UNDER-STAND...
...MY TRUE, UNBRIDLED SOUL!!
THAT'S A SUR-PRISE.
DIDN'T FIGURE YOU WERE THE TYPE FOR A JOURNEY OF SELF-DISCOVERY.
KEH KEH...
TRUE.
BUT I'M JUST GETTING STARTED.

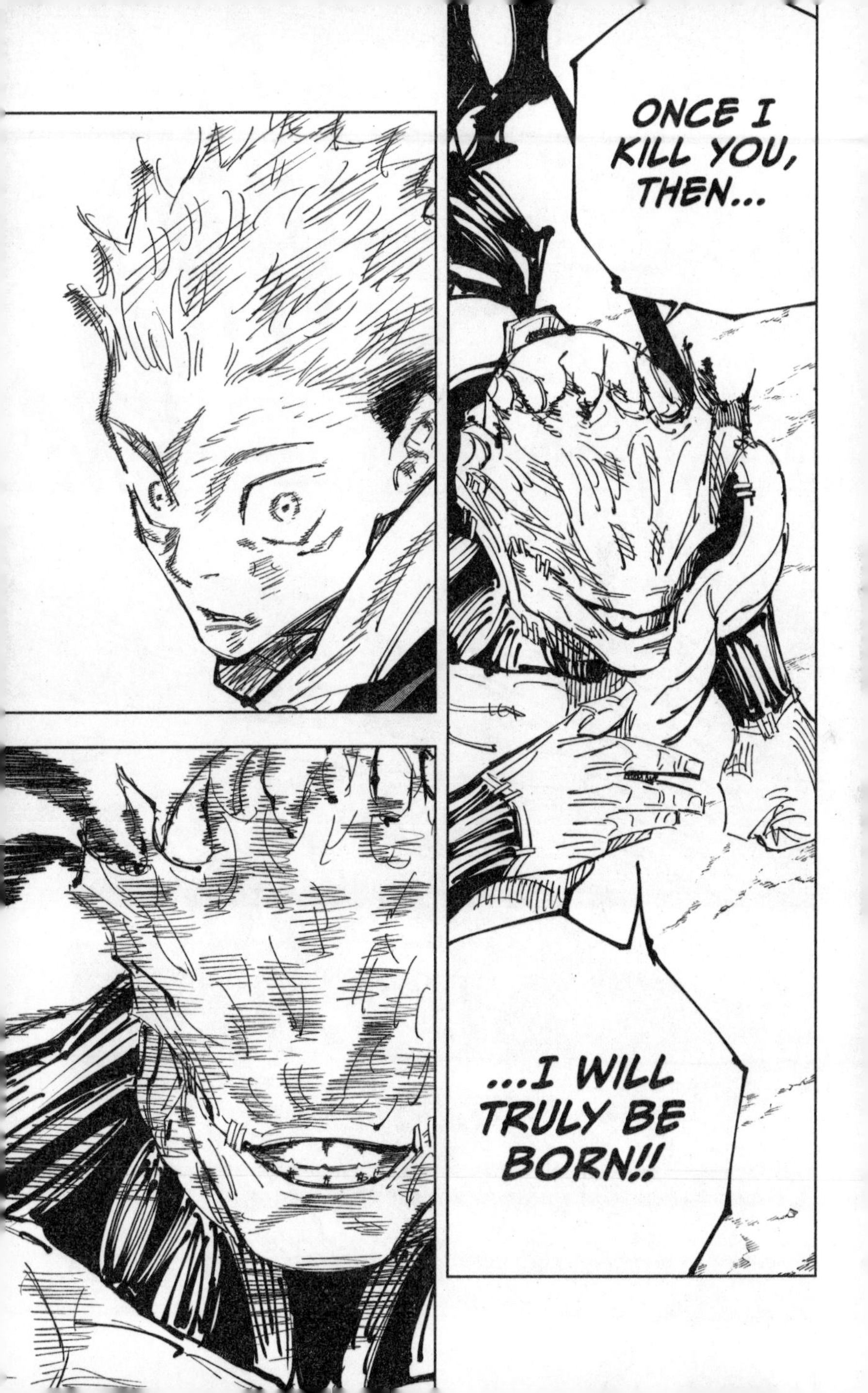
ONCE I KILL YOU, THEN...
...I WILL TRULY BE BORN!!

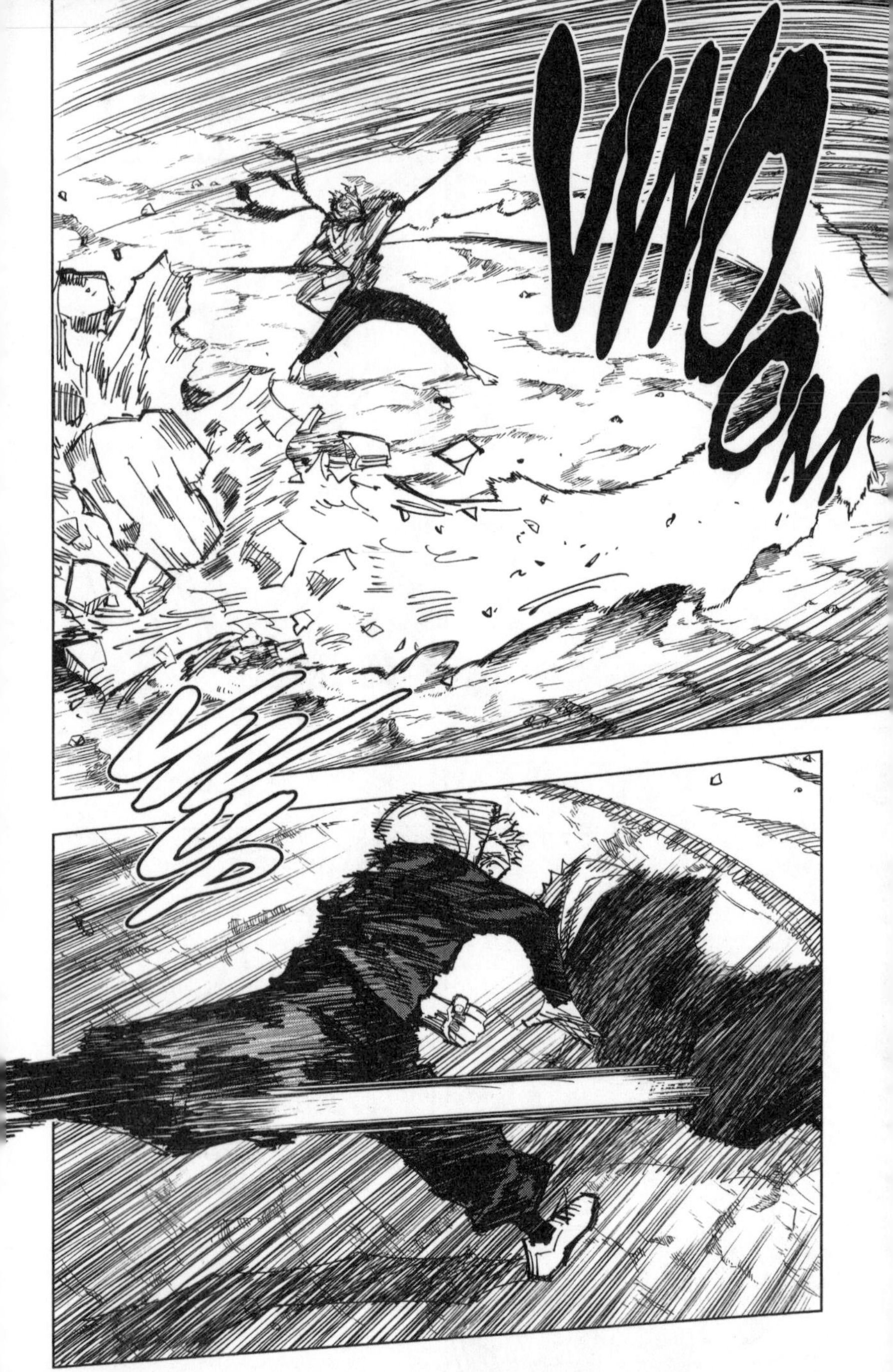
VWOOM

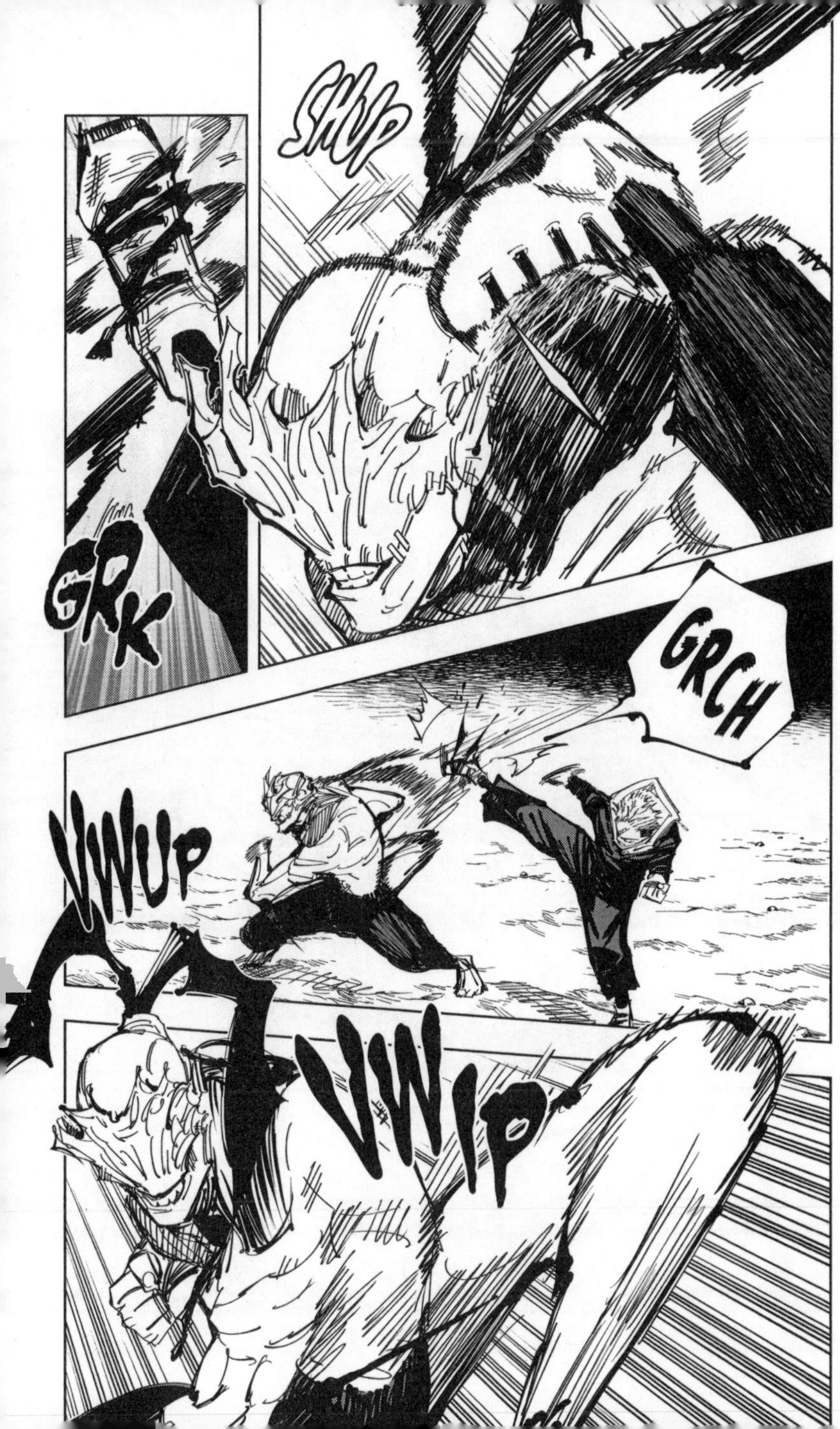
SHLUP
GRK
GRCH
VWUP
VWIP

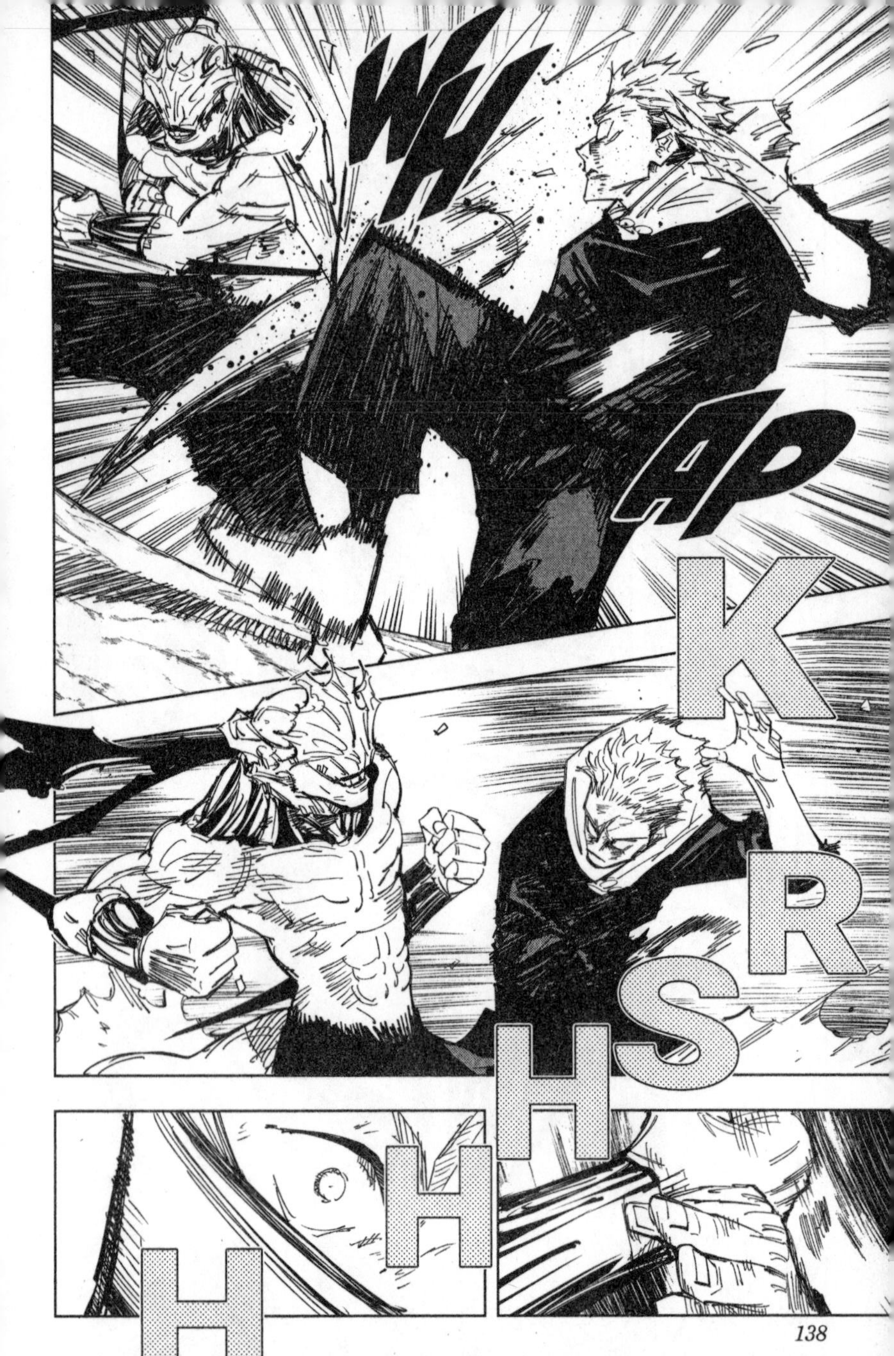
WHAP
KRSHHH

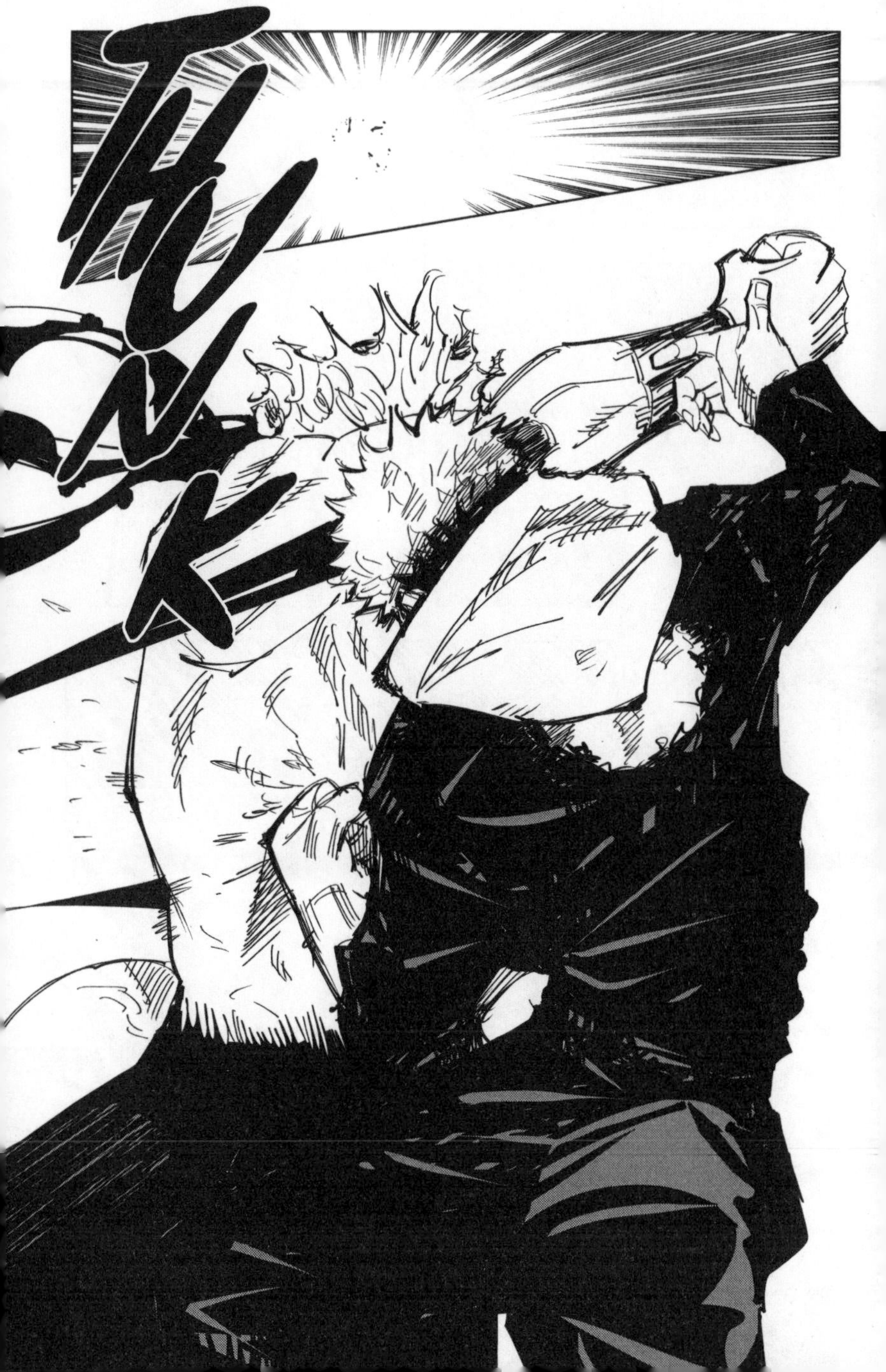
THUNK

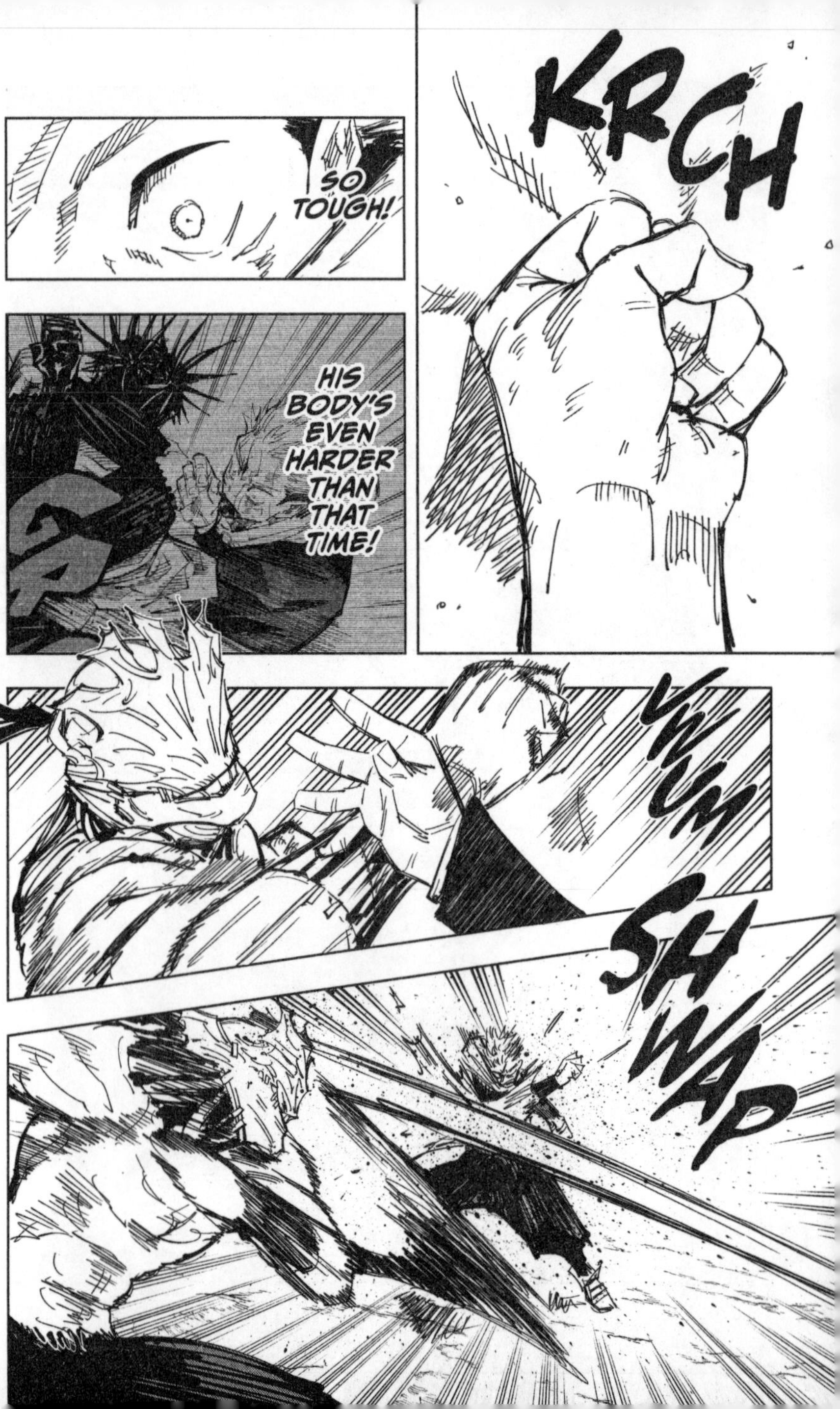
KRCH
SO TOUGH!
HIS BODY'S EVEN HARDER THAN THAT TIME!
VWUM
SHWAP

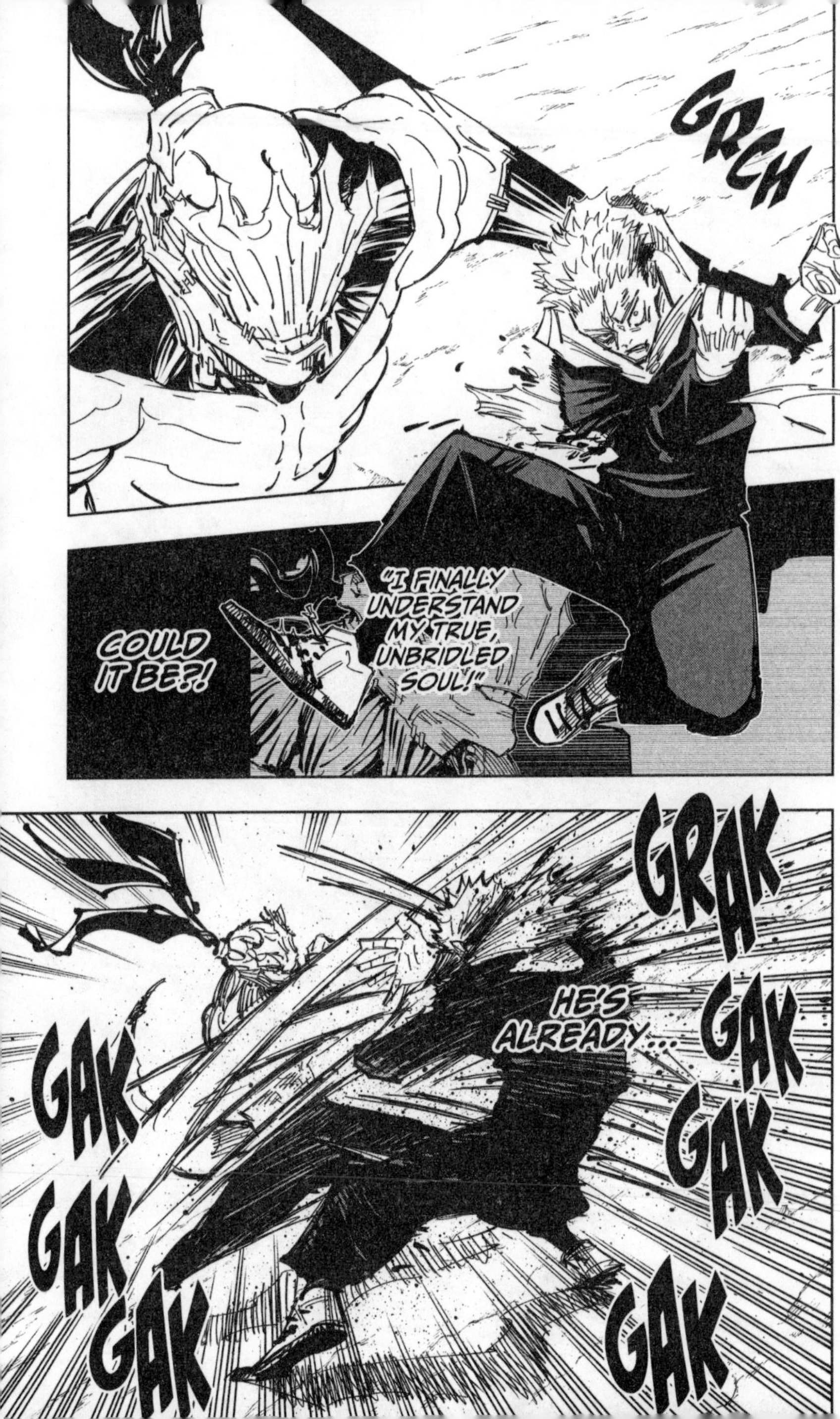
GRCH
"I FINALLY UNDERSTAND MY TRUE, UNBRIDLED SOUL!"
COULD IT BE?!
GRAK
GAK
GAK
GAK
HE'S ALREADY...
GAK
GAK
GAK

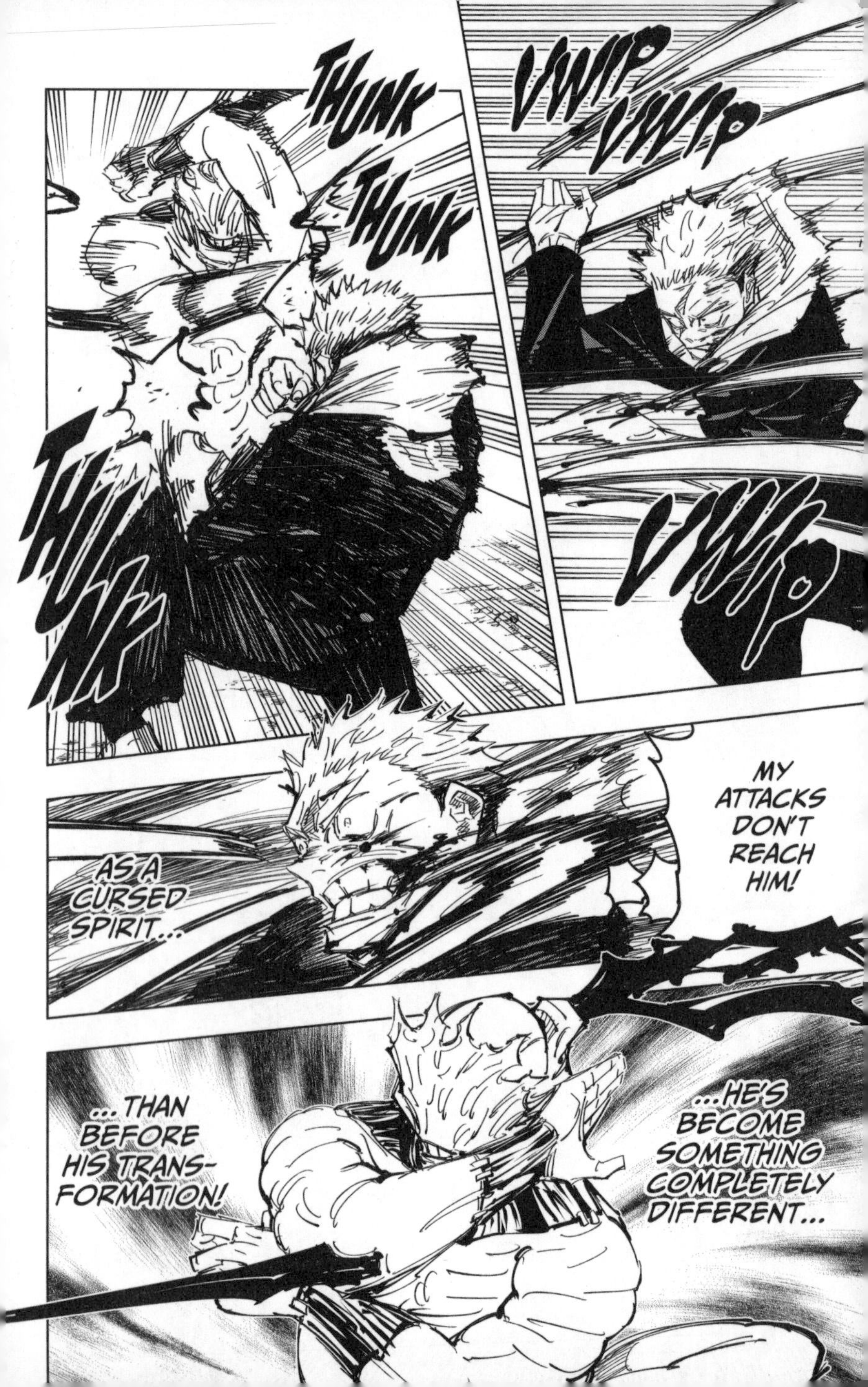
VWIP
VWIP
VWIP
THUNK
THUNK
THUNK
MY ATTACKS DON'T REACH HIM!
AS A CURSED SPIRIT...
...HE'S BECOME SOMETHING COMPLETELY DIFFERENT...
...THAN BEFORE HIS TRANS-FORMATION!

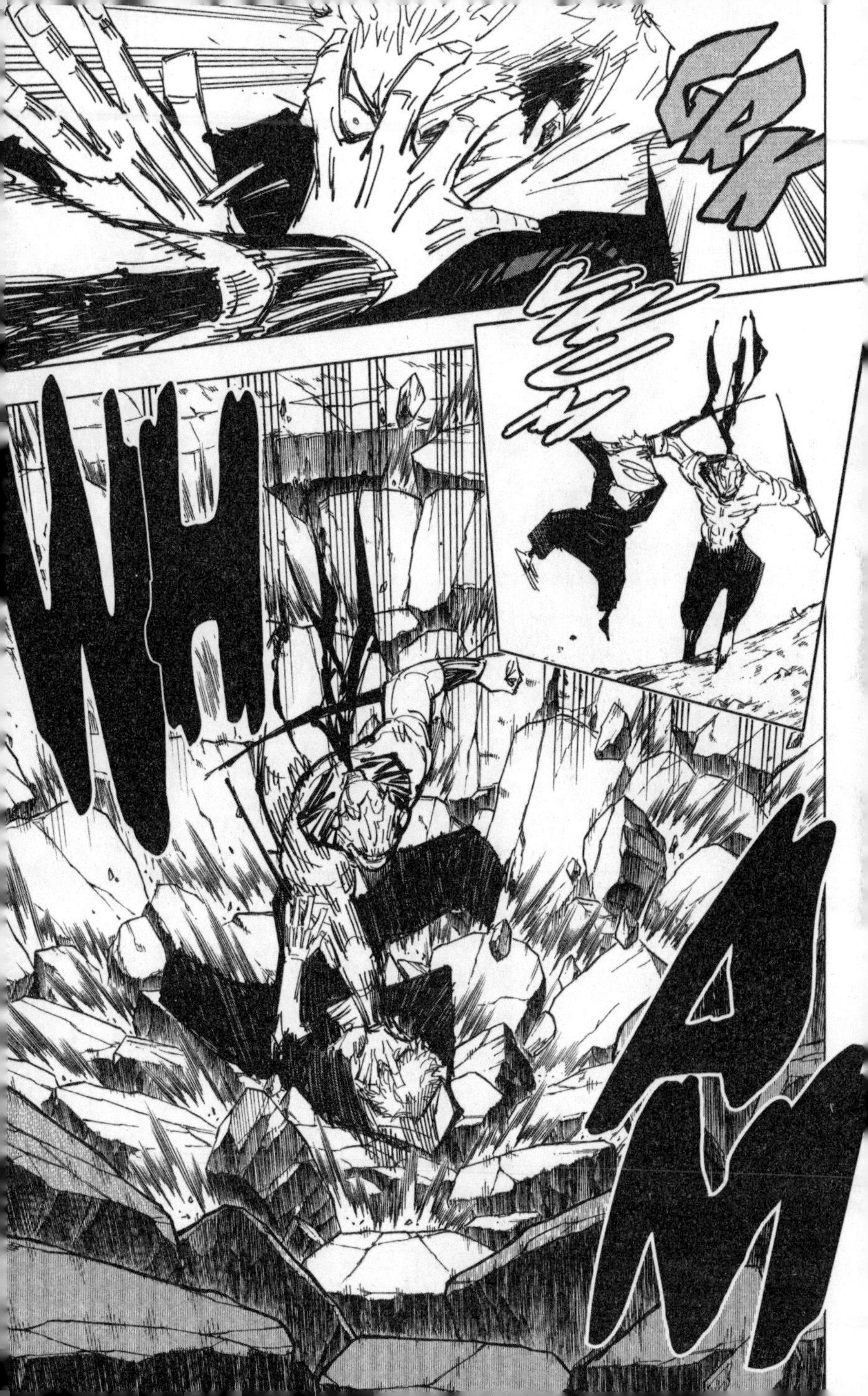
GRK
WHAM

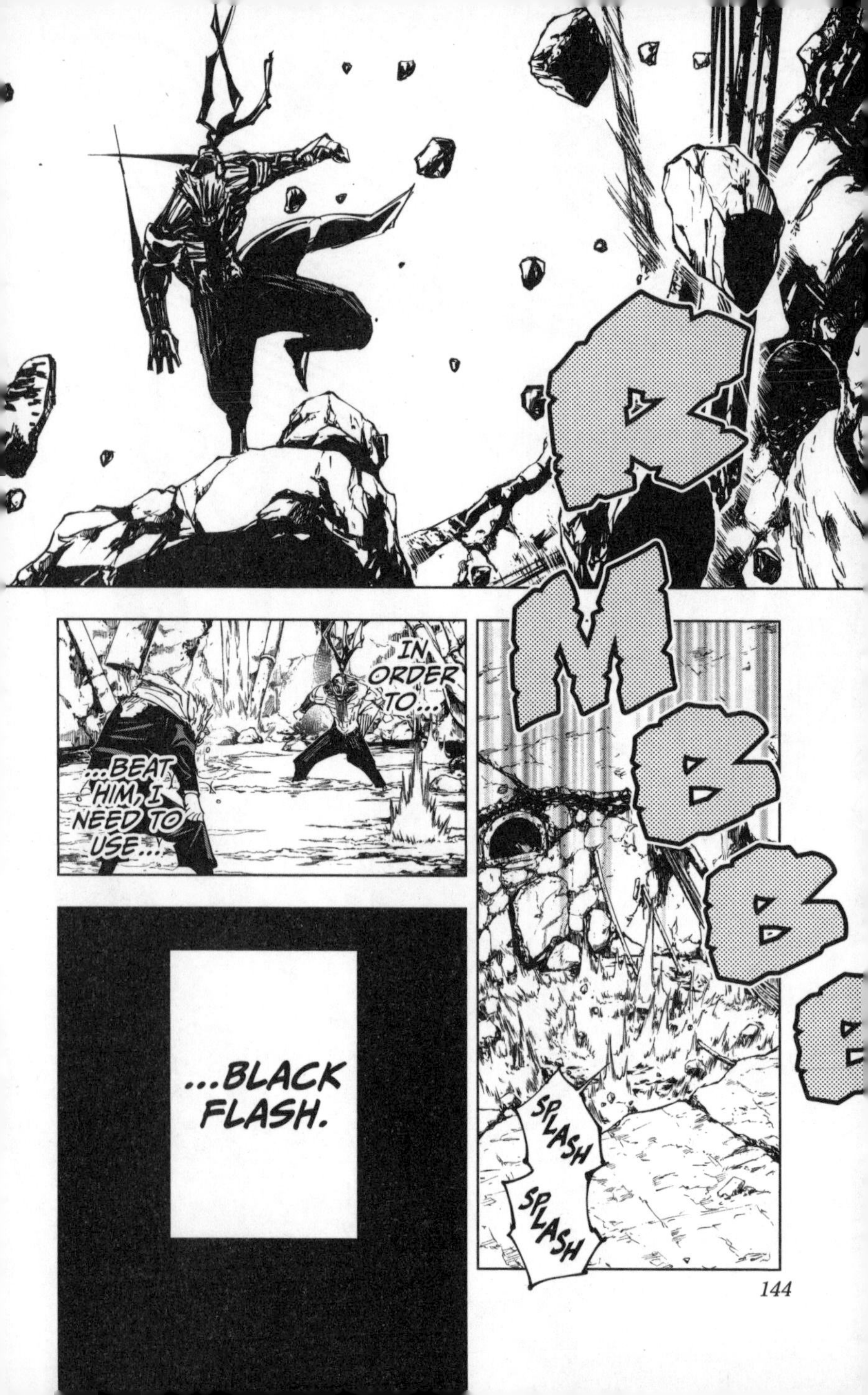
ZMBB
SPLASH
SPLASH
IN ORDER TO...
...BEAT HIM, I NEED TO USE...
...BLACK FLASH.

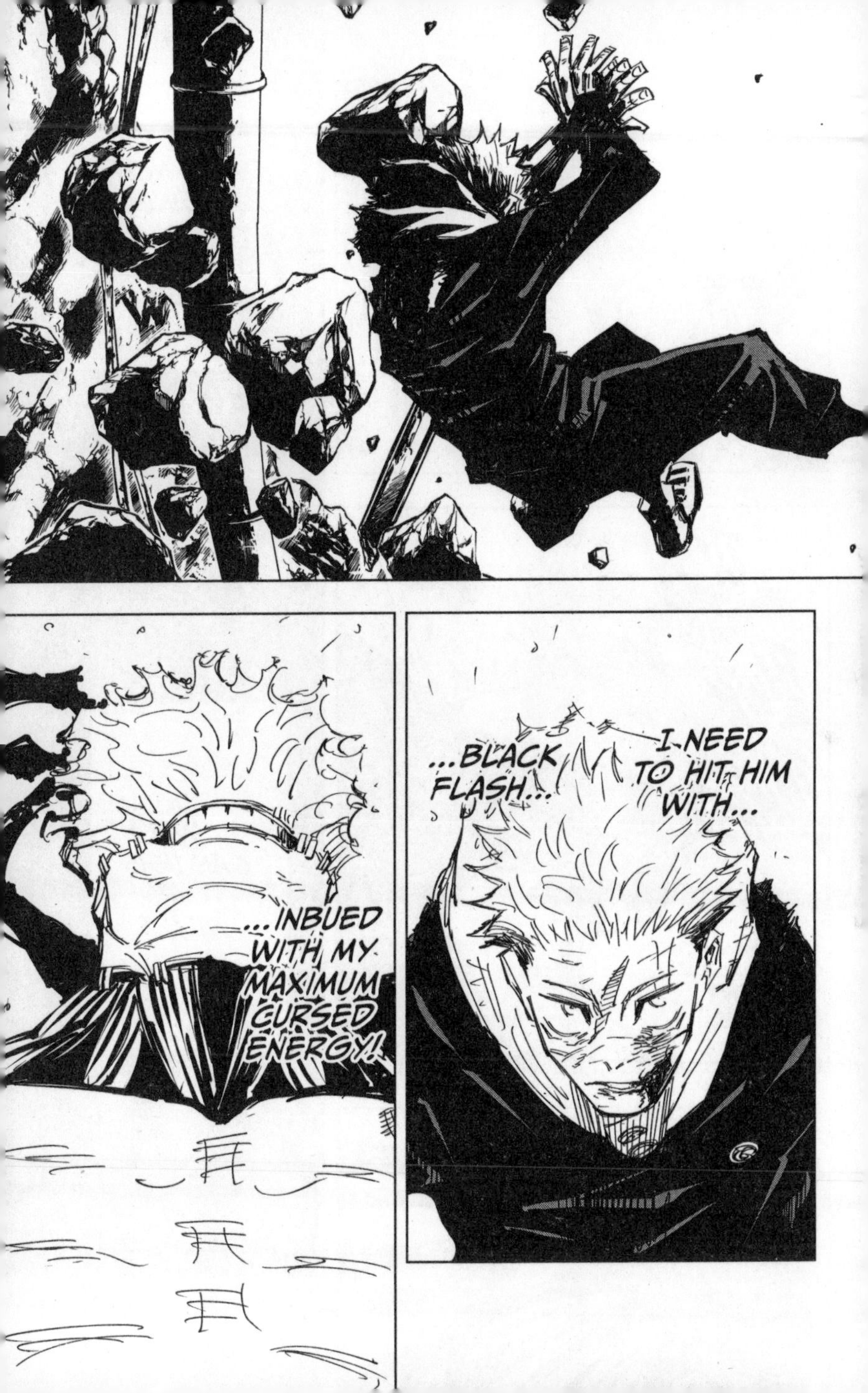
I NEED TO HIT HIM WITH...
...BLACK FLASH...
...INBUED WITH MY MAXIMUM CURSED ENERGY!

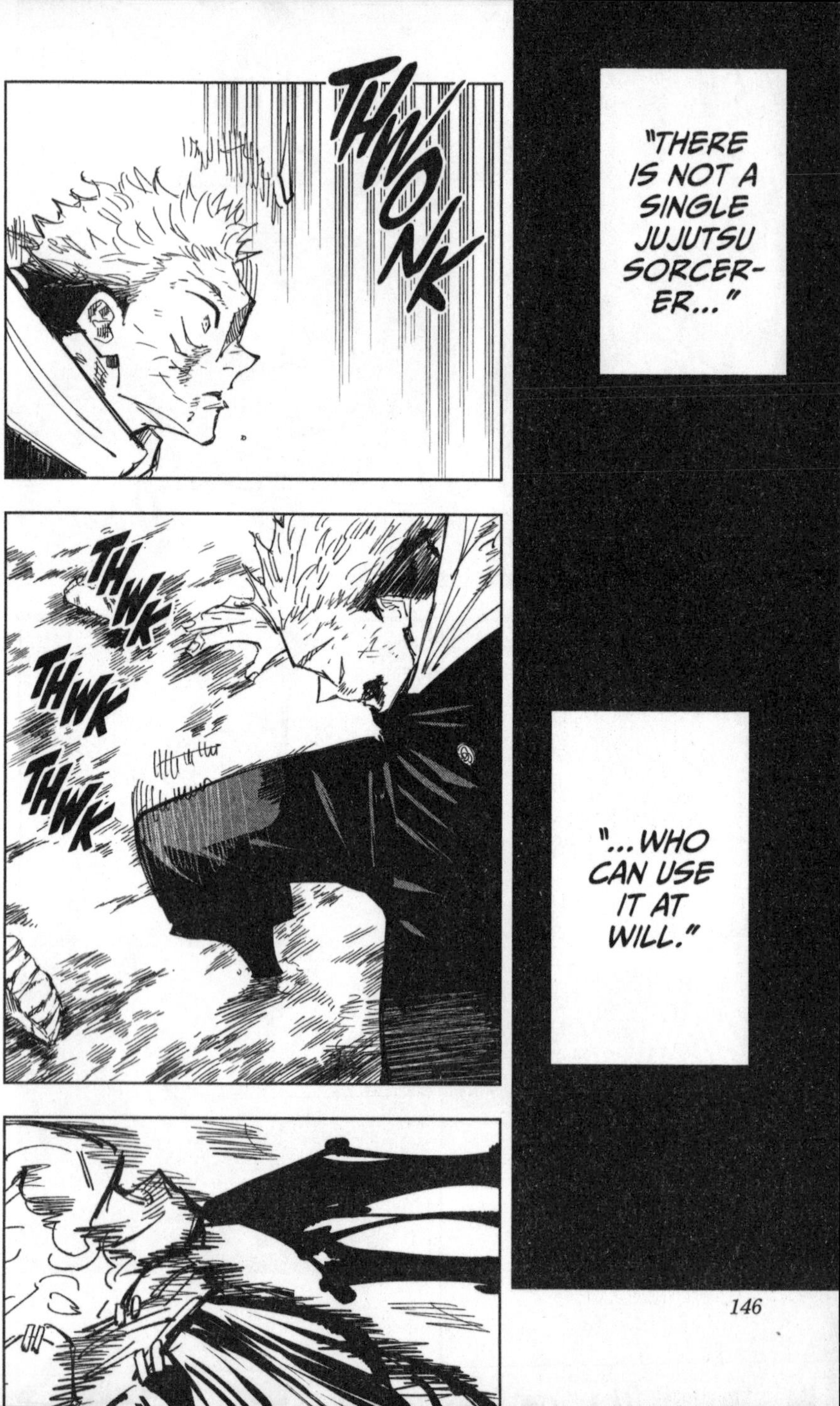
"THERE IS NOT A SINGLE JUJUTSU SORCERER..."
THWONK
"...WHO CAN USE IT AT WILL."
THWK
THWK
THWK

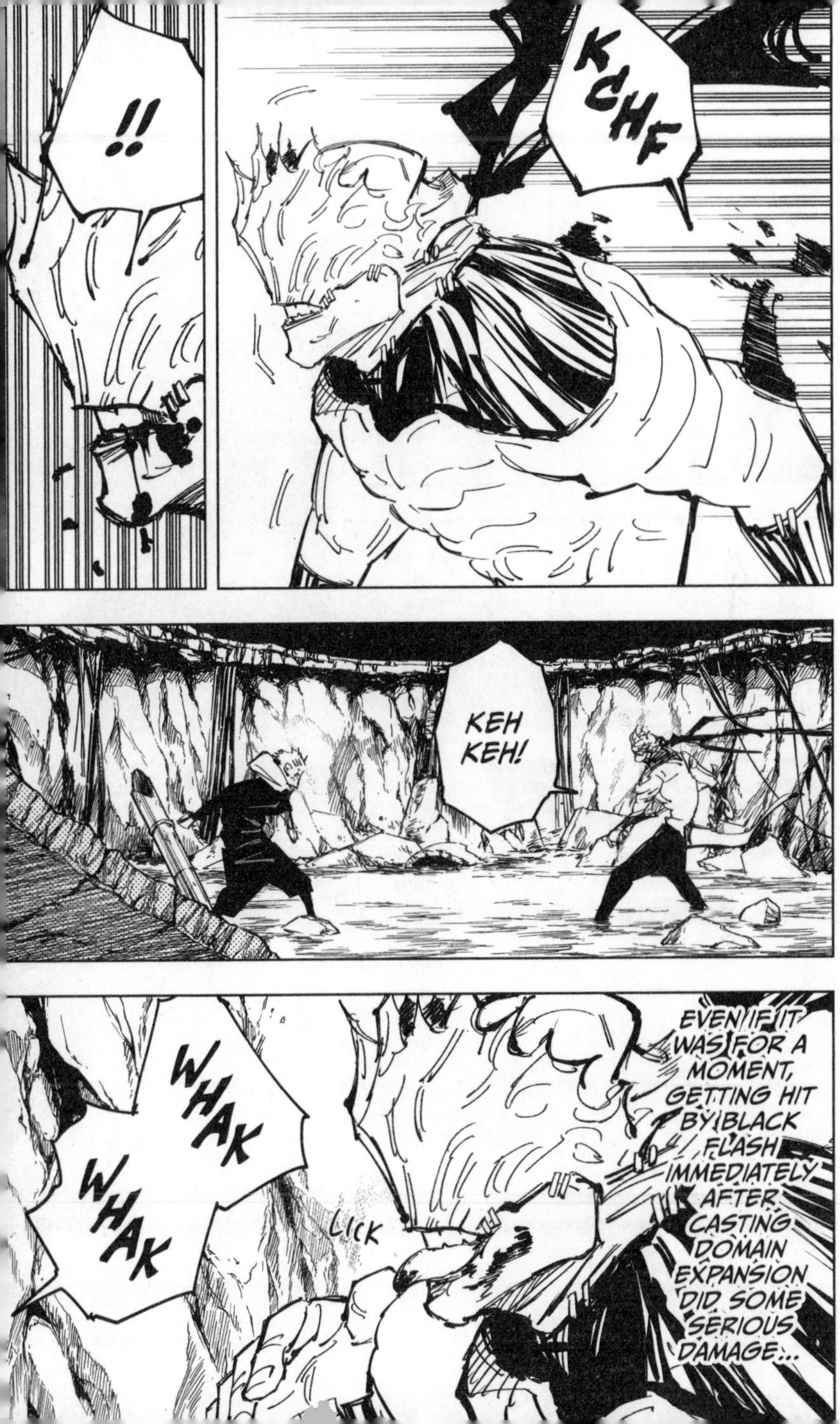
KCHF
!!
KEH KEH!
EVEN IF IT WAS FOR A MOMENT, GETTING HIT BY BLACK FLASH IMMEDIATELY AFTER CASTING DOMAIN EXPANSION DID SOME SERIOUS DAMAGE...
LICK
WHAK WHAK
WHAK

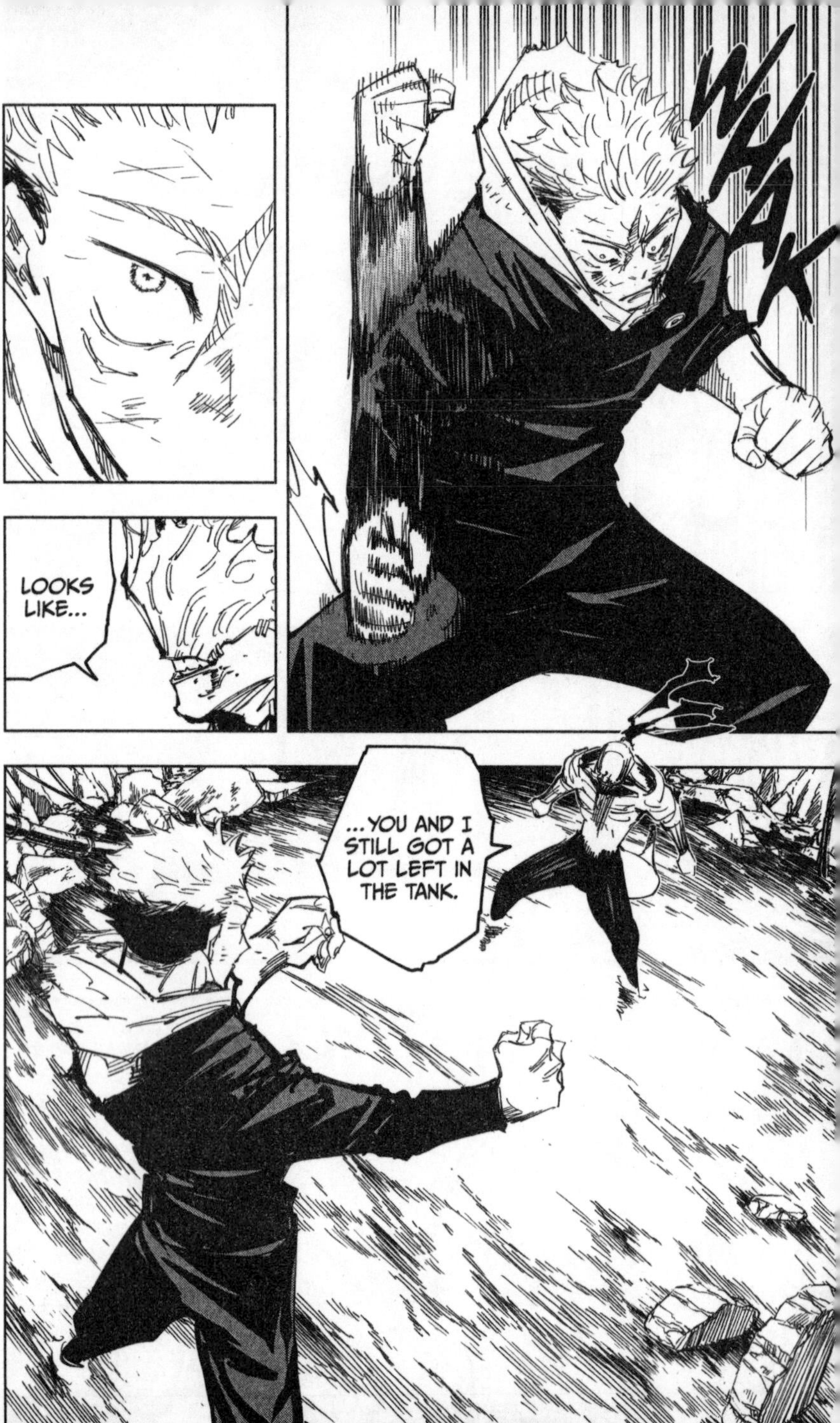
WHAK
LOOKS LIKE...
...YOU AND I STILL GOT A LOT LEFT IN THE TANK.

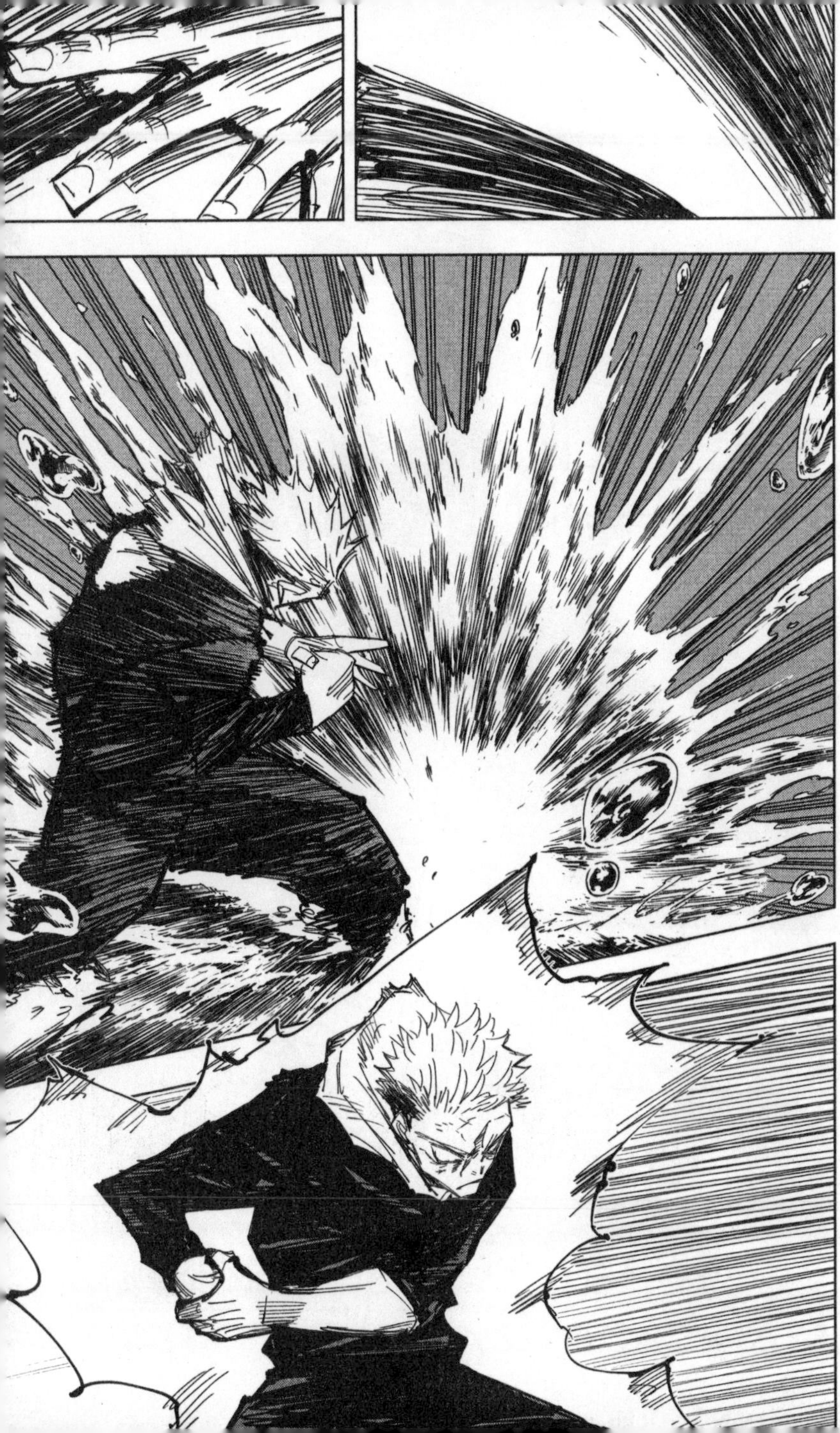

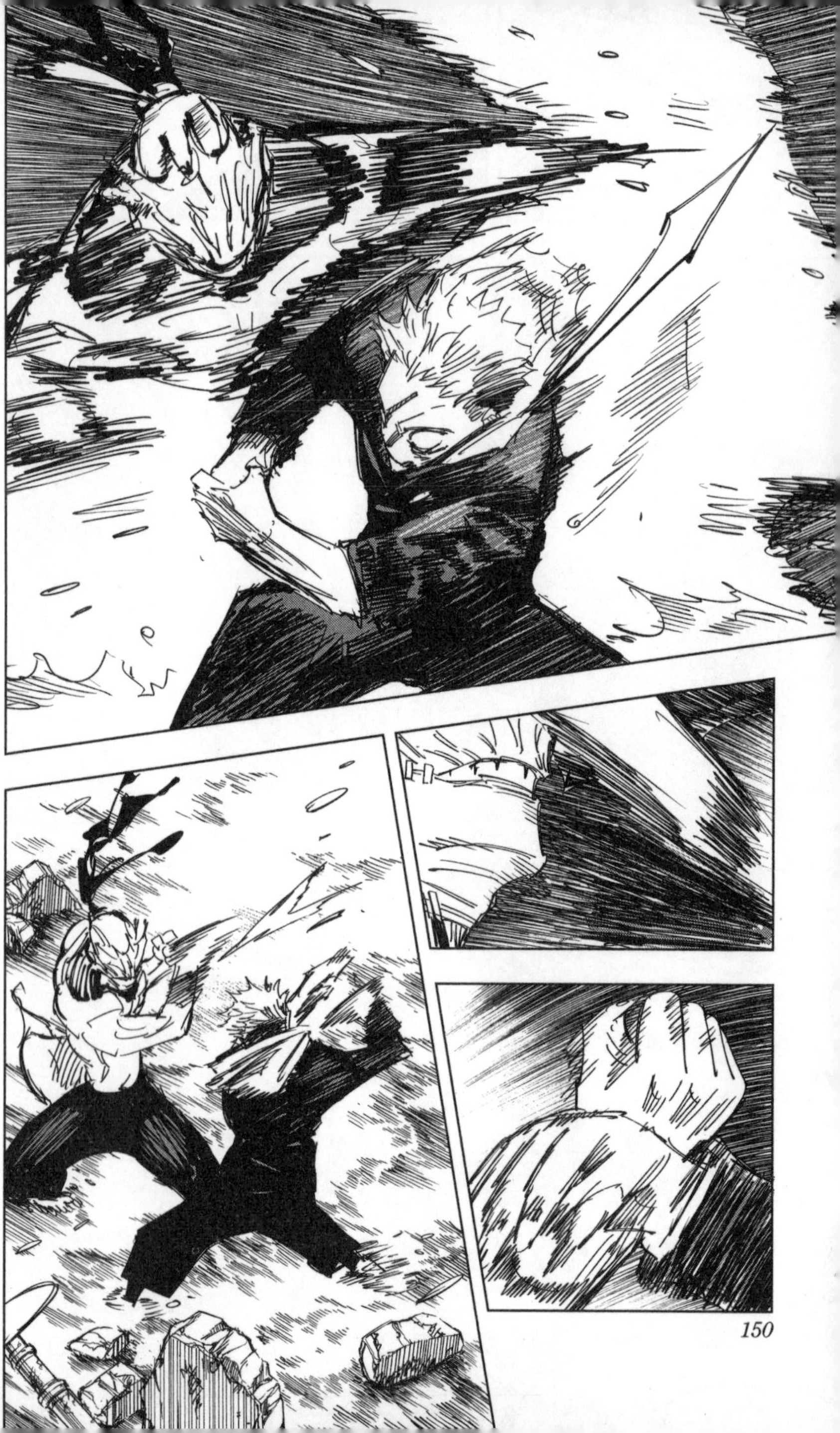

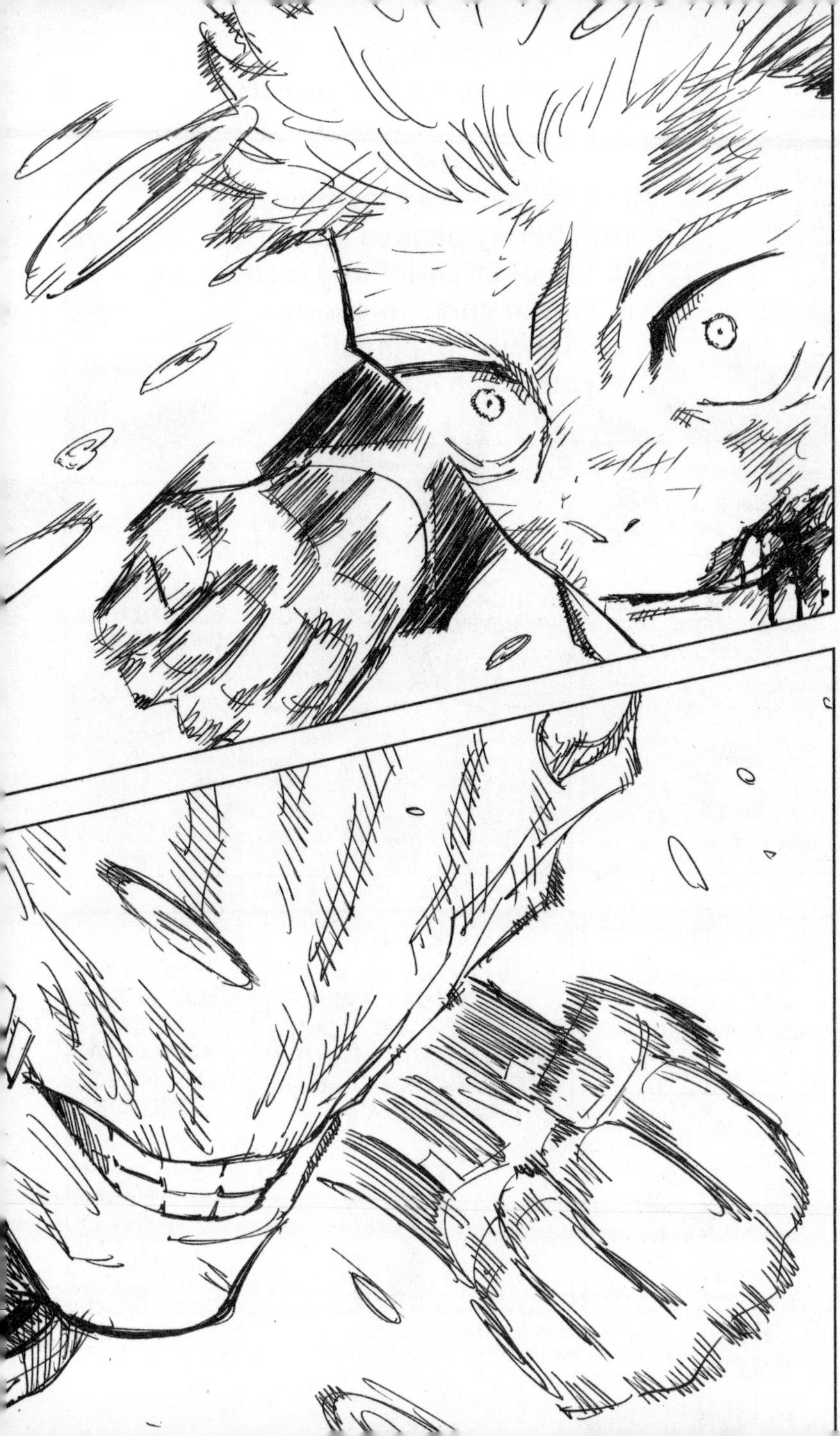

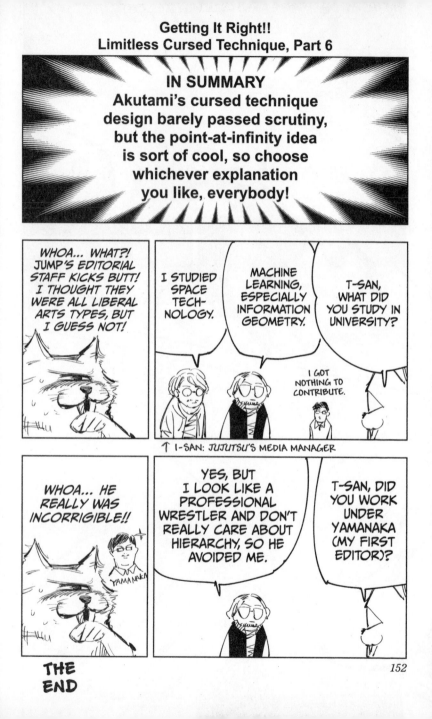

Getting It Right!!
Limitless Cursed Technique, Part 6

IN SUMMARY
Akutami's cursed technique design barely passed scrutiny, but the point-at-infinity idea is sort of cool, so choose whichever explanation you like, everybody!

T-SAN, WHAT DID YOU STUDY IN UNIVERSITY?
MACHINE LEARNING, ESPECIALLY INFORMATION GEOMETRY.
I STUDIED SPACE TECH-NOLOGY.
I GOT NOTHING TO CONTRIBUTE.
WHOA... WHAT?! JUMP'S EDITORIAL STAFF KICKS BUTT! I THOUGHT THEY WERE ALL LIBERAL ARTS TYPES, BUT I GUESS NOT!
↑ I-SAN: JUJUTSU'S MEDIA MANAGER
T-SAN, DID YOU WORK UNDER YAMANAKA (MY FIRST EDITOR)?
YES, BUT I LOOK LIKE A PROFESSIONAL WRESTLER AND DON'T REALLY CARE ABOUT HIERARCHY, SO HE AVOIDED ME.
WHOA... HE REALLY WAS INCORRIGIBLE!!
YAMANAKA

THE END

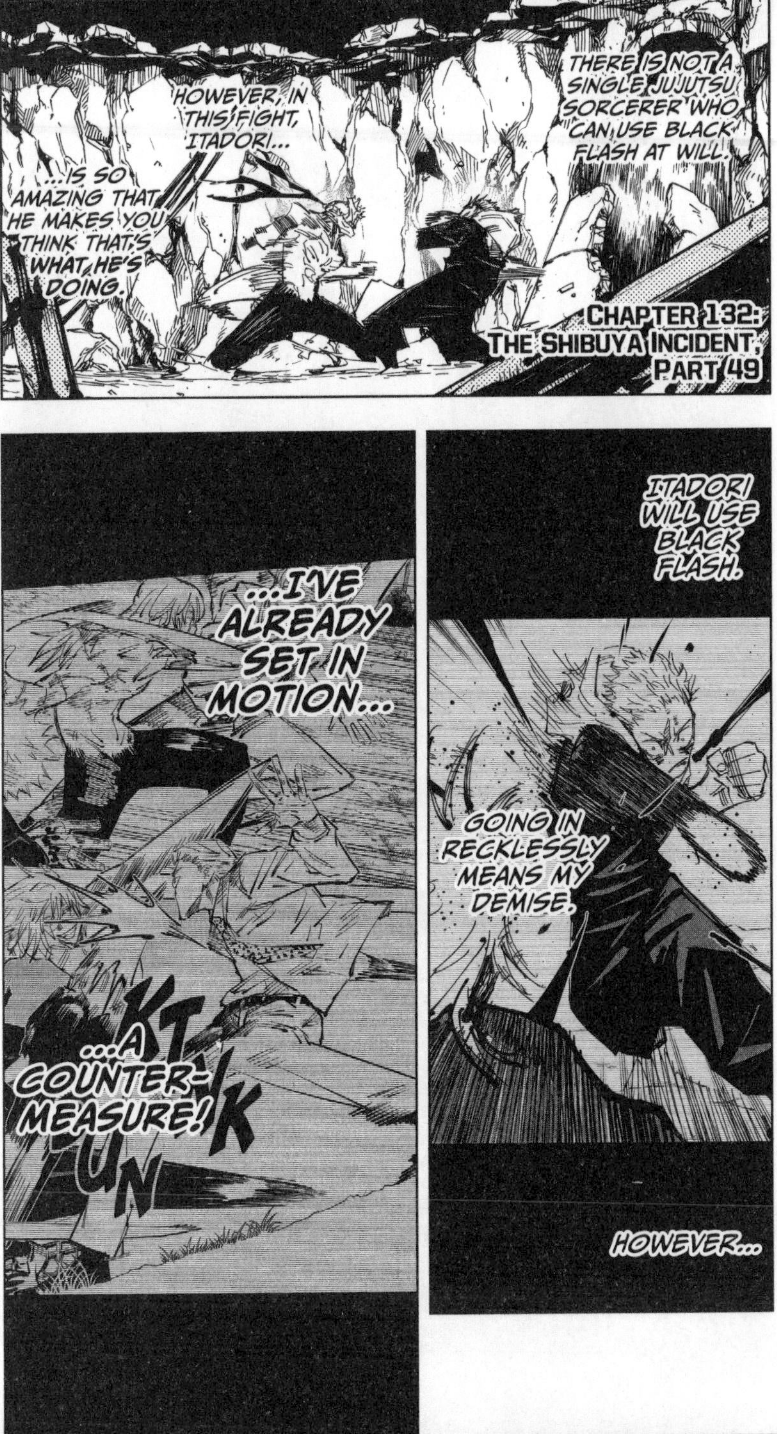
THERE IS NOT A SINGLE JUJUTSU SORCERER WHO CAN USE BLACK FLASH AT WILL.
HOWEVER, IN THIS FIGHT, ITADORI...
...IS SO AMAZING THAT HE MAKES YOU THINK THAT'S WHAT HE'S DOING.
CHAPTER 132: THE SHIBUYA INCIDENT, PART 49
ITADORI WILL USE BLACK FLASH.
GOING IN RECKLESSLY MEANS MY DEMISE.
HOWEVER...
...I'VE ALREADY SET IN MOTION...
...A COUNTER-MEASURE!
KTUNK

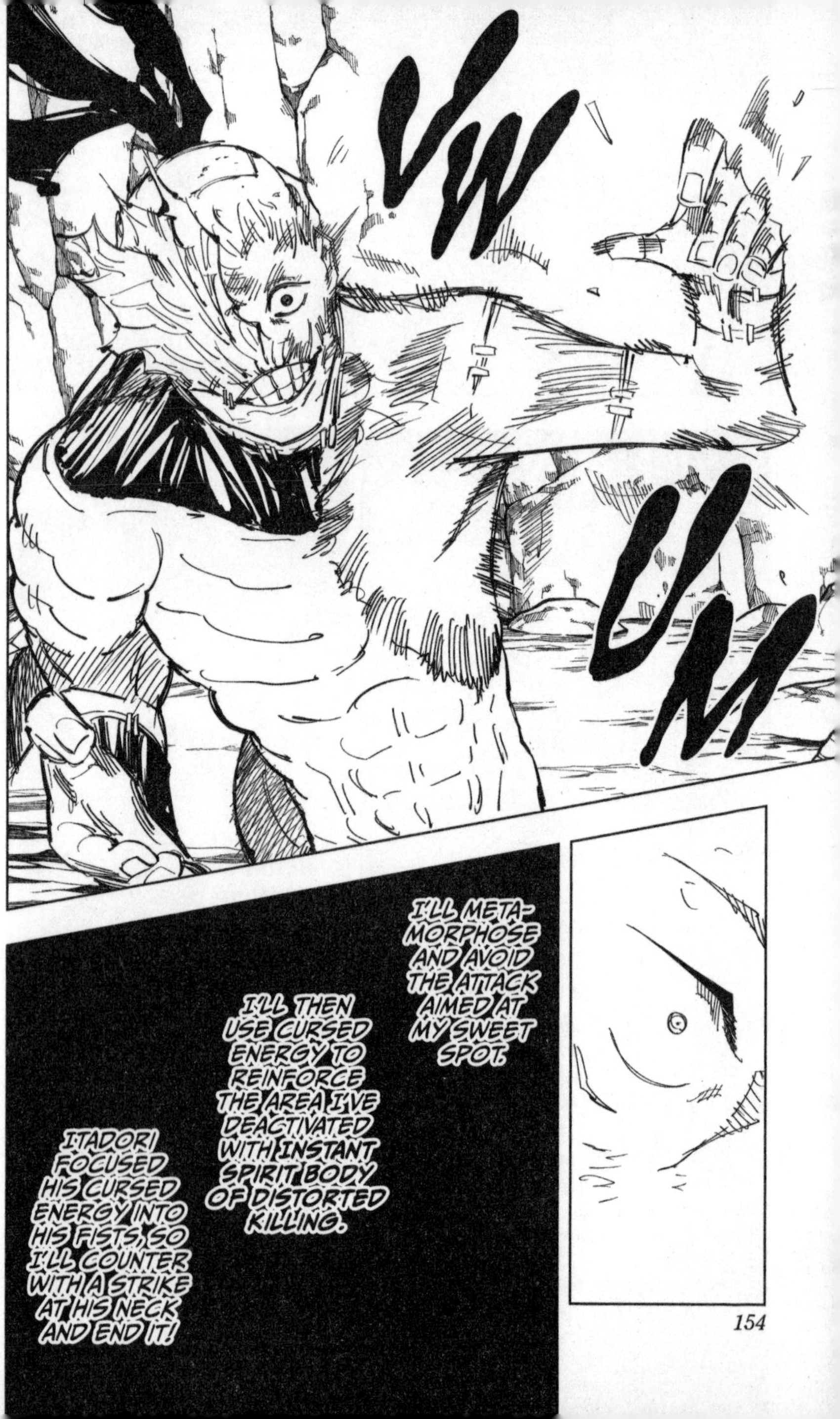
VWUM
I'LL METAMORPHOSE AND AVOID THE ATTACK AIMED AT MY SWEET SPOT.
I'LL THEN USE CURSED ENERGY TO REINFORCE THE AREA I'VE DEACTIVATED WITH INSTANT SPIRIT BODY OF DISTORTED KILLING.
ITADORI FOCUSED HIS CURSED ENERGY INTO HIS FISTS, SO I'LL COUNTER WITH A STRIKE AT HIS NECK AND END IT!

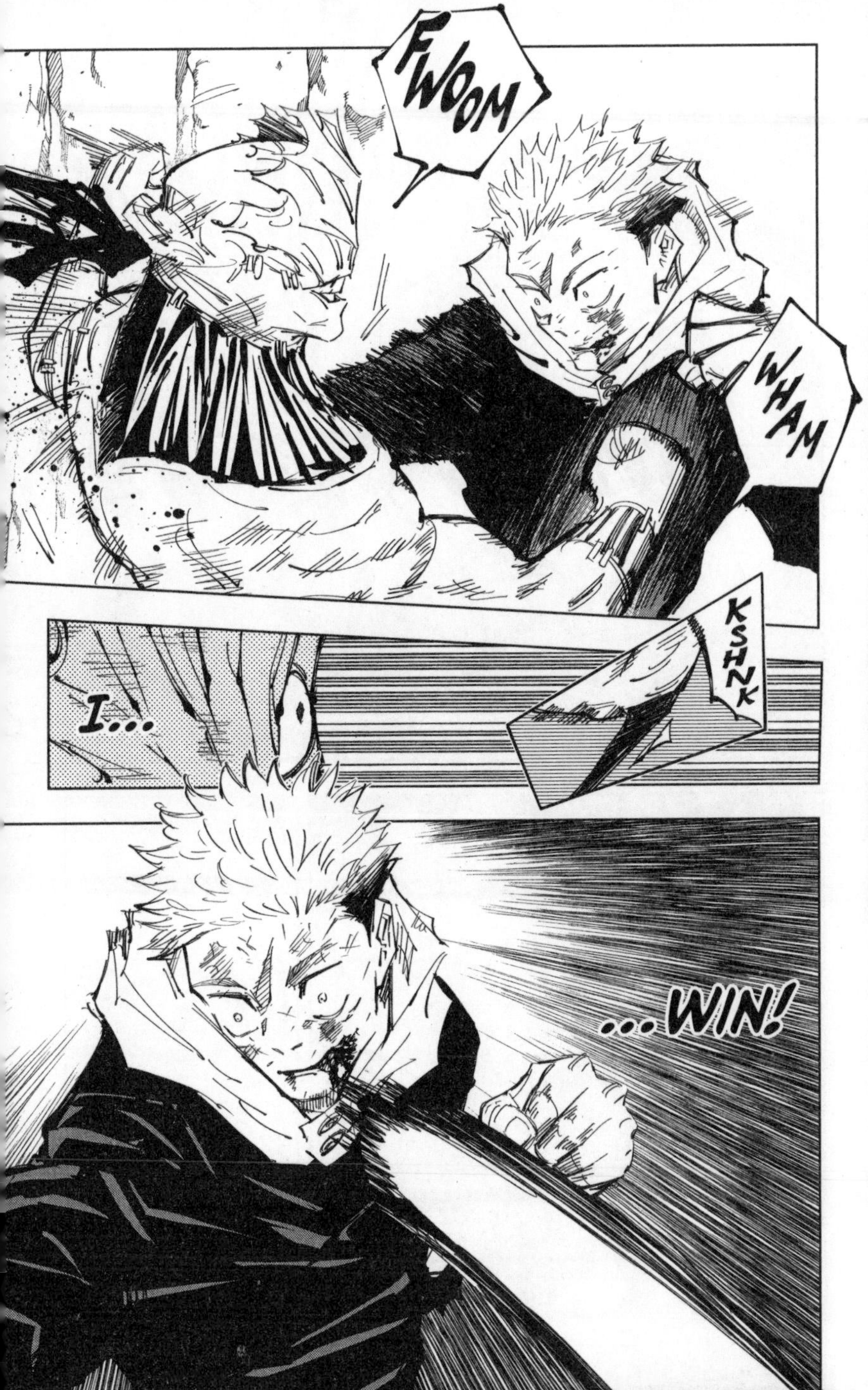
FWOOM
WHAM
KSHNK
I...
...WIN!

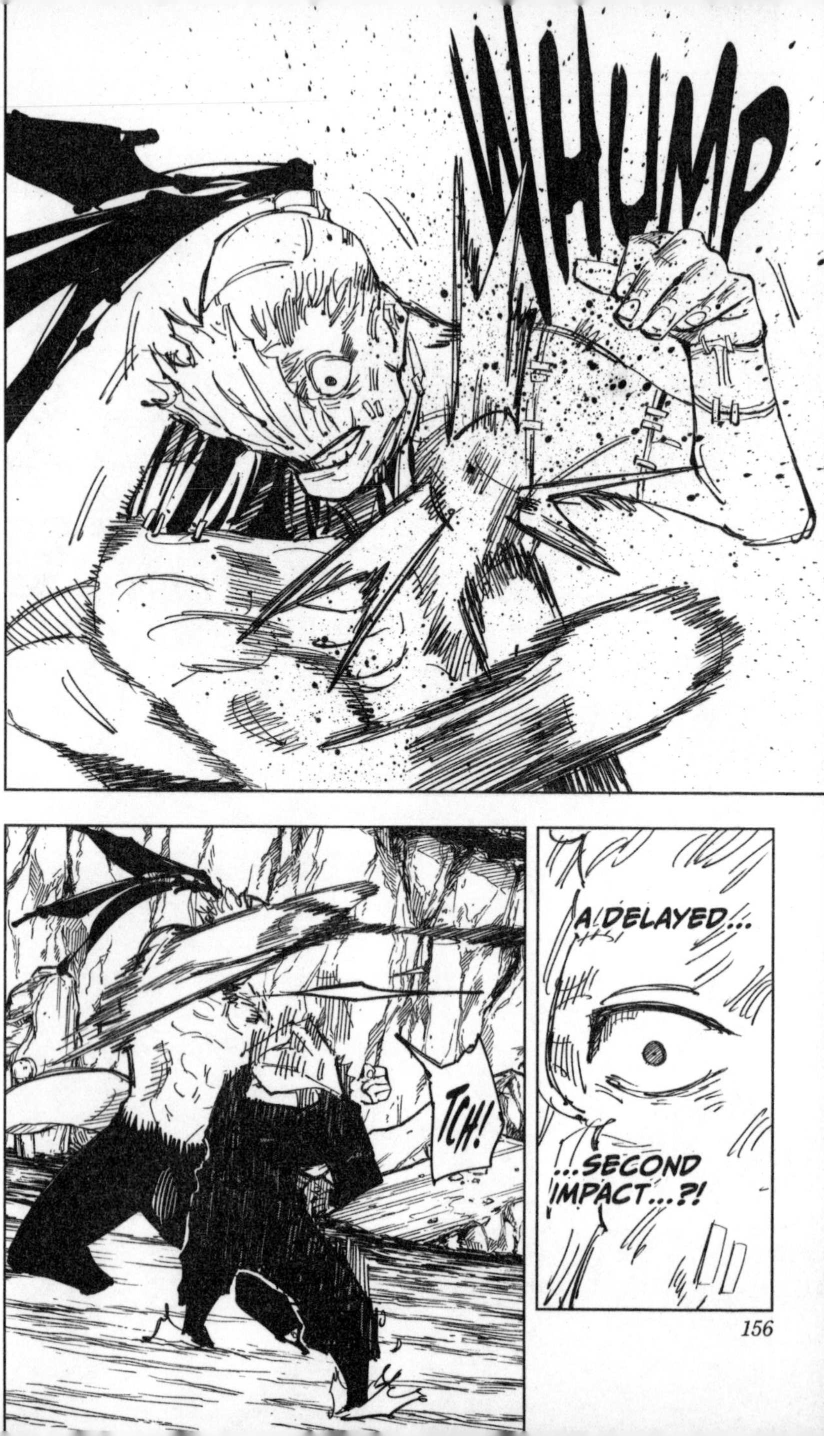
WHUMP
A DELAYED...
...SECOND IMPACT...?!
TCH!

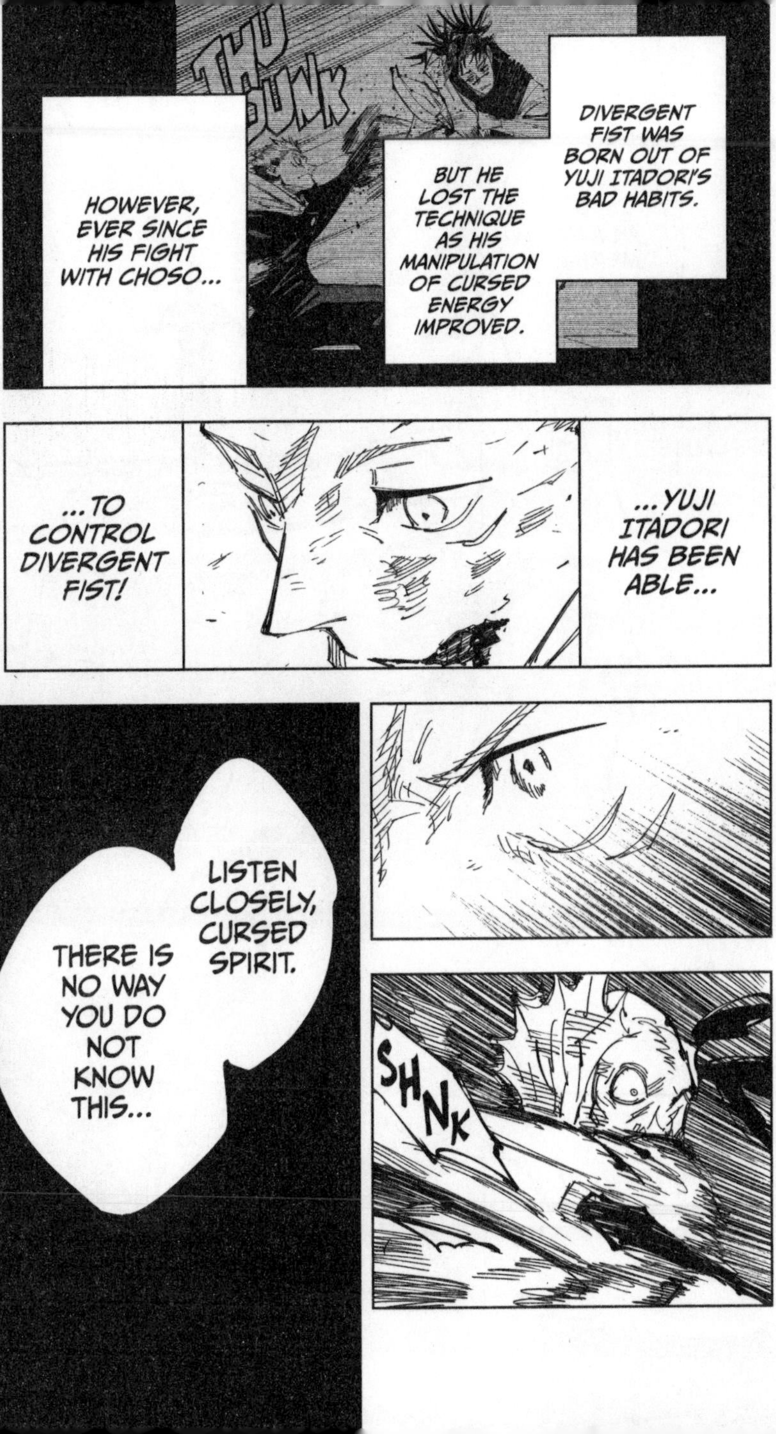
DIVERGENT FIST WAS BORN OUT OF YUJI ITADORI'S BAD HABITS.
BUT HE LOST THE TECHNIQUE AS HIS MANIPULATION OF CURSED ENERGY IMPROVED.
THUNK
HOWEVER, EVER SINCE HIS FIGHT WITH CHOSO...
...YUJI ITADORI HAS BEEN ABLE...
...TO CONTROL DIVERGENT FIST!
SHNK
LISTEN CLOSELY, CURSED SPIRIT.
THERE IS NO WAY YOU DO NOT KNOW THIS...

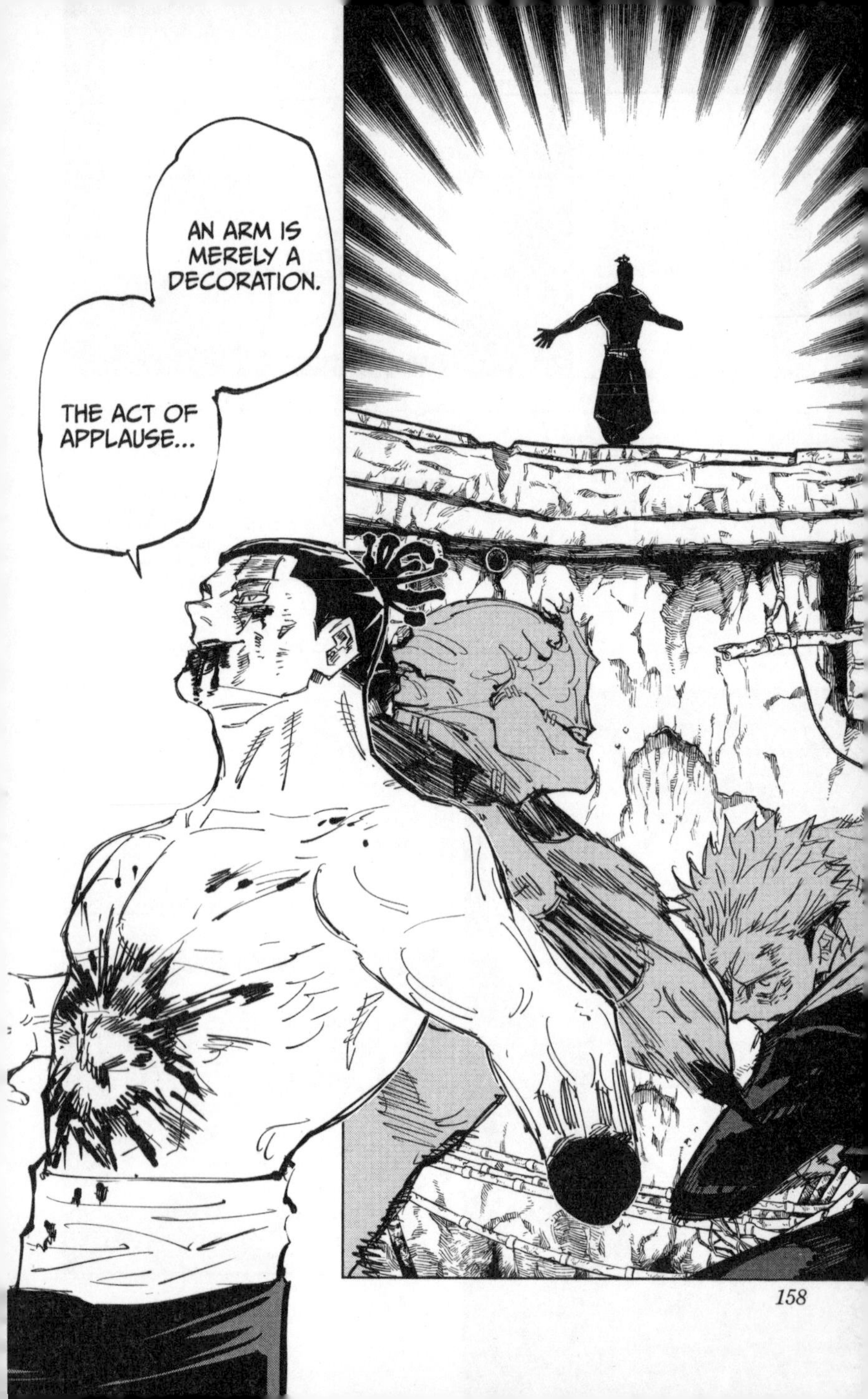
AN ARM IS MERELY A DECORATION.
THE ACT OF APPLAUSE...

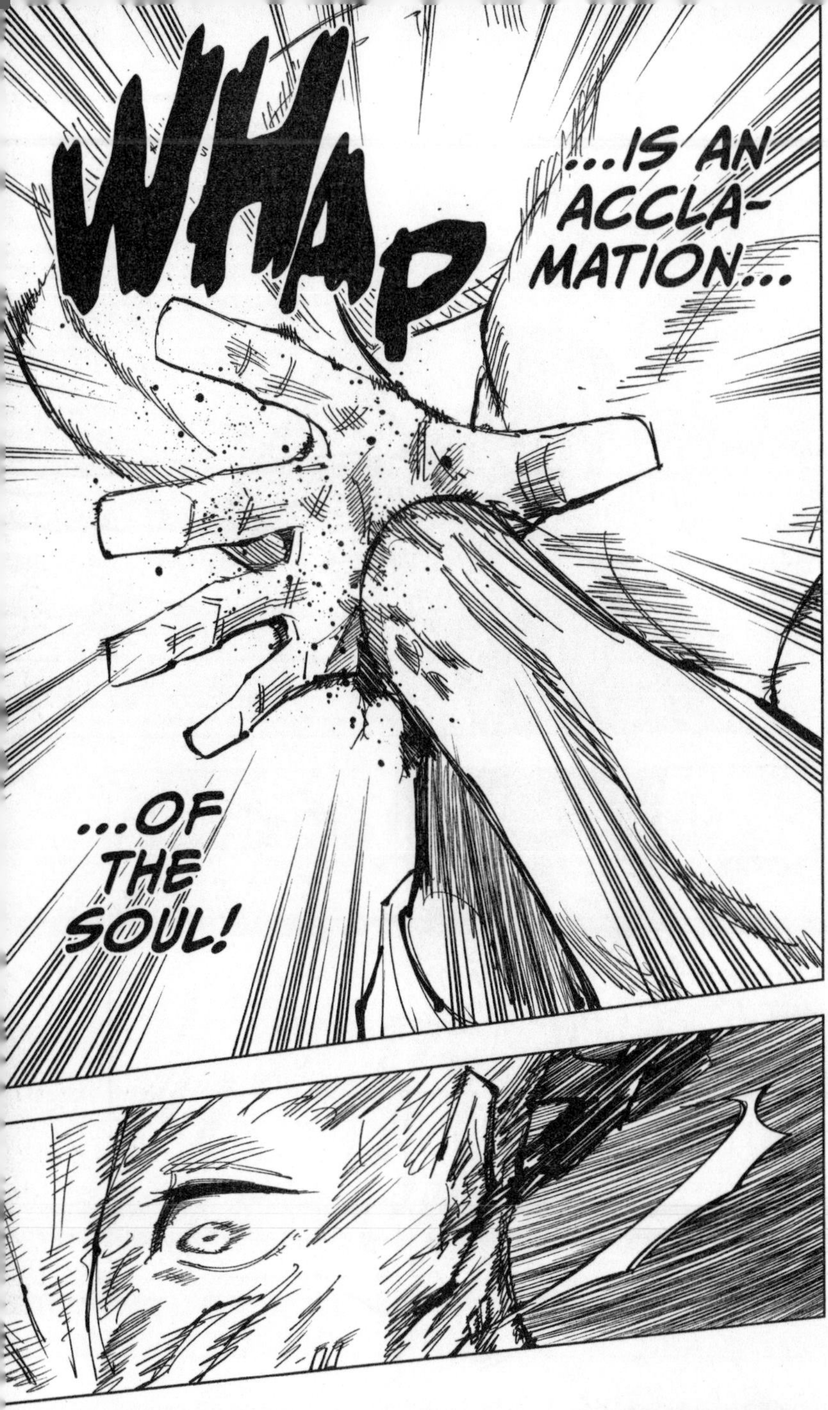
...IS AN ACCLA-MATION...
WHAP
...OF THE SOUL!

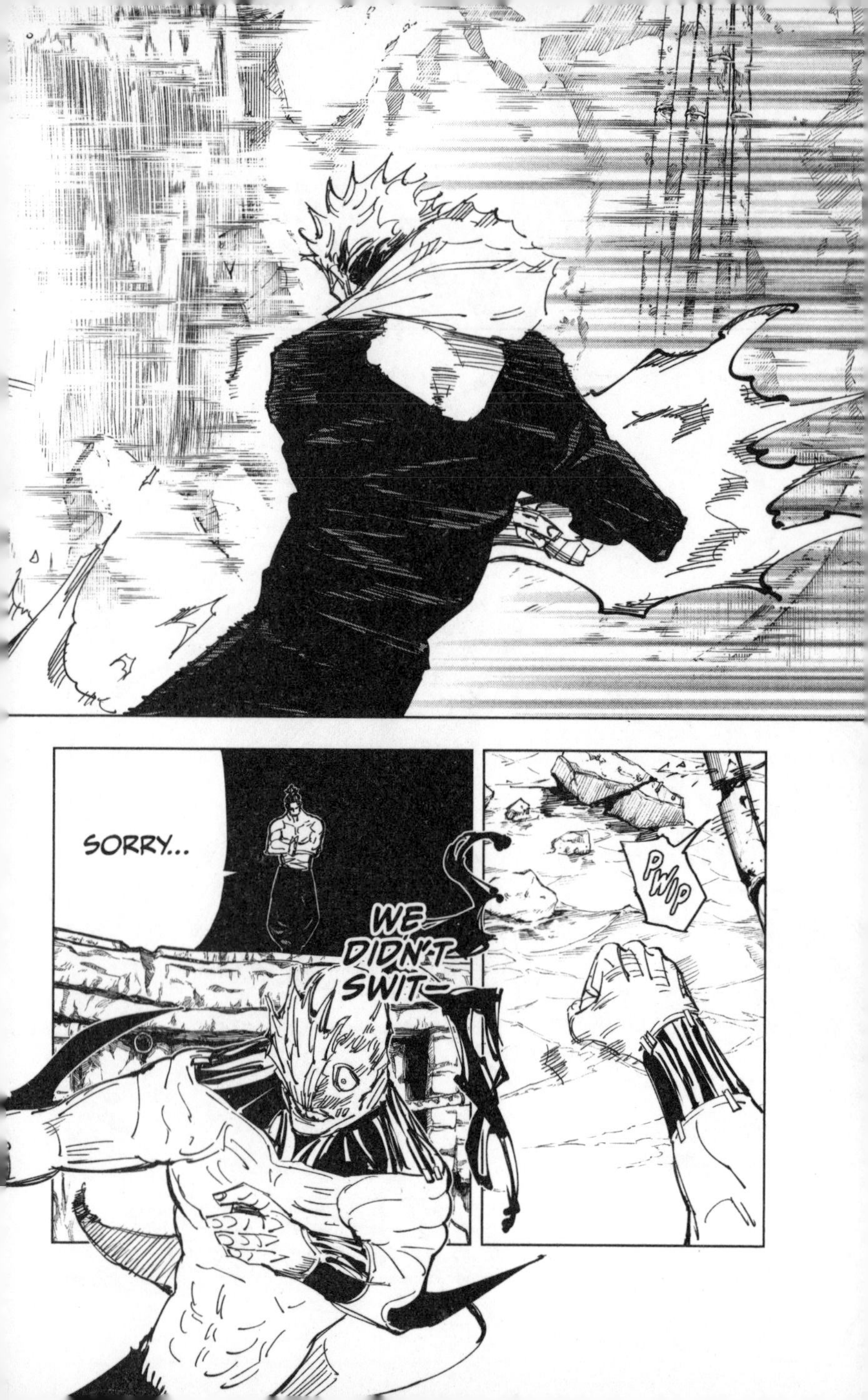
PWIP
SORRY...
WE DIDN'T SWIT—

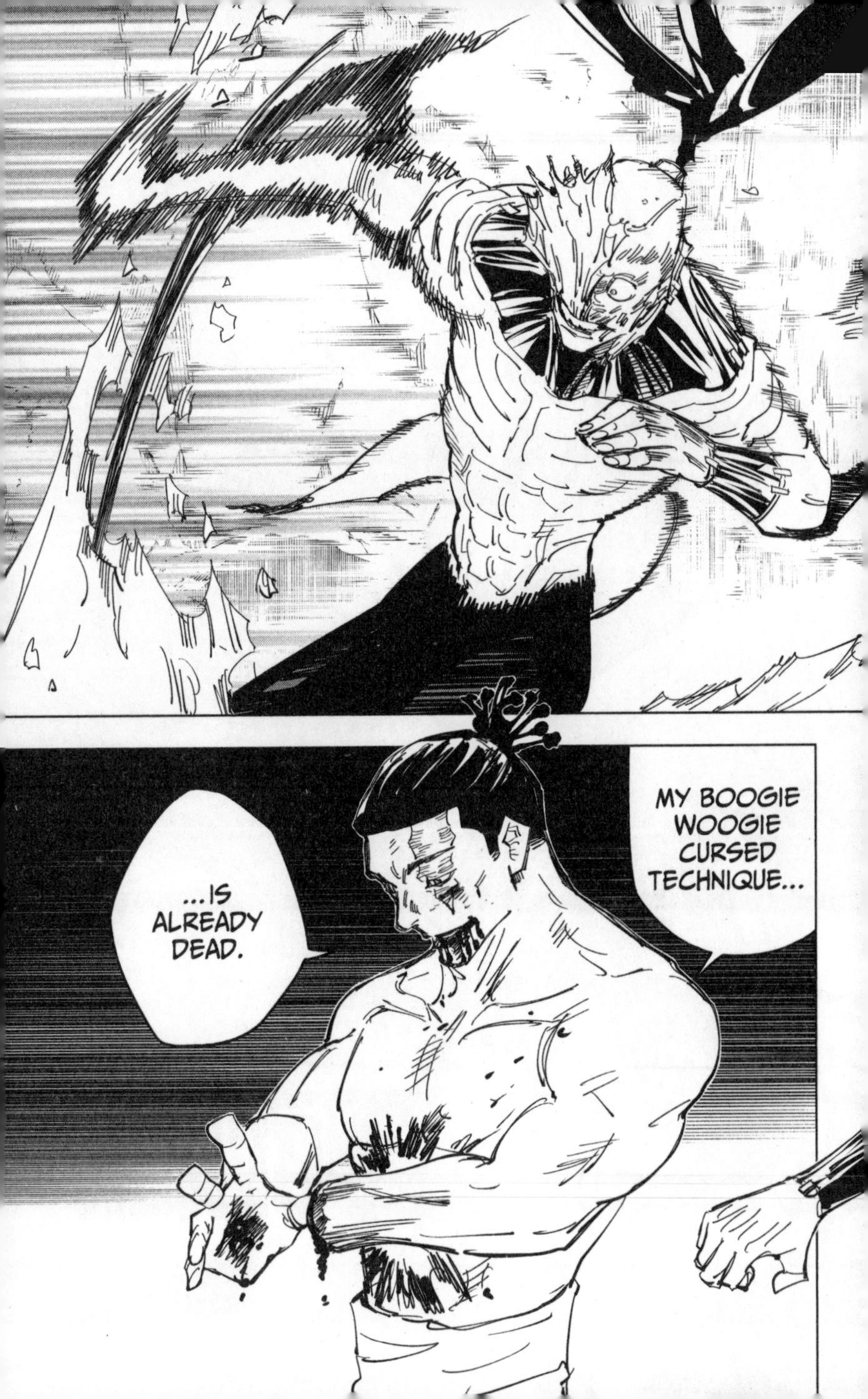
MY BOOGIE WOOGIE CURSED TECHNIQUE...
...IS ALREADY DEAD.

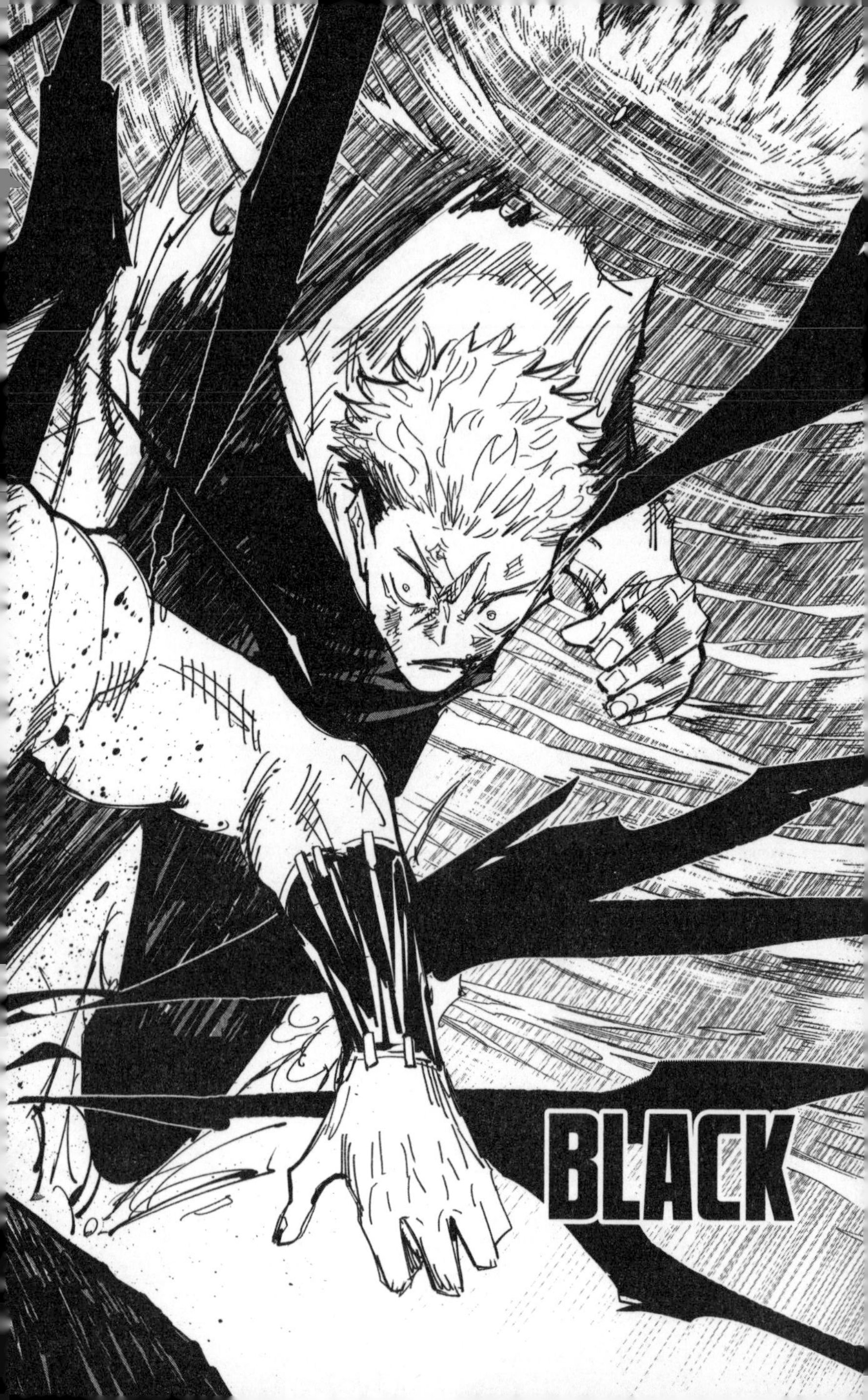
BLACK

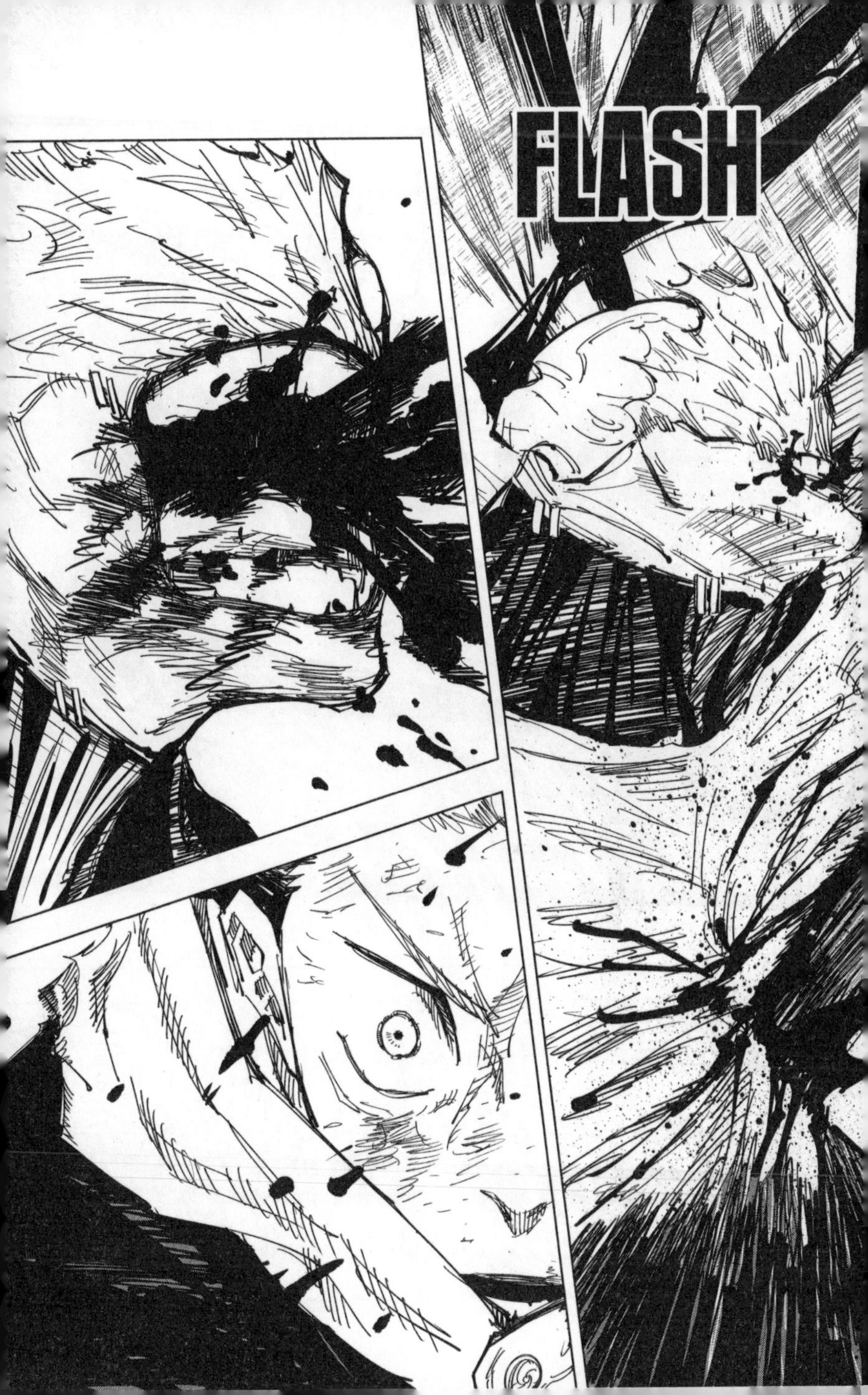
FLASH

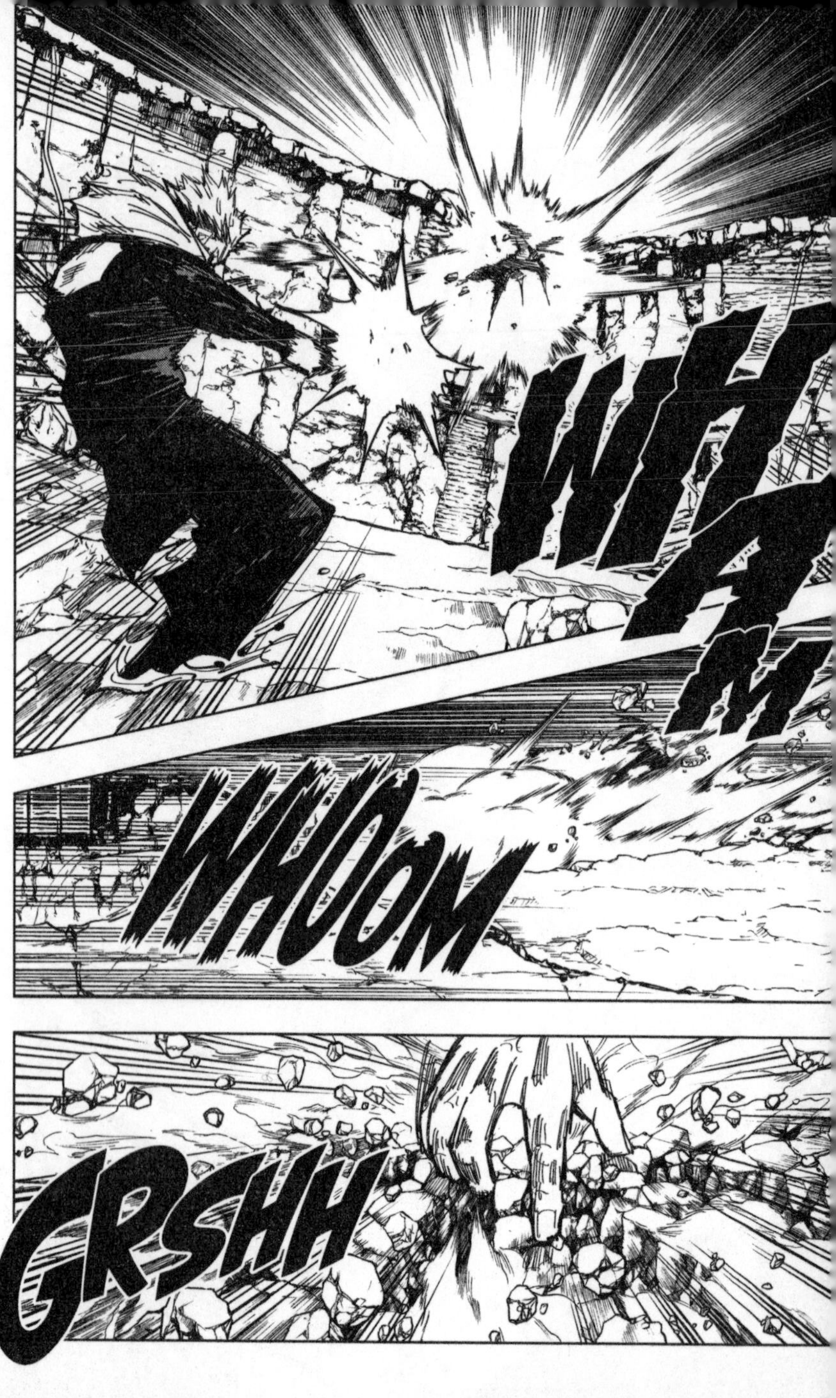
WHAM
WHOOM
GRSHH

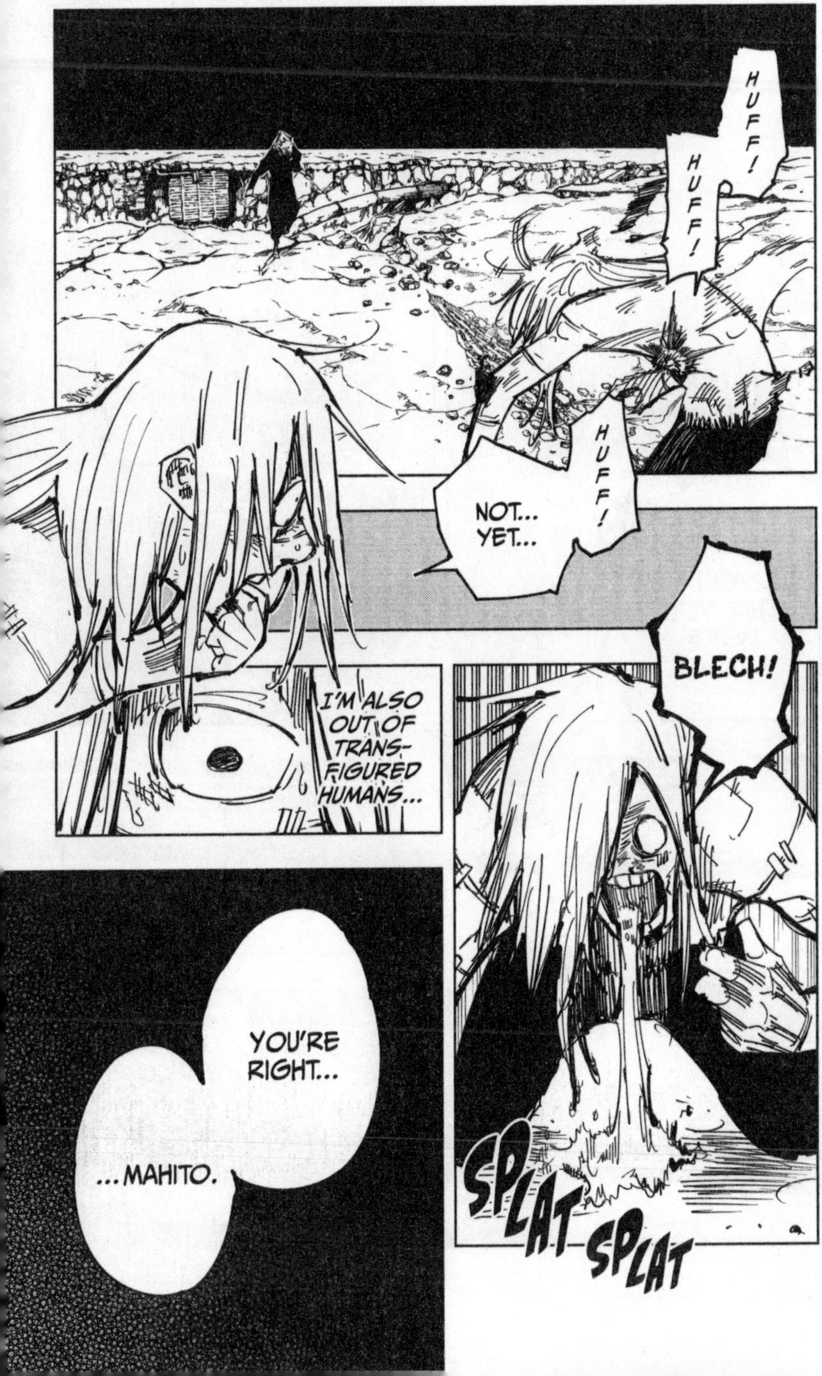
HUFF! HUFF!
HUFF! HUFF!
NOT... YET...
BLECH!
SPLAT SPLAT
I'M ALSO OUT OF TRANS-FIGURED HUMANS...
YOU'RE RIGHT...
...MAHITO.

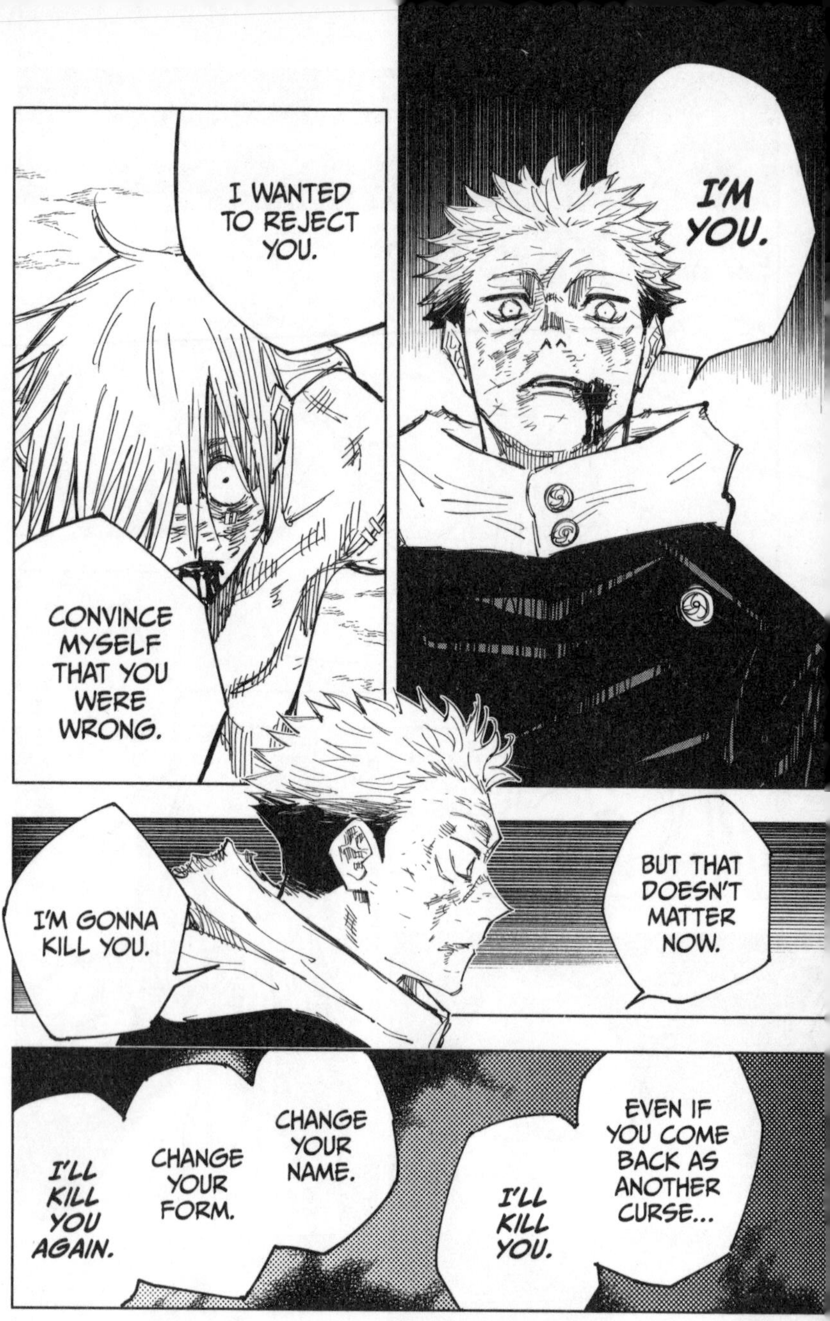
I'M YOU.
I WANTED TO REJECT YOU.
CONVINCE MYSELF THAT YOU WERE WRONG.
BUT THAT DOESN'T MATTER NOW.
I'M GONNA KILL YOU.
EVEN IF YOU COME BACK AS ANOTHER CURSE...
I'LL KILL YOU.
CHANGE YOUR NAME.
CHANGE YOUR FORM.
I'LL KILL YOU AGAIN.

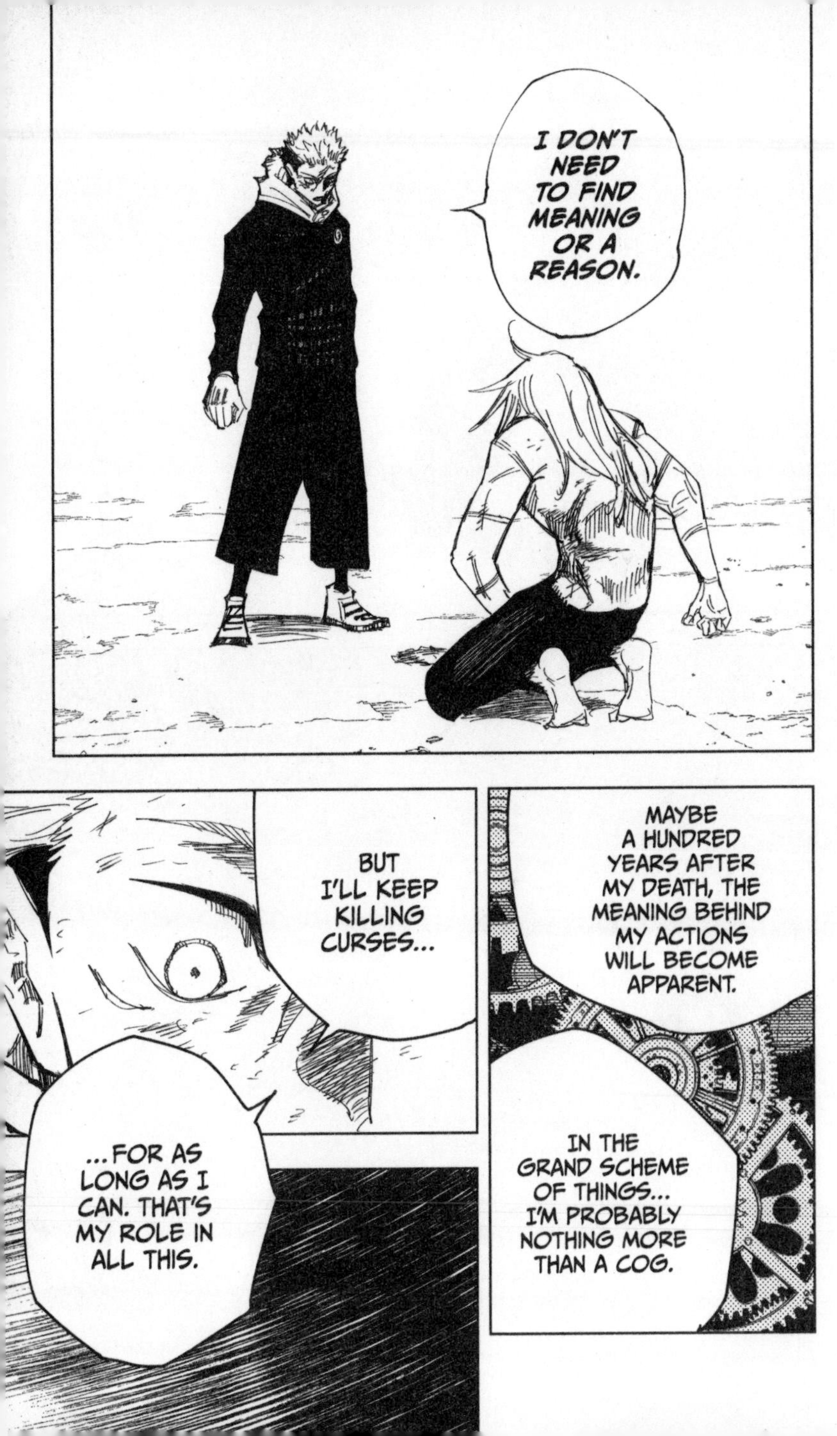
I DON'T NEED TO FIND MEANING OR A REASON.
MAYBE A HUNDRED YEARS AFTER MY DEATH, THE MEANING BEHIND MY ACTIONS WILL BECOME APPARENT.
IN THE GRAND SCHEME OF THINGS... I'M PROBABLY NOTHING MORE THAN A COG.
BUT I'LL KEEP KILLING CURSES...
...FOR AS LONG AS I CAN. THAT'S MY ROLE IN ALL THIS.

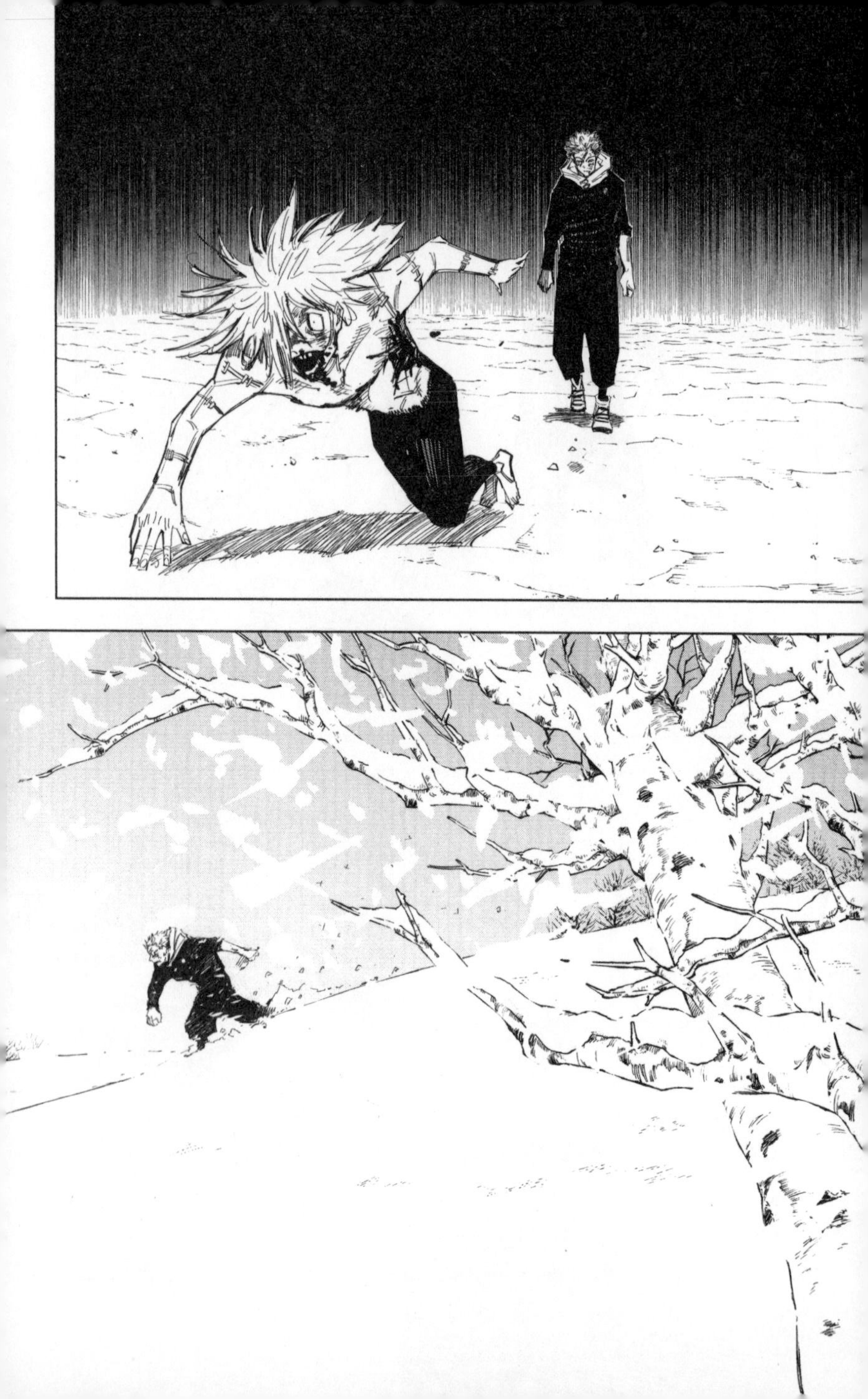

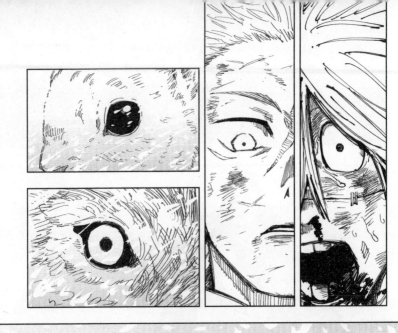

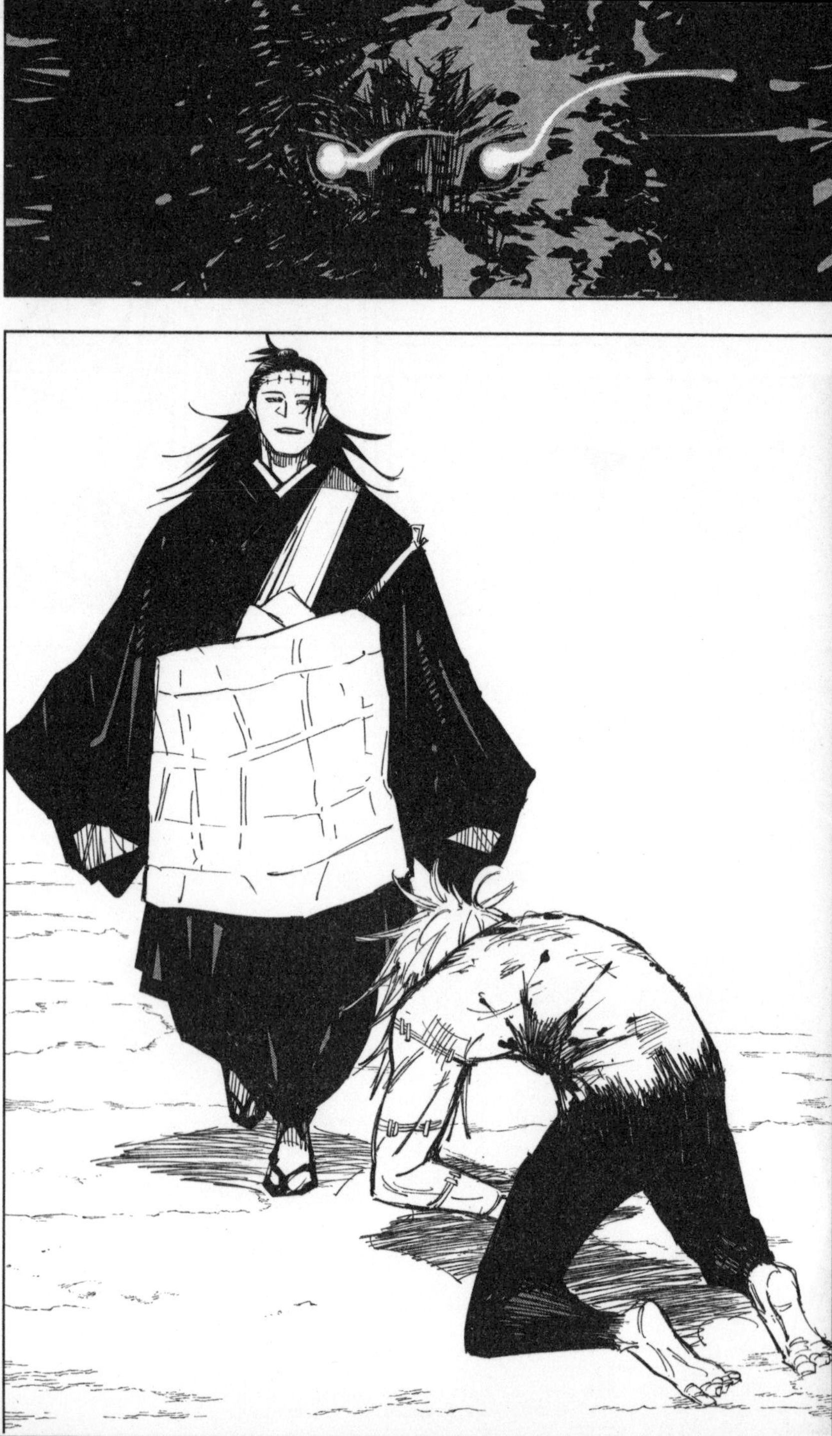

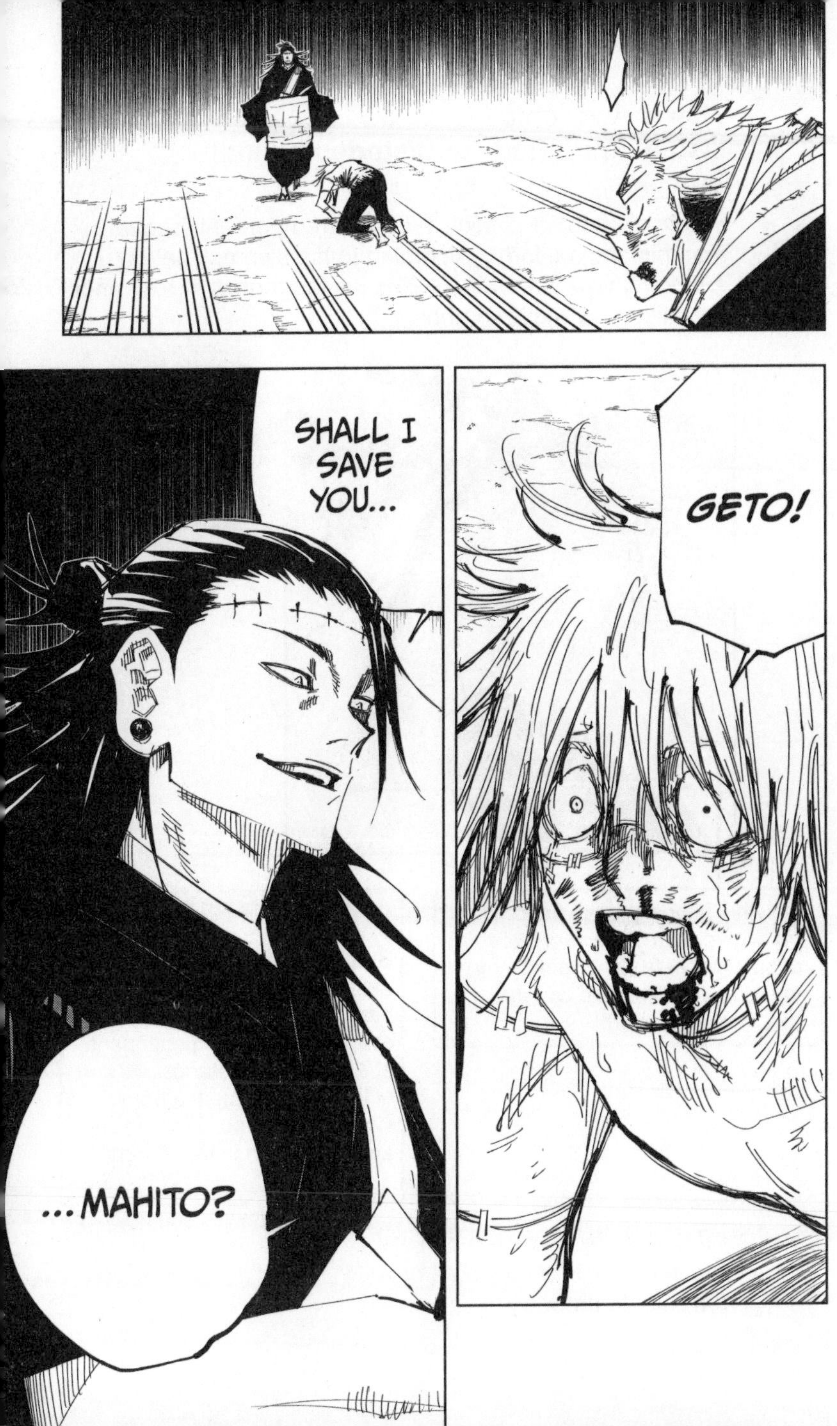
GETO!
SHALL I SAVE YOU...
...MAHITO?

This Is Awesome!!
Instant Spirit Body of Distorted Killing!!

• Mahito's unbridled soul. Two hundred percent tougher than his original form (according to his own estimates). A binding vow further increases his toughness in exchange for halting his metamorphosis.

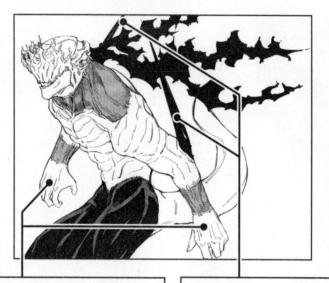

Only his hands are like their original form. In other words, even when in Instant Spirit Body of Distorted Killing, he can use Idle Transfiguration!!

Blades
Due to a binding vow shortening the metamorphosis cycle, he hardly sacrafices any toughness even when catching opponents at a moderate distance. It's sort of like Senku Kogetsu from *World Trigger*, so I didn't include an explanation in the manga!

• If Itadori hadn't nailed him with Black Flash, Mahito would have torn him to shreds.

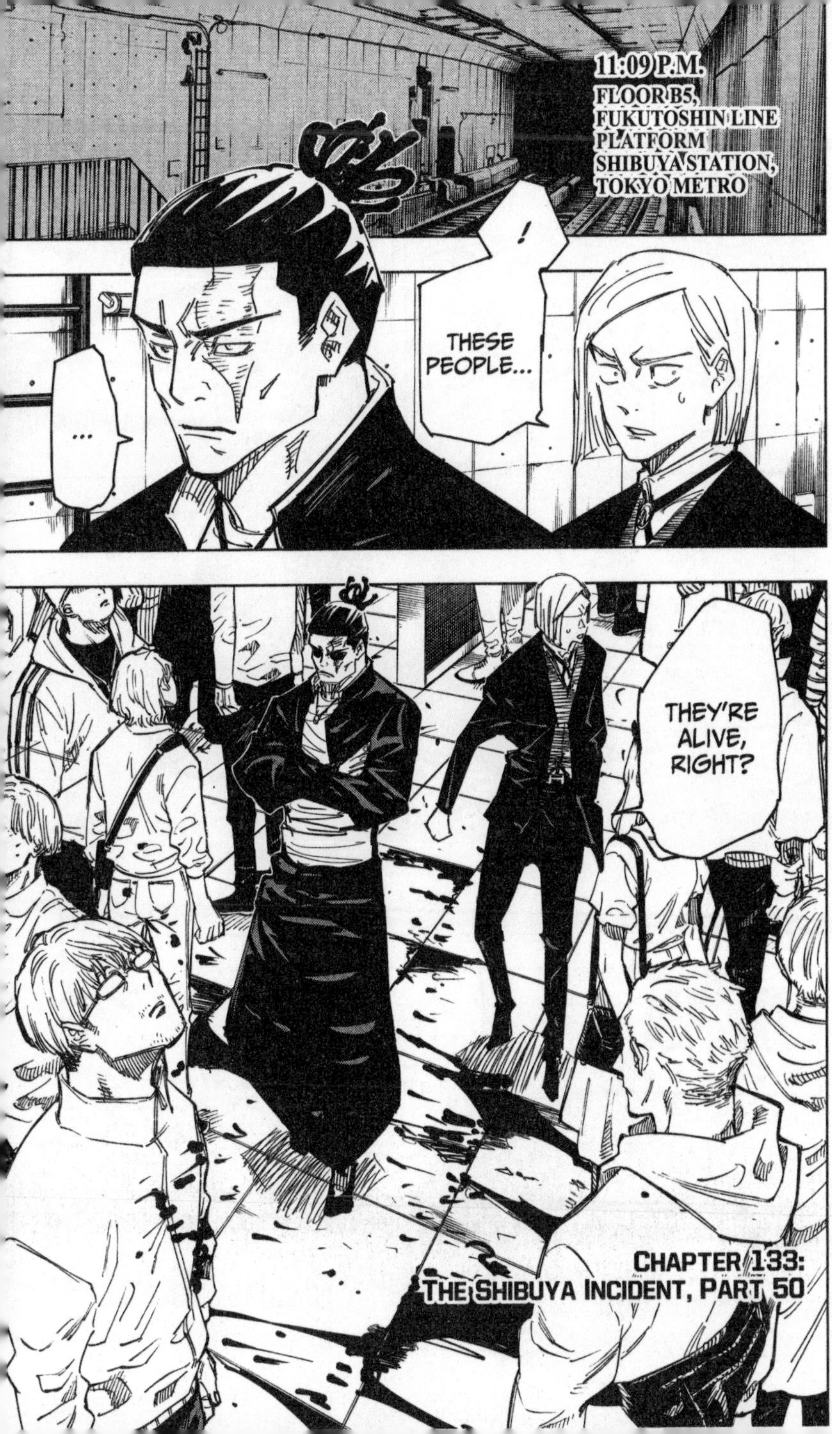
11:09 P.M.
FLOOR B5, FUKUTOSHIN LINE PLATFORM SHIBUYA STATION, TOKYO METRO
!
THESE PEOPLE...
...
THEY'RE ALIVE, RIGHT?
CHAPTER 133: THE SHIBUYA INCIDENT, PART 50

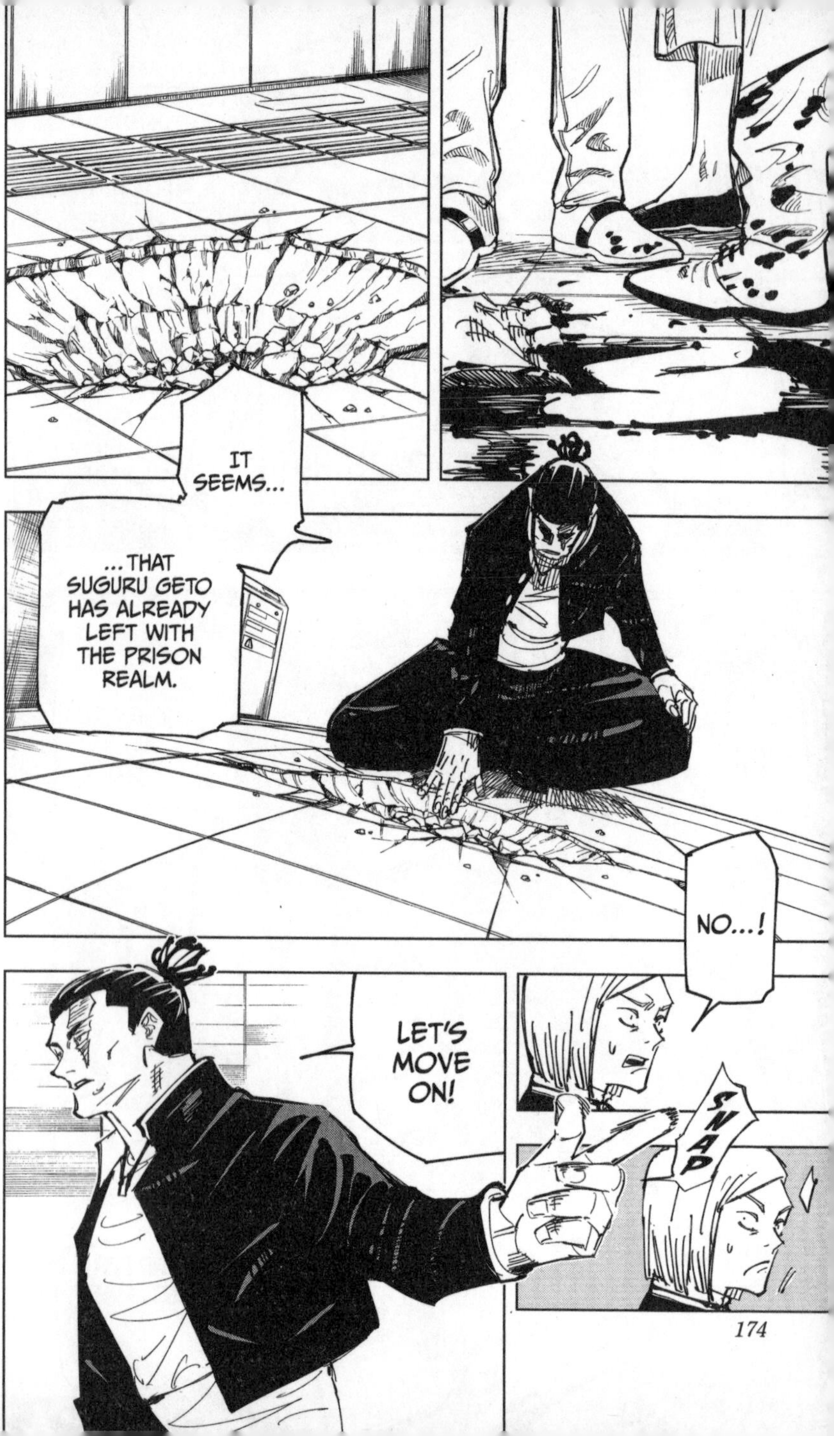
IT SEEMS...
...THAT SUGURU GETO HAS ALREADY LEFT WITH THE PRISON REALM.
NO...!
LET'S MOVE ON!
SNAP

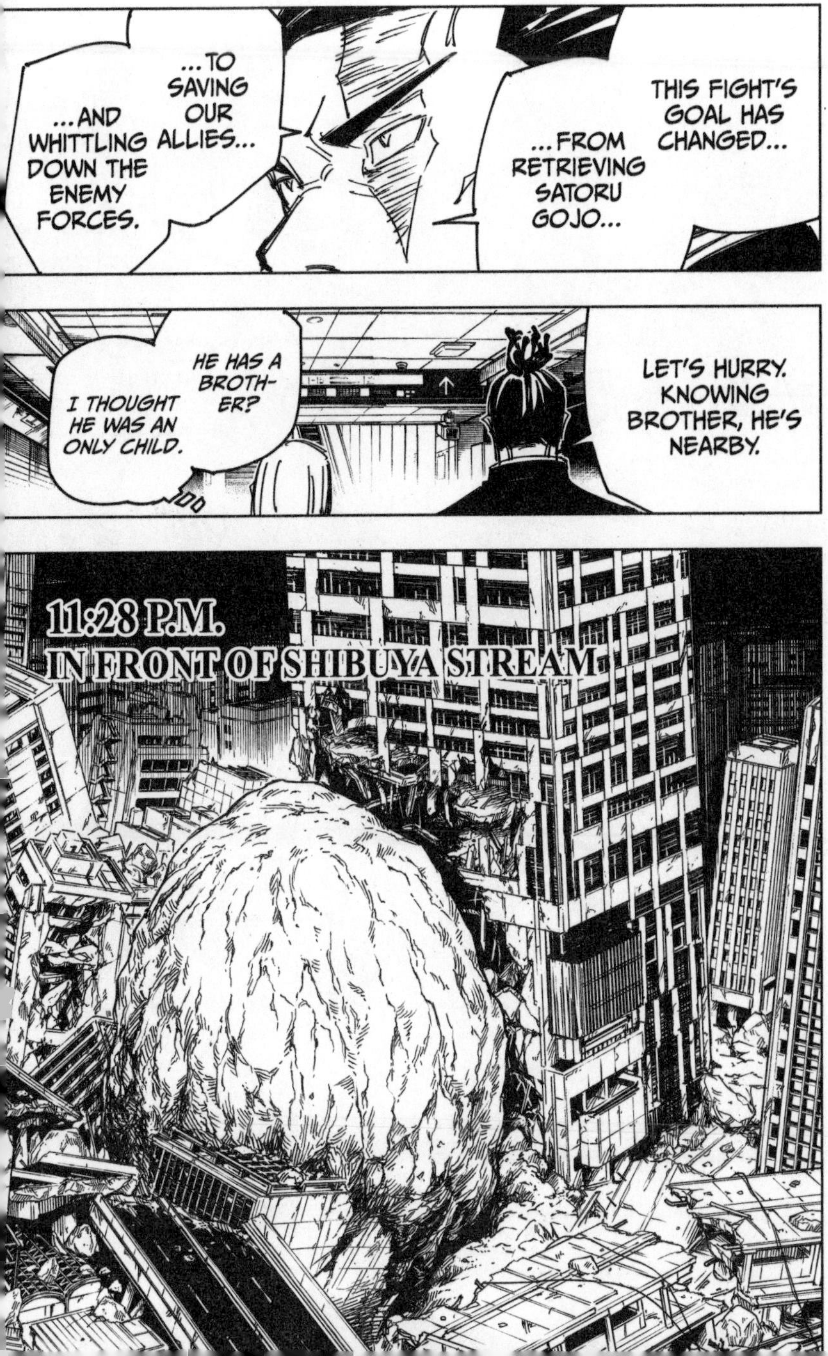
THIS FIGHT'S GOAL HAS CHANGED...
...FROM RETRIEVING SATORU GOJO...
...TO SAVING OUR ALLIES...
...AND WHITTLING DOWN THE ENEMY FORCES.
LET'S HURRY. KNOWING BROTHER, HE'S NEARBY.
HE HAS A BROTHER?
I THOUGHT HE WAS AN ONLY CHILD.
11:28 P.M.
IN FRONT OF SHIBUYA STREAM

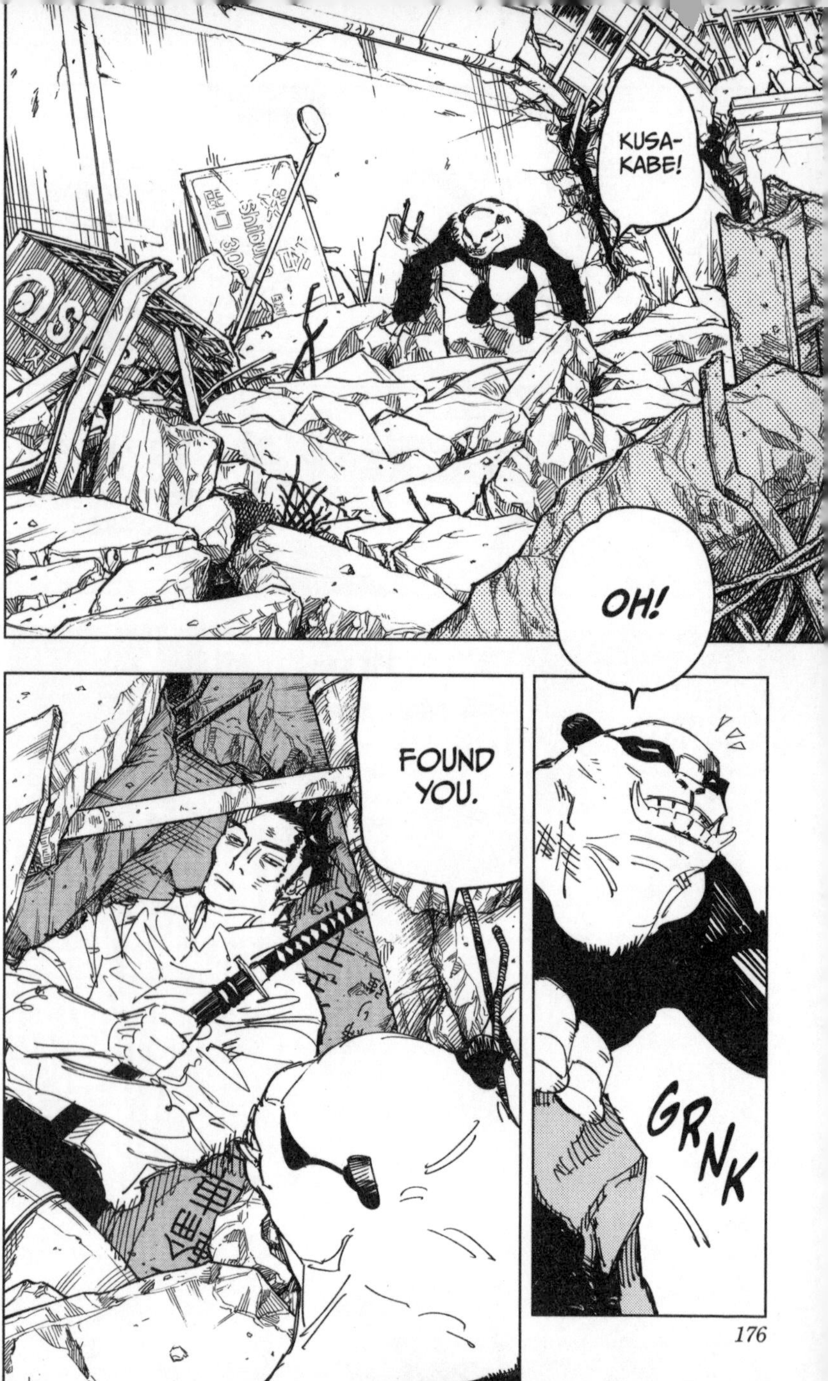
KUSA-
KABE!
OH!
GRNK
FOUND
YOU.

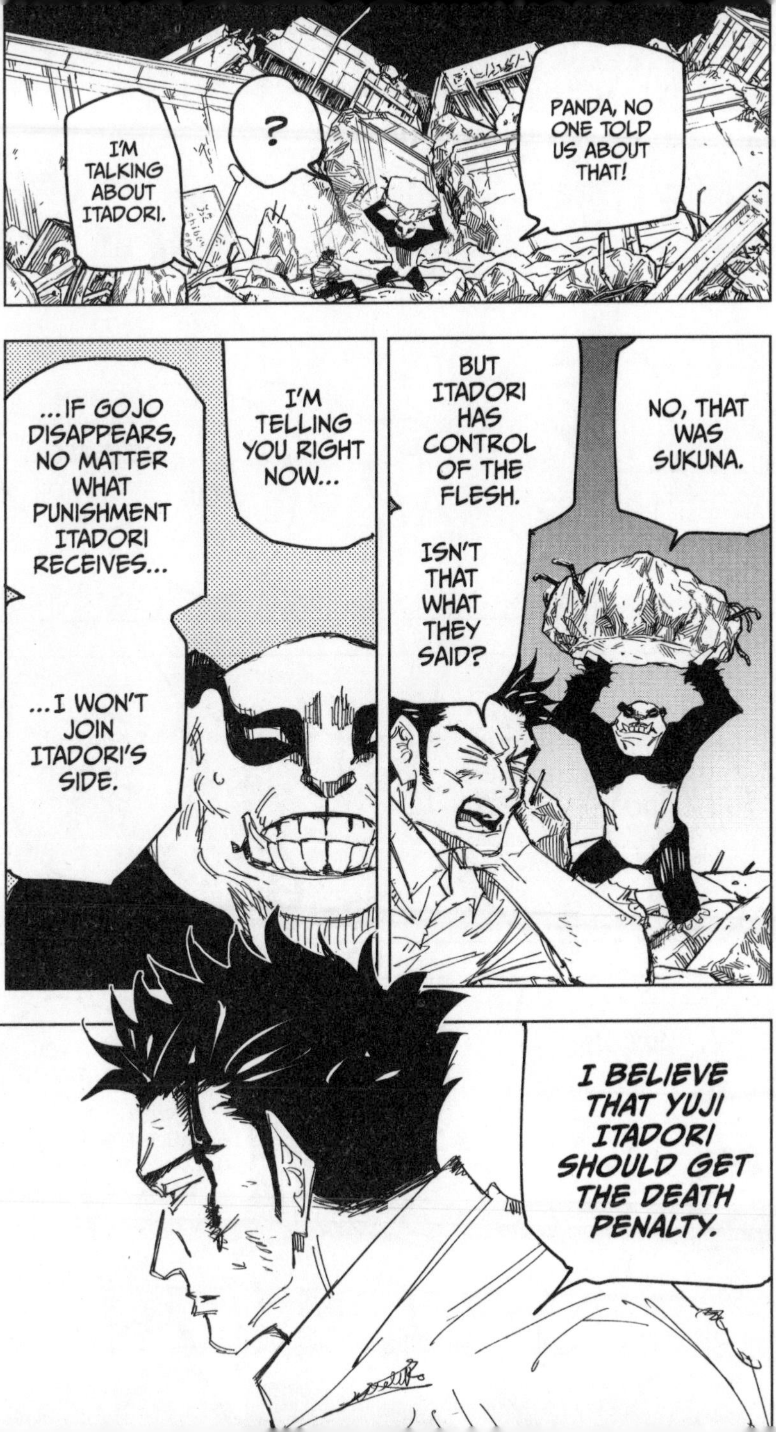
PANDA, NO ONE TOLD US ABOUT THAT!
?
I'M TALKING ABOUT ITADORI.
NO, THAT WAS SUKUNA.
BUT ITADORI HAS CONTROL OF THE FLESH.
ISN'T THAT WHAT THEY SAID?
I'M TELLING YOU RIGHT NOW...
...IF GOJO DISAPPEARS, NO MATTER WHAT PUNISHMENT ITADORI RECEIVES...
...I WON'T JOIN ITADORI'S SIDE.
I BELIEVE THAT YUJI ITADORI SHOULD GET THE DEATH PENALTY.

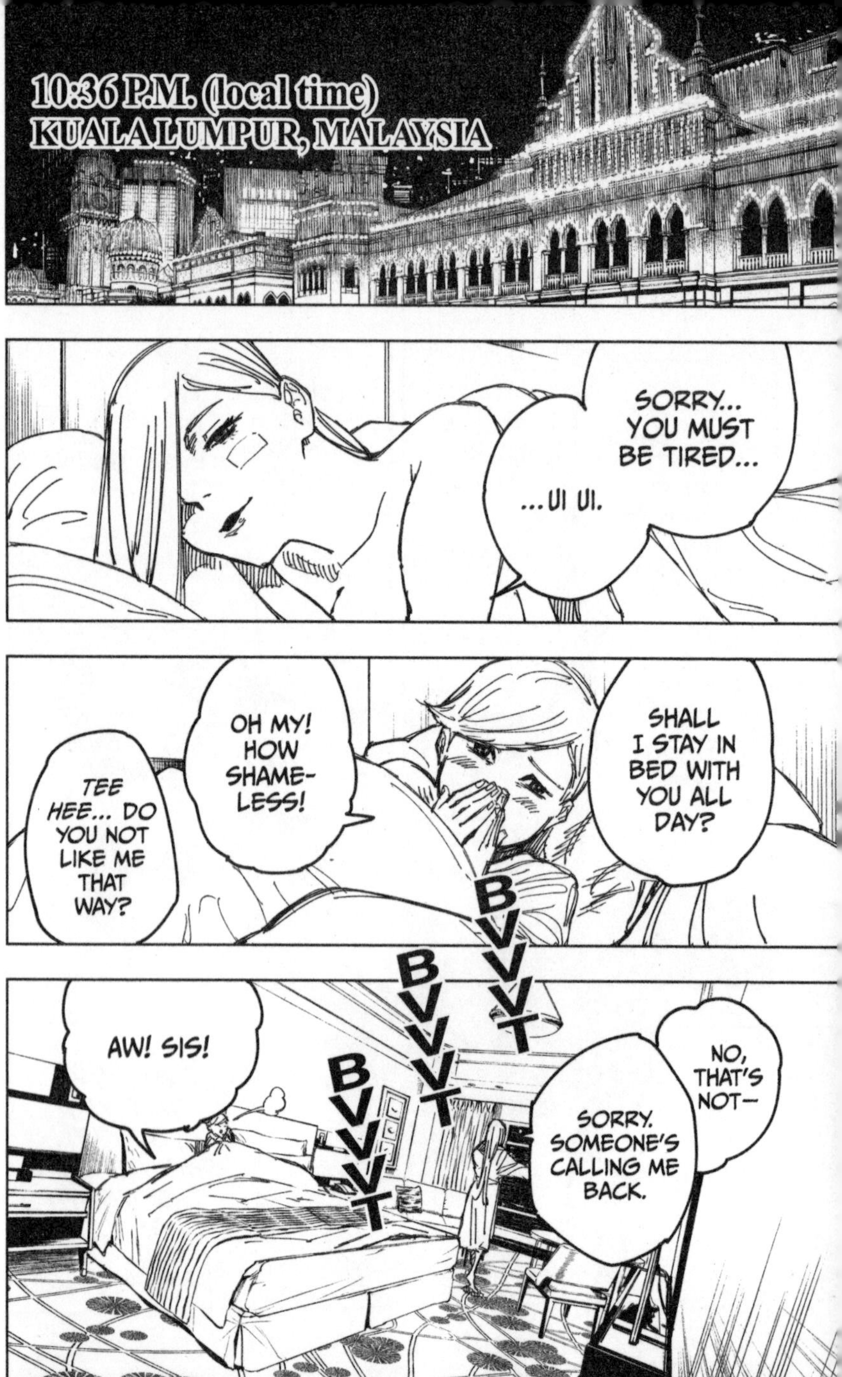
10:36 P.M. (local time)
KUALA LUMPUR, MALAYSIA
SORRY... YOU MUST BE TIRED...
...UI UI.
SHALL I STAY IN BED WITH YOU ALL DAY?
OH MY! HOW SHAME-LESS!
TEE HEE... DO YOU NOT LIKE ME THAT WAY?
BVVVT
NO, THAT'S NOT—
SORRY. SOMEONE'S CALLING ME BACK.
BVVVT
BVVVT
AW! SIS!

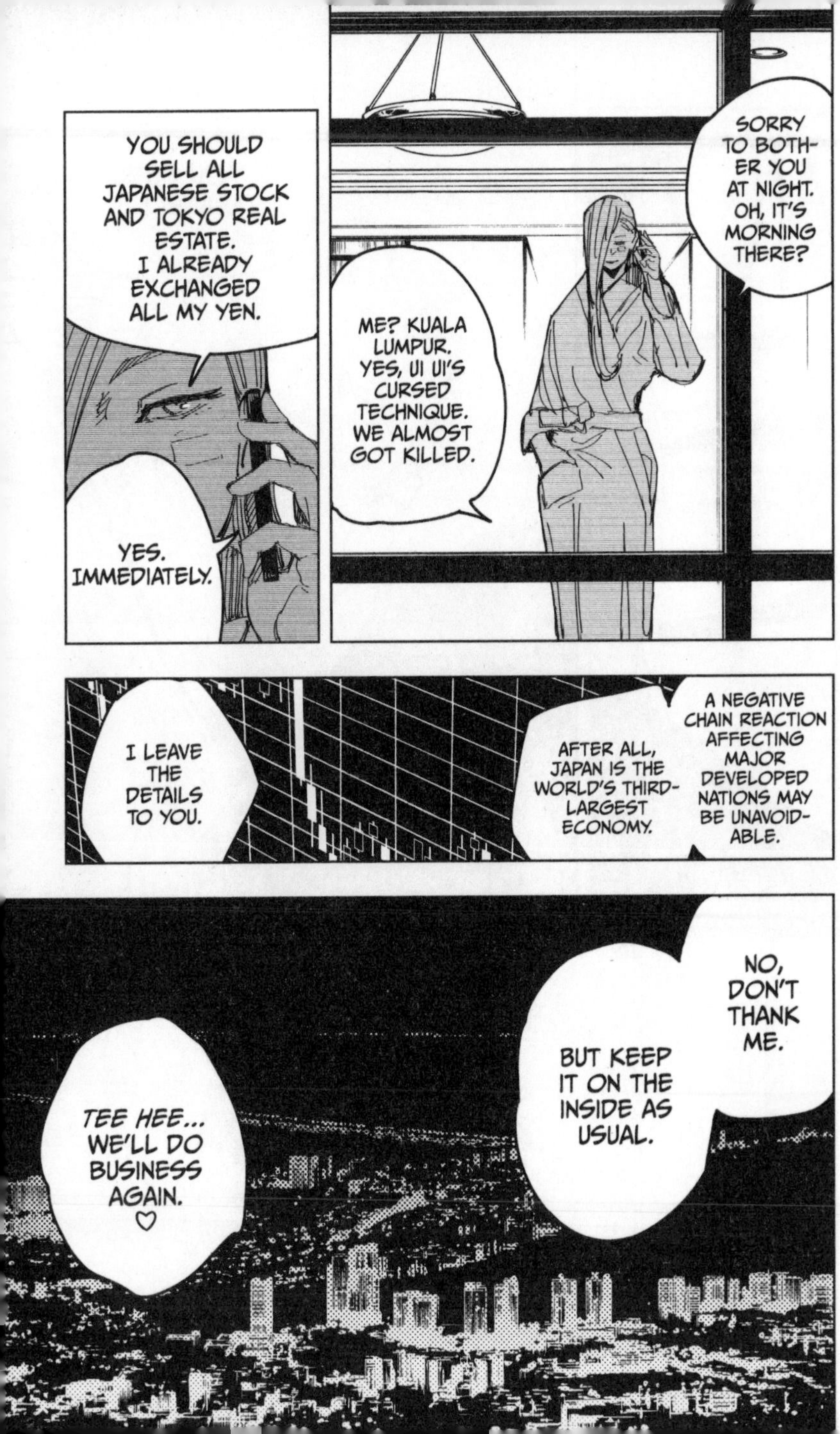
SORRY TO BOTHER YOU AT NIGHT. OH, IT'S MORNING THERE?
ME? KUALA LUMPUR. YES, UI UI'S CURSED TECHNIQUE. WE ALMOST GOT KILLED.
YOU SHOULD SELL ALL JAPANESE STOCK AND TOKYO REAL ESTATE. I ALREADY EXCHANGED ALL MY YEN.
YES. IMMEDIATELY.
A NEGATIVE CHAIN REACTION AFFECTING MAJOR DEVELOPED NATIONS MAY BE UNAVOIDABLE.
AFTER ALL, JAPAN IS THE WORLD'S THIRD-LARGEST ECONOMY.
I LEAVE THE DETAILS TO YOU.
NO, DON'T THANK ME.
BUT KEEP IT ON THE INSIDE AS USUAL.
TEE HEE... WE'LL DO BUSINESS AGAIN. ♡

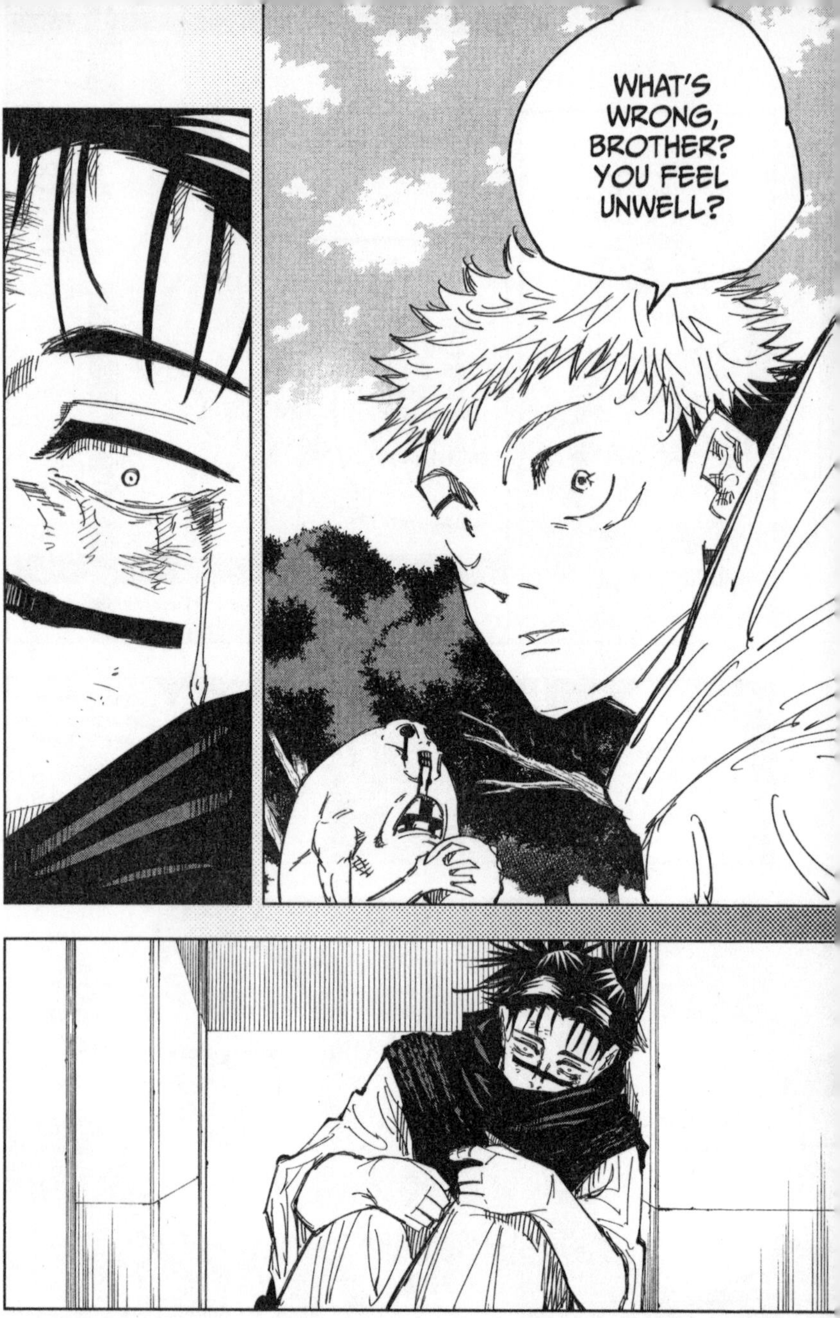
WHAT'S WRONG, BROTHER? YOU FEEL UNWELL?

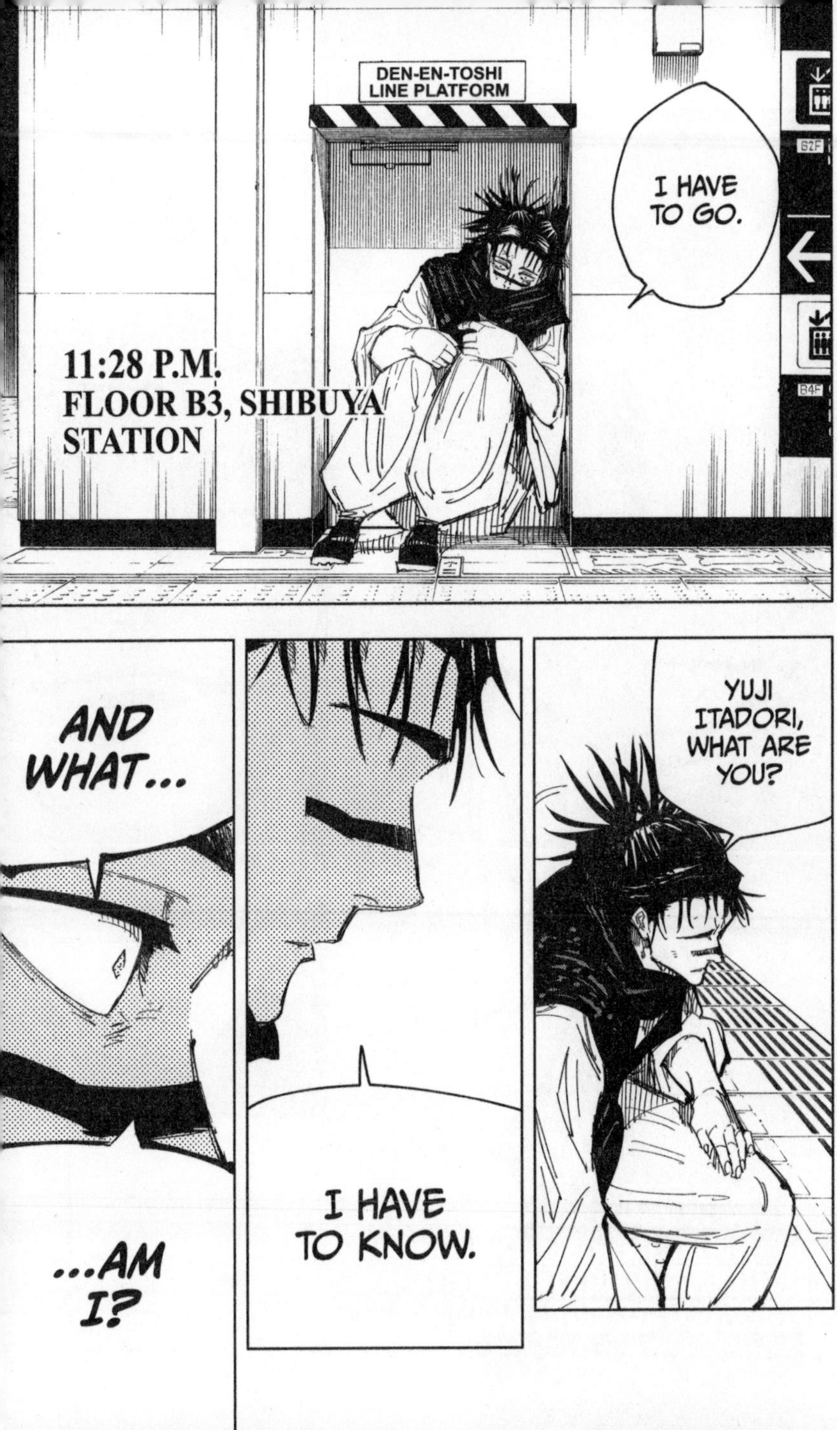
DEN-EN-TOSHI
LINE PLATFORM
B2F
B4F
I HAVE TO GO.
11:28 P.M.
FLOOR B3, SHIBUYA STATION
YUJI ITADORI, WHAT ARE YOU?
I HAVE TO KNOW.
AND WHAT...
...AM I?

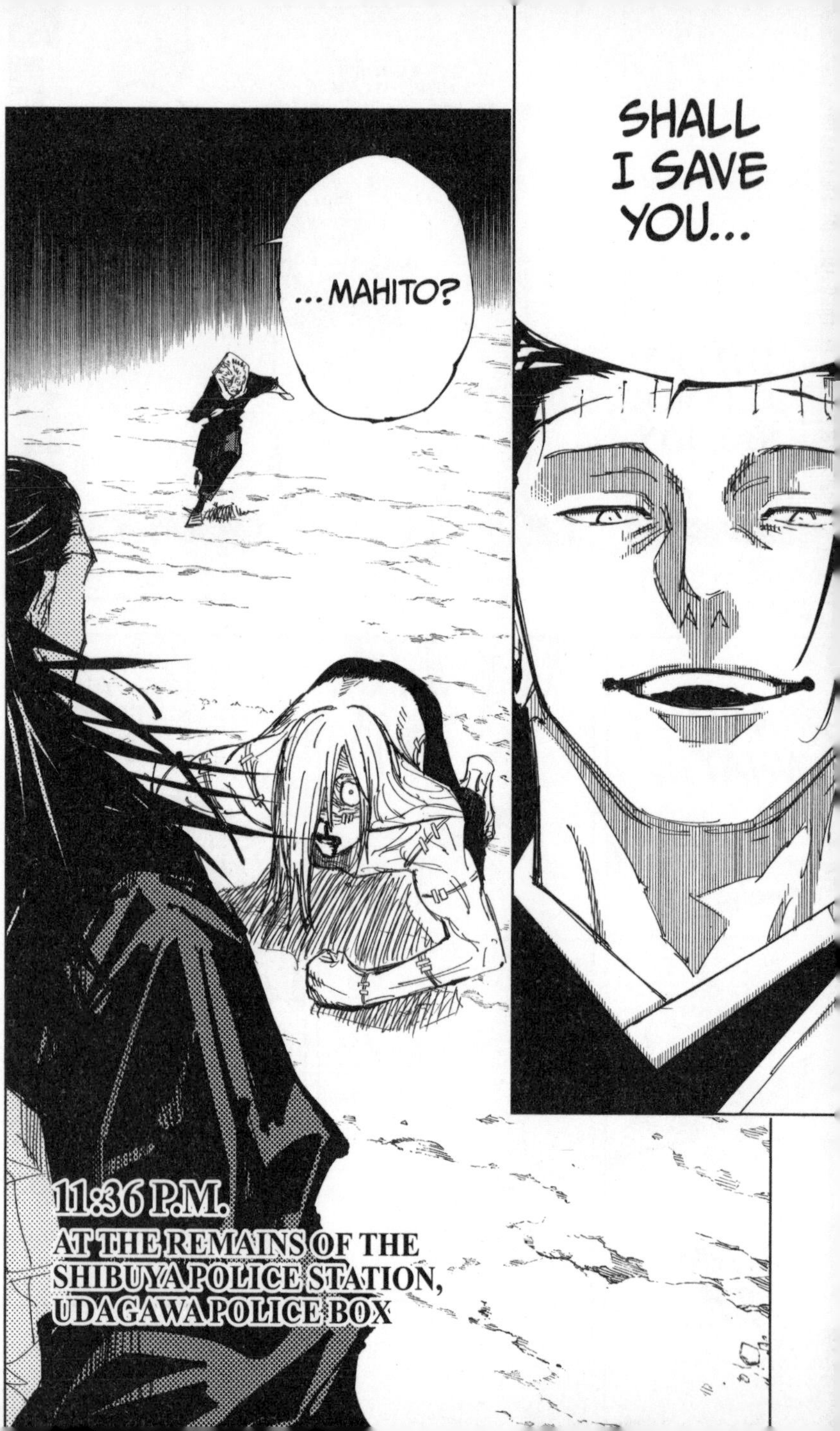
SHALL I SAVE YOU...
...MAHITO?
11:36 P.M.
AT THE REMAINS OF THE SHIBUYA POLICE STATION, UDAGAWA POLICE BOX

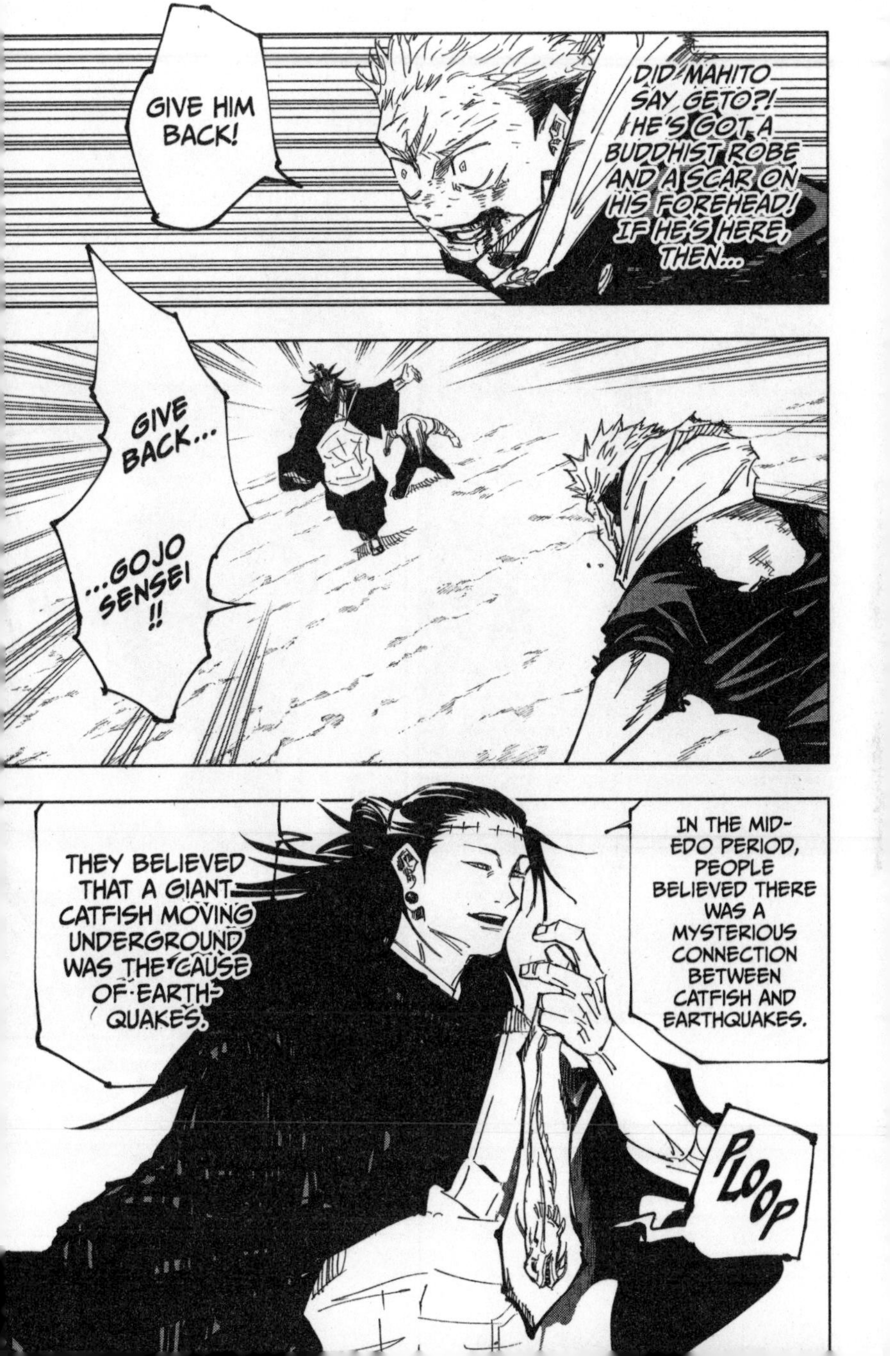
DID MAHITO SAY GETO?! HE'S GOT A BUDDHIST ROBE AND A SCAR ON HIS FOREHEAD! IF HE'S HERE, THEN...
GIVE HIM BACK!
GIVE BACK...
...GOJO SENSEI!!
IN THE MID-EDO PERIOD, PEOPLE BELIEVED THERE WAS A MYSTERIOUS CONNECTION BETWEEN CATFISH AND EARTHQUAKES.
PLOOP
THEY BELIEVED THAT A GIANT CATFISH MOVING UNDERGROUND WAS THE CAUSE OF EARTHQUAKES.

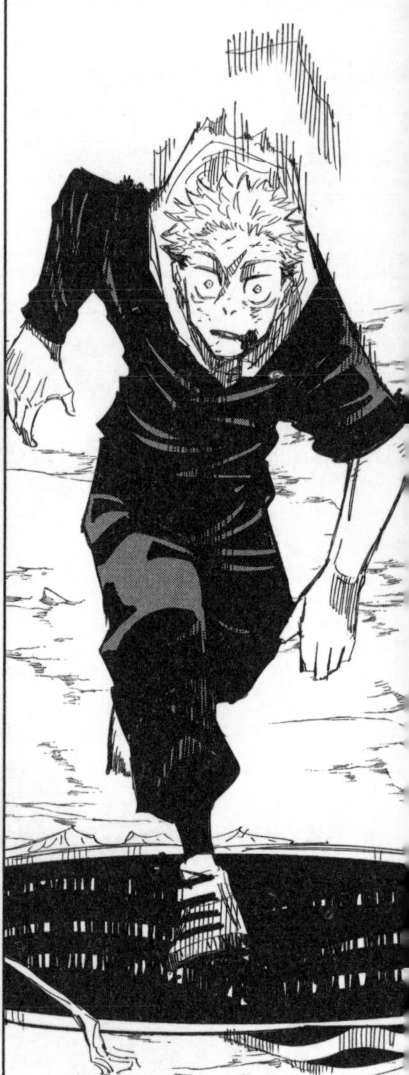
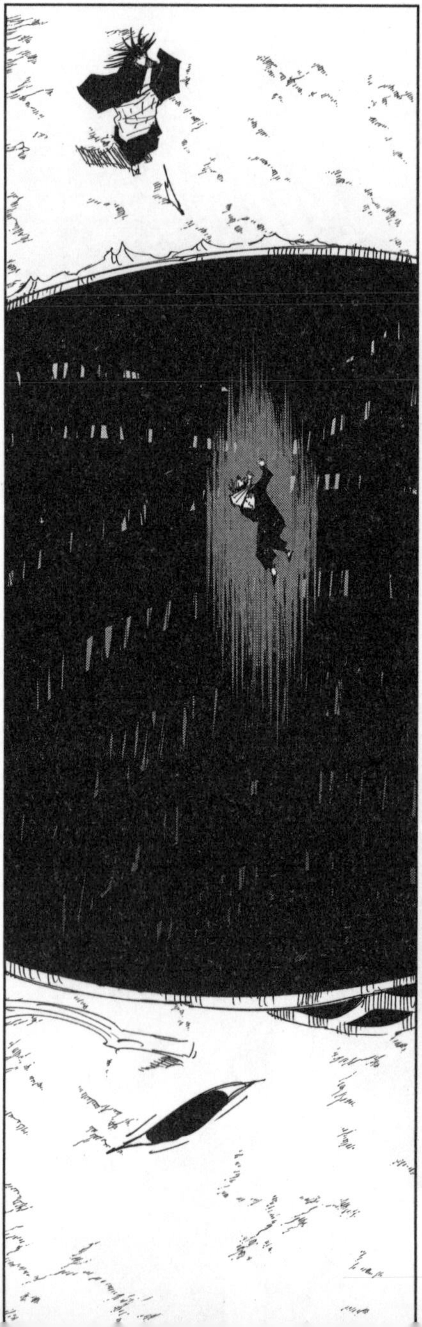

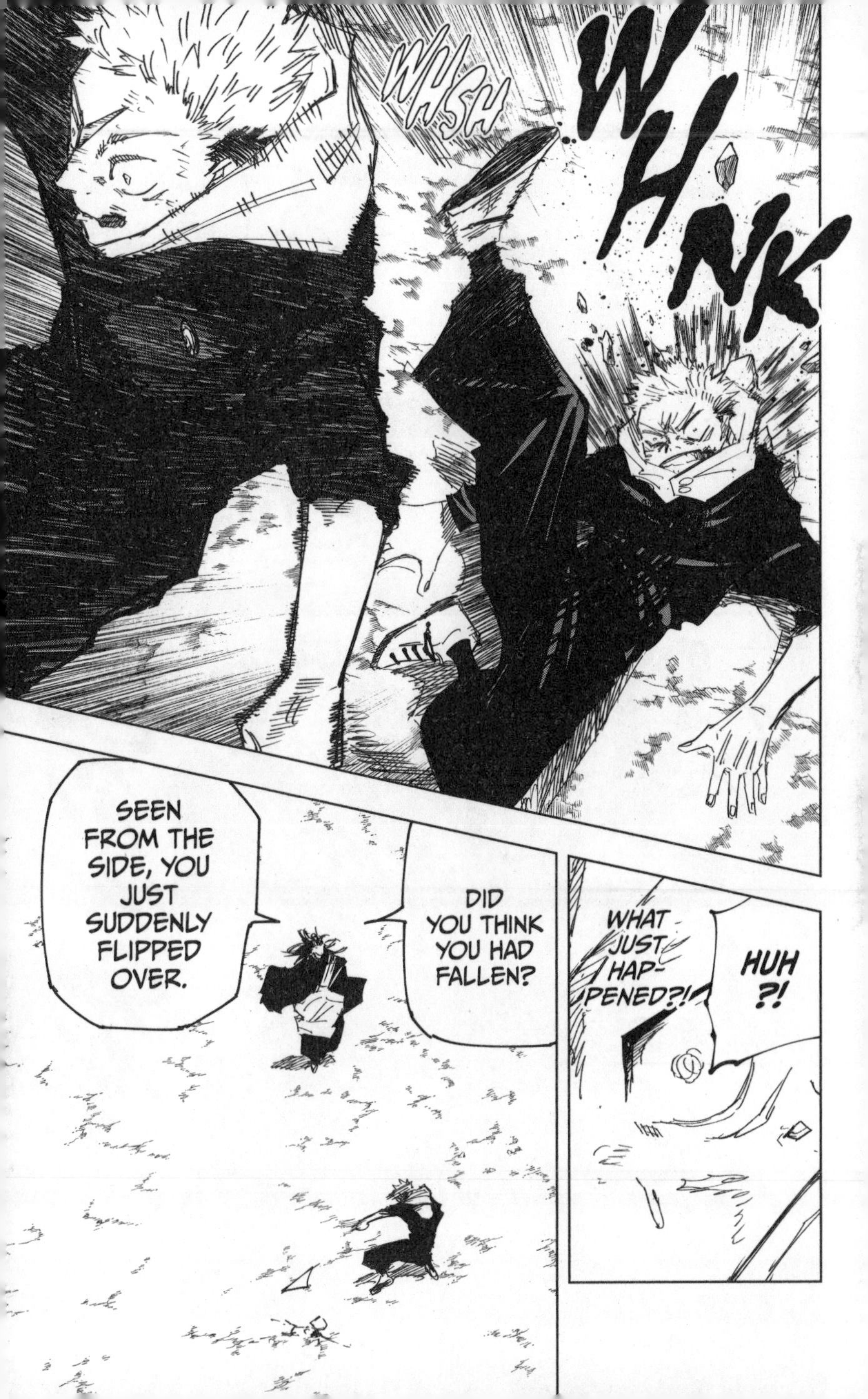
WHINK
WHSH
HUH ?!
WHAT JUST HAP-PENED?!
DID YOU THINK YOU HAD FALLEN?
SEEN FROM THE SIDE, YOU JUST SUDDENLY FLIPPED OVER.

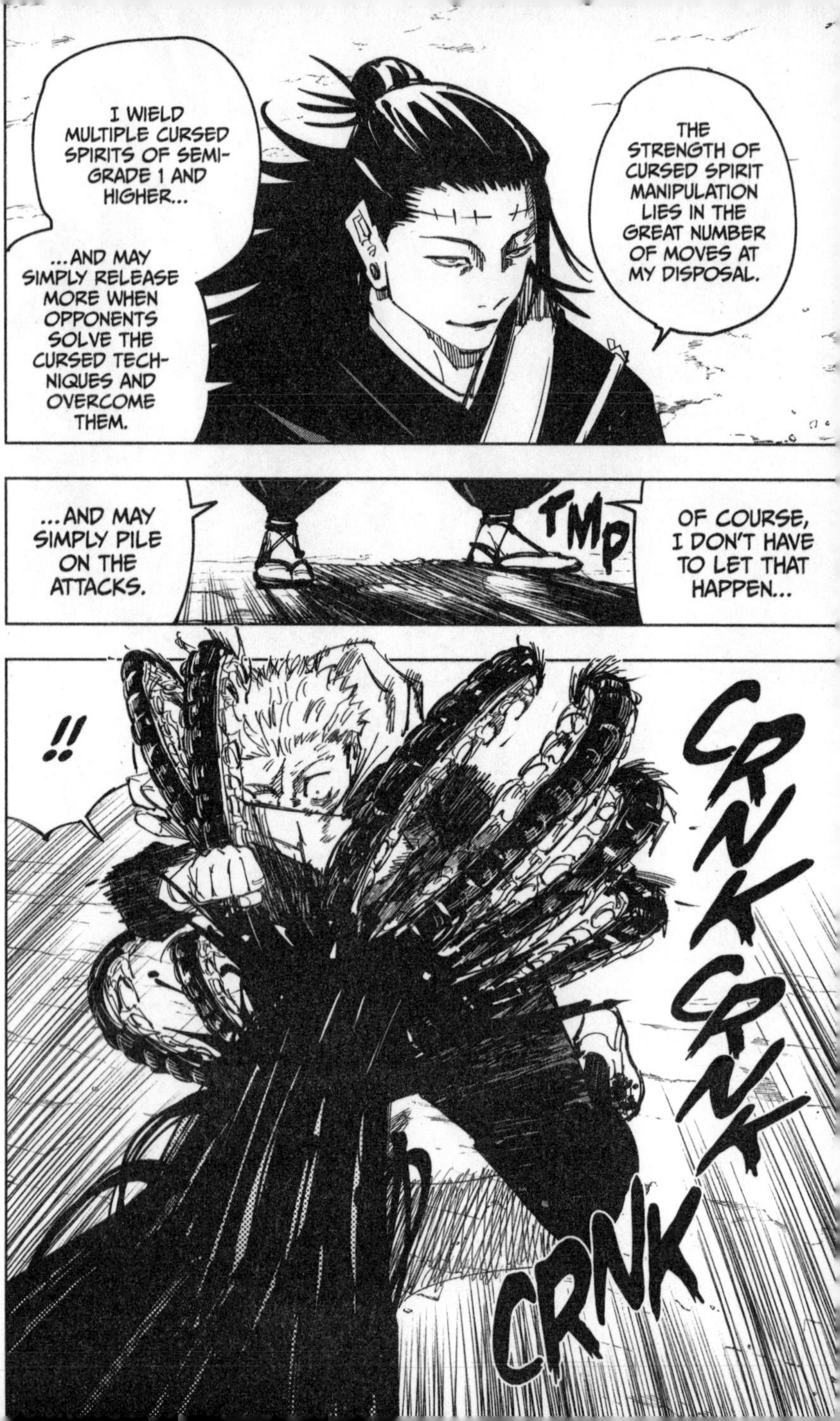
THE STRENGTH OF CURSED SPIRIT MANIPULATION LIES IN THE GREAT NUMBER OF MOVES AT MY DISPOSAL.
I WIELD MULTIPLE CURSED SPIRITS OF SEMI-GRADE 1 AND HIGHER...
...AND MAY SIMPLY RELEASE MORE WHEN OPPONENTS SOLVE THE CURSED TECH-NIQUES AND OVERCOME THEM.
OF COURSE, I DON'T HAVE TO LET THAT HAPPEN...
TMP
...AND MAY SIMPLY PILE ON THE ATTACKS.
CRNK
CRNK
CRNK
CRNK
!!

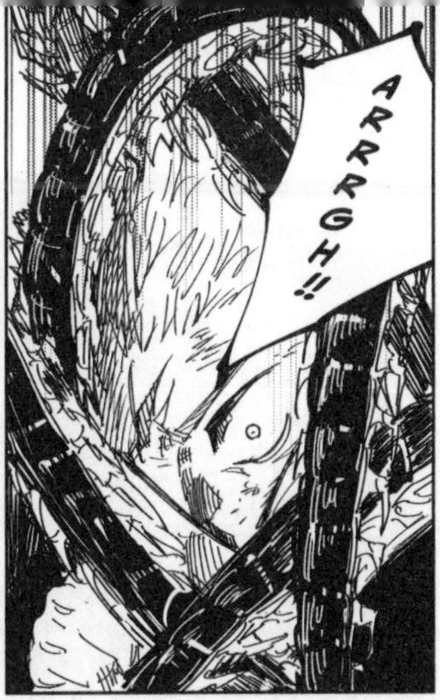
ARRRGH!!
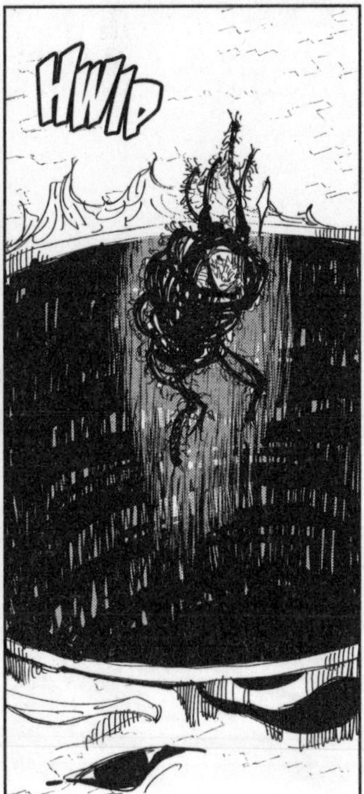
HWIP
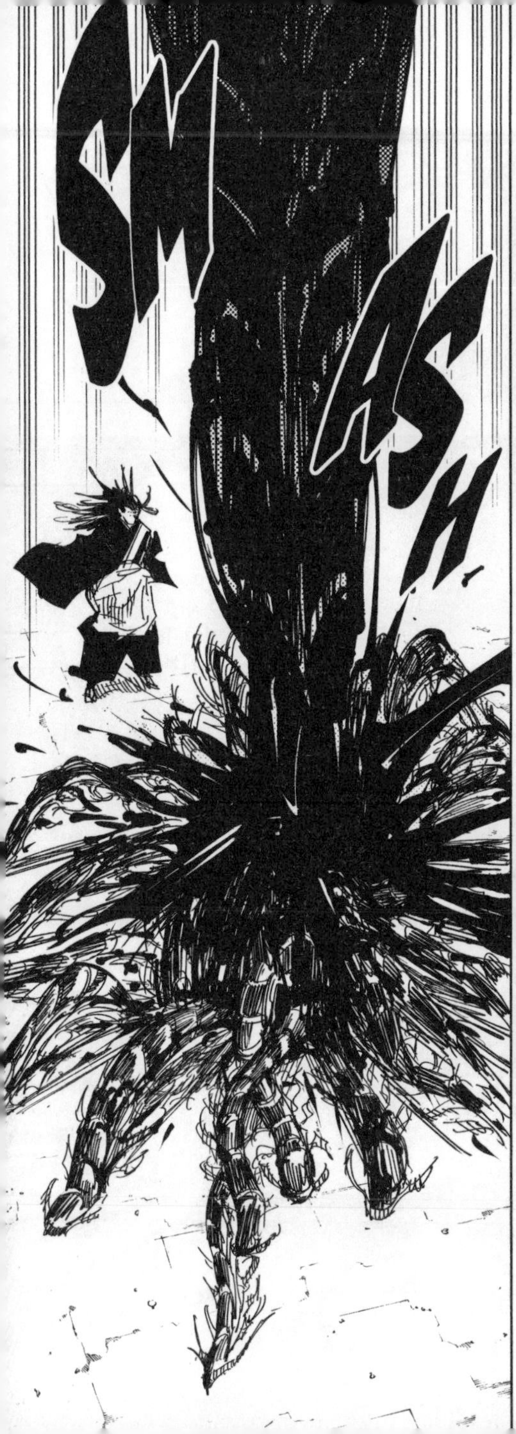
SMASH

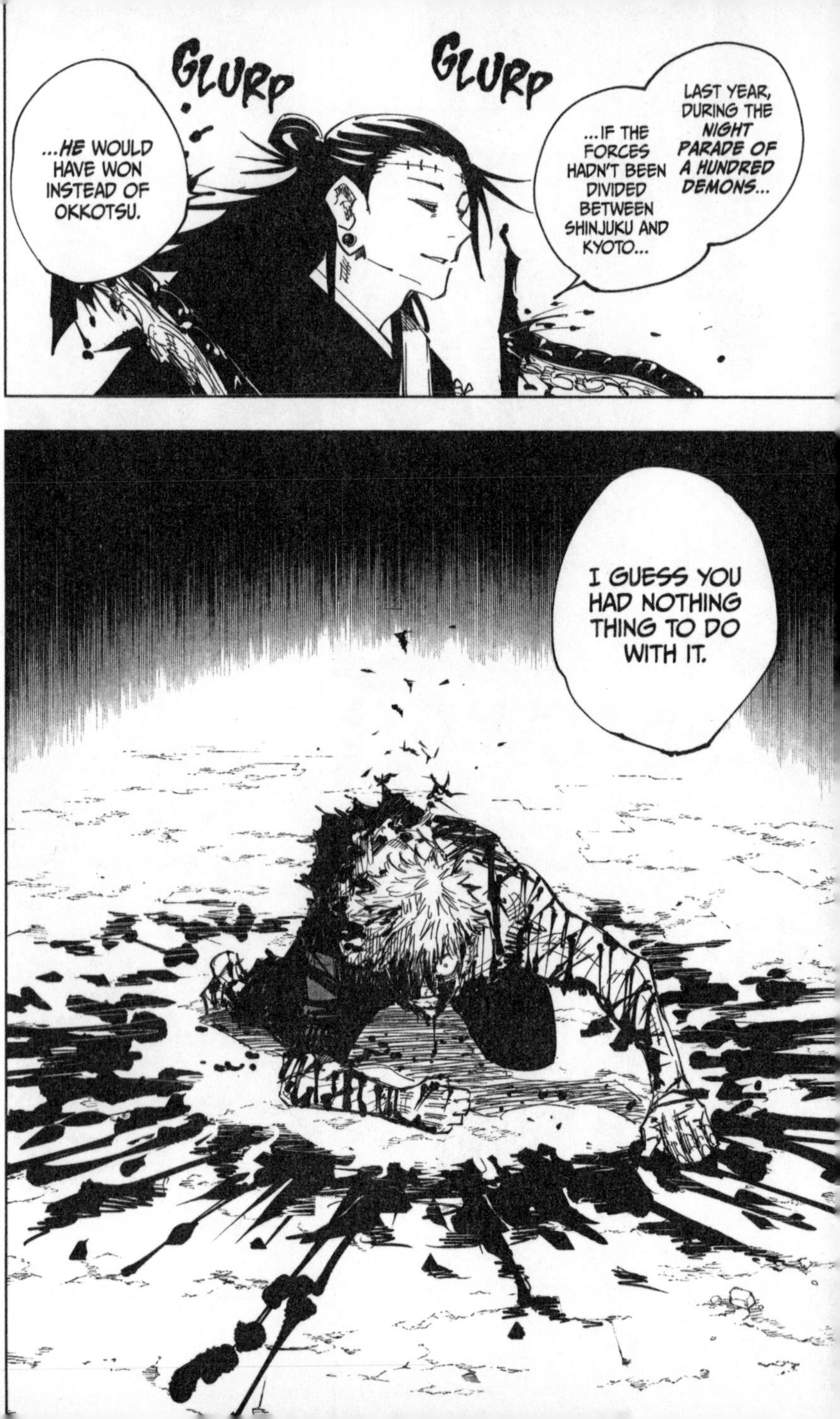
LAST YEAR, DURING THE NIGHT PARADE OF A HUNDRED DEMONS...
...IF THE FORCES HADN'T BEEN DIVIDED BETWEEN SHINJUKU AND KYOTO...
GLURP
GLURP
...HE WOULD HAVE WON INSTEAD OF OKKOTSU.
I GUESS YOU HAD NOTHING THING TO DO WITH IT.

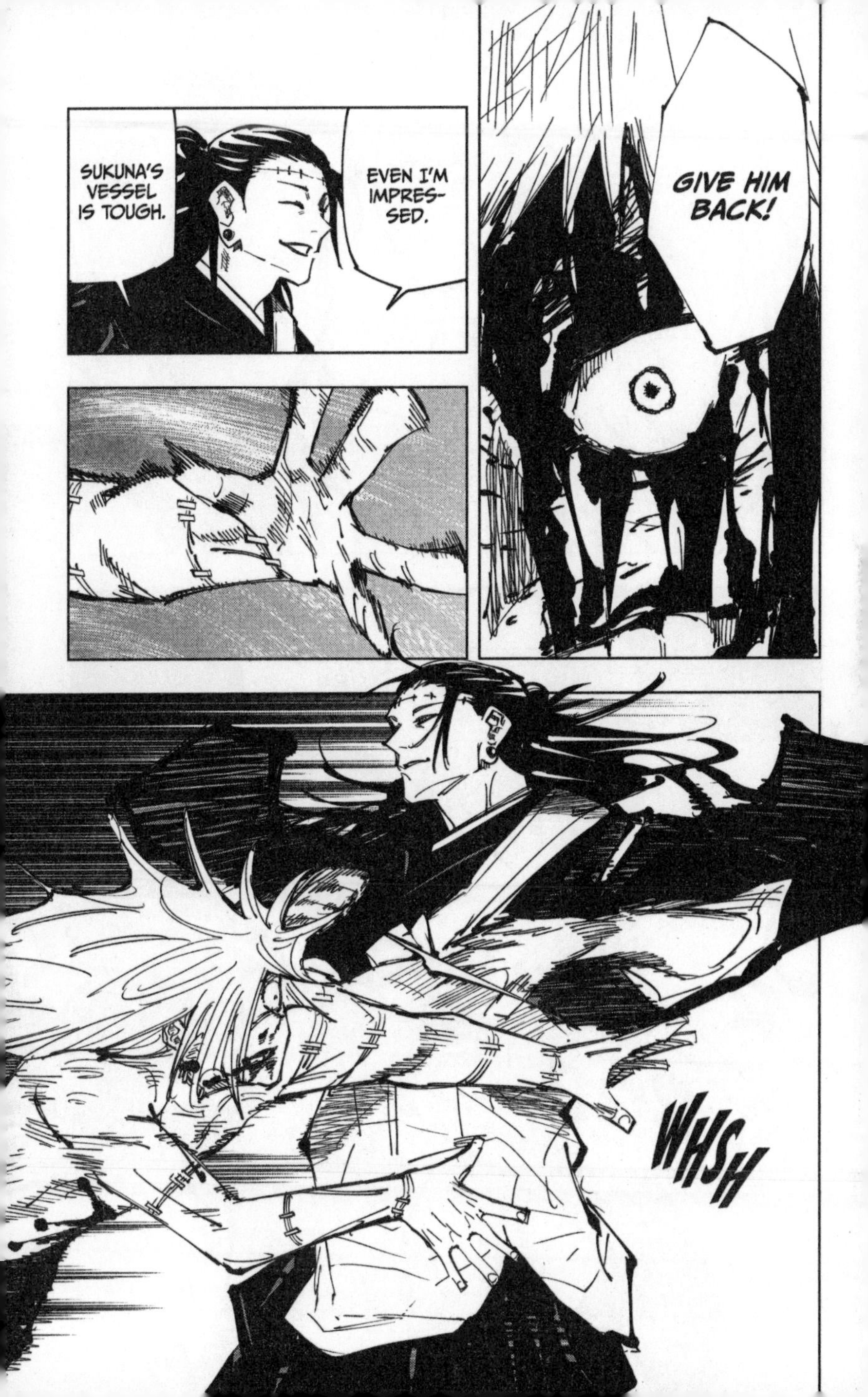
GIVE HIM BACK!
EVEN I'M IMPRES-SED.
SUKUNA'S VESSEL IS TOUGH.
WHSH

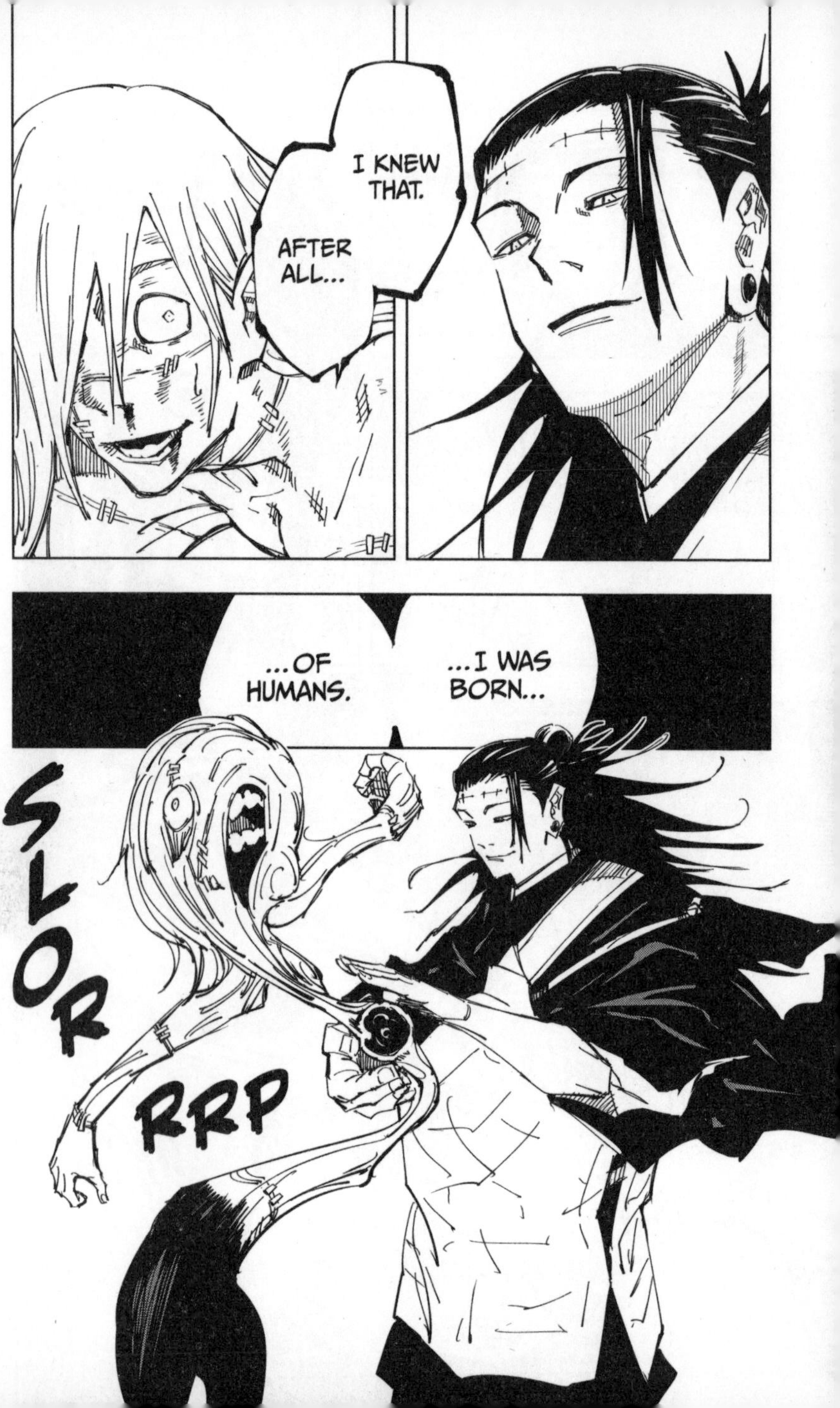
I KNEW THAT.
AFTER ALL...
...I WAS BORN...
...OF HUMANS.
SLORRRP

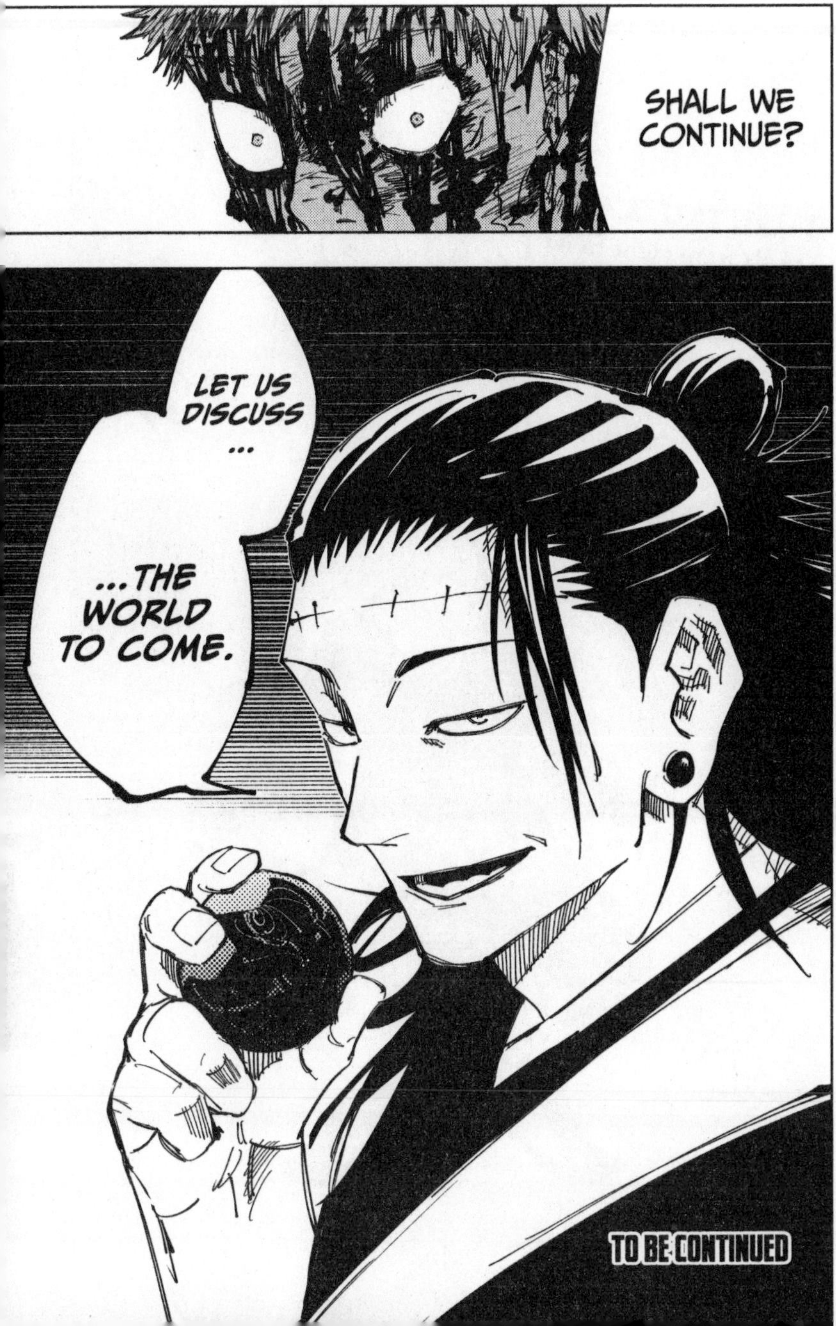
SHALL WE CONTINUE?
LET US DISCUSS ...
...THE WORLD TO COME.
TO BE CONTINUED

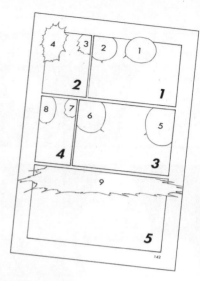

JUJUTSU KAISEN

reads from right to left, starting in the upper-right corner. Japanese is read from right to left, meaning that action, sound effects, and word-balloon order are completely reversed from English order.